D0163112

WITHDRAWN

PLATO'S RECEPTION OF PARMENIDES

B
395
.P66
1999

Plato's Reception of Parmenides

JOHN A. PALMER

#39985645
MNGA

CLARENDON PRESS · OXFORD

1999

11-13-00 CT

Oxford University Press, Great Clarendon Street, Oxford OX2 6DP

Oxford New York

Athens Auckland Bangkok Bogotá Buenos Aires Calcutta
Cape Town Chennai Dar es Salaam Delhi Florence Hong Kong Istanbul
Karachi Kuala Lumpur Madrid Melbourne Mexico City Mumbai
Nairobi Paris São Paulo Singapore Taipei Tokyo Toronto Warsaw
and associated companies in
Berlin Ibadan

Oxford is a registered trade mark of Oxford University Press

Published in the United States
by Oxford University Press Inc., New York

© John A. Palmer 1999

The moral rights of the author have been asserted

First published 1999

All rights reserved. No part of this publication may be reproduced,
stored in a retrieval system, or transmitted, in any form or by any means,
without the prior permission in writing of Oxford University Press.
Within the UK, exceptions are allowed in respect of any fair dealing for the
purpose of research or private study, or criticism or review, as permitted
under the Copyright, Designs and Patents Act, 1988, or in the case of
reprographic reproduction in accordance with the terms of the licences
issued by the Copyright Licensing Agency. Enquiries concerning
reproduction outside these terms and in other countries should be
sent to the Rights Department, Oxford University Press,
at the address above

British Library Cataloguing in Publication Data
Data available

Library of Congress Cataloging-in-Publication Data
Palmer, John Anderson, 1965–
Plato's reception of Parmenides / John A. Palmer.
Includes bibliographical references and indexes.
1. Plato. 2. Parmenides—Influence. 3. Sophists (Greek
philosophy) I. Title.
B395.P66 1999 184—dc21 98–46615
ISBN 0–19–823800–2

1 3 5 7 9 10 8 6 4 2

Typeset by Graphicraft Limited, Hong Kong
Printed in Great Britain
on acid-free paper by
Bookcraft (Bath) Ltd
Midsomer Norton, Somerset

For Francesca

Preface

THE origin of the present work can be traced back to the dissatisfaction I felt with what I was taught about Parmenides when I began studying the Presocratics at Cambridge. This dissatisfaction subsequently expressed itself in a paper on the relation between Xenophanes and Parmenides which I wrote for David Furley's seminar on the Presocratics at Princeton in the spring of 1990. I want to thank him for encouraging what were in fact some rather hazy thoughts—and for his continued kindness, good sense, and open-mindedness as those thoughts subsequently developed in different directions. This process began during André Laks's Princeton seminar on Parmenides and Anaxagoras in the Spring of 1992. He was a sympathetic critic at the time and continued to offer acute comment and advice as my ideas developed into my 1996 doctoral dissertation, 'Aspects of Plato's Reception of Parmenides'. I owe him particular thanks for helping me clarify the problems and potential advantages of my somewhat unorthodox approach to the history of ancient philosophy.

Much of the central argument of Part I took shape during the Fall of 1993, when I returned to Cambridge under the auspices of a Donald and Mary Hyde Fellowship. It was during this time that I decided to focus exclusively on Plato's encounter with Parmenides. A Mellon Dissertation Year Fellowship provided a period of uninterrupted work following my return to Princeton. In the Spring of 1995 I was fortunate to attend Alexander Nehamas's seminar on Parmenides and Plato, which helped to solidify certain ideas as I was moulding them into a coherent form. I want to thank him for his sensitive and searching criticisms both at that time and since. I also want to express my debt to Myles Burnyeat and Michael Frede for their invaluable comments and insights at various stages of the project. Discussions with Charles Brittain, Verity Harte, Rachel Barney, and Andrew Ford were invariably stimulating and helped me work out certain key ideas. I want to thank the President and Fellows of Clare Hall, Cambridge, for electing me to the Research Fellowship that has given me the opportunity to revise the dissertation in a friendly and stimulating intellectual environment. My greatest debt is to Malcolm Schofield, under whose guidance I began seriously studying ancient philosophy. What I owe to his example and encouragement is impossible to express. Perhaps I can just say that I look forward to continuing to learn from him well into the future.

I have seen fit to drop the first two words of my earlier title because I have now taken into account how Plato represents Parmenides' consideration of his own hypothesis in the second part of the *Parmenides*. This has led me to rethink, revise, and substantially reorganize my earlier account of

Parmenides' influence on Plato's later thought. The resulting account still cannot be claimed exhaustive. However, this is now due less to my own hesitation in the face of this daunting and yet undeniably crucial text than to the irrecoverable depth of the Platonic engagement with Parmenides itself. I have also removed much of the dissertation's material on the Xenophanes reception, a revised version of which will now be published separately.

Although in what follows I presume a certain familiarity with Parmenides and Plato, what I have to say should be readily intelligible to a reader with such knowledge of these philosophers as one might get from a good undergraduate course. I have made a serious effort to make what I say accessible to the Greekless reader by translating all Greek in the main body of the text, with the occasional minor exception of temporarily postponing translation when actually discussing how a particular phrase or passage is to be translated. Even these discussions are, I hope, comprehensible. To be equally accommodating to the reader with some Greek, I have often included the text of a phrase or passage alongside its translation. With only a few exceptions, I have avoided transliteration since it tends to be an unsightly compromise that satisfies neither audience.

To my editors Peter Momtchiloff and Robert Ritter I am indebted for their keen interest in the project and for their patient and skilful guidance of the book through the press. I want to express a special debt of thanks to my parents, who have always encouraged and supported my intellectual adventures. Finally, I owe the deepest possible gratitude to Francesca Simkin, for lifting my spirits at a particularly trying time and for continuing to do so to this day. I dedicate this book to her with love.

J.A.P.

Contents

Editions and Abbreviations

ABBREVIATIONS of Greek authors and texts are as per Liddell, Scott, and Jones, *A Greek–English Lexicon* (Oxford: Clarendon Press, 1925–40). For Parmenides and the other Presocratics, I have followed the text of DK except where indicated in the notes (not noted are minor changes in punctuation adopted from Cordero 1984 and Coxon 1986). For Gorgias, I have employed T. Buchheim, *Gorgias von Leontini: Reden, Fragmente und Testimonien* (Hamburg: Felix Meiner, 1989), which marks a substantial improvement over earlier editions. For Plato, I have used the Oxford Classical Texts, volumes ii–v, ed. J. Burnet (1901–7), and volume i, ed. E. A. Duke, W. F. Hicken, W. S. M. Nicoll, D. B. Robinson, and J. C. G. Strachan (1995). The line numbering of the new edition of volume i unfortunately does not correspond to that of Burnet's earlier edition, which will make some references seem strange, but I have followed it none the less. For Aristotle, I have used the editions in the Oxford Classical Texts, or, where these are unavailable, in the Teubner series. The Greek commentators on Aristotle are cited by page and line number from the relevant volumes of the *Commentaria in Aristotelem Graeca* (*CAG*). The texts of other authors I have quoted, rather than simply referred to, are indicated in the list of abbreviations.

Alex. Aphr.	Alexander of Aphrodisias. *in Metaph.* = *in Aristotelis Metaphysica commentaria* (*CAG* I); *in Top.* = *in Aristotelis Topicorum libros octo commentaria* (*CAG* II. ii)
Ammon.	Ammonius. *in Cat.* = *in Aristotelis Categorias commentarius* (*CAG* IV. 4); *in Porph.* = *in Porphyrii Isagogen* (*CAG* IV. iii)
Anon. *in Tht.*	*Anonymi commentarius in Platonis Theaetetum*
Arist.	Aristotle. *De an.* = *De anima*; *Cael.* = *De caelo*; *GC* = *De generatione et corruptione*; *HA* = *Historia animalium*; *Metaph.* = *Metaphysica*; *Ph.* = *Physica*; *Rh.* = *Rhetorica*; *SE* = *Sophistici elenchi*; *Top.* = *Topica*
Aristocl.	Aristocles. *De phil.* = *De philosophia*
Clem. Al.	Clement of Alexandria. *Strom.* = *Stromateis*
Dam.	Damascius. *Pr.* = *De principiis*
David	*in Porph.* = *in Porphyrii Isagogen commentarium* (*CAG* XVIII. ii)
DG	*Doxographi Graeci*, ed. H. Diels (Berlin, 1879)
DK	H. Diels, *Die Fragmente der Vorsokratiker*, 6th edn., rev. and ed. W. Kranz, 3 vols. (Berlin, 1951–2)
DL	Diogenes Laertius, *Vitae philosophorum*, ed. H. S. Long, 2 vols. (Oxford, 1964)

Elias	*in Porph.* = *in Porphyrii Isagogen commentaria* (*CAG* XVIII. i); *in Cat.* = *in Aristotelis Categorias commentaria* (*CAG* XVIII. i)
Emp.	Empedocles
Eus.	Eusebius. *PE* = *Praeparatio evangelica*, ed. K. Mras (Berlin, 1954–6)
Gorg.	Gorgias. *Hel.* = *Helena*
Hdt.	Herodotus
Herm.	Hermias. *in Phdr.* = *in Platonis Phaedrum scholia*, ed. P. Couvreur (Paris, 1901)
Hes.	Hesiod. *Op.* = *Opera et Dies*; fr. = *Fragmenta Selecta*, 3rd edn., ed. R. Merkelbach and M. L. West (Oxford, 1990)
Hom.	Homer. *Il.* = *Iliad*; *Od.* = *Odyssey*
Hp.	Hippocrates. *Epid.* = ἐπιδημίαι; *Morb. Sacr.* = περὶ ἱερῆς νούσου; *VM* = περὶ ἀρχαίης ἰητρικῆς, ed. H. Kuehlewein (Leipzig, 1894)
Isoc.	Isocrates. *Orat.* = *Orationes*
KR	G. S. Kirk and J. E. Raven, *The Presocratic Philosophers* (Cambridge, 1957)
KRS	G. S. Kirk, J. E. Raven, and M. Schofield, *The Presocratic Philosophers*, 2nd edn. (Cambridge, 1983)
MXG	Pseudo-Aristotle, *De Melisso Xenophane Gorgia*
OF	O. Kern, *Orphicorum Fragmenta* (Berlin, 1922)
Parm.	Parmenides
Phlp.	Philoponus. *in Ph.* = *in Aristotelis Physica commentaria* (*CAG* XVI, XVII)
Pl.	Plato. *Alc.* I = *Alcibiades* I; *Ap.* = *Apologia Socratis*; *Cra.* = *Cratylus*; *Ep.* = *Epistles*; *Euthd.* = *Euthydemus*; *Euthphr.* = *Euthyphro*; *Hp. Ma.* = *Hippias Major*; *Hp. Mi.* = *Hippias Minor*; *Men.* = *Meno*; *Phd.* = *Phaedo*; *Phdr.* = *Phaedrus*; *Phlb.* = *Philebus*; *Prm.* = *Parmenides*; *Prt.* = *Protagoras*; *R.* = *Republic*; *Smp.* = *Symposium*; *Sph.* = *Sophist*; *Tht.* = *Theaetetus*; *Ti.* = *Timaeus*
Plot.	Plotinus, *Enneads*
Plu.	Plutarch. *Col.* = *Adversus Colotem*, ed. M. Pohlenz and R. Westman (Leipzig, 1959); *Virt. mor.* = *De virtute morali*, ed. J. Dumortier and J. Defradas (Paris, 1975)
Porph.	Porphyry. *VP* = *Vita Pythagorae*
Procl.	Proclus. *in Prm.* = *in Platonis Parmenidem commentarii*, ed. V. Cousin (Paris, 1864; repr. Hildesheim, 1961), supplemented by William of Moerbeke's Latin translation of the end of Book 7, ed. R. Klibansky and C. Labowsky (London, 1953); *in Cra.* = *in Platonis Cratylum commentarii*, ed. G. Pasquali (Leipzig, 1908); *in Ti.* = *in Platonis Timaeum commentarii*; *Theol. Plat.* = *In Platonis theologiam*, ed. L. G. Westerink (Paris, 1968–81)

SE   Sextus Empiricus. *M.* = *Adversus mathematicos*, ed. R. G.
            Bury (Cambridge, Mass., and London, 1935–49); *P.* =
            Outlines of Pyrrhonism
Simp.   Simplicius. *in Cael.* = *in Aristotelis de Caelo commentaria*
            (*CAG* VII); *in Cat.* = *in Aristotelis Categorias commentar-
            ium* (*CAG* VIII); *in Ph.* = *in Aristotelis Physica commentaria*
            (*CAG* IX and X)
Thphr.   Theophrastus. *Phys. Op.* = Φυσικαὶ δόξαι; *Sens.* = *De sens-
            ibus*; *Sign.* = *De signis tempestatum*
Tz.   John Tzetzes. *H.* = *Historiarum variarum chiliades*, ed. T.
            Kiessling (Leipzig, 1826)
X.   Xenophon. *An.* = *Anabasis*; *Cyr.* = *Cyropaedia*; *Mem.* =
            Memorabilia
Xenoph.   Xenophanes

PART I

Plato's Middle Period Reception of Parmenides

Introduction

Everything must be studied from the point of view of itself, as near as we can get to this, and from the point of view of its relations, as near as we can get to them.

Samuel Butler (1835–1902)

Parmenides is, after Socrates, the philosopher who exercised the greatest influence on Plato's thought. Parmenides arguably had an even more profound influence than Socrates on Plato's overall metaphysical outlook, especially in the later stages of his career. In the *Sophist*, Plato allows an Eleatic pupil of Parmenides' to assume Socrates' traditional role as the dialogue's primary questioner. Parmenides himself, in the dialogue bearing his name, is allowed to question Socrates, posing problems for a theory similar to Plato's own middle period theory of forms. Parmenides then undertakes an elaborate examination of his own views regarding the one being to help Socrates form a more adequate conception of the nature of intelligible reality. The historical Parmenides had also substantially influenced the theory his fictional namesake is made to criticize in this dialogue, so that understanding Plato's engagement with Parmenides at this stage of his career is a prerequisite to understanding the later engagement. At present, the influence at neither stage is well understood.

One point that has been increasingly appreciated is that Plato's middle period forms resemble a plurality of Parmenidean beings. In an important study, Friedrich Solmsen drew attention to the parallels between the *Symposium*'s description of the form of Beauty and Parmenides B8's account of the attributes of Being.[1] The details of

---

[1] Solmsen 1971(*a*), 64–70. Cf. e.g. Sprague 1971; Seligman 1974, 6; Teloh 1976(*a*), 23–5, and 1976(*b*), 125–7; Nehamas 1979, 98–103; Seligman 1982, 23; Coxon 1986, 26–7; Miller 1986, 30–1; Kahn 1988, 253; Curd 1998, 228–41. Although Solmsen's study was the first to make the point forcefully to the English-speaking world, it was already fairly common in German scholarship: cf. e.g. Liebrucks 1949, 37–8; Gadamer 1950, 60; Prauss 1966, 38–9; Friedländer 1969, 24; Krämer 1969, 6–7. See also Krämer 1959, ch. 5 *passim*, where Parmenides' influence on Plato's theory of separate, intelligible forms is recognized but made somewhat secondary to the influence of the Eleatic theory of being upon the One as the ultimate ground of being in the Platonic Prinzipienlehre. Solmsen's apparent originality is due in part to his nowhere citing these studies.

Solmsen's comparison may be summarized (and supplemented) as follows. Diotima tells Socrates that one who has been properly educated in matters of love will finally reach the goal of all his previous labours and glimpse something wonderfully beautiful in its nature. First of all, she says, this 'always is and neither comes to be nor passes away' (ἀεὶ ὂν καὶ οὔτε γιγνόμενον οὔτε ἀπολλύμενον, *Smp.* 211a1). This bears comparison with the first declaration in Parmenides' programmatic summary of the attributes of Being, 'that Being is ungenerated and imperishable' (ὡς ἀγένητον ἐὸν καὶ ἀνώλεθρόν ἐστιν, B8. 3). Having offered some initial support for this declaration, Parmenides' goddess concludes that Justice has allowed it 'neither to come to be nor to perish' (οὔτε γενέσθαι | οὔτ' ὄλλυσθαι, B8. 13–14) and, a little later, that its 'coming-to-be has been extinguished, and perishing is not to be heard of' (γένεσις μὲν ἀπέσβεσται καὶ ἄπυστος ὄλεθρος, B8. 21; cf. B8. 27–8). Diotima continues that this Beauty is 'neither increasing nor decreasing' (οὔτε αὐξανόμενον οὔτε φθίνον, *Smp.* 211a1–2). Likewise, Parmenides' goddess asks, 'How and whence was it increased?' (πῇ πόθεν αὐξηθέν; B8. 7), and she argues that what-is cannot have grown (and, by a presumed parallel logic, cannot diminish). Diotima goes on to say that the form of Beauty is 'not beautiful in one respect and ugly in another, nor at one time beautiful but not at another, nor beautiful in one relation but ugly in another, nor beautiful here and ugly there' (*Smp.* 211a2–4). One may compare this characterization with Parmenides' assertions that Being 'is all alike' (B8. 22), that it is 'neither any more in some place nor any less' (B8. 23–4), and again that 'it is necessary that it be neither any greater nor any smaller in this way or that' (B8. 44–5; cf. B8. 47–8). Beauty itself, Diotima says, 'is always itself in itself with itself of a single kind' (αὐτὸ καθ' αὑτὸ μεθ' αὑτοῦ μονοειδὲς ἀεὶ ὄν, *Smp.* 211b1–2), which recalls Parmenides' description of Being as 'of a single kind' (μουνογενές,[2] B8. 4) and his declaration that 'remaining the same and in the same in itself it lies' (ταὐτόν τ' ἐν ταὐτῷ τε μένον καθ' ἑαυτό τε κεῖται, B8. 29). Finally, Diotima's affirmation that the form of Beauty 'neither comes to be any smaller or greater nor suffers any change' (μήτε τι πλέον μήτε ἔλαττον γίγνεσθαι μηδὲ πάσχειν μηδέν, *Smp.* 211b4–5) may be compared with the assertions by Parmenides' goddess that

[2] Since there are several attested variants for B8. 4a, Solmsen 1971(*a*), 68–9, expresses doubts as to which reading Plato's text may have contained. Because of the uncertainty of the text, Hackforth 1955, 81, prefers to compare μονοειδές here and at *Phd.* 78d5 and 80b2 to πᾶν ὁμοῖον at B8. 22. However, Plato's repeated use of μονοειδές in these passages, in which he adapts the Parmenidean vocabulary, may itself indicate that he found something similar in his text of Parmenides, i.e. μουνογενές.

Being is 'unshaken' (ἀτρεμές, B8. 4), that is, 'changeless' (ἀκίνητον, B8. 26, 38).

Similarly, the language Plato employs elsewhere to describe the forms is often reminiscent of Parmenides. In the *Phaedo*, for example, Socrates at one point asks Cebes: 'the Equal itself, the Beautiful itself, what each thing itself is, what-is (τὸ ὄν)—do they ever admit any change whatsoever? Or does what each of them is, being of a single kind itself in itself (μονοειδὲς ὂν αὐτὸ καθ' αὑτό), always remain constantly the same, and does this never admit any alteration in any respect or in any way?' (78d3–7, cf. 80b1–3).[3] Although one could cite numerous other passages in which Plato speaks of the middle period forms in Eleatic language, it is more important to ask what we are to make of this connection. To begin answering this question, we must take some view on the extent to which Parmenides may have influenced Plato's general distinction, especially as it figures in the arguments at the end of *Republic* 5, between being as the object of knowledge and becoming as the object of *doxa* or mere opinion.

While scholars have recognized a general debt, they tend to depict Plato as making a crucial departure from Parmenides in so far as they assume that Parmenides denied the existence of the world of our ordinary experience. The assessment by W. K. C. Guthrie, in the discussion of Plato's philosophical influences which introduces the volumes on Plato in his *History of Greek Philosophy*, is fairly representative. Acknowledging Parmenides' considerable influence on Plato, he says that Parmenides' 'challenging thesis that by all rational argument motion and change were impossible had to be met without evading his apparently unassailable premisses. . . . Plato modified the harsh dichotomy of Parmenides . . . by introducing an intermediate ontological category between being and non-being, namely the world of becoming. Not having the status of full, unchanging being, it could not be the object of full knowledge but only of *doxa*, belief or opinion. Nevertheless, the "beliefs of mortals" were not wholly false as Parmenides had claimed (B1. 30), but somewhere between knowledge and ignorance as their subject was between the being of the Forms and sheer nonentity.'[4] The brevity and the general nature of Guthrie's assessment is also representative, at least of those who have not slighted the relation altogether;[5] and it reflects the widespread

---

[3] On certain Parmenidean elements in the *Phaedo*, cf. Hackforth 1955, 84, Guthrie 1965, 38, and 1975, 352.   [4] Guthrie 1975, 34–5.

[5] Thus Zeller 1922, 645 ff. and 655–7, who, like many others to follow, described Plato's distinction between being and becoming broadly as a fusion of Eleatic and Heraclitean perspectives. Cf. e.g. Grube 1935, 4, for a sceptical assessment, and Raven

failure to engage in the preliminary exploration of the dynamic of Plato's appropriations that should serve as the basis for any serious assessment of the relation.[6] Such efforts in this direction as one does find all too often proceed by the methodologically unsound course of adopting from the outset an independent interpretation of Parmenides and then attempting to assess Plato's use of his predecessor with reference to this interpretation. An obvious failing of this procedure is that it assumes that the meaning of Parmenides' notoriously underdetermined and malleable poem is somehow sufficiently transparent for us to assume that Plato would have arrived at the same interpretation of it as the modern scholar, even though this scholar typically assumes himself to be equipped with various tools of historical, philological, and philosophical analysis unavailable to Plato. Blindness to this error manifests itself most notably in the presumption, visible in Guthrie and repeated frequently elsewhere, that Plato must be breaking radically with Parmenides in his account of *doxa* and the ontological status of its object—despite the equally frequent, indeed, often simultaneous, assertion that Parmenides is the single most important influence on Plato's distinction between the intelligible and the sensible.[7]

The essential questions—whether and to what extent Plato's conception agrees with or departs from Parmenides'—are rarely even posed. One who has at least asked the question is Theodor Ebert. In a brief section of his book on knowledge and belief in Plato entitled 'Epigone oder Kritiker des Eleatismus?', he argues that Plato's treatment in *Republic* 5 of the relation between these cognitive states is in

---

1965, 7, for a more charitable general view. Most other general studies of Plato's middle period metaphysics have even less to say about Parmenides' influence on the distinction than the general remarks of these authors.

[6] Something of an exception is Krämer 1969, 7 ff., who, in attempting a historical elucidation of Plato's enigmatic claim at *R*. 6. 509b8–10 that the Good is 'beyond being', and having noted the general Parmenidean character of the forms, proceeds to explore 'ob und inwieweit *innerhalb* der eleatischen Problemstellung eine Differenzierung möglich war, die auf den platonischen Seinsüberwurf (ἐπέκεινα τῆς οὐσίας) hinführte'. I find untenable, however, Krämer's assumption that Plato's conception of Eleaticism at this period is not based directly upon Parmenides' poem, where the primary antithesis is between being and not-being, but is mediated via its Zenonian (and, to a lesser extent, Melissan) development, in which the primary antithesis becomes unity versus plurality (though Krämer requires this assumption to find any Eleatic pedigree for the thesis that the Good/One is beyond Being).

[7] Cf. e.g. Cornford 1933, 101–2; Brown 1945, 172–3; Librizzi 1950, ch. 4 (esp. 40–1, 45); Friedländer 1969, 24; Guthrie 1965, 26, 38, and esp. 75; Prauss 1966, 37–8; Robin 1968, 86; Levi 1970, 30–1 (cf. Levi 1948, 80); Solmsen 1971(*a*), 68; Guthrie 1975, 492, 496–7; Reale 1978, 26.

fact intended as a critique rather than a development of Parmenides.[8]
Unfortunately, Ebert's conclusion is based on certain features of Karl
Reinhardt's (not Plato's) interpretation of Parmenides—and worse,
on an unpersuasive reading of *Republic* 5. To resolve the discrepancies between the way in which Plato distinguishes between knowledge
and belief here and in the *Meno* and *Theaetetus*, Ebert adopts the
extreme position that *Republic* 5. 476e4–8 indicates that the arguments
to follow, in which knowledge and belief are demarcated in such a way
that no transition from the latter to the former is possible, are not to
be taken as representing Plato's own view.[9] Plato's 'critique' of Parmenides, then, amounts to an implicit criticism of the unmediated
opposition between knowledge and belief that forms the cornerstone
of his theory of *doxa*. That is, Ebert supposes from the outset a
genuine continuity between Plato's theory of the relation between
knowledge and *doxa* in *Republic* 5 and Parmenides' view, but because
Plato's theory here is not Plato's theory, he concludes that its presentation represents a criticism of Parmenides.

An alternative possibility is that such problems as Ebert detects
within the *Republic* 5 theory may be explained, at least in part, genet-
ically—that is, as a function of Plato's appropriation of Parmenides.
Such is the view of Arpad Szabó, whose brief remarks constitute one
of the few presumptions of structural continuity at all levels between
Plato's theory and Parmenides'.[10] He suggests that the theory of
knowledge, ignorance, and belief expounded by Socrates at *Republic*
5. 476e7 ff. is so 'conspicuously mechanical', particularly in its denial
that what-is-not can be an object of belief, that a historical explanation must be sought for Plato's adoption of it. The origins of the view
of knowledge and ignorance here, he argues, are essentially Eleatic:
he quotes Parmenides B2. 5–8 as 'der Ursprung des Platonischen

---

[8] Ebert 1974, 131–2 (cf. 116).

[9] Ibid. 118. A more recent variation of this view may be found in Stokes 1992,
who argues that Socrates' arguments with the sight-lovers are wholly 'dialectical'
and therefore that 'we should not saddle Plato himself with any other than the *literary* responsibility for either the course or the conclusions of the argument' (104).
(If one were to extend this criterion of dialecticality, one might well wonder for
which of his arguments Plato might be presumed to bear more than a 'literary'
responsibility.)

[10] Szabó 1955, 99–102. Another who comes close to assuming a serious continuity between the respective theories of *doxa* and its objects is Findlay 1974,
14, who in a rather vague statement notes that for Parmenides the 'changeable
world of the senses . . . existed not in truth but only in the "Opinions of Mortals", a
view which probably did not mean that it was just nothing: it had perhaps a certain shadowy, dependent half-being of which Plato was later to make use in his own
theory'.

Gedankens'. Likewise, he thinks that *doxa* occupies the same position in Parmenides as in Plato's classification: here he quotes B6. 4–9 for comparison. He concludes by asserting that the very distinction in Plato between the visible and the intelligible is Eleatic in origin. However, in supposing that all one need do to prove that 'die Meinung bei Parmenides dieselbe Rolle hat, wie in der Platonischen Rangordnung' (whatever, exactly, he means by this) is juxtapose the two texts, Szabó, like the other authors to whom I have referred, fails to recognize that what is actually required is a serious effort to comprehend how Plato understood Parmenides. Szabó's easy presumption of continuity is as naive in its approach as the more common presumption of radical discontinuity.

Before proceeding, then, I want to say something about how I believe we must approach the question of Parmenides' influence on Plato. I have already noted the principal error vitiating most appraisals of this influence, namely the assumption that one can base an appraisal upon an interpretation of Parmenides developed independently of the actual Platonic reception. Such attempts at assessing this specific case of intellectual influence are particularly unfortunate, since many modern treatments of Parmenides have, either implicitly or explicitly, endeavoured to avoid any interpretation of his philosophy that might appear too 'Platonic', afraid that attributing to him anything like Plato's own distinction between the sensible world of becoming and the intelligible realm of being would be anachronistic. The paradox involved in then addressing Parmenides' influence on Plato, based on a view of Parmenides that deliberately avoids seeing him as Plato might have done, should be apparent. Now, those who avoid a 'Platonic' reading of Parmenides tacitly recognize that it is indeed possible to understand Parmenides as articulating the type of epistemological and ontological categories fundamental to Platonism—as well they should, since such an understanding was fairly common among later Platonists in antiquity. Therefore, even if one were unwilling to accept an interpretation along these lines as representing a proper understanding of Parmenides himself, one would nevertheless have to admit that the 'Platonic' understanding had its historical effect and, as such, deserves attention. One might even believe that Plato himself would have subscribed to the 'Platonic' understanding of Parmenides.

   The principal error that I have indicated undermines most appraisals of Parmenides' influence on Plato owes its prevalence to the all too common tendency among historians of Greek philosophy to rely upon an unreflective model of intellectual influence. Here we need to distinguish between two broad varieties of project in which the historian of philosophy engages. In the first, the historian attempts to give the best possible account of the thought of a particular philosopher in its own right (perhaps in a particular work or on a particular topic). In the second, the historian undertakes to give an account of the process of change between one philosopher or period and the next, or, in the more specific case, of the influence of one thinker (or thinkers) upon a later thinker. Perhaps because they tend to concern themselves primarily with the first type of project, historians too often operate on the assumption that it has a direct bearing on the second. In the case with which we are concerned, this view of the relation between the two types of project leads to the assumption that a better understanding of Parmenides' thought in its own right necessarily places one in a better position to understand his influence on later philosophers, which amounts to the assumption that what Parmenides meant to say somehow reveals itself monologically in each subsequent encounter with his poem.

Stated in these terms, the inadequacy of any such assumption should be apparent. The first variety of historical project does not have a necessary connection with the second. Again, in the case with which we are concerned, it is simply a mistake—one might term it the 'essentialist fallacy'—to privilege Parmenides' intended meaning as the determining factor in his subsequent influence. I therefore want to make it clear that I shall not be concerned in what follows with arguing that Parmenides himself should be understood in a certain way. Instead, I assume that what Parmenides himself may have intended is largely irrelevant to an account of his influence on Plato. (This is of course not necessarily the case—Plato may have understood Parmenides roughly as he intended to be understood. But it will not be part of my project to argue that this is so.) Concentration on the project of reconstructing what Parmenides meant to say has resulted in an uncritical assumption that such a reconstruction may serve without modification as the basis for discussing his later influence. Attempting to explain Plato's engagement with Parmenides as a response to an interpretation that there is little guarantee he would have accepted results at best in distortion and, at worst, in a fiction that bears little relation to the actual character of the encounter. One must, consequently, attempt to establish the recoverable features of Plato's reception and attempt to understand the view of Parmenides presupposed by these features before one will be in a proper position to address the question of his actual influence on Plato. In short, I want to shift the frame of discussion away from talk of 'influence', implying as it does the essentialist view that Parmenides' intended meaning somehow flows easily and naturally into each subsequent encounter, to take a properly reception-orientated approach. Thinking in terms of reception demands that one devote close attention to how Plato takes over elements of Parmenides' thought that he saw as conformable to his own philosophical purposes. Plato's actual use or reception of Parmenides must itself be our guide to the historically relevant interpretation.

That Parmenides' intended meaning may bear little relation to his actual influence might seem rather unlikely, so I shall try to explain why I think this is in fact a natural assumption. If we consider Parmenides' poem as an act of communication, it is evident that it has various conditions for success, which in certain circumstances are easy to satisfy, while in other circumstances they may fail to be met for various reasons. One also needs to appreciate that the (broadly construed) grammatical or purely semantic content of Parmenides' utterances is not by itself sufficient to determine their meaning unambiguously. These utterances (or indeed, any utterances) are often underspecified in that they can convey more than their direct propositional content. We should resist attempts to reduce or limit the possibilities of what his verses *can* mean by arguing on purely grammatical grounds that such and such is what they *must* mean. Paul Grice, for one, has taught us to appreciate that what a speaker may mean by uttering a particular sentence and what that sentence itself means need not be closely related. Here linguists speak of a distinction between 'speaker-meaning' and 'sentence-meaning'. The potential gap between speaker-meaning and sentence-meaning has its analogue at the audience or recipient's end. The potential gaps in fact multiply once we introduce this third element into our basic description of communicative acts. Thus what a recipient understands as meant by an utterance need not be closely related to the purely semantic content of that utterance (receiver-meaning ≠ sentence-meaning); or a recipient might take an utterance's literal meaning to be what its speaker intended to convey in a situation where this is not in fact the case (receiver-meaning = sentence-meaning ≠ speaker-meaning); or, most radically, and perhaps what occurs most often in Plato's reading of Parmenides, what a recipient understands as meant by an utterance may conform neither to its literal meaning nor to what its speaker in fact intended to convey (receiver-meaning ≠ sentence-meaning ≠ speaker-meaning).

The greater the historical distance between the original speaker (or author) and the eventual audience or recipient, the greater the likelihood that these potential discrepancies between meaning (intended or literal) and interpretation will increase. This is true for a number of reasons. First, whatever original performative dimension the utterance may have had is lost, with a resultant loss of all information the speaker may have originally conveyed via extra-linguistic means. What remains is a text constituting a record of an original performance. Second, the shared cultural presuppositions that facilitated understanding of the speaker by his original or target audience, and upon which he will have relied in conveying his meaning, will be diminished if not completely lost. Third, the historically distant recipient's own cultural presuppositions, unenvisaged by the original speaker, will unavoidably influence understanding of the speaker's message. Fourth, the historically distant recipient's interest in the text may be centred more upon the *use* he can make of it rather than simply upon achieving an accurate understanding of it. Although one could obviously introduce other factors, these are some of the more important and the ones on which I want to focus. The first pair of factors concerns the progressive loss of access to the speaker's intentions; the latter pair, the progressively greater effect of the recipient's own presuppositions and intentions.

When Parmenides originally performed his poem, the knowledge and beliefs he shared with his audience must have allowed him to convey meanings that went beyond the purely semantic content of his utterances. By situating his verse within (or in opposition to) certain poetic, religious, and philosophical traditions, he would have been able to guide his audience's expectations and foster in them certain presuppositions that he would have felt to be essential to the apprehension of his message. We can, even now, see that the proem of his poem would have been crucial to achieving this purpose, for it contains numerous cues or indications of the context within which Parmenides wants his message to be understood. We can still identify many of these cues even if we can only speculate on their original significance. For instance, Parmenides clearly expected his audience to perceive the identity of the horses he describes as conveying him and of the path on which they carried him, which he describes as 'far-fabled' (πολύφημον, B1. 2). He would also have relied on his target audience to understand why he describes this as 'the path of the divinity' (ὁδὸν . . . δαίμονος, B1. 2–3),[11] who the 'sun-maidens' (Ἡλιάδες κοῦραι, B1. 9) guiding him are, where and what the House of Night

---

[11] Accepting δαίμονος, as *ap.* SE, *M.* 7. 111, in preference to the emendation, δαίμονες, accepted by DK.

he describes himself as having gone to is, and who the goddess is who addresses him on his arrival there and in whose voice he presents the remainder of the poem.

One might feel secure in the identification of some of these elements, but then I have drawn attention to elements standardly discussed in treatments of the proem. Perhaps there are cues we no longer recognize as such. Is it, for example, significant that Parmenides describes in such detail the action of his chariot's axle and its wheels? Or that he so elaborately describes the gates through which he enters the House of Night and their movement? Sextus Empiricus, who has preserved the proem for us, was one who did consider these elements significant. Even if we are successful in making the relevant identifications, we still face the more difficult and uncertain task of explaining how these and other such elements bear upon Parmenides' message in the rest of the poem. Presumably how they do so would have been clearer to his target audience, so that it would probably have had a better idea than we do of the identity of the subject he speaks so fervently about in what follows.

I of course do not mean to deny that if one wanted to understand Parmenides, one should do one's best to recover as much of the original context of his poem as possible, for this is an important step in successfully carrying out the first kind of historical project.[12] I think it is clear, however, that a historically distant recipient will probably not possess all or even most of the knowledge Parmenides relied upon sharing with his target audience. Furthermore, the unforeseen beliefs and presuppositions of the later recipient will almost certainly result in his understanding Parmenides as saying things he did not in fact mean. This divergence will be all the greater when the recipient reads the poem with the intention of using it in the context of an already established set of concerns and problems, as was the case with Plato. The same sentence can express different propositions on different occasions, even when it is uttered by the same speaker. When a speaker other than the original speaker utters that sentence—and this is in effect what the eventual recipient does when he subsequently uses or reads the text—in a different cultural context, with a set of assumptions influencing his view of its meaning different from those assumed by the original speaker, and with the aim of employing the sentence for ends that speaker did not or even could not envisage, then the like-

---

[12] The single most enlightening attempt to recover and explain the cultural context of Parmenides' poem by focusing on these and other such elements in the proem remains Burkert 1969, aspects of which are developed in Furley 1973. See also Pellikaan-Engel 1974 and Feyerabend 1984.

lihood that it will be taken to express a proposition other than the one it was originally meant to express would appear almost guaranteed. If what Parmenides meant by a specific statement is determined to some extent by how he used that statement, then when he is no longer the one using that statement but is replaced in this role by a later recipient of his text, then that recipient's presuppositions, intentions, and goals become the more important factors in determining the meaning of the statement.

All of this is by way of clarifying my claim that what Parmenides may have meant to say does not necessarily play a role in his subsequent influence. I hope that most of what I have said will simply seem commonsensical. For I am less interested in articulating a specific methodology (and even less in applying the methodology of a specific school or movement, be it philosophical, literary critical, or linguistic) than I am interested in what results from pursuing an idea the essential point of which can be stated simply enough: we must try to understand Parmenides as Plato did if we are to be in any position to speak meaningfully about Parmenides' influence on Plato. This rather basic principle leads to quite complex results in application. For it involves us in the often difficult process of inferring Plato's understanding of Parmenides from his actual use of him. Plato nowhere simply sets out his view of Parmenides. We are therefore always forced to piece together his interpretation from his integrated use of Parmenides at various periods, with all the difficulties this involves. These difficulties are multiplied by the fact that Plato is, as we shall see, also concerned with contemporary or near-contemporary uses of Parmenides that are in conflict with his own. This fact is, I hope, one of the more interesting things to emerge from the present study, for it serves as a reminder of the polyphony in Parmenides' reception even at its earliest stages.

Although the readings of Parmenides that will emerge from our examination of the Platonic reception are often rather different from most currently on offer, it is not my intention to argue that they are essentially correct or even more plausible than other interpretations of Parmenides. I do nevertheless spend some time developing readings of certain Parmenidean passages within the framework set by Plato's reception both to facilitate understanding of this reception and to show that it presumes a coherent reading of Parmenides. I thus take issue only obliquely with the numerous studies of Parmenides in his own right, primarily to counter claims that he cannot be read in this way. One might believe that understanding the history of Parmenides' ancient reception, and Plato's reception in particular,

should lead to a better understanding of Parmenides himself.[13]
Although I once found this idea attractive, I no longer feel it important to make such a claim here. If one wants a better understanding of
Parmenides, one should engage directly in the first variety of historical project. The decision to devote my attention here to the second
variety of project vis-à-vis Parmenides should by no means be
thought of as a challenge to the legitimacy of this different, more traditional type of project. In fact, I necessarily continue to engage in
it myself, for taking the approach to Parmenides I do here demands
engaging in the first kind of project vis-à-vis Plato. Which is to say
that this study is first and foremost a study of Plato.

Although I think that the arguments at the end of *Republic* 5 are the
only middle period text in which Plato's engagement with Parmenides
is clear and sufficiently sustained for us to recover the understanding

---

[13] This is the type of mistake made by Osborne 1987. She advocates returning to
the authors who quote what we have of the Presocratics and reading the quotations
within the framework supplied by these later authors. She is clearly correct in pointing out that we need to pay greater attention to the context in which our fragments
of the Presocratics are quoted and to the interests of the authors quoting them, interests which will have governed their selection of the texts they have preserved for us.
However, despite her introduction's frequent and promising calls for a reception-
orientated approach to the Presocratics, she eventually succumbs to the temptation
of supposing that the type of deep recontextualization advocated constitutes a proper
method for arriving at a better understanding of the early authors themselves (in this
case, Empedocles and Heraclitus). The result is what may most charitably be viewed
as an unresolved tension in her conception of her project, to which reviewers have
rightly drawn attention (see esp. Barnes 1988 and Schofield 1988). She also ends up
making extravagant claims for the worth and status of the quoting author's (in this
case, Hippolytus') interpretation. For example: 'No subsequent reading based on the
words [authors such as Hippolytus] quote can have greater validity than their own
readings' (23). Here Osborne betrays her desire that study of the later reception will
yield a more valid or accurate understanding of the Presocratics in their own right,
as she does elsewhere in her willingness to speak of accounting for the quoting author's
interests so that his biases may be 'defused' (9). Osborne's basic mistake consists
in failing to keep distinct the two types of historical project. Hippolytus' use of the
Presocratics is interesting and very much worth exploring in its own right. But
this exploration should not be mistaken for a guide to a better understanding of the
Presocratics in *their* own right. Cf. Kahn 1988, who makes the same kind of mistake
vis-à-vis the specific case with which we are concerned: Plato 'was in a better position than we are to understand what Parmenides had in mind. Since Plato has given
us a much fuller and more explicit statement of his own conception of Being, this
conception, if used with care, may help us interpret the more lapidary and puzzling utterances of Parmenides himself' (237). Kahn in fact does not move as far in
a reception-orientated direction as this might suggest; instead, he first sets out an independent reading of Parmenides' use of the verb 'to be' and then seeks confirmation
of this reading in Plato.

that lies behind Plato's use, we can nevertheless recognize that Plato's concern with Parmenides in the middle period dialogues extends to a number of doctrines and motifs most characteristic of this period that do not overtly figure in *Republic* 5. I begin, then, with some of these elements, arguing in particular that the theory of recollection presents a response to Meno's paradox analogous to what Plato will have seen as Parmenides' own response to Xenophanes' empiricist doubts about the possibility of knowledge. After the *Symposium* passage already mentioned, Plato's most striking middle period appropriation of Parmenides comes in the argument at *Republic* 5. 467e–477b, which is recognizably Parmenidean in details of phrasing, in overall structure, and in the epistemological and ontological distinctions it aims to establish. This passage employs an important type of argument that Aristotle attributes to both Plato and Parmenides. I accordingly explore how this argument functions here and how it may be seen as functioning in Parmenides. Plato's argument is directed towards winning over a recalcitrant group of thinkers he dubs the lovers of sights and sounds. I argue that it employs certain assumptions the sight-lovers would not have been prepared to accept by discussing the views of certain of Plato's predecessors who might reasonably be thought to have belonged to this class. Here Gorgias emerges as particularly important, for we shall see that he attempted to refute the argument of Parmenides that Plato is adopting in *Republic* 5. I conclude the discussion of Plato's middle period use of Parmenides with an analysis of how Plato's description of the sight-lovers and the views he attributes to them draw upon Parmenides' criticism of mortals and their misguided beliefs.

It is much more difficult to untangle the various strands of Plato's later engagement with Parmenides, where his philosophy comes to be encapsulated in the formulae, 'being is one' and 'the all is one'. I begin trying to do so by showing how the *Theaetetus* and the initial exchanges between Socrates, Zeno, and Parmenides in the *Parmenides* problematize the understanding of these formulations. In the latter dialogue in particular, Plato presents Parmenides as an object of conflicting understandings and appropriations. Zeno is made to characterize his own treatise as an *ad hominem* response to certain reductive attacks upon his master's philosophy, thereby indicating the inadequacy of their underlying view of that philosophy as equivalent to the strict monistic thesis that only one thing exists. Aspects of Plato's own view of Parmenides in the middle period dialogues are marked as inadequate by Parmenides himself, and yet certain essential elements of Plato's earlier use are allowed to stand. Plato emphasizes this by allowing Parmenides to respond to Gorgias' attack on his philosophy and by having him re-articulate the basic argument he had taken over from Parmenides in *Republic* 5. The Gorgianic perspective on Parmenides' philosophy also figures crucially in the First Deduction of the subsequent exercise in which Parmenides undertakes an examination of his own theory. Plato has Parmenides reject this reductive perspective, thereby providing us with a crucially important instance of how Plato is concerned with combating certain sophistic appropriations of Parmenides so as to recover him for the uses he himself wants to make. This dynamic of reappropriation becomes increasingly important as we continue to examine Plato's later period reception.

This theme in fact guides my discussion of the complex representation of Parmenides in the *Sophist*, where I argue that Plato's efforts to define the Sophist so as to discriminate between this figure and the Philosopher are accompanied by an attempt to recover Parmenides from sophistic appropriations that challenge certain of the key distinctions of Plato's middle period metaphysics. I therefore take issue with the common view that Plato in the *Sophist* is determined to 'refute' Parmenides. The Sophist's denial of the viability of the distinctions between truth and falsehood and between reality and appearance employ the logic of Parmenides in ways Plato himself finds unacceptable. Plato's own view of Parmenides in this dialogue emerges in the ontological doxography in which Parmenides is significantly associated with Xenophanes and in the subsequent interrogation of this doxography's first two groups. The interrogation of the Eleatics in particular has important connections with various deductions in the *Parmenides*'s dialectical exercise. These connections make it possible to see where in each dialogue Plato is concerned with sophistic appropriations of Parmenides and where he is engaging with him in ways that reflect his own understanding. This understanding is reflected to some extent in portions of the *Timaeus* but most directly and importantly in the *Parmenides*'s Second Deduction. I therefore conclude this study by describing how Plato will have understood Parmenides' account of the attributes of Being in B8 and the relation of this account to the cosmology he presented alongside it, and I explain how this understanding is reflected in the Second Deduction.

2

Eschatology and Epistemology

Plato's middle period concern with Parmenides is not limited to the passages in which he describes the forms. Rather, it seems to have had its effect upon many of the doctrines most characteristic of this period. Here I want to show how Plato's adoption of a strongly anti-empiricist epistemology seems to be prompted in part by his reading of Parmenides. Scholars have noted certain Parmenidean elements in the middle period dialogues apart from the descriptions of forms, but no one has properly integrated these isolated allusions into anything like a systematic picture of Plato's engagement with Parmenides during this period.[1] Before turning to a detailed examination of the relation between Parmenides' and Plato's arguments at the end of *Republic* 5, I will therefore present an overview of the pervasive though only sporadically acknowledged involvement with

[1] The most rewarding and important study of the middle period's Parmenideanism is to be found in the first three chapters of Prauss 1966. The first chapter presents the theory of forms as a response, deeply influenced by Parmenides, to the problem of the ontological status of universals raised by the repeated *aporiai* of the Socratic search for definitions. Prauss sees Parmenides' influence manifesting itself generally at both the epistemological level, in the conception of true knowledge as transcending the sensible world, and at the ontological level, in the conception of the forms themselves as a plurality of Parmenidean beings. But the 'logische Eleatismus' of his title is tied more closely to his principal theme: the emergence in Plato's thought of the conception of things as substances with attributes, and the concomitant emergence of a conception of *logoi* as predicative statements. Prauss argues in his second and third chapters that, prior to developing this conception, Plato conceived of things as mere aggregates of characters or *dunameis*, of *logoi* as enumerations of the elements of such aggregates, and of knowledge as the process of referring the individual *dunameis* of a thing to their corresponding forms. The Eleaticism of this theory, Prauss maintains, is manifest both in its exclusive division between the forms as absolute unities versus things as absolute pluralities and in the separation of the forms from each other as absolute unities. As his consequent definition of 'logical Eleaticism' (11, cf. 41, 124) shows, Prauss is not interested in the details of Plato's interaction with Parmenides *per se*; instead, 'Eleaticism' for him verges on becoming merely a metaphor (witness his inclusion of the theories of Empedocles, Anaxagoras, and the Atomists as also exemplifying it) that allows him to address certain problems in Plato's development. Also worth mentioning, despite readings often ranging from idiosyncratic to perverse, since it nevertheless presents probably the most sustained attempt at an analysis of the Eleaticism of Plato's middle period, is Liebrucks 1949.

Parmenides that forms part of the background against which those arguments are made.

I will begin, then, with the *Phaedrus* myth. In his second speech in this dialogue, Socrates undertakes to show that love is a type of divine madness. The demonstration requires that he discuss the nature of the soul and its various activities and experiences, a discussion he begins by arguing that the soul is immortal given its character as a self-mover. Although, he says, the soul's immortality may be established by argument, its nature could only be adequately described by a god —humans must be content with describing its nature by analogy and comparison. Thus his famous comparison of the soul to a charioteer with a pair of winged horses (246a3–b4). In his commentary on the dialogue, Syrianus' pupil Hermias connected Plato's image of the soul chariot with, among others, the chariot of Parmenides' proem: 'Plato was not the first to employ the charioteer and horses, but prior to him the inspired poets Homer, Orpheus,[2] and Parmenides did so' (Herm. *in Phdr*. 122, 19–21). Modern scholars have, as one would expect, taken up positions both for and against there being any serious connection, the weight of opinion perhaps leaning against.[3] From the point of view of the Platonic reception, however, the absurdity of Leonardo Tarán's representative assertion that 'in Parmenides nothing suggests the comparison of the chariot with the soul' will be obvious. Suggests to whom? Certainly not to one who would have recognized, for example, the parallels between the proem and Orphic accounts of the initiate's experience of the afterlife. Moreover, those denying any Parmenidean inheritance here have taken too narrow a focus: the substance of Plato's image is itself so slight as to make the question of the intertextual relation unanswerable on this basis alone. What seems to confirm the debt is the subsequent use of the chariot image in the description of the purified soul's ascent to the hyperouranian region and its consequent vision of reality. Here Plato's appropriation of

---

[2] Hermias appears to be confused about Orpheus. Later, at *in Phdr*. 142, 13–18, he speaks of the horses of Phanes and quotes the verse from the Orphic Rhapsodies: 'conveyed here and there by golden wings' (χρυσείαις πτερύγεσσι φορεύμενος ἔνθα καὶ ἔνθα, *OF*, fr. 78). Hermias is most likely, under the influence of Plato's own image, projecting a pair of winged horses for Phanes from what is actually the standard description of Phanes himself as winged.

[3] Among those confident of the derivation are Diels 1897, 22; Natorp 1903, 72; Frutiger 1930, 264; and Ferguson 1963, 191. The differences between Plato's imagery and Parmenides' are stressed by Robin 1954, lxxix n. 2 (who sees a source in the plastic arts as more likely); Hackforth 1952, 76–7 (who thinks the account of the soul in the *Republic* a sufficient source); and Tarán 1965, 18–19. De Vries 1969, 126 ad *Phdr*. 246a7, is non-committal.

Parmenides' proem is more evident and begins to reveal itself as a genuinely philosophical engagement.

Even before the chariot image is introduced, one finds, as Paul Friedländer has noted,[4] Parmenidean language in the description of the soul in the proof of its immortality. The soul, as source of motion and change for all other things, must itself be ungenerated (ἀγένητον, 245d1); since it is ungenerated, it must necessarily also be imperishable (ἀδιάφθορον, d4). This is to attribute to the soul features that Parmenides had attributed to Being when he said: 'Being is ungenerated and imperishable' (ἀγένητον ἐὸν καὶ ἀνώλεθρόν ἐστιν, B8. 3). It is possible, Socrates continues, for such a self-mover 'neither to be destroyed nor to come to be' (οὔτ' ἀπόλλυσθαι οὔτε γίγνεσθαι, 245d7–8), echoing Parmenides' conclusion that Being has been allowed by Justice 'neither to come to be nor to perish' (οὔτε γενέσθαι | οὔτ' ὄλλυσθαι, B8. 13–14). The Parmenidean echoes are particularly interesting in so far as the proof as such probably derives from Alcmaeon (cf. Arist. *De an.* 1. 2. 405ª29 ff.). Their presence may be explained by comparing the position of the *Phaedo* (also recalling Alcmaeon) that the soul 'most resembles that which is divine, deathless, intelligible, single in kind, indissoluble, and forever the same in the same state as itself' (τῷ μὲν θείῳ καὶ ἀθανάτῳ καὶ νοητῷ καὶ μονοειδεῖ καὶ ἀδιαλύτῳ καὶ ἀεὶ ὡσαύτως κατὰ ταὐτὰ ἔχοντι ἑαυτῷ ὁμοιότατον εἶναι, *Phd.* 80b1–3; cf. *R.* 10. 611e2–3). Here in the *Phaedo* (as later in the *Phaedrus*) Plato describes the forms in Parmenidean language, and it is only to be expected that he would transfer this terminology to the soul in so far as it is presumed to resemble them. But in no other description of the soul are the borrowings so clear, which suggests an intention to evoke Parmenides from the outset of the *Phaedrus* myth. There may also be some more subtle preparation when Socrates prefaces his account of the hyperouranian region by saying that, while no poet has ever sung of it as it deserves, one must nevertheless tell the truth about it, especially when one is speaking about the truth (*Phdr.* 247c3–6). We might well wonder if any poet ever sang of this place, and the only suitable candidate seems to be Parmenides. Similarly, Socrates' designation of his subject as 'about the truth' (περὶ ἀληθείας) recalls Parmenides' designation of the first portion of his exposition as 'about the truth' (ἀμφὶς ἀληθείης, B8. 51, cf. B1. 29). Both allusions (if such they are) are so oblique as to be negligible in themselves, but occurring in close proximity to one another, and in the context in which they do, are perhaps meant to be recognizable.

---

[4] Friedländer 1969, 371 n. 19.

The reader is prepared in these various ways to recognize the structural similarity between the voyage to a revelation of Being described in Parmenides' proem and Plato's description of the soul's journey upon death to the hyperouranian region where it attains a vision via *nous*, the soul's governing part, of the 'real Being' (οὐσία ὄντως οὖσα) that is the true object of all true knowledge (247c7–8). Paul Natorp in fact gave greater emphasis to this portion of the myth than to the chariot image itself.[5] He recognized that the description of the forms as 'complete, simple, and unshaken' (ὁλόκληρα δὲ καὶ ἁπλᾶ καὶ ἀτρεμῆ, 250c2–3) is yet another reminiscence of the Parmenidean attributes of Being. Furthermore, he felt there to be an especially strong Eleatic influence upon the earlier opposition, in the account of the soul's vision, between that which really is Being (ὅ ἐστιν ὄν ὄντως) and the things which we now call beings (247d–e). He thought this to be as close as Plato ever comes to the Eleatic denial of becoming and of the existence of the sensible world. Plato's point, however, in saying that the soul passes beyond 'the things that we now say "are"' to a vision of 'what really is' (249c3–4) is not that we are mistaken in saying that the objects of the sensible world exist but rather that they cannot be said to be without restriction, in other words that they do not possess the same absolute mode of being enjoyed by what really is. Equally Parmenidean is the description of those souls unable to attain the vision of real Being as going away to feed 'on the food of opinion' (τροφῇ δοξαστῇ, 248b4–5). These relations are all worked out more fully, and in even more distinctly Parmenidean terms, in the presentation of the distinctions between knowledge and *doxa*, being and becoming, in *Republic* 5. The *Phaedrus* myth, however, incorporates these elements into the context of a revelation of pure Being transcending the world of ordinary experience that recalls the revelation granted Parmenides.[6]

The *Phaedrus* myth thus suggests how Plato may have read Parmenides' proem. I would, therefore, disagree with J. S. Morrison's view that the *Republic*'s myth of Er indicates that Plato read the proem, not as an ascent to the realm of pure Being, but as a *katabasis* or journey to the underworld.[7] Morrison supports the *katabasis* interpretation

    [5] Natorp 1903, 72.
    [6] Cf. Solmsen 1971(a), 69–70, who notes a comparable structural similarity whereby Parmenides' account of Being and Plato's in many ways analogous account of the Beautiful in the *Symposium* are each presented as the 'revelation' of mysterious female figures, the goddess and Diotima.
    [7] Morrison 1955, 59–60. Those who have supposed that Parmenides' proem describes an *anabasis* rather than a *katabasis* have sometimes also seen a parallel in

of the proem by comparing its imagery to that of Hesiod, *Theogony*
744 ff.; he supposes that the observable connections between the
two texts establishes Parmenides' destination as 'the familiar region
of poetic tradition about the underworld'. While I agree that the
Hesiodic parallels (and others Morrison cites) make it highly probable that Parmenides' proem does in fact describe a *katabasis*, there
are insufficient signs in the myth of Er itself to indicate that Plato took
it as such. Morrison makes the common mistake of gauging the
Platonic reception via an independent interpretation of Parmenides.
With the possible exception of the account of the structure of the
cosmos at 616b–617c, upon which Morrison focuses, Plato does not
actually appear to make any significant use of Parmenides' proem in
the myth of Er. Such use as he may be thought to make in this particular passage suggests an understanding of the proem as describing an *anabasis* or ascent rather than a *katabasis*. The most direct
connection Morrison makes is between the 'yawning chasm' (χάσμ'
ἀχανές, B1. 18) formed by the opening of the gates of Night and Day
in Parmenides and the pairs of chasms or χάσματα in earth and heaven
through which souls pass to and from the regions above and below in
the myth of Er (*R.* 10. 614c).[8] Parmenides, with the maidens, chariot
and horses, passes through this chasm (B1. 21–2) before he comes
to the place where he receives the goddess's revelation. If there is a
comparable revelation in the *Republic* myth, it would seem to occur
when the souls journey to a place, apparently at the extremity of
the heaven,[9] from which they observe the mechanism of the cosmic

---

the *Republic*'s myth of the cave; cf. Librizzi 1950, 45; Ballauff 1963. More generally,
cf. Burkert 1972, 357–68, on astral immortality from the earliest period of speculation about the soul's nature and post-mortem existence through to the Platonic myths.

  [8] Morrison 1955, 60.
  [9] The troublesome word is ἄνωθεν at *R.* 10. 616b4. Morrison 1955, 66, notes the
apparent parallel with *Phd.* 110b5 ff., where the earth is described as it would appear
if seen from above—εἴ τις ἄνωθεν θεῷτο. He maintains, however, that 'there is no
indication in the *Republic* that the souls reach such an elevation in the journey
described' and accordingly prefers to construe ἄνωθεν, not with καθορᾶν which it
immediately follows, but with τεταμένον. But Plato says the souls do not merely reach
a place where they can observe the great rainbow-like light διὰ παντὸς τοῦ οὐρανοῦ
καὶ γῆς τεταμένον (616b4–5)—which Morrison properly renders as 'stretched *over*
[not through] the whole heaven and earth' so as to interpret the light not as the cosmos's axis but as a surrounding bond holding it together (cf. 616c1–4)—but, after
another day's journey, the souls actually reach this light itself (εἰς ὃ [sc. τὸ φῶς]
ἀφικέσθαι προελθόντες ἡμερησίαν ὁδόν, 616b6–7). To save himself from inconsistency,
Morrison should be willing to admit that the souls do indeed observe the workings
of the cosmos from an elevated position—from the extreme boundary of the cosmos
itself—although this would begin to undermine his *katabasis* interpretation.

revolutions (*R.* 10. 616c–617b). This revelation, however, is only of the physical structure of the heavens. Plato hints at another kind of revelation, more in line with the revelation of real Being in the *Phaedrus* myth, when he says that the souls returning from the heavens told of having witnessed sights of inexpressible beauty (615a3–4). Even Morrison thinks it 'seems certain that Plato here has in mind something like the procession of souls which he describes so vividly in the *Phaedrus*'.[10] Each revelation in the *Republic* takes place only after the souls' journey to an ouranian (possibly hyperouranian) region. If either is supposed to have a Parmenidean analogue—that is, if the myth of Er does indeed draw upon Parmenides—then, contrary to Morrison, but consistent with the *Phaedrus* myth, it implies an interpretation of the proem as ascent.

If one accepts the relation between Parmenides' proem and the *Phaedrus* myth (and, to a lesser degree, the myth of Er), the intertextual relation is nevertheless not precise enough to allow us to infer with confidence what view Plato took of the earlier text. He may indeed, as I have been suggesting, simply have understood the proem as describing an ascent. Or he may have thought Parmenides' House of Night is, as the Hesiodic parallels suggest, located at the 'roots' of Earth, Tartarus, the ocean and the heavens but transferred the place of revelation in his own account from the ends of the earth to the boundary of the heavens. Or he may have recognized the Hesiodic parallels but still understood the proem as an ascent, understanding Parmenides himself as having transformed the traditional topography. This uncertainty does not mean that there is no recognizable Parmenidean influence operating in the *Phaedrus* myth. One can still perceive the traces of that influence even if one cannot be confident of the interpretation that lies behind them.

Even though the precise details of Plato's reading of the proem are beyond recovery, one important point is clear: Plato interpreted the proem epistemologically. By this I do not mean that he took it as Sextus Empiricus does, as an extended epistemological allegory in which each element has its literal analogue in an account of the cognitive faculties and the search for knowledge (SE, *M.* 7. 112–14). Nor as the less extreme modern allegorizers such as Bowra do. I mean instead that he would have found in Parmenides a counterpart to his own view that ultimate apprehension of pure being is available to the human soul only after death. Because of the presence in the proem of imagery of the Orphic initiate's post-mortem experience

10 Morrison 1955, 66.

as described in the verses on the gold lamellae from southern Italy, Crete, and Thessaly,[11] it would be straightforward for Plato to interpret the proem as Parmenides' account of his own afterlife experience (or something analogous to it such as a dream). The connections between Parmenides' proem and Plato's myths are unlikely to be merely a function of their having a common source in Orphic and Pythagorean eschatology, for there is little indication in our sources that the Pythagoreans or the Orphica, despite promoting ritual purification of the soul so that it might obtain a blessed state after death, taught of any specific post-mortem revelation of things cosmic and divine. Indeed, the development one can trace within Plato's eschatological myths from the almost exclusive concern with the system of rewards and punishments in the *Gorgias*, through the balanced fusion of the judgement and revelation themes in the *Phaedo* and *Republic*, to the final ascendancy of the revelation theme in the *Phaedrus* myth (at which point the soul's vision is not merely of the physical workings of the cosmos but of Being itself) runs parallel to the signs, in these myths and elsewhere, of Plato's increasing interest in Parmenides. This is no coincidence. Parmenides would have seemed unique in providing a model for both the content and the conditions of the unfettered soul's vision of Being.

The theoretical component of this post-mortem vision is, of course, Plato's view that learning essentially involves a process of recollection. The symbiosis between the recollection theory and the revelation theme is clearest at *Phaedrus* 249b6–c4, where Socrates describes proceeding from numerous perceptions and collecting them into one by reasoning as 'recollection of those things our soul once saw when, journeying with God and peering above the things which we now say are, it lifted its head up to what really is'. The increasing prominence of the revelation theme in Plato's eschatology points to development within the theory of recollection itself. The engagement with Parmenides is important to this development, for Plato's theory is analogous to what he would have seen as the Parmenidean response to Xenophanes' doubts about the possibility of knowledge. Plato also addresses the inadequacies of what begins in the *Meno* as an essentially Pythagorean theory by grafting onto it more specifically Parmenidean features.

Meno states the problems of learning as follows: 'but how, Socrates, will you search for something that you do not in the least know what is? Which of the things you do not know will you establish as

---

[11] See Burkert 1969, Feyerabend 1984.

the object of your search? *Or, even if you were to chance directly upon it, how will you know that this is what you did not know?* (ἢ εἰ καὶ ὅτι μάλιστα ἐντύχοις αὐτῷ, πῶς εἴσῃ ὅτι τοῦτό ἐστιν ὃ σὺ οὐκ ᾔδησθα;)' (*Men.* 80d5–8). This lemma to Meno's formulation of the problem directly echoes Xenophanes B34:

> καὶ τὸ μὲν οὖν σαφὲς οὔτις ἀνὴρ ἴδεν οὐδέ τις ἔσται
> εἰδὼς ἀμφὶ θεῶν τε καὶ ἄσσα λέγω περὶ πάντων·
> εἰ γὰρ καὶ τὰ μάλιστα τύχοι τετελεσμένον εἰπών,
> αὐτὸς ὅμως οὐκ οἶδε· δόκος δ᾽ἐπὶ πᾶσι τέτυκται

(and so the clear truth not any man has seen, nor will there be any who knows about the gods and such things as I say about all things: *for even if one were to chance directly to say what has been brought to pass, nevertheless one does not oneself know*—but opinion has been made for all).

Although Diels and Fränkel identified the parallel,[12] subsequent commentators have failed to take it up. One reason for this neglect is that when Socrates equates Meno's problem with the eristic argument that it is impossible for a person to search for either what he knows or what he does not know (cf. *Euthd.* 276d7 ff.), he seems to be addressing only the first part of Meno's statement. Commentators have thus questioned whether Socrates' subsequent theory responds to the lemma at all[13] and, in searching for the paradox's antecedents, have neglected what should be understood as Plato's own signal that it is a sophistic transformation of the Xenophanean problem.[14] It is in fact easy to see how a sceptically inclined fifth-century thinker could have construed Xenophanes B34 as asserting the impossibility of knowledge and, in particular, how such a thinker could have constructed a dilemma around verses 3–4a.

One might nevertheless object that despite the close verbal parallels, there need be no specific allusion to Xenophanes because the prob-

---

[12] DK, i. 137 n. on 21B34. 2; Fränkel 1925, 186 and n. 2; cf. Lesher 1992, 186.

[13] Thus e.g. Moravscik 1970, 57: 'Meno . . . adds the question of how one would know that what is found is the information sought initially. This second problem . . . is not mentioned by Socrates. The reason for this is presumably that as he interprets the puzzle this question need not arise.' Sharples 1985, 143 ad *Men.* 80d5–e6, thinks however that Socrates' theory is as much a response to Meno's lemma as to the sophistic paradox: 'the theory of Recollection shows how we can know that we have reached an answer, and it shows that there is some point in undertaking the enquiry'.

[14] Thus e.g. Bluck 1961, 272 ad *Men.* 80d6 (with no comment on the lemma): 'It is impossible to tell who originated this ἐριστικὸς λόγος, as Socrates calls it. It bears an obvious similarity to the sort of questions that are asked in the *Euthydemus.* . . . One thinks of the Megarians, and in particular of Eubulides (Diog. L. II, 108).' It is unclear, however, from the portion of Diogenes he cites, why one might think of Eubulides.

lem of Meno's lemma had long been a widespread topos. Thus, for example, the author of the Hippocratic treatise *On Ancient Medicine*, in the context of distinguishing medicine from those sciences that appeal in their investigations to things that are non-apparent and problematic: 'if one were to speak of and understand these non-apparent things as they are, they would be clear neither to the person speaking of them nor to his audience—whether or not they are true. For there is nothing against which one can compare them to know the clear truth' (ἃ [sc. τὰ ἀφάνεα] εἴ τις λέγοι καὶ γινώσκοι ὡς ἔχει, οὔτ᾿ ἂν αὐτῷ τῷ λέγοντι οὔτε τοῖς ἀκούουσι δῆλα ἂν εἴη, εἴτε ἀληθέα ἐστὶν εἴτε μή. οὐ γὰρ ἔστι πρὸς ὅ τι χρὴ ἀνενέγκαντα εἰδέναι τὸ σαφές, Hp. *VM* 1). To infer from this text, however, that there was nothing particularly Xenophanean in maintaining that even if one were to hit upon the truth one would have no means of knowing so would, I think, be mistaken. As Jonathan Barnes notes, the connections between the language of this Hippocratic text and Xenophanes B34 are too close to be coincidental. This leads him to conclude that we have here 'an early and favourable exegesis of Xenophanes' fragment'.[15] *On Ancient Medicine* therefore suggests that Xenophanes' statement was famous enough for Plato to have relied upon his audience to appreciate the allusion in Meno's lemma.

Whereas Xenophanes' doubts are firmly rooted in the traditional demarcation between divine and human apprehension,[16] Parmenides in his poem describes himself as overcoming the limitations on human understanding so as to attain via direct divine revelation knowledge such as the gods themselves possess. While Xenophanes says there neither is nor will be a 'man who knows' (ἀνὴρ εἰδώς) the truth about the divine and cosmic matters[17] of which he speaks, Parmenides positions himself directly as a 'knowing man' (εἰδὼς φώς, B1. 3). Perhaps most importantly, Xenophanes relegated his entire system to the cognitive status of mere opinion or δόκος: because no human being has certifiable access to the truth, he says in B34, this is all that is available to humans. James Lesher has recently pointed out how

[15] Barnes 1982, 139; cf. Fränkel 1925, 191.
[16] Cf. e.g. Hom. *Il.* 2. 484–6, Hes. *Op.* 483–4, Theognidea 141–2, Semonides 1. 3–5, Solon 13. 65–70, fr. 17, Pindar, *Olympian* 7. 24–6, Heraclitus 22B78 DK, Alcmaeon 24B1 DK (which resembles Xenoph. B34 in expression), Philolaus 44B6 DK. For a general overview of the theme, see Snell 1953, ch. 7; for an overview tied specifically to Parmenides, see Mansfeld 1964, ch. 1. Note that Barnes 1982, 139, suggests that the metrical clause preceding Arius Didymus' quotation of Xenoph. B34. 4b—θεὸς μὲν οἶδε τὴν ἀλήθειαν ('God knows the truth')—may be a genuine fragment.
[17] This seems the most probable range of ἅσσα λέγω περὶ πάντων.

commentators, through focusing on the similarities between Xenophanes' one God and Parmenides' Being, have generally neglected
what he sees as 'the close correspondence between the "skeptical" conclusion of fragment 34 and the attack on mortal *doxa* from which
Parmenides begins his own account'.[18] Lesher provides a valuable
sketch of Parmenides' response to Xenophanes, centred around the
idea that Parmenides accepts Xenophanes' position that reliance upon
sense perception can only result in δόκος and as a consequence
demands an alternative path to knowledge. Where we must depart
from Lesher is in his view that Parmenides was not merely dissatis-
fied with the limitations of empirical knowledge but went the further
step of denying the very existence of its objects.[19] Although this could
possibly be a correct account of Parmenides' response per se, there
are reasons to doubt even this. There is, at least, no motivation for a
denial of the cosmos's existence in Parmenides' acceptance of the
Xenophanean view that there can be no certain knowledge in cosmic
matters. It at any rate seems that Plato would have viewed Parmenides as simply relegating his cosmological account to the same
status as Xenophanes relegated his own system. Plato places certain
qualifications upon the accuracy of his own cosmological accounts,
saying for example at the conclusion of the *Phaedo* myth that one who
possessed *nous* or true understanding would not hold fast to all the
details of this account (*Phd.* 114d1–2) and describing the cosmology
of the *Timaeus* as a 'likely story' (εἰκὼς μῦθος, *Ti.* 29d2, cf. 30b7). These
reservations seem directly analogous to the qualification Xenophanes
places upon his own account when he says in B35: 'let these be believed
as like true things' (ταῦτα δεδοξάσθω μὲν ἐοικότα τοῖς ἐτύμοισι).
Plato could easily have understood Parmenides as placing a similar
qualification on the status of his cosmological account when he has
the goddess say that 'to you I relate this entire likely ordering of things'
(τόν σοι ἐγὼ διάκοσμον ἐοικότα πάντα φατίζω, B8. 60).[20]

　　In seeing Parmenides as attempting to overcome the limitations
Xenophanes placed on empirical knowledge by positing a fundamentally different mode of understanding, Lesher nevertheless hits
upon the essential point, for reflection upon this particular dialectical relation is likely to have contributed to Plato's own adoption of

---

[18] Lesher 1992, 183. One exception is DK, i. 137 n. ad 21B34. 4.

[19] Here Lesher follows a view of Parmenides' response already articulated by
Fränkel 1925, 192.

[20] Cf. Procl. *in Ti.* 105 A–B (commentary on *Ti.* 29c1–3). Cf. also Wilamowitz-
Möllendorff 1899, 204–5; Cornford 1937, 30.

an anti-empiricist epistemology. One could respond to Xenophanes' (and Meno's) doubts about the possibility of human knowledge by developing a more thorough empiricist epistemology. Aristotle eventually approached the problem in this way, and it is possible that Alcmaeon and the author of *On Ancient Medicine* did so before Plato.[21] Such an approach was available to Plato, and yet he rejects it, perhaps most famously at *Phaedo* 96b where he outlines a theory, only to set it aside, according to which the brain furnishes us with perceptions, from which arise memory, opinion, and eventually, when these have attained a degree of stability, knowledge. In spite of this rejection, he at times seems to come surprisingly close to the empiricist view. At *Phaedrus* 249b6–c1 he says that we come to grasp universals by proceeding from numerous perceptions and collecting them into one by reasoning. Similarly, at *Phaedo* 74b4–6, he says that we have formed our conception of equality from seeing equal sticks, stones, and so on. It seems one of the oddest features of the middle period epistemology that, having proceeded this far along the empiricist path, Plato abandons it to describe the final intuition of the universal as 'recollection'. The apparently empiricist excerpt from the *Phaedo* comes, of course, in the midst of the recollection argument; while in the sentence of the *Phaedrus* immediately following that just referred to, he declares: 'this is recollection of those things which our soul once saw in its journey with god' (249c1–3). Among the numerous factors conditioning this move may be what Plato perceived to be Parmenides' equally radical response to the problem of learning. Like Parmenides, he accepts a Xenophanean view on the limits of empirical inquiry and yet denies that opinion or *doxa* is the highest cognitive state available to humans. He does so by asserting that it is possible to attain a higher state of apprehension via a post-mortem experience furnishing us with knowledge such as the gods themselves possess.

Although I am claiming that Plato perceived there to be a Parmenidean response to Xenophanes B34 analogous in many respects to his own response to Meno's paradox, and although one might think there are some Parmenidean elements in the *Meno*,[22] I would hesitate to suggest that the recollection theory as propounded in this dialogue makes any particular use of Parmenides. In fact, as Socrates'

---

[21] Cf. Barnes 1982, 140 and 149–50, for the idea that the empiricist view of medical knowledge adopted in *VM* and Alcmaeon's genetic epistemology (for which he finds evidence in comparing *Phd.* 96b with Thphr. *Sens.* 26) are positive developments of Xenoph. B18.   [22] So Vlastos 1965, 154–5 and 161.

introduction of the theory indicates, in this dialogue it most clearly displays its Pythagorean origins:

Those relating this theory belong to those priests and priestesses who are concerned with being able to give an account of the matters in which they engage. Pindar also speaks of it, as do many others among the divinely inspired poets. . . . They say that the human soul is immortal and that at one time it comes to an end—which humans call dying—and at another is born again, and it never finally perishes. . . . Therefore the soul, being immortal and having been born many times, has seen all things both here and in Hades, and there is nothing it has not learned. So it is not surprising if it can recollect what it already knew before about virtue or anything else. For since all nature is akin, and the soul has learned everything, nothing prevents someone who has recollected just one thing—indeed this is what humans call learning—from finding out all the rest so long as he is persistent and does not tire of searching: for the process of searching and learning is simply recollection (*Men.* 81a10–d5).

In the theory thus formulated revelation is conspicuously absent. Socrates makes no distinction between the means of acquiring knowledge in Hades and on earth. The soul has had no special vision of reality in the afterlife. Rather, its knowledge comes from simply having been around long enough to have experienced everything—it 'has seen all things both here and in Hades'. There are a number of problems that result from this conception. Why do we need the intervention of recollection when we were, apparently, once able to come to know via direct experience?[23] There is also apparently no distinction made regarding the type of knowledge recoverable by recollection: the soul is simply said to have previously seen and learned 'all things' (81c6–7, d1). It is also unclear exactly what stages in the learning process constitute 'recollection'.

I shall not review the various proposals that have been made to salvage the *Meno* theory by explaining away such problems, for there are signs that Plato himself recognized its inadequacies. At the conclusion of the demonstration with the young slave, Socrates says he would not want to commit himself to all the theory's details, only to its conclusion that one should believe in the possibility of learning what one does not yet know (86b6–c2). He maintains a comparable distance from the theory's potential problems by presenting it at the outset as, not his own theory, but that of the priests and poets. It is not unreasonable to presume that the problems and inconsistencies of the theory are due in part to its being imported without sufficient

---

[23] Cf. Allen 1959, 166.

modification from Pythagorean sources. Empedocles B129 speaks of Pythagoras[24] as a 'man of exceeding knowledge' (ἀνὴρ περιώσια εἰδώς, cf. Xenoph. B34. 1–2, Parm. B1. 3) who possessed a great store of intelligence and was experienced in all manner of wisdom because 'whenever he would reach out with all his intelligence, he could easily see each of all the things that are (τῶν ὄντων πάντων λεύσσεσκεν ἕκαστον) in ten and even twenty human lifetimes'.[25] Robin has stressed that since Pythagoras' power of recalling his past experiences was presented as remarkable (as was Empedocles': cf. B117), we should be careful in speaking of any general theory of recollection in Pythagoreanism.[26] Without doing so, I simply want to point out that in such evidence as we possess one finds the same basic problems that I have singled out in the *Meno* theory. Nothing suggests that during (and possibly between) his past incarnations Pythagoras engaged in anything but the same basically empirical brand of inquiry that he practised in his most recent life;[27] and the range of things he came to know is all-encompassing.

The main reason, however, why I think the efforts to patch up the problems with the *Meno* theory within its own framework are ultimately misdirected is that the subsequent formulations of the theory in the *Phaedo* and *Phaedrus* address precisely these problems by introducing features not found in the *Meno*. What is important for our purposes is that these features would appear to reflect Plato's engagement with Parmenides. In the *Phaedo*/*Phaedrus* theory it is specifically knowledge of the forms that is acquired by recollection, and consequently the stages via which one proceeds to apprehension of universals can be demarcated in a way that makes clear precisely where recollection is involved. Secondly, it is presumed that the soul in its previous experience of the afterlife had a direct revelation of the forms that constitutes a fundamentally different type of cognitive access to truth than is typical of its experience in this world. The moment at which one, after a series of perceptions, intuits the

[24] Porph. *VP* 30, where the fragment is preserved, presumes it to refer to Pythagoras, and the majority of scholars have accepted this (for references, cf. Cameron 1938, 20 n. 1; Guthrie 1962, 161 n. 1). DL 8. 54, however, reports that some took the verses to refer to Parmenides.

[25] Cf. Heraclides Ponticus *ap.* DL 8. 4: Pythagoras in his former life as Aithalides was granted by Hermes the ability to remember his experiences through both life and death, so that 'in life he could remember all things (πάντων), and when he died, he could preserve this memory'.   [26] Robin 1919, 451.

[27] Cf. Heraclitus B129, where Pythagoras is said to have been the greatest practitioner of inquiry or ἱστορίη, and B40, where he is grouped with Xenophanes as (roughly) an empiricist.

universal or form is a re-enactment or 'recollection' of part of that rev-elation. Parmenides, of course, provides no model for this movement from perception to recollection of the universal, but he does provide a model for both the idea of a post-mortem experience of direct access to truth as well as for the idea that a special type of knowledge is thus acquired. In this sense, the modified recollection theory in the *Phaedo* can be seen as already taking on a certain Parmenidean form: but it is only with the integration of this theory into the *Phaedrus* myth, whose Parmenidean inheritance we have outlined above, that the influence of this engagement is finally, if still obliquely, acknowledged.

At this point, then, I want to end this introductory sketch of those aspects of Plato's middle period engagement with Parmenides not specifically related to the characterization of the forms. By briefly dis-cussing the recollection theory, I have tried to give some indication of how Plato's engagement with Parmenides grows throughout the course of the middle period dialogues. Many points I have made must remain merely speculative, but I would defend the value of such spec-ulation, first, by pointing out that my ultimate purpose has not been to uphold each particular connection as such but rather to suggest cer-tain ways in which the middle period engagement with Parmenides runs deeper than has generally been acknowledged. The unavoidably speculative quality of some of the points made here should not be taken as a sign that this engagement is less substantial than claimed but, just the opposite, as a consequence of our own inability to gauge its actual depth. One final note: by using the terms 'involvement' and 'engagement' I have attempted to avoid suggesting that purely historical factors—Parmenidean 'influence'—led Plato to adopt any of his characteristic middle period views. Philosophical motivations should remain primary in any genetic account. What I have, though, wanted to suggest is that Plato's philosophical reflections during this period may often have proceeded via reflection upon Parmenides' poem. He will have come to see his predecessor's concerns as con-tinuous in significant respects with his own and therefore will have found the poem a useful spur to the formulation of his own views. Having to this point discussed aspects of the reception that suggest in general terms how Plato would have seen his own concerns as continuous in some perhaps less than obvious ways with those rep-resented in Parmenides' proem, I now want to turn to the text rep-resenting the most direct and extended middle period appropriation of Parmenides. It will allow us to explore in some detail the reading of Parmenides that led Plato to regard him as his most important Presocratic predecessor.

3

The Argument from the
Possibility of Knowledge

In the final movement of *Republic* 5, Plato presents certain arguments intended to persuade a group he calls 'the lovers of sights and sounds' that they are mistaken in assuming that the attention they devote to the ordinary objects of experience furnishes them with knowledge. Plato characterizes the mode of being of these objects as inherently unstable, from which he infers that the cognitive state resulting from apprehension of these objects must likewise be unstable. Plato argues, however, that there *is* a class of objects with an absolutely stable mode of being that provides the foundation for genuine knowledge. The core of Plato's argument, its characterization of the opponent, and both the virtues and failings of its general epistemological and ontological perspective all reflect Plato's use of Parmenides. It is particularly unfortunate, then, that none of the principal modern discussions undertakes any systematic exploration of Plato's engagement with Parmenides in this text. For the end of *Republic* 5 is perhaps the only middle period text in which the engagement is specific and sustained enough to show how Plato read certain key passages of Parmenides' poem.

The first argument Plato gives to Socrates to persuade the sight-lover that what he takes to be knowledge is mere *doxa* proceeds as follows (*R.* 5. 476e4–477b11):

(i)   one who knows knows something that is, rather than nothing or what-is-not, for
(ii)   one can have no apprehension at all of something that is not;
(iiia)   what-completely-is (τὸ παντελῶς ὄν)[1] is completely knowable, while

---

[1] For a summary of the proposed ways of understanding the sense of the verb εἶναι ('to be') in this phrase and in the overall argument, i.e. whether it has an existential, predicative, or some form of veridical sense, see Reeve 1988, 288 n. 13. I have not allowed the increasingly dated debate over the senses of εἶναι to dominate my discussion. The categories employed in this debate, however useful for our own attempts at understanding, were not Plato's own. Hintikka 1980, 7, draws the proper conclusion regarding attempts to detect among Greek philosophers distinctions of the

- (iiib) what-is-not-in-any-way is altogether unknowable;
- (iv) what both is and is not lies between what genuinely or completely is and what-is-not-at-all;
- (v) the cognitive state corresponding to what-absolutely-is is knowledge (γνῶσις or ἐπιστήμη), that corresponding to what-absolutely-is-not is complete ignorance (ἀγνωσία or ἄνοια), and that which has as its object what both is and is not is opinion or *doxa*.

Glaucon's response securing the premiss in (ii) establishing (i) is as direct an echo of Parmenides as is manageable without direct quotation: πῶς γὰρ ἂν μὴ ὄν γέ τι γνωσθείη; ('for how could one know something that is not?', Pl. *R.* 5. 477a1) ≈ οὔτε γὰρ ἂν γνοίης τό γε μὴ ἐόν

type made by Frege and Russell among the senses of 'is': 'If there is any unequivocal moral to be drawn from recent scholars' work, it is that no real distinction between the three allegedly different senses of "is" or *estin* is made by any of the Greek philosophers. On the contrary, it is dangerously anachronistic to try to project the distinction back to the Greeks.' The designation τὸ παντελῶς ὄν ('what-completely-is') is capable of encompassing e.g. both the existential and predicative senses of εἶναι, such that what is so designated will both exist at all times and will be fully F rather than F and not-F. Such inclusiveness is what one would expect of what is described as being 'completely' (παντελῶς), 'in every way' (πάντως, 478d7), and 'absolutely' (εἰλικρινῶς, 477a7, 478d6, 479d5). The necessity of such an inclusive understanding is stressed by Kahn 1981, who explores the thesis that 'the uses of εἶναι in Plato . . . are often *overdetermined*: several grammatical readings of a single occurrence are not only possible but sometimes required' (105); cf. Kahn 1988, 240–1. (Brown 1986 has advanced a similar thesis in arguing that εἶναι in Plato often needs to be understood as a verb of 'variable polyadicity'.) Kahn takes as one of his main examples *Smp*. 210e–211a (the description of the form of Beauty in which Solmsen 1971(*a*) saw such strong Parmenidean influence). He notes that in the phrase ἀεὶ ὄν ('always being') the participle ὄν has an obvious existential value but that the subsequent predicative phrases such as οὐ τῇ μὲν καλόν, τῇ δ'αἰσχρόν ('not beautiful in one respect but ugly in another'), 'permit us to go back and see that ἀεὶ ὄν can be read not only as "this beautiful thing is forever" but also as "this thing is forever beautiful". The existential use in ἀεὶ ὄν is pregnant with the incomplete copula. But it would be a mistake to *eliminate* the first construal in favour of the second. . . . We must recognize both the absolute construction (explicitly) and the copula syntax (implicitly) as part of the total meaning of the text. And so likewise for αὐτὸ καθ' αὐτὸ μεθ' αὐτοῦ μονοειδὲς ἀεὶ ὄν at 211b1–2: both "it is always uniform" and also "it is eternal, exists forever"' (Kahn 1981, 108). When he comes to discuss *R.* 5. 476e ff., however, Kahn is much less free with his concept of overdeterminacy, arguing that a veridical reading gives the best sense until 479a7 ff., at which point there is a shift to a predicative construction (112–13; cf. Kahn 1988, 255–6). I prefer to extend Kahn's concept to this passage as well and assume that, in so far as τὸ παντελῶς ὄν and its correlatives are used in roughly the same contexts as the bare τὸ ὄν, it is preferable to remain sensitive at the outset to all possible senses of the verb while noting those places in the subsequent argument where one sense or the other is brought to the fore. Cf. the defence of an existential/predicative reading of 'being' in this passage by Gonzalez 1996 *contra* the restricted veridical reading of Fine 1978 and 1990.

('for neither could you know what-is-not', Parm. B2. 7a).[2] Although this is the most direct echo in the passage of Parmenides' actual language, the entire argument is recognizably Parmenidean both in its overall structure and in the set of distinctions it draws. Socrates' initial question, whether the person who knows knows something-that-is or something-that-is-not, corresponds to the choice in Parmenides B2 between the two possible paths towards understanding. Socrates' dismissal of what-is-not-in-any-way as 'completely inapprehensible' (πάντῃ ἄγνωστον) recalls the goddess's dismissal of the second path as 'completely unknowable' (παναπευθέα, B2. 6). Similarly, Socrates' introduction of a third possible mode of being situated between complete being and complete non-being, that which both is and is not (εἶναί τε καὶ μὴ εἶναι), would seem to have its analogue in Parmenides' description of the mode of being of the objects upon which mortals have fixed their thought as what both is and is not (τὸ πέλειν τε καὶ οὐκ εἶναι, B6. 8). Finally, the conclusion of Socrates' argument assigning the cognitive states of knowledge and *doxa* respectively to what-completely-is and what both is and is not mirrors Parmenides' own deployment of the terms 'intellect' or *nöos* and *doxa*. This network of correspondences provides an initial indication that Plato understood Parmenides to be ascribing an imperfect mode of being to the objects of ordinary experience and as thus relegating apprehension of these objects to a lower cognitive plane.

In two remarkable statements in the *De caelo* and *Metaphysics M*, Aristotle attributes an argument to Parmenides and Plato that isolates the essential dynamic of the Platonic argument at *Republic* 5. 476e4–477b11 and its Parmenidean background. We may first cite what Aristotle says about Parmenides in *De caelo* 3. 1. As an overture to his own treatment of the sublunary elements, he is surveying his predecessors' views on generation:

Some earlier philosophers abolished coming to be and passing away. Melissus and Parmenides, for example, say that none of the things-that-are either comes to be or perishes but only appears to us to do so. Even if in other respects they say some excellent things, nevertheless one should not suppose them to speak in a manner appropriate to natural science. For that some things-that-are do not come to be and are completely free from change is a thesis that belongs instead to another inquiry prior to natural science. But since they supposed there is nothing else besides the being of perceptibles,

---

[2] Cf. Kahn 1988, 255: 'The echo of Parmenides B2. 7 is unmistakable.' Crystal 1996, 357–60, detects seven allusions to Parmenides in *R.* 5. 476d8–480a13 (some of which are decidedly tenuous) but overlooks this most obvious one of all.

and since *they were the first to understand that some natures of this sort are required if there is to be any knowledge or intelligence* (τοιαύτας δέ τινας νοῆσαι πρῶτοι φύσεις, εἴπερ ἔσται τις γνῶσις ἢ φρόνησις), for these reasons they transferred to these objects descriptions appropriate to higher objects (*Cael.* 3. 1. 298ᵇ14–24).[3]

One cannot take the view of Parmenides in this passage to be Aristotle's unqualified view, for there are elements that conflict with his more involved treatments of Parmenides elsewhere. In *Metaphysics A*, for example, he is much more cautious about attributing to Parmenides, as he seems to do here, the absolute denial of all generation and destruction. He is also much more sceptical there about associating Parmenides so directly with Melissus. Such difficulties aside, the importance of this passage for our purposes lies in its attribution to Parmenides of what we may call 'the argument from the possibility of knowledge' (APK). This argument may be simply stated: if knowledge is to be possible, there must be eternal and changeless entities to serve as its objects. In one of his main accounts of Plato's motivation for positing the existence of forms, Aristotle also attributes APK to Plato:

The view concerning the forms occurred to those who espoused it because they were convinced of the truth of the Heraclitean arguments that all perceptibles are always in flux, so that *if there is to be knowledge and intelligence about anything, there must be certain other enduring natures besides the perceptibles* (εἴπερ ἐπιστήμη τινὸς ἔσται καὶ φρόνησις, ἑτέρας δεῖν τινὰς φύσεις εἶναι

---

[3] Kerferd 1991 provides a valuable discussion of this passage that moves towards a reception-orientated approach. He criticizes those who have dismissed what Aristotle says here as an anachronistic misinterpretation (in particular, Cherniss 1935, 63 n. 258; Tarán 1965, 283–4; Guthrie 1965, 112; others are referred to at Kerferd 1991, 4 n. 4), and he calls for 'a closer scrutiny of what Aristotle says, in relation to what we know of Parmenides' doctrines' (4). However, rather than taking this passage as a point of departure for a proper study of Aristotle's reception of Parmenides (which is still awaited, despite e.g. Natorp 1890, Mansion 1953, Gershenson and Greenberg 1962, Bicknell 1964, and Spangler 1979), Kerferd scrutinizes Aristotle's remarks via discussion of part of Simplicius' commentary on the passage (*in Cael.* 558, 11–17). There Simplicius attempts to reconcile Aristotle's statements with his own view that Parmenides 'clearly transmitted to us, on the one hand, the unitary nature of the intelligible, which is what-really-is (τὸ ὄντως ὄν), and on the other hand, with the same clarity, the way in which sensible objects are arranged throughout the world'. Although Simplicius, particularly in his commentary on Aristotle's *Physics*, provides information on the controversies over Parmenides in the 4th cent. BC that is invaluable for a proper understanding of Aristotle's views here and elsewhere, Aristotle's view of Parmenides should be distinguished from Simplicius'. Not, of course, that Simplicius' view is not worth exploring in its own right. For this, see e.g. Bermann 1979, Guérard 1987, Stevens 1990.

παρὰ τὰς αἰσθητὰς μενούσας), for there is no knowledge of things in flux (*Metaph. M.* 4. 1078^{b}12–17).

Aristotle's phrasing in the argument he here attributes to Plato is virtually identical to that in the argument he attributes to Parmenides in the *De caelo*.

If Aristotle attributes APK to both Parmenides and Plato, and if Plato does in fact employ the argument in his appropriation of Parmenides, as we shall see that he does at the end of *Republic* 5, then it would seem more than likely that Plato himself understood Parmenides as employing a form of the argument. Before examining in detail what Plato would have seen as Parmenides' version of the argument, we should note one peculiar and crucial feature of APK's basic structure. Again, the argument as Aristotle presents it states that *if* there is to be knowledge, there must be certain eternal and unchanging entities. One might well ask why the possibility of knowledge should entail the existence of such entities. The argument implies that if there were no eternal, unchanging entities, there would be no knowledge. But why should this be the case? It is not difficult to see that the argument Aristotle attributes to Parmenides and Plato depends upon a restricted conception of knowledge, that is, upon an unstated assumption that knowledge in the strict sense must be directed towards objects with a certain highly qualified mode of being. With such an assumption the argument is sound. Without it, it has no force at all. The significance of this feature of the argument will become clearer as we work through the details of Parmenides' and then Plato's employment of APK.

The Platonic argument at *Republic* 5. 476e–477b outlined above corresponds structurally to the portion of Parmenides' poem providing the foundation for the full description of Being in B8, the portion represented for us by B2, B3, and B6. In developing a reading of these fragments conditioned by Plato's use of them, we need to focus not only upon their logical and ontological aspects but also, since this is central to Plato's appropriation, upon the equally prominent epistemological aspect. Plato will have understood *nöos* and its cognates in Parmenides as signifying a strong form of apprehension, the object of which has a restricted mode of being. One might suppose that *nöos* in Parmenides could just as well have been understood by Plato as a cognitive faculty capable of being directed towards any object, even though it is most successful when it has Being (τὸ ἐόν) as its object. This objection in effect suggests that Parmenides' strict ontology should not be seen as determined by, but as itself determining, his strict epistemology. The alternative scenario suggested by this objection might seem to make it easier to explain Parmenides' attribution of a 'wandering understanding' (πλαγκτὸν⁴ νόον) to mortals in B6. 6, for the attribution apparently grants *nöos* to those whose thought is not focused upon Being. All this attribution actually indicates, however, is that mortals possess, like Parmenides, the basic capacity to apprehend Being. This need not mean that they apprehend the things they do via *nöos*. Rather, they have attempted to direct their *nöos* towards things that cannot properly serve as its objects. Their *nöos* has consequently wandered or gone astray. They end up not merely failing to exercise this capacity properly but not exercising it at all. They are thus described as 'knowing nothing' (εἰδότες οὐδέν, B6. 4), and they are left in a state of mere *doxa*.

More decisive in excluding this alternative scenario is that the somewhat uncharacteristic manner in which Plato employs the cognitive terms *dianoia* ('understanding'), *gnōmē/gnōsis* ('knowledge'), and *doxa* in *Republic* 5 makes it highly unlikely that he would have understood *nöos* in Parmenides as capable of having anything except Being as its object. *Dianoia* is here a general cognitive faculty capable of being exercised on a variety of objects. It encompasses both *gnōsis* and *doxa* (476d5–6). When Socrates says that the sight-lovers' *dianoia* is incapable of apprehending the nature of the Beautiful itself (476b4–8), the implication may be that *dianoia* is most successful when directed towards forms. It nevertheless remains the case that such apprehension as the sight-lovers do have involves an exercise of *dianoia*. *Dianoia*, in other words, is conceived of along the lines of our objector's suggestion regarding the sense of *nöos* in Parmenides. However, in the Platonic argument at 476e–477b outlined above, it is not *dianoia* but *gnōsis* that picks up the Parmenidean term *nöos*. *Gnōsis* is specified as the apprehension of what-is, while *doxa* is assigned to what-is-and-is-not. Their object-specific character becomes even clearer in the argument that follows at 477b11–478d12, where *epistēmē* (substituted for *gnōsis* at 477a9–b1 and thenceforth the more frequent term for 'knowledge') and *doxa* receive strictly intentional definitions. These definitions rule out the possibility of either faculty being directed towards anything except its proper object. Plato's manner of distinguishing the various terms in this portion of the *Republic* entails that one cannot have *gnōsis* of the objects of ordinary experience. Any apprehension of them is de facto *doxa*. Conversely, one might suppose

⁴ For a defence of πλαγκτόν versus πλακτόν, see Sider 1985, 364–5, and Coxon 1986, 185.

it possible to have beliefs about a form or what-is, but any true belief about a form or what-is will de facto be a case of *gnōsis*. (It would seem that a false belief concerning a form or what-is constitutes no apprehension at all.) If the analogue of Platonic *gnōsis* is Parmenidean *nöos*, then Plato will have understood *nöos* in Parmenides as a cognitive faculty that has the analogue of what-completely-is (τὸ παντελῶς ὄν) as its proper object. One may note that Socrates describes what-completely-is as 'completely knowable' (παντελῶς γνωστόν, 477a3) but assiduously avoids describing the intermediate mode of being as the object of some intermediate form of *gnōsis*.

I have taken some pains to indicate that *gnōsis* in *Republic* 5 is a particularly restricted variety of understanding, such that it can only be exercised in the presence of what fully or completely is, and that Plato will have understood *nöos* in Parmenides in an analogous fashion because the argument from the possibility of knowledge requires such a conception of knowledge. If knowledge or *gnōsis* is possible, and given that *gnōsis* is conceived of as directed towards objects with the absolute mode of being Plato designates as what-completely-is, this possibility entails the existence of objects with this absolute mode of being.

It is fitting that Plato understood Parmenides' use of *nöos* in the way indicated, for Parmenides may reasonably be thought, even independently of Plato's perspective, to have elicited certain radical implications from his own predecessors' use of the term and its cognates. The Homeric poems already employed the verbs *noein* and *gignōskein* in certain contexts for the recognition of what something really is.[5] This sense becomes so prominent among the Presocratics that Bruno Snell identified it as the primary sense of *gignōskein* in early philosophic writings; he likewise identified 'Einsicht' as an equally prominent sense of *gnōmē*, a sense in which the term is virtually synonymous with *nous*

---

[5] Von Fritz 1943 argues that the original and fundamental concept underlying the use of νοεῖν is the realization of a situation, a sense which was extended to special cases (e.g. Hom. *Il.* 3. 395 ff., 19. 112, *Od.* 1. 322, 4. 653) where 'the first recognition or classification turns out to be deceptive and has to be replaced by another and truer recognition which, so to speak, penetrates below the visible surface to the real essence of the contemplated object'. Lesher 1981, 8–10, rightly criticizes von Fritz's assumption that the semantic fields of νοεῖν and γιγνώσκειν, particularly in the region of this deeper recognition, do not overlap, citing the use of γιγνώσκειν at Hom. *Il.* 10. 340–50 [*sic*—the key phrase, γνῶ ῥ' ἄνδρας δηΐους, actually occurs at 358] and *Od.* 17. 549 ff. as counter-examples (cf. the examples in Lesher 1983, 161–2 and 166). Nevertheless, despite this criticism of von Fritz, and despite his insistence on the close ties of both forms of knowing with sight, Lesher still sees recognizing the true nature of a situation as an increasingly prominent sense of both verbs (14–15).

or *nöos*.[6] With Heraclitus, one finds an incipient distinction between *noein* and *gignōskein* such that the former takes on something of the more strictly intentional aspect I am claiming Plato would have seen in Parmenides. In Heraclitus *gignōskein* typically has the sense of recognizing what something really is, as in his criticism of Hesiod in B57—'who did not recognize (οὐκ ἐγίνωσκεν) day and night; for they are one'—and in his criticism of the observers of traditional religious practices in B5—'not even recognizing (οὔ τι γινώσκων) the nature of gods and heroes' (cf. B17, B86, B188). *Gnōsis* in B56 and *gnōmē* in B78 likewise denote insight into the true nature of things. Thus Charles Kahn can conclude that Heraclitus uses *gignōskein* and its cognate nouns 'for "cognition" in a privileged sense, for the insight which men lack and which his own discourse attempts to communicate'.[7] As for *nöos*, although Heraclitus uses the term less frequently, where he does it too marks a deep understanding of reality or the 'divine law' of the cosmos (B114), an understanding that runs deeper than that of the poets and sages most people consider wise (B40, B104).[8] What distinguishes the terms is that the object of *gnōsis* in Heraclitus is not always the universal truth of the *logos*,[9] whereas this does seem to be the case with *nöos*. Parmenides seems to presume a similar distinction. *Gnōmē*, which like *nöos* represents for him a recognition of what something really is, need not be directed towards Being or τὸ ἐόν (cf. especially B8. 61), whereas *nöos* has Being as its special object. Accompanying this distinction in Parmenides is the idea we have already noted that the object of *nöos* will have an absolute mode of being. That is, in Parmenides the sense of *nöos* shifts from 'recognizing what something (anything) really is' to 'recognizing what *is really*'. A similar shift in the philosophical use of *nöos* is implied in Heraclitus' description of the eternal being of the *logos* (B1, cf. B30). Plato, therefore, may have been genuinely justified in seeing Parmenides' use of *nöos* as conformable to his own strictly intentional specification of *gnōsis/epistēmē*.

What type of reading of the relevant lines of Parmenides' poem does Plato's use in *Republic* 5 presume? In B2 the goddess indicates to Parmenides what are the only possible modes of being for an object of νόος (*nöos*):

εἰ δ' ἄγ' ἐγὼν ἐρέω, κόμισαι δὲ σὺ μῦθον ἀκούσας,
αἵπερ ὁδοὶ μοῦναι διζήσιός εἰσι νοῆσαι·

---

[6] Cf. Snell 1924, 28 f. and 35 f., on γιγνώσκειν and γνώμη respectively.
[7] Kahn 1979, 104–5.   [8] Cf. von Fritz 1945–6, 35–43.
[9] Lesher 1983, 160, makes this point with special reference to B28 and B56.

ἦ μὲν ὅπως ἔστιν τε καὶ ὡς οὐκ ἔστι μὴ εἶναι,
πειθοῦς ἐστι κέλευθος, ἀληθείη[10] γὰρ ὀπηδεῖ,
ἦ δ' ὡς οὐκ ἔστιν τε καὶ ὡς χρεών ἐστι μὴ εἶναι,
τὴν δή τοι φράζω παναπευθέα ἔμμεν ἀταρπόν·
οὔτε γὰρ ἂν γνοίης τό γε μὴ ἐόν, οὐ γὰρ ἀνυστόν,
οὔτε φράσαις

(Come now, I will tell you, and you preserve my tale once you have heard it, those which are the only paths in the search for knowing. The one, that it is and it is not possible for it not to be, is the path of persuasion, for truth attends upon it. The other, that it is not and it is necessary that it not be, this I tell you is a completely unknowable path. For neither could you know what-is-not, for this cannot be accomplished, nor could you pick it out).

The second verse is most often translated along the lines of A. H. Coxon's 'those ways of enquiry which are alone conceivable'.[11] Understanding the line in this way poses an immediate problem. For the goddess appears to introduce a third path at B6. 3–5:

πρώτης γάρ σ' ἀφ' ὁδοῦ ταύτης διζήσιος <εἴργω>,
αὐτὰρ ἔπειτ' ἀπὸ τῆς, ἣν δὴ βροτοὶ εἰδότες οὐδὲν
πλάζονται,[12] δίκρανοι

(For <I hold you back> first from this path of inquiry, and next from *this one*, along which mortals who know nothing wander, two-headed).

How can the goddess call the paths in B2 the only ones conceivable when she subsequently distinguishes yet another path? Few who adopt some form of the standard translation of B2. 2 address this problem. A promising avenue has been opened by Nestor-Luis Cordero and Alexander Nehamas, who have argued independently that Parmenides does not in fact distinguish a third way but that the path of mortal *doxa* should be assimilated to the path of not-being specified in B2. 5.[13] The supplementation of the lacuna at the end of B6. 3 with εἴργω ('I hold back') proposed by Diels (via a supposed analogy with εἶργε νόημα at B7. 2) does indeed make it appear that the goddess *bars* Parmenides from two distinct paths, the one she has already warned him against in B2 plus a path previously unmentioned.

---

[10] For a defence of the reading ἀληθείη as *ap.* Simp. and Procl. vs. Bywater's emendation ἀληθείη, see Sider 1985, 363.

[11] Coxon 1986, 52. Similarly e.g. Diels 1897, 33; Cornford 1933, 98; Untersteiner 1958, 129; Guthrie 1965, 13; Tarán 1965, 32; Barnes 1982, 157 and 159; KRS 245; O'Brien 1987(*a*), 16.

[12] See Sider 1985, 363–5, and Coxon 1986, 183, for a defence of the common epic form πλάζονται against the MS πλάττονται.

[13] Cordero 1984, ch. 3 (expanding parts of Cordero 1979); Nehamas 1981. For a less attractive variety of two-path view, see Couloubaritsis 1987.

Cordero, however, proposes supplementing the lacuna with the verb ἄρξει ('you will begin')—in the second person to pick up the goddess's exhortation in B6. 2b and in the future tense because she is clearly pointing forward to the expositions of B8. 1–50 and 51 ff. In the earlier portion of the line he thus prefers the reading τ' of codices B and C of Simplicius to σ' found in D, E, and F, given that the elision of σύ to σ' is unlikely.[14] The result is: πρώτης γάρ τ' ἀφ' ὁδοῦ ταύτης διζήσιος <ἄρξει>—'car *tu commenceras* par ce premier chemin de la recherche'. On this reading, the two paths mentioned in B6 can be identified with the two already introduced in B2. Nehamas proposes the supplement ἄρξω ('I will begin') and suggests that σ' should be understood as an elision of σοι instead of σε (citing for comparison Hom. *Il.* 1. 170–1). The result: πρώτης γάρ σ' ἀφ' ὁδοῦ ταύτης διζήσιος <ἄρξω>—'For, first, *I will begin for you* from this way of inquiry'. This reading allows Nehamas to draw the conclusion that 'B6 does not therefore reject any way of inquiry. On the contrary, it says that the goddess will follow (demonstrate) two methods of inquiring into nature.'[15] These two methods are, again, to be identified with the paths already specified in B2. According to both Cordero's and Nehamas's interpretations, then, B6 does not introduce any third path, and B2 can continue to be understood as specifying the only conceivable paths of inquiry.

Although one might well find these two-path views attractive,[16] this is a case where one must set aside an interpretation that is perhaps preferable in its own right in order to reconstruct Plato's understanding of Parmenides. In this case, the structure of the argument at *Republic* 5. 476e–477b strongly suggests that Plato saw Parmenides as distinguishing three separate paths. Having asked Glaucon whether one who knows knows something or nothing (476e7), Socrates elaborates this alternative into a disjunction between the two extreme modes

---

[14] Cordero 1984, 168–75 (esp. 174). On pp. 138–44 he criticizes as merely apparent the parallels between B6. 3 and B7. 2. He also shows that Diels's εἴργω has its roots in the reading εἴργε νόημα in the Aldine edition of Simp. *in Ph.* (Venetus 1526), which was accepted by scholars with various resulting modifications of the earlier and better-attested portion of B6. 3, until Diels's 1882 edition of Simplicius' commentary on the *Physics* (*CAG* IX).

[15] Nehamas 1981, 104–5. Nehamas's ἄρξω is perhaps preferable to Cordero's ἄρξει given that the goddess herself goes on to set out the results of following each path in turn.

[16] It may even be the case that there was already a two-path view in antiquity, if 'both' in Theophrastus' statement that Parmenides 'proceeded on both paths' (ἐπ' ἀμφοτέρας ἦλθε τὰς ὁδούς, ap. Alex. Aphr. *in Metaph.* 31, 7–9) means that there were *only* two paths.

of being, what-completely-is and what-is-not-at-all (477a2–4). This portion of the argument corresponds to Parmenides B2, which sets out a similar choice between the extremes of possible modes of being. Only after having set out these two extremes and having ruled out the second as 'completely unknowable' (πάντῃ ἄγνωστον ≈ Parm. B2. 6, παναπευθέα) does Plato then introduce the possibility of a third, mixed mode of being (477a6 ff.) that will become the object of *doxa*. Parmenides likewise postpones introducing an intermediate mode of being until B6. 4–9. Plato in no way equates this third mode, what-is-and-is-not, with either of the first two, and there is no reason to suppose he would have seen any such equation in Parmenides. It is therefore highly unlikely that he would have seen Parmenides as having somehow equated the mixture of being and not-being specified at B6. 4–9 with either of the modes specified in B2.[17]

If there are three possible paths of inquiry presented in the poem, as the structure of the *Republic* 5 argument indicates Plato took there to be, it will not do to understand B2. 2 as stating that there are only two conceivable paths of inquiry. The restriction marked by 'only' (μοῦναι) must be different from that presumed by the usual translation. In keeping with Plato's concern to demarcate a strict mode of knowledge, we may understand this verse as introducing the only paths in the search for knowledge. More precisely, taking διζήσιος as a subjective genitive with its basic sense of 'search' (which the corresponding verb at B8. 6 possesses), and taking νοῆσαι as a datival infinitive retaining a degree of its original sense of purpose, translate: 'those which are the only paths in the search for knowing' (i.e. for the attainment of knowledge).[18] The goddess tells Parmenides that there are only two genuine paths in the search for νόος or true understanding. Although mortals may have mistaken it as an avenue to such understanding, the goddess deliberately avoids presenting the third path as such when she introduces it in B6.

---

[17] Cf. Cornford 1933, 101–2, on the structural 'analogy between the three realms of the *Republic* and Parmenides' three Ways'. There is at least a latent contradiction, however, in Cornford employing the analogy with Plato to support the identification of three paths in Parmenides while simultaneously asserting that Plato departs from Parmenides over the status of the third path's objects.

[18] Cf. Kahn 1969, 703, 'what are the only ways of search there are for knowing or understanding', a translation defended at 703 n. 4; and Cordero 1984, 48, 'quels sont les seuls chemins de la recherche (qui existent) pour penser'. Cordero goes on to present a critical survey of alternatives and adduces Emp. B3. 12b, ὁπόσῃ πόρος ἐστὶ νοῆσαι ('by whichever there is a channel for knowing'), in support of his view that 'les chemins de la recherche proposés en 2,2 sont des chemins "pour penser", c'est-à-dire des chemins le long desquels la pensée, la connaissance, peuvent, *a priori*, cheminer'.

Why is the second path rather than the third presented as a potential path in the search for knowledge? It might appear that one could
have some knowledge of what-is-and-is-not, but Parmenides in B2.
7–8 rules out the possibility of knowing the object of the second path
by declaring that one may not apprehend (γνοίης) what-is-not. It
seems inconsistent to present the path in B2. 5 as one possible path
in the search for knowledge and then deny that one can know what-
is-not. There is a similar tension in the parallel argument in *Republic*
5. Socrates never suggests that what-is-and-is-not might be knowable (γνωστόν). He does, however, initially hold forth the possibility
that what-is-not might be an object of knowledge. After Glaucon has
already answered that one knows something rather than nothing, he
asks the seemingly odd question, whether one knows what-is or what-
is-not (476e10), despite going on to declare that what-is-not-at-all is
completely unknowable. The apparent oddity of identifying what-
is-not as a potential object of knowledge indicates that Parmenides'
conception of knowledge or νόος as viewed by Plato entails a certain
formal restriction on its object's mode of being. What necessarily is
not satisfies the formal condition that the object of knowledge enjoy
an absolute mode of being. Absolute not-being is an absolute and
unchanging mode of being, even if in the end there can be no νόος of
what is in this way. The second path's specification of the possible
object's mode of being, then, satisfies this formal condition of knowledge in a way that the third path's does not.

How are we then to understand B2. 3 and B2. 5's formulations of
the two possible paths in the search for knowledge? The first major
difficulty that confronts one in an attempt to understand these lines
is that 'is' (ἔστιν) in B2. 3a and 'is not' (οὐκ ἔστιν) in B2. 5a have no
expressed subject. The fragment's first two lines provide the necessary context for the identification of the subject of these seemingly
enigmatic utterances. These initial lines indicate that the subject is
simply the object of the search for knowledge. This reading may be
seen as a narrower version of those interpretations that identify the
subject broadly as any possible object of thought—narrower because
'knowing' (νοῆσαι) in B2. 2 is understood as a strong form of cognition. G. E. L. Owen's identification of the implied subject as 'what
can be talked or thought about'[19] exemplifies the broad interpretation. The present, restricted reading is more akin to that advanced by
Charles Kahn, who is more careful to search for the implied subject

[19] Owen 1960, 60; similarly e.g. Barnes 1982, 162–3.

in what has come before. He concludes that both the proem and B2. 1–2 suggest that 'the subject of Parmenides' thesis is the object of knowing, what is or can be known'.[20] Attempts have also been made to supply 'Being' as the subject—either implicitly, following Diels and Karl Reinhardt, or even, in Francis Cornford's case, by explicit emendation[21]—appealing for support to the fact that this becomes Parmenides' subject in the following portions of the poem (B4. 2, B6. 1, B8. 3, 19, 25, 32). But Cordero is surely correct in pointing out that one must take care to distinguish between the subject presumed in B2. 3a and B2. 5a and the eventual subject of the poem itself.[22] The present identification of the subject as the object of the search for knowledge adheres to this constraint.[23] Although the introduction of 'Being' or τὸ ἐόν as subject is unjustified, the impulse to connect the use of ἐόν in the subsequent exposition with the specification of the first path in B2. 3 is fundamentally correct, and it directs us to a point that will be of some significance as we proceed. Although τὸ ἐόν proves an accurate *description* of the subject, it would be a mistake to infer that it therefore must be the unexpressed grammatical subject in B2. The correct inference is that Parmenides subsequently uses the designation ἐόν or τὸ ἐόν in certain contexts as an abbreviated way of referring to the mode of being of the object of the way of truth. One may compare how at B8. 16 he restates the original choice presented in B2 via the abbreviated 'it is or it is not' (ἔστιν ἢ οὐκ ἔστιν, cf. B8. 11). Just so Plato will often use 'what-is' (τὸ ὄν) as shorthand for 'what-completely-is' (τὸ παντελῶς ὄν) or some other, fuller expression of absolute being.

[20] Kahn 1969, 710; cf. 710 n. 13, where he notes that this follows even more directly if one takes νόησις at B2. 2 in the strong sense. However, he ends up retreating from the interesting avenues opened by his emphasis on the poem's epistemological concerns by taking εἶναι in the 'veridical sense' (711–13); though see the somewhat more generous view of Kahn 1988.

[21] Diels 1897, 33; Reinhardt 1916, 35–6; cf. Tarán 1965, 33, and Cordero 1984, 55 ff., for references to those who have followed this line. Cornford 1939, 30 n. 2, proposed emending B2. 3a to ἡ μὲν ὅπως ἐὸν ἔστι καὶ ὥς, κτλ.

[22] Cordero 1984, 54. This is somewhat more subtle than Owen 1960, 55: 'there is a conclusive reason why this subject will not do. The reason is that it turns the *éstin* into a mere tautology and the *ouk éstin* correspondingly into a flat contradiction, whereas Parmenides thinks it necessary to *argue* for *éstin* and against *ouk éstin*.' The extent to which Parmenides argues for the theses of B2. 3 and B2. 5 is debatable. Cf. also Mansfeld 1964, 58, and Lesher 1984, 12–16.

[23] It also obeys a further constraint formulated by Cordero 1984, 60: 'Il est évident qu'il n'est pas obligatoire de proposer un sujet pour l'ἔστι parmenidien, *mais* une fois que l'on décide de l'énoncer, ce sujet doit être *le même* dans les deux cas (en 2,3a et 2,5a).'

The second major difficulty on which scholars have focused regards the sense of the verb 'to be' in these lines. Rather than being
drawn into this somewhat dated debate, however, we may reasonably
presume that the verb potentially encompasses various aspects of the
senses that have been distinguished, that is to say that it is (to use
Kahn's term) 'overdetermined' or, more technically, that it conforms
to Lesley Brown's description of the Greek verb εἶναι as a verb of
variable polyadicity.[24] That one can opt for virtually any of the senses
that have been detected in the verb εἶναι (the existential, predicative,
veridical, or what have you) and run it through the poem in an eventually consistent fashion is itself some indication that the enterprise
of determining Parmenides' particular use of the verb has somehow
been misdirected. What I want to draw attention to instead is the
additional qualifications placed upon 'it is' (ἔστιν) by B2. 3b and 'it is
not' (οὐκ ἔστιν) by B2. 5b, for these qualifications (rather than some
special sense of the bare verb itself) determine the restricted or absolute mode of being enjoyed by the object of each path. B2. 3—ὅπως
ἔστιν τε καὶ ὡς οὐκ ἔστι μὴ εἶναι—first asserts that the object of knowledge is and then specifies its necessary or absolute mode of being.
The second half of the line places the requisite modal qualification on
ἔστιν in the first.[25] The structure of B2. 5—ὡς οὐκ ἔστιν τε καὶ ὡς
χρεών ἐστι μὴ εἶναι—is essentially the same. It first denies that the
object of knowledge is but nevertheless similarly specifies it as having a necessary mode of (non-)being. Translate: 'that it (the object of
knowledge = "O") is and it is not possible for it (O) not to be' and 'that
it (O) is not and it is necessary that it (O) not be'.[26] Again, the second

---

[24] Much of what I have already said (above, n. 1) regarding the parallel debate in
the interpretation of Pl. *R.* 5. 476e ff. applies here as well. Although scholars have
perhaps been more willing to allow for some fusing of senses in Parmenides than in
Plato, this has in some cases entailed attributing a certain degree of confusion to
Parmenides. Cf. e.g. Calogero 1932, ch. 1; Furth 1968; Furley 1973, 13–14; KRS 246;
O'Brien 1987(*a*), 168–79.

[25] One might think there is a problem with saying that there is a modal qualification placed on ἔστιν by B2. 3b, for χρεών, the adverbial participle expressing necessity, occurs only in B2. 5b, whereas in B2. 3b one finds merely οὐκ ἔστι μὴ εἶναι. But
the parallel structure of B2. 3b and B2. 5b indicates that ἐστι in B2. 3b must have a
value symmetrical to that of χρεών ἐστι in B2. 5b. More simply, ἐστι, when used with
subject infinitive in parallel fashion to the quasi-impersonal verbs δεῖ and χρή, has,
like them, a modal sense: '(it) is possible'.

[26] One may construe μὴ εἶναι at B2. 3b and B2. 5b as complementary infinitives
and take the subject of ἐστι to be the same as that of ἔστιν in B2. 3a and B2. 5a, viz.
the proper object of νόος, yielding the translations: 'and that it is not for not being',
and 'and that it necessarily is for not being'. Or, more properly, one may take μὴ εἶναι
as a subject infinitive with the quasi-impersonal ἐστι and understand the unexpressed

path of inquiry, rather than the third, is presented as the genuine alternative to the first because it meets the formal requirement that a proper object of knowledge possess a necessary and absolute mode of being (in this case absolute not-being). Understanding knowledge or *νόος* as a strong cognitive mode requiring of its proper object an absolute mode of being avoids the apparent absurdity of having Parmenides say that one cannot even think about something that fails to satisfy the requirement that it is not possible for it not to be. He does not say that one cannot have any apprehension of something that exists (or is F) at time t_1 but not at t_2, or that is F in one context but not in another. It is simply that apprehensions of this type will not constitute knowledge.

Such a reading affects the character of the initial argument in an important way. The basic line of reasoning is as follows: the object of knowledge must have a stable or necessary mode of being. There are two possible modes of being that meet this requirement, specified in B2. 3 and B2. 5. The second possibility is ruled out on the grounds that there can be no apprehension of an object that necessarily is not (B2. 7–8). But there is a crucial gap at the point where the goddess sets Parmenides upon the first path. That there can be no knowledge (indeed no apprehension at all) of what-necessarily-is-not (B2. 5–8) by no means entails that there exists something that necessarily is, despite her declaring this to be the case in B2. 3. *It may simply be that there is no such knowledge. It remains a genuine possibility that there is no proper object of knowledge* and thus no such object as the one she will go on to describe in B8. Despite the goddess's warnings, one might still 'choose' the second path. Such a choice would in effect constitute a denial of the possibility of knowledge. Because of this gap, it is impossible to reconstruct an inescapable logic by which the goddess bars Parmenides from the second path. One might therefore suppose that her argument is as much rhetorical as logical: she simply declares the first path to be the path of persuasion upon which truth attends (B2. 4). But it would be more accurate to say that the argument relies upon the crucial premiss that knowledge is possible. It is reasonable to suppose this possibility is already presumed when the goddess directs Parmenides in B2. 2 towards the search for knowledge. All of

---

subject of *μὴ εἶναι* to be the same as that of *ἔστιν* in B2. 3a and B2. 5a, yielding the translations given here. Supplying the unexpressed subject of *μὴ εἶναι* in this way seems to yield better sense than allowing *μὴ εἶναι* to stand alone as the subject—as do e.g. Tarán 1965, 32, who accordingly translates B2. 3b and B2. 5b as: 'it is not possible not to exist' and 'not to exist is necessary'; and Cordero 1984, 70, who translates: 'ne pas être n'est pas possible' and 'ne pas être est nécessaire'.

which is to say that Parmenides' argument in B2 is an argument from the possibility of knowledge.[27]

Elements of this basic argument recur in various forms at three points in the remainder of the poem. B3, τὸ γὰρ αὐτὸ νοεῖν ἐστίν τε καὶ εἶναι ('for the same thing is there for knowing and for being'), is a straightforward statement of the possibility of knowledge's ontological consequence. What 'is there for knowing', namely the proper object of knowledge, is 'there for being' or exists. Here Parmenides attempts to counter the possible objection to APK and close the gap isolated above by asserting that there must be an object that meets the demands of knowledge.

The same is true of B6. 1: χρὴ τὸ λέγειν τὸ νοεῖν τ' ἐὸν ἔμμεναι. Leonardo Tarán's research on the text of Simplicius' commentary on Aristotle's *Physics*, where B6 is preserved, has shown that all the manuscripts give τὸ νοεῖν, not τε νοεῖν as first conjectured by Simon Karsten in 1835. Karsten's conjecture was subsequently accepted by Diels in his edition of the Presocratics without notice of the manuscript reading and thus accepted uncritically by subsequent editors and commentators.[28] Even with the text restored, certain syntactic and semantic difficulties prevent the sense of the line from being immediately apparent. The suggestion that λέγειν functions as an equivalent of φράζειν, and thus that τὸ λέγειν means something along the lines of 'what is there to pick out', is weak.[29] However one eventually construes it, the verb must retain its usual connotation of 'speaking'. Before publication of the new text, a widely endorsed construal of

---

[27] Hintikka 1980, who sees both Plato and Parmenides as assuming the close dependence of thinking on its object, perhaps comes closest to actually attributing such an argument to Parmenides: 'What Parmenides wanted to establish is that a successful thought-act presupposes that its object exists. . . . We do not assume that a thought is a thought only if its object exists, but we do assume that knowledge is knowledge only if it is true, that is, if its propositional object (fact) exists. In formal terms the following implication is valid: (1) (a knows that *p*) ⊃ *p*. The validity of this principle [which Hintikka sees as directly expressed in B2. 8b] thus encouraged Parmenides to assume that the direct object of any knowledge-act likewise has to exist' (9). Hintikka sees the natural character of this assumption for Parmenides as explicable in terms of an assimilation of the veridical use of 'is', and the concomitant concern with propositional objects, with the existential sense and its concern with knowledge of particulars or 'direct objects'.

[28] Cf. Tarán 1985, 253–4; Cordero 1979, 1 and 24 n.1; 1984, 110 n. 1; and 1987, 19–20.

[29] Robinson 1975, 626, taking the conjunction of λέγειν with νοεῖν here as parallel to the conjunction of γνοίης and φράσαις in B2. 7–8, concludes that λέγειν 'is being used in its primitive sense of "pick out"'. Unfortunately, it is not clear that λέγειν ever means 'pick out' in earlier Greek literature in the same way as φράζειν. A closer parallel for the conjunction of λέγειν and νοεῖν is οὐ γὰρ φατὸν οὐδὲ νοητόν at B8. 8.

B6. 1 preserving this sense of λέγειν was: 'it is necessary that what is there for speaking and for thinking is there for being'.[30] Although the new text precludes such a reading, I mention it to demonstrate the difficulties in attempting to construe λέγειν and νοεῖν here (even on the old text) as dand infinitives like those at B2. 2 and B3. The problem is that it is difficult to find the necessary form of the verb 'to be' for which they may serve as complements. If one takes this to be ἔμμεναι, the participle ἐόν is left without a proper grammatical function. To get the desired sense, the participle should be another datival infinitive, so that the sense of ἐὸν ἔμμεναι could be 'is there for being' as in the case of the phrase ἔστι γὰρ εἶναι immediately following. Such difficulties make it preferable, especially in light of the newly restored manuscript reading τὸ νοεῖν, to take τὸ λέγειν and τὸ νοεῖν as articular infinitives functioning as the subjects of χρή and to take ἐὸν ἔμμεναι as an indirect statement (subject accusative plus infinitive) governed by them. Translate: 'it is necessary to declare and to know that being is'.[31]

If B6. 1 is not a statement of APK per se, it nevertheless declares the necessity of the condition upon which knowledge is possible—namely that Being (ἐόν), that which enjoys the mode of being specified

---

[30] So basically e.g. Burnet 1930, 174 ('It needs must be that what can be spoken and thought is'); Cornford 1939, 31 ('What can be spoken of and thought must be'); Owen 1960, 60 ('What can be spoken and thought of must exist'); Barnes 1982, 158 ('What is for saying and for thinking of must be'); and KRS 247 ('What is there to be said and thought must needs be'). These translations obscure what, precisely, is being made of ἐὸν ἔμμεναι.

[31] Cf. Cordero 1984, 111: 'Peu de chose s'oppose . . . à ce que τὸ λέγειν τὸ νοεῖν τ' soient les sujets de χρή, et à ce que ἐὸν ἔμμεναι soit une proposition complétive qui dépend des deux infinitifs: "il est nécessaire de dire et de penser qu'il y a de l'être" (ou que "l'être existe").' Even before the restoration of the manuscript reading, the line was understood along these lines by Cornford 1933, 99, 'That it is necessary to say and think: that which is, is'; and Kranz in DK, 'Nötig ist zu sagen und zu denken, daß nur das Seiende ist', though of course there is nothing in the text corresponding to his 'nur' (cf. Cordero 1984, 111, for further references). Cordero adopts this translation in spite of the fact that the use of the articular infinitive as the subject of the quasi-impersonal χρή is insufficiently attested. The lack of a parallel is not decisive, however, since the case is complicated by the absence of an articular infinitive in the Homeric poems: it may simply be that Parmenides' fondness for the new form of expression led him to certain usages that became anomalous by the classical period. The construction here is at any rate not so different from what one finds e.g. at Pl. *Cra.* 433c9: οὐκ ἀρέσκει γέ με τὸ φάναι ὄνομα μὲν εἶναι. An alternative construal is provided by O'Brien 1987(*a*), 24 (defended at 26, cf. 197 ff., 207 ff.), who takes τό in each case to be demonstrative, announcing the proposition ἐὸν ἔμμεναι, and thus takes λέγειν and νοεῖν to be simple infinitives governed by χρή: 'Il faut dire ceci et penser ceci: l'être est'. While the explanation I give of the grammatical structure is to be preferred, O'Brien's construal yields much the same sense.

at B2. 3, *is* and consequently is there to be known. Why is this necessary? Not because of what is said in B6. 1b–2a—ἔστι γὰρ εἶναι, | μηδὲν δ᾽ οὐκ ἔστιν ('for it is there for being, while nothing is not'). These words simply restate the original disjunction between the two paths in B2. Rather, it is necessary because accepting that knowledge is possible involves accepting that its object, Being, is.[32] B6. 1 simply asserts the necessary existence of this object. This necessity is not established by a logical chain of argumentation but in the original choice of the path described at B2. 3, a choice that affirms the possibility of knowledge. The beginning of B6 reaffirms the need to make this decision.

The essentials of APK receive perhaps their clearest statement at B8. 34–6a:

> ταὐτὸν δ᾽ ἐστὶ νοεῖν τε καὶ οὕνεκεν ἔστι νόημα·
> οὐ γὰρ ἄνευ τοῦ ἐόντος, ἐφ᾽ ᾧ πεφατισμένον ἐστίν,
> εὑρήσεις τὸ νοεῖν

(The same thing is there for knowing and is that because of which[33] there is knowledge: for not without being, with reference to which it [knowledge] is expressed,[34] will you find knowledge).

---

[32] This reading avoids ascribing to Parmenides the fallacy of shifting from the assertion that 'it can exist' (B6. 1b) to 'it must exist' (B6. 1a), the so-called fallacy of the *de re* interpretation of modal statements detected by Owen 1960, 60 and 60 n. 47. Similar fallacies are found by Furth 1968, 245, and Furley 1973, 11. Tugwell 1964, 36–7, tries to meet Owen's objection by arguing against separating 'the potential εἶναι from the existential to an anachronistic extent'; cf. Coxon 1986, 174. I have some sympathy for this suggestion, according to which ἔστι γὰρ εἶναι, 'it is for being', should be taken as an assertion of its existence rather than as equivalent to 'it can be'.

[33] This is to take οὕνεκεν as equivalent to οὗ ἕνεκα, as at Hom. *Il.* 9. 505 and *Od.* 3. 60, rather than as a synonym for ὅτι. Thus e.g. von Fritz 1945–6, 45–7; Vlastos 1946, 68 n. 15. Cf. Parmenides' use of οὕνεκεν at B8. 32 and of τοῦ εἵνεκεν at B8. 13.

[34] The sense of B8. 35b is notoriously difficult. For an overview of the attempts to understand this clause, cf. Tarán 1965, 123–7. It seems that the antecedent of ᾧ must be found in τοῦ ἐόντος, in which case the subject of ἐστίν must be τὸ νοεῖν. Thus e.g. Kranz in DK; Verdenius 1942, 40. The sense of the verb φατίζω is not in itself obscure. It means 'tell of', 'relate', or 'express', as at B8. 60, τόν σοι ἐγὼ διάκοσμον . . . φατίζω ('to you I relate this ordering of things'). But if one accepts, as most do, the reading ἐν ᾧ, it is difficult to see how knowing is supposed to be 'expressed', 'ausgesprochen' (Kranz), or 'uttered' (Verdenius) *in* Being. Cordero 1984, 113 n. 15, argues that ἐφ᾽ ᾧ, found in all the MSS of Procl. *in Prm.*, is preferable to ἐν ᾧ, found in Simp. *in Ph.* and printed in DK without mention of the reading known to Proclus. I accept this reading and translate in what I hope is a straightforward manner. The sense of the somewhat parenthetical declaration that knowledge is expressed with reference to Being is simply that the expression of one's knowledge will be an account of Being. It may even be, if we place weight on the perfect tense of the participle and translate 'with reference to which it has been expressed', that the goddess is here referring to the account of Being given thus far, which itself constitutes the knowledge she imparts to Parmenides.

Parmenides here declares that what can be known and is the cause of knowledge is Being (τὸ ἐόν), again, the object with the necessary or absolute mode of being introduced in B2. 3. The two halves of B8. 34 make related but distinct points. The assertion that Being is there to be known makes the ontological point that the object of knowledge exists, in much the same way as B3. The assertion that Being is the cause of knowledge makes the epistemological point that it is only the existence of something with this mode of being that makes knowledge possible.[35] B8. 35–6a then give grounds for making the ontological assertion: one would not be able to attain true knowledge if there were nothing possessing this absolute mode of being. The conditional form of the goddess's statement here is extremely interesting. Even after leading Parmenides to make the original choice in B2, she continues at this latter stage to mark the ultimately unsupported assumption on which her entire exposition rests, namely that νόος or knowledge in the strict sense is possible. Being (τὸ ἐόν), which is the cause and ground of knowing (B8. 34b), must exist and exist to be known (B8. 34a), for without it knowledge would be impossible (B8. 35–6a). The crucial premiss, unstated but directly implied at this point, is that knowledge is indeed possible.

Let me repeat, then, that there is an important gap in the overall argument, one that the goddess herself comes close to acknowledging. The search for knowledge or νόος may potentially be a vain one, for it may be that there is nothing with the absolute mode of being that she demands its object must have. This possibility is, in effect, the threat posed by the introduction of the second path in B2. 5. The goddess cannot bar Parmenides from this path via an inescapable logic. She can only denounce it as a path along which he would never achieve genuine knowledge. For all she says in B2, B3, B6. 1–2a, and B8. 34–6a, it remains possible to reply: 'yes, but one will never achieve knowledge as you conceive it because there is no such thing as your Being.'

If we return now to the corresponding argument in Plato, we shall find that it also attempts, with questionable success, to conceal a similar gap. There is a common presumption that since the arguments at the end of *Republic* 5 are directed at the sight-lovers, they

---

[35] Coxon 1986, 209, supposes that Parmenides' language here 'foreshadows and is likely to be a source of Plato's account of the Form of the Good, which is also both the object and the end or cause of philosophical knowledge'. Plato describes the form of the Good as 'being the cause of knowledge and truth' (αἴτιον δ᾽ ἐπιστήμης οὖσαν καὶ ἀληθείας, *R*. 6. 508e; cf. *Smp*. 211c).

must proceed via premises acceptable to them.[36] This assumption is problematic on several counts and should be rejected as a constraint upon interpretation of the arguments. For one, the scope of the principle is ambiguous. Commentators tend to introduce it first in a weak form, imposing the mild constraint that the arguments can make no appeal to forms, given that the sight-lovers are introduced as not admitting their existence. In this weak and rather innocuous form, the constraint must surely be accepted. For any appeal here to the existence of forms would obviously be begging the question. But when commentators say that the arguments directed towards the sight-lovers must proceed via premises acceptable to them, they in fact presume a much stronger constraint, namely that *all* the premises of the arguments must be acceptable to the sight-lovers. In this strong form, the constraint is intensely problematic, for it presumes at the outset that the arguments are successful and must be interpreted as such. By 'successful' here I do not mean that the arguments are not without their minor fallacies but that they can be considered adequate to winning over the sight-lovers. By adopting the strong form of the constraint, commentators have forced themselves into the often difficult position of having to explain even the more obscure and potentially difficult premisses of the arguments as things anyone, even a sight-lover, would accept. Thus Julia Annas describes premiss (iiia) at 477a2–4, that what-completely-is (τὸ παντελῶς ὄν) is completely knowable (παντελῶς γνωστόν), as 'clearly taken to be acceptable without prejudging the issue'. Although she supposes Plato found this principle a truism, she simultaneously admits that to our ears it 'sounds bizarre' and 'seems far from obvious—indeed, not even true'.[37] Similarly, Annas says that the premiss that knowledge and *doxa* are capacities in the following argument 'is meant to be obvious, indeed trivial'.[38] Why, then, does Socrates go to the lengths he does to explain what he means by a 'capacity' and to secure Glaucon's acceptance that knowledge and *doxa* conform to his definition? These premisses are problematic. If we find them so, we should not presume that Plato constructed the figure of the sight-lover as a puppet opponent who would graciously

[36] So e.g. Gosling 1968, 120–1; Fine 1978, 123; Annas 1981, 195 and 196; Cooper 1986, 233; Reeve 1988, 62; Fine 1990, 87; Stokes 1992, 109; Gonzalez 1996, 249–53; and cf. Murphy 1937, 74–5. Benitez 1996 presents a valuable corrective to this common presumption of a 'dialectical requirement' that the arguments must be conducted on grounds acceptable to the sight-lovers, though he, like Stokes 1992 and Ebert 1974, ends up denying that Plato is himself committed to his arguments here.

[37] Annas 1981, 196 and 199. Cf. Reeve 1988, 63, who supposes the premiss 'is intended to be obvious and irresistible'.   [38] Annas 1981, 201.

accept them. Since the strong form of the constraint has at best questionable grounding in the text and imposes artificial pressures on interpretation of Plato's arguments, it is best abandoned. I think it is in fact crucial to recognize that Plato's arguments appeal to premisses the sight-lover will not be prepared to accept.

Socrates begins, again, by asking whether one who knows knows something that is rather than nothing or what-is-not. Since in his initial question securing this premiss—'[Does one know] what-is or what-is-not?' ($\Pi \acute{o} \tau \epsilon \rho o \nu$ ὄν ἢ οὐκ ὄν; 476e10)[39]—there is no modal qualification placed on 'what-is', the sight-lover can go along with Glaucon's response. When the sight-lover says that one must know what-is, by 'what-is' he need mean no more than something that is in the way Socrates goes on to say the object of *doxa* is, namely something that is in one respect but may not be in another or that exists at one time but may not at another. But Socrates then shifts from the bare 'what-is' ($\tau \grave{o}$ ὄν) to 'what-completely-is' ($\tau \grave{o}$ $\pi a \nu \tau \epsilon \lambda \hat{\omega} s$ ὄν), which he says is absolutely knowable. *Although the sight-lover might well accept that something that is absolutely would be absolutely knowable, there is no reason for him to accept that there actually is anything possessed of the absolute mode of being Socrates designates as 'what-completely-is'.* Plato's shift from 'what-is' to 'what-completely-is' corresponds to the gap in Parmenides' own attempt to establish the existence of a proper object of knowledge. Seeking to show the sight-lover that there is knowledge in a higher and more restricted sense than he has been willing to accept, Plato simply posits the existence of what-completely-is to serve as such knowledge's proper object. In much the same way, Parmenides' goddess had set him on the path towards a knowledge loftier than that recognized by mortals by indicating to him the necessity of asserting that there is in fact an object of such knowledge that possesses a similar absolute being.

Socrates abruptly breaks off the argument in *Republic* 5 that is based on the tripartite division of the modes of being and starts afresh with a second argument that proceeds from an analysis of the various cognitive faculties. This shift brings the overall strategy into conformance with the thrust of APK, which proceeds from an epistemological premiss to an ontological conclusion. The shift also suggests an awareness that the ontological hierarchy has been set up too hastily and, in particular, that there are problems with positing the existence of what-completely-is in the manner of the first argument. (Note the

[39] Cf. the form of his question to Simmias at *Phd.* 65d4–5: 'do we say that Justice itself is something or nothing?' ($\phi a \mu \acute{\epsilon} \nu$ $\tau \iota$ εἶναι δίκαιον αὐτὸ ἢ οὐδέν;)

return to the bare 'what-is' in the conclusion broken off at 477b11.) Socrates' new argument (477b11–478d12) seeks to establish the onto-logical hierarchy via an analysis of basic epistemological concepts:

(i) a capacity (*dunamis*) must be specified by reference to its par-ticular class of objects (477c6–d6);

(ii) both knowledge and *doxa* are capacities (477d7–e3);

(iii) knowledge and *doxa* are different (477e4–478a2). Therefore,

(iv) knowledge and *doxa* must be specified by reference to differ-ent classes of objects (478a3–5). Since

(v) the object of knowledge is what-is (478a6–7), via (iv):

(vi) the object of *doxa* is something other than what-is (478a8–b5). However,

(vii) the object of *doxa* cannot be what-is-not *simpliciter*; since, via (vi), the object of *doxa* is something (τι), while what-is-not is not anything (478a6–c2).

The conclusions drawn at 478c3–d12 recapitulate the main points of 476e4–477b11: complete ignorance (ἄγνοια) is the cognitive state whose object is what-is-not, while knowledge (γνῶσις) is that whose object is what-is. Since *doxa* as a cognitive state is agreed to lie between knowledge and ignorance, its object must be what was previously char-acterized as lying between what-genuinely-is and what-completely-is-not, namely what-is-and-is-not.

There are premises here as well that the sight-lover will not be prepared to accept. He will have particular problems with Plato's distinction between knowledge and *doxa* as capacities. To see why this is the case, however, we shall first have to say something more about the sight-lover's particular perspective. At this point, there-fore, we may simply note that, whereas we were initially led to expect that this argument would be persuasive to the sight-lover, what we in fact observe is an increasing relativization of the conclusions to Socrates and Glaucon alone. There are signs of this relativization in the increasingly frequent 'brackets' placed upon the key premises. For example, (iii) is established when Socrates says to Glaucon, 'But a little earlier [sc. at 477b5] *you agreed* that knowledge and *doxa* are not the same' (477e4–5). After Glaucon endorses the premiss, Socrates again stresses their agreement: 'it is clear that *doxa is agreed by us* to be different from knowledge' (477e8–478a1). Significantly, Socrates does not simply say *doxa* is different from knowledge but brackets the premiss by referring to his agreement with Glaucon that this is so. Most importantly, when Glaucon at 478a12–b2 recapitulates the essentials of the argument thus far, he qualifies premises (i)–(iii) in

a similar way: 'it is impossible [sc. that the same thing will be apprehended by knowledge and by *doxa*], *based on what we have agreed. If
one capacity is of a nature to be directed to one thing, and *doxa* and
knowledge are both capacities, but each one is different, *as we say*,
based on these points it is not possible that what is apprehended by
knowledge and what is apprehended by *doxa* are the same.' This type
of relativization already figured in the brief argument at 475e–476a that
Socrates had used to explain to Glaucon what he means by saying that
philosophers, as opposed to sight-lovers, love the vision of truth. This
vision of truth amounts to the apprehension of forms, and Socrates
had prefaced his argument for their existence by remarking that what
he means would not be easy to explain to someone else—including the
sight-lover—but he thinks Glaucon will agree with him on what follows (475e6–7).

It is fairly typical of Plato to mark key premisses as controversial
by emphasizing that they are accepted primarily on the basis of agreement between Socrates and his interlocutor. Perhaps the most salient
example occurs in the last step of the *Phaedo*'s final argument for the
soul's immortality. In a carefully worded passage, Socrates elicits from
Cebes the crucial premiss that what is deathless (ἀθάνατον), in the
sense in which the soul has been agreed to be deathless (namely, not
admitting death so long as it exists), is also indestructible (ἀνώλεθρον).
Socrates clearly indicates the point at issue at 106c9–d1 (cf. 106b2–
3): 'now then, as for what is deathless, *if* it is *agreed by us* to be indestructible as well, then the soul would, in addition to being deathless,
also be indestructible'. Cebes gives his full assent to the necessary premiss. Philosophers as far back as the Peripatetic Strato of Lampsacus
(3rd cent. BC) have pointed out the argument's apparent fallacy,
objecting that all that has actually been shown is that the soul is 'deathless', in the sense in which this has been understood in the argument
thus far, but not thereby indestructible. Socrates, however, is willing
to take the agreement reached with Cebes as an indication of the
truth of the conclusion even though he is fully aware of what has and
has not been shown. The conclusion is established on the basis of
Socrates' and Cebes' agreement to the crucial premiss. This agreement
is presented by Plato in a way that marks the controversial premiss.
The effect is to relativize the conclusion to those actually participating in the discussion. Simmias, one notes, is not convinced. The
capacity argument in *Republic* 5 has a similar character. To reach the
conclusion that knowledge is the special form of apprehension that
has what-is for its object, Socrates and Glaucon agree to a number
of things in such a way that it becomes increasingly unclear whether

Plato in the end supposes the argument effective in persuading the sight-lover that there is indeed a higher cognitive arena than he had been prepared to accept. At the beginning of the next book, Socrates significantly says things would have been clearer if they could have devoted more time to these topics (484a5–6).[40]

I have suggested that Plato's arguments here, although directed towards persuading the sight-lover, rest on certain assumptions he would not in fact accept. Scholars have rightly pointed out that these arguments should be interpreted in such a way as not to rely on the Platonic distinction between forms and particulars. The primary assumptions that I have singled out, however, that knowledge and *doxa* differ in the way Socrates says they do, and that there is something one may designate as 'what-completely-is' such that it may serve as the proper object of knowledge, are of a more fundamental nature. They may lead to, but do not necessarily involve, the form/particular distinction. One might nevertheless object that these assumptions are not actually controversial at all. One might suppose that any ordinary Greek would accept that knowledge and opinion or belief are different, however he or she might want to specify the distinction. One might want to say that Plato simply draws upon what he presumes to be this common distinction and so is not depending on his own

---

[40] Other places where APK occurs in Plato include *Cra.* 439b10–440c1 and *Ti.* 51d3–e2. In the *Cratylus* passage, Socrates argues that if there is to be genuine knowledge, then there must be entities with a stable mode of being to serve as its objects. At one point in this argument Socrates comes quite close to articulating the Parmenidean principle that leads Glaucon to reject the possibility of knowing what-is-not (440a3–4). Socrates' argument displays the same type of gap as the one that occurs in the *Republic* 5 version, so that he is finally as ineffective at winning over Cratylus as we shall see he is at persuading the sight-lovers (see 440d8–e2). Aristotle, furthermore, in the fragments of his lost treatise, 'On Ideas' (Περὶ ἰδεῶν), attributes to Plato an argument for the existence of forms with a structure similar to that of APK. The argument is referred to as the second argument from the sciences (*ap.* Alex. Aphr. *in Metaph.* 79, 8–11): 'furthermore, the objects of the sciences exist. But the sciences have as their objects certain other things besides the particulars. For particulars are indefinite and indeterminate, whereas the sciences are concerned with things determinate. There are therefore certain things besides the particulars, and these are the Ideas.' The argument likewise proceeds from a formal specification of the mode of being required of objects of knowledge (the sciences are of determinate things), denies that particulars possess this mode of being (they are indefinite and indeterminate), and concludes that the objects of the sciences exist, which amounts to an assertion of the possibility of knowledge. On the intricacies of this argument, see Fine 1993, 70–6. She agrees (although this is not Aristotle's objection) that there is the same sort of gap in the argument as the one we have identified in APK: 'Without the assumption that there are objects of knowledge, it does not follow that there are any objects besides *kath' hekasta*: perhaps there are only *kath' hekasta* and so no objects of knowledge' (71).

philosophic understanding of the terms to make the distinction. Additionally, it might seem that positing something that fully or completely is as what is fully knowable is not a particularly Platonic move but one characteristic of Greek thinkers both before and after Plato. From the start it was presumed that one understands what things really are, rather than merely perceiving how they appear to be, when one understands that things are essentially water, or air, or some combination of these and/or other elements. Aristotle too, even in the midst of criticizing the Platonic hypothesis of separately existing universals, says that there is neither definition nor demonstration and thus no knowledge of the being of individual perceptibles because their involvement with matter causes them both to be and not to be (*Metaph. Z.* 15. 1039^{b}27–30). Ultimately, however, I do not think one can successfully maintain that what I have marked as the controversial assumptions of these arguments were in truth universally accepted.[41] In particular, I do not think that the sight-lover accepts these assumptions. But to argue for this view in the face of objections such as have been presented, we must attempt to be more precise about who this figure is. Our pursuit of him will eventually lead us back to Plato's engagement with Parmenides.

---

[41] In the *Timaeus*'s version of APK, which should be compared with the *Republic*'s capacity argument, Plato himself may seem to be alluding to certain thinkers who were unprepared to accept the distinction between knowledge and *doxa*. Having asked whether 'all the things we always speak of as beings themselves (αὐτὰ καθ' αὐτὰ ὄντα)' actually exist, or whether there are only such things as we perceive with our senses, such that any reference to the intelligible form of each thing would be nothing but empty talk (51b7–c5), Timaeus presents the following brief argument: '*if* intelligence (νοῦς) and true opinion (δόξα ἀληθής) are two distinct kinds, then by all means there are these things in themselves, forms imperceptible by us but intelligible only. But *if, as it seems to some*, true opinion does not differ at all from intelligence, then all such things as we perceive via the body must be posited as the things most stable. They [sc. νοῦς and δόξα] must, in fact, be said to be two things, given that they are distinct in origin and unlike in character' (51d3–e2). Here, again, the existence of a class of eternal and changeless entities is made conditional upon the possibility of a strict form of knowledge distinct from opinion, a distinction which Timaeus indicates some were not prepared to accept.

4

Sight-Lovers, Mortals, and *Doxa*

ANTISTHENES

Who are the 'lovers of sights and sounds'? Some may think this a question better left unasked given the extremes to which nineteenth-century scholarship, particularly in Germany, went in trying to detect in such labels veiled allusions to Plato's contemporary rivals. The fashion for such identifications stretches back to the beginnings of modern Platonic scholarship. Friedrich Schleiermacher detected a polemic against Aristippus in the *Theaetetus*'s refutation of the thesis that knowledge is perception. He saw traces of a parallel polemic against Antisthenes in the remainder of the dialogue, particularly in the 'dream theory' at 201e–202c.[1] Antisthenes was a pupil of Socrates' and a key figure in the early history of Cynicism. He attacked his younger contemporary Plato in the scurrilously entitled *Sathōn* (a crude pun on 'Plato' meaning, roughly, 'little willy').[2] He has been the second most frequently proposed target of Plato's criticism in the dialogues after Isocrates. Plato's treatment of the views of the 'opsimaths' or 'late-learners' in the *Sophist*, for instance, has been widely accepted as a direct reference to Antisthenes. This is in part because of a similar allusion in Isocrates that is reminiscent of certain remarks by Aristotle on Antisthenes. 'Some people have grown old', Isocrates says, 'denying the possibility of speaking falsely, or contradicting, or making two opposing statements about the same things'; and he asks who is such a late-learner (ὀψιμαθής) so as not to know that such nonsense may be found in the writings of Protagoras and the other sophists (*Orat.* 10. 1–2). Aristotle's reports that Antisthenes denied the possibility of falsehood and contradiction (*Metaph. Δ.* 29. 1024ᵇ29–34, *Top.* 1. 11. 104ᵇ20–1) in turn led to the assumption that Antisthenes is lurking behind a number of the sophistic arguments propounded in Plato's *Euthydemus*. An elaborate network of ever more complex cross-references and probabilistic reasoning grew up to support

---

[1] See the introduction to the translation of the *Theaetetus* in Schleiermacher 1855.
[2] Giannantoni 1990, V A 147–59, collects the testimonia concerning the *Sathōn* and the ancient reports which most likely reflect its contents; cf. V A 27–30 for anecdotal evidence of the rivalry between Plato and Antisthenes. The material has recently been discussed in Brancacci 1990, ch. 6.

such identifications,[3] eventually resulting in a backlash against the Antisthenes hunters. G. C. Field militated against the 'idea that any character in [Plato's] dialogues represents in detail a contemporary person'.[4] His reaction, although a valuable corrective, went too far in the opposite direction. Today a more non-committal stance generally prevails: while it is admitted that there are probably some criticisms of Antisthenes in the dialogues, it is felt that few if any passages can be certainly identified as such.[5] The parties in this long debate have focused too exclusively on the possibility of making precise, one-to-one identifications. In this particular case, the question should not be whether by 'sight-lover' Plato means Antisthenes. The label 'sight-lover(s)' is designed to encompass a broad class of thinkers.[6] The proper question, therefore, is whether Antisthenes may be thought to belong to the general class of thinkers so designated.

Simplicius is one of several late authors who report more or less the same version of the following anecdote regarding an Antisthenean criticism of Plato:

Some of the ancient thinkers, such as Antisthenes, completely did away with qualities, while accepting that what is qualified exists. Once, when engaged in a dispute with Plato, he said, 'Plato, I can see a horse, but "Horseness" I do not see'. 'Because', replied Plato, 'you have the kind of sight by which a horse is seen, but you have not yet attained the kind by which "Horseness" is beheld' (*in Cat.* 208, 28–32; cf. 211, 15–21).[7]

This text provided the primary evidence for the identification of the sight-lover with Antisthenes.[8] Although any such exclusive identification should be avoided, this anecdote may still secure Antisthenes

---

[3] For a detailed summary of the 19th-cent. debate, with citations of these and other Platonic passages that were thought to cloak anti-Antisthenean polemics, plus references to scholars *pro* and *contra*, see Natorp 1894, 2543–4.   [4] Field 1930, 190.

[5] Thus e.g. Guthrie 1971, 310; cf. Denyer 1991, 27–8.

[6] Dümmler 1889, 40–3, took the singular ὁ χρηστός ('the good fellow') at *R.* 5. 479a1 as indicating that Plato has a specific individual in mind (*contra* Dümmler, cf. Zeller 1922, 296 n. 2). Adam 1963, i. 337 ad loc., although generally more cautious, feels forced to admit that the deictic οὗτος ('this man') at *R.* 5. 476d3, 8 supports Dümmler's thesis. However, the person indicated by these singular forms need not be Antisthenes, or any other individual, but simply that person, whoever he might be, who takes the kind of view attributed to the sight-lover. It is in any case misleading to cite these singulars in support of an exclusive identification, for Plato first speaks of 'sight-*lovers*' and 'sound-*lovers*' (475d2–3) and continues throughout to refer to them in the plural (476a9–10, b4–5, 479e1–2) as well as the singular.

[7] Cf. Giannantoni 1990, V A 149, and Brancacci 1990, 175–6, for the other versions *ap.* Ammon. *in Porph.* 40, 6–10; Elias, *in Porph.* 47, 14–19, *in Cat.* 108, 15–109, 3 and 220, 28–30; David, *in Porph.* 109, 12–16; and Tz. *H.* 7. 605–9.

[8] So e.g. Dümmler 1882, 40 ff., who also cites DL 6. 53; there, however, the anecdote, with different examples, is recounted of Diogenes of Sinope. Field 1930, 168, oddly objects that the criticism is not well attested for Antisthenes, on the rather shaky

membership in the group. In interpreting Antisthenes' objection as rooted in the distinction between a quality (ποιότης) and what is qualified (τὸ ποιόν), Simplicius appears to be drawing upon Aristotle's evidence that the Antistheneans denied the possibility of defining what something is (τὸ τί ἐστιν) and allowed only that one may indicate of what sort something is (ποῖον τί ἐστιν, *Metaph. H.* 3. 1043[b]23–8). This thesis is part of the more general Antisthenean position that a simple entity cannot be defined but only indicated by its own proper account or οἰκεῖος λόγος (cf. Arist. *Metaph. Δ.* 29. 1024[b]32–4). The objection Antisthenes is reported to have made against Plato, however, does not (*pace* Simplicius) belong directly to this context. Rather, saying 'I see a horse, but not "Horseness"' is in effect a denial of the reality of universals. Ammonius understood Antisthenes' point in this way (*in Porph.* 40, 6–10). Along with John Tzetzes, he gives a fuller version of the objection than Simplicius, adding 'I see a man but not "Manness"'. Ammonius takes the point to be that genera and species are not themselves real but exist as mere thoughts or conceptions (ψιλαὶ ἐπινοίαι; cf. Tzetzes' ψιλαὶ ἐννοίαι).[9] This criticism of Plato makes Antisthenes a suitable candidate for membership in the class of those who are described in *Republic* 5 as accepting the existence of beautiful things but not of Beauty itself. Indeed, such an inference may already have been made in antiquity. The source of Plato's 'reply' to Antisthenes as reported by Simplicius is problematic. The *Sathōn* might seem the most likely known source for Antisthenes' reported point against Plato, but it is difficult to believe that in this (or any other) work he would have given Plato the opportunity to make the reported rejoinder. Plato's 'reply' is thus in all probability an invention of the subsequent tradition concocted on the basis of Plato's own works. The most direct parallel, and thus the potential source of this invention, is Socrates' description of the sight-lovers as possessing an intelligence incapable of seeing the nature of the Beautiful itself (*R.* 5. 476b6–8; cf. 479e1–2).

The concluding arguments of *Republic* 5 make certain key assumptions that the sight-lover would not be prepared to accept. These are principally (i) that there is anything that enjoys the absolute mode of being Plato designates as 'what-completely-is' (τὸ παντελῶς ὄν), (ii) that knowledge and *doxa* may be distinguished in the purely

ground that it is not attributed to any particular work, and therefore (wrongly) infers from DL 6. 53 that a genuinely Diogenean remark was fathered upon his presumed master.

[9] Cf. Brancacci 1990, 190 ff., on the possible relation between this criticism and Pl. *Prm.* 132b4–c8.

intentional manner Plato adopts in these arguments, and (iii) that knowledge as he consequently conceives it is possible. Even without examining Antisthenes' views more deeply than we have (we will have occasion to return to him), one can see that he would not have accepted this first assumption. He is thus unlikely to have followed Plato's strictly intentional distinction between knowledge and *doxa*. Unfortunately, we cannot safely go farther. Antisthenes does appear to have discussed epistemological matters in some detail. Among the logical treatises in Diogenes Laertius' catalogue of his works (DL 6. 15–18), there is listed a treatise in four books entitled, 'On Opinion and Knowledge' (Περὶ δόξης καὶ ἐπιστήμης). Although it has been suggested that the treatise contained his theory of definition, or that it presented an account of knowledge as true opinion with an account, or even that in it Antisthenes attempted to reduce knowledge to *doxa*, there is in the end insufficient foundation for conjecture regarding how (or even if) Antisthenes actually distinguished knowledge and *doxa*. I therefore want to turn now to others, perhaps more important than Antisthenes, who also belong to the general class of sight-lovers.

HIPPIAS

There is in fact an intertextual relation within the Platonic corpus itself that provides a perspective on the character of the sight-lovers that is, in the end, more informative than any connections one might make with Antisthenes. Socrates twice describes the sight-lover as one whose attention is focused solely upon beautiful things and who is unable to conceive of Beauty itself even if someone should attempt to lead him towards apprehension of it (*R.* 5. 476c2–4, 479e1–2). As Myles Burnyeat has taught us to appreciate, Hippias as portrayed in the *Hippias Major*[10] is precisely such a figure.[11] A much debated

---

[10] For overviews of the debate regarding the dialogue's authenticity, cf. Soreth 1953, 1–4; and Woodruff 1982, 93–103 (also Kahn 1985, 267–73, for a dissenting voice amidst the increasing trend towards acceptance). Although I shall treat it as genuine, the points I make would stand even if it were written, as most athetizers would have it, by a student within the Academy during Plato's lifetime (a view proposed by Röllig 1900; adopted by Wilamowitz-Möllendorff 1919, ii. 328; and maintained most systematically by Tarrant 1928). It is worth noting that Aristotle's discussion at *Top.* 6. 7. 146ᵃ21–32 of the definition of beauty (τὸ καλόν) as 'what is pleasant to the sight or hearing' suggests he knew the dialogue, for this is tantamount to the final definition of the beautiful proposed in the *Hippias Major* (298a).

[11] The view of Hippias and his connection with the sight-lovers presented here derives substantially from that set out by Burnyeat in his 1988 Cambridge lectures on the *Hippias Major*. (As one might expect, some have detected Antisthenes lurking behind Plato's Hippias; cf. Dümmler 1889, 184 f. and 203 f.; Joël 1893, 441–2.)

issue, which bears directly upon the question of the dialogue's date of composition, has been whether it contains allusions to middle period Platonic metaphysics.[12] Yet no one in this debate has suggested that there may be significant parallels between the *Hippias Major* and *Republic* 5.[13] This oversight is somewhat surprising given that there are both thematic and specific parallels between the two texts.

The *Hippias Major* opens with a discussion of Hippias' political service as ambassador on behalf of his native Elis. During the course of this discussion Socrates remarks upon Gorgias' and Prodicus' similar service to their respective cities. The arguments directed at the *Republic*'s sight-lovers are similarly, and, of course, more explicitly, framed by a debate over who is properly equipped to manage political affairs. The entire 'digression' of the *Republic*'s central books is a defence of Socrates' claim that only true philosophers are so equipped, a defence in which he both argues that they are the only ones who possess genuine knowledge and demonstrates what this knowledge consists of. The opening of the *Hippias Major* suggests, albeit on a much smaller scale, that the discussion that follows may have a similar political dimension. From this point of view, it is noteworthy, if only for its irony, that in the *Hippias Major* Socrates refers to Hippias' supposed expertise in astronomy, geometry, and arithmetic (285b5 ff.). For these subjects form the core of the guardians' educational programme in *Republic* 7. The introductory conversation of the *Hippias Major* concludes with Hippias' account (286a3–c2) of his successful speech before the Spartans on the pursuits appropriate for a young man desirous of a fair reputation to engage in, again providing an ironic counterpoint to the *Republic*'s discussion of the type of education that produces the knowledge necessary for political activity.

More specific parallels underscore the relation between the two dialogues. For example, Glaucon describes the sight-lovers as 'ones

---

[12] For example, some (e.g. Tarrant 1955, 53) have seen in the principle that all beautiful things are beautiful by the beautiful (τὰ καλὰ πάντα τῷ καλῷ ἐστι καλά, 287c8–d1) an echo of *Phd.* 100d7–8—'Do all beautiful things become beautiful by the beautiful?' (τῷ καλῷ πάντα τὰ καλὰ [γίγνεται] καλά;) Those presuming an early date (cf. e.g. Grube 1926, 141–2; Soreth 1953, 12 ff.), however, argue that despite the superficial similarity, the formulation in the *Hippias Major* need imply no more serious metaphysical doctrine than the comparable phrase at *Euthphr.* 6d9–11, where Socrates asks Euthyphro to instruct him concerning 'the form itself by which all pious things are pious' (αὐτὸ τὸ εἶδος ᾧ πάντα τὰ ὅσια ὅσιά ἐστιν). Stylometric analyses have suggested the *Hippias Major* most likely belongs, not with the earliest dialogues, but among those of the middle period leading up to the *Republic*; see Brandwood 1990 and 1992.

[13] Malcolm 1968, 192–3, and Woodruff 1982, 153 and 178–9, come closest by positing a few minor connections.

who would not willingly engage in arguments and this kind of exercise' but who instead make the rounds of all the festivals (*R.* 5. 475d). The implied contrast between the typical arena of the sophists' epideictic displays and the more intimate exchanges in which Plato thinks wisdom best pursued is thoroughly general and familiar from other dialogues. The contrast is, however, particularly relevant to Hippias as he is portrayed in the two dialogues bearing his name. In the *Hippias Major*, as we shall see, he resists Socrates' attempts to engage him in an argument regarding the nature of the beautiful (τὸ καλόν—it is surely no coincidence that this same term figures so prominently in *Republic* 5), and in the opening of the *Hippias Minor* he gives a proud account of his successful display at the Olympic festival. The alternative description of the sight-lovers as 'lovers of the practical arts' (φιλοτέχνους καὶ πρακτικούς, *R.* 5. 476a10, cf. 475e1) is seemingly pointless until one recalls that Hippias' self-avowed polymathy encompassed knowledge of all the various crafts: he came to the festival at Olympia wearing nothing he had not made himself (*Hp. Mi.* 368b–c).

Oversight of the connection between the *Hippias Major* and *Republic* 5 is remarkable, given that Hippias is, as we shall see, a paradigmatic sight-lover in that he is unable or unwilling, despite Socrates' best efforts at guiding him, to understand what is meant by 'the Beautiful itself' or αὐτὸ τὸ καλόν. When Socrates asks Hippias for assistance with the question, 'What is the beautiful (τὸ καλόν)?' (286d1–2), and then, after a preliminary exchange, restates the question more formally, Hippias asks whether this is not equivalent to the question, 'What is beautiful (καλόν)?' (287d2–5). Already Schleiermacher assumed that Hippias somehow misunderstands Socrates' question.[14] This assumption has persisted to the present day. Paul Woodruff, for example, finds Hippias' response 'puzzling': 'Apparently he understands [the question], for he answers Socrates' catechism at 287cd without hesitation; but apparently he does not, for he assures Socrates that the matter is a trifle and proceeds to trivialize the question by substituting "something fine" (*kalon*) for "the fine" (*to kalon*).'[15] I believe Hippias is neither confused nor trivializing in his response. Hippias and Socrates simply understand different

---

[14] Thus Schleiermacher 1855, iii. 282, commenting on the different character of Hippias' responses from those of interlocutors in dialogues like the *Euthyphro* and *Laches*: 'muss wol Jeder sich selbst fragen, wie kommt wol Platon dazu, den nicht unberühmten Sophisten in einem so unerhörten Grade von Dummheit darzustellen, als wäre er nicht einmal im Stande gewesen die Frage, wie ein Wort zu erklären sei, auch nur zu verstehen?'   [15] Woodruff 1982, 43. Cf. Nehamas 1975, 298.

things by 'the beautiful'. When Socrates asks him what is the beautiful (τὸ καλόν), Hippias takes this in a perfectly straightforward manner to mean: 'what is that which is beautiful?' Thus he naturally sees Socrates' question as equivalent to 'what is beautiful (καλόν)?' One will only suppose Hippias confused if one (confusedly) supposes in advance that Hippias must, somehow, understand 'the beautiful' or τὸ καλόν as Socrates does, namely as designating some kind of universal. But Socrates deliberately avoids telling Hippias precisely what he himself means by this. If it is thus clear how Hippias understands the question, what is not clear at this stage (if we follow what is actually said in the dialogue and not import assumptions about what Socrates means from our knowledge of other dialogues) is precisely why Socrates thinks the questions differ. When Hippias asks how they do, Socrates offers no explanation but merely turns the question back upon him by asking, 'Do you not think they do?' (287d7–8). Anyone who has read any Plato of course knows that they do, but it does not seem that Hippias has done so. Supposing that he misunderstands Socrates' question amounts to having entered into the Socratic project. Hippias, however, when faced with the question 'What is the beautiful?' and denied a proper explanation of what Socrates means, is amenable enough to provide an answer in conformance with the way he has taken the question: 'a beautiful maiden', he says, 'is (something that is) beautiful' (ἔστι . . . παρθένος καλὴ καλόν, 287e3–4). Only in the course of Socrates' argument against this response does it begin to emerge with any clarity what he himself had meant by 'the beautiful'.

Hippias' acceptance of the principle that 'all beautiful things are beautiful by the beautiful (τῷ καλῷ)' (287c8–d1) might suggest that he does in fact understand that Socrates means 'the beautiful' to pick out a form or universal. But from Hippias' point of view this principle can easily be understood as meaning that all beautiful things are beautiful because of the beauty they possess—not by somehow sharing in the form of Beauty or something that is in all cases beautiful. It is irrelevant to Hippias' understanding that the use of an instrumental dative such as τῷ καλῷ to express a universal or form's causal role will seem familiar to a reader of Plato (from e.g. *Euthphr.* 6d11 or *Phd.* 100d7). To make such comparisons is, again, to ally oneself too readily with Socrates' perspective. Likewise, all Hippias need understand by the rather vague statement that the beautiful is 'something that is' (ὄν τι, 287d1–2) is that the beauty things possess that makes them beautiful is something (presumably, their beauty). Throughout this opening exchange, then, both Socrates and Hippias have their own private understanding of the key terms on which their discussion turns.

They are talking at cross purposes even though they appear to be in agreement. Socrates, moreover, does not examine Hippias *in propria persona* but places his questions and criticisms in the mouth of an absent and unidentified interlocutor. This device underscores the difficulties of communication between Socrates and someone like Hippias. Woodruff sees the questioner device as 'a wonderfully convenient buffer between the two antagonists'.[16] I take its significance to be rather different. The device emphasizes the fundamental incompatibility between Hippias' and Socrates' two perspectives.[17] The inversely corresponding device in *Republic* 5, whereby Glaucon answers on the sight-lover's behalf, signals a similar incompatibility.

The main argument against Hippias' first 'definition' (288b8–289c5) is designed to show that a beautiful maiden is only relatively beautiful. Although a beautiful maiden is admittedly beautiful, a beautiful mare is also beautiful, as is a beautiful lyre and even a beautiful pot. But, Hippias says, a beautiful pot does not deserve to be considered beautiful in comparison with a beautiful horse or maiden. Socrates' questioner then seizes upon his admission that a beautiful pot is only relatively beautiful to point out that, should one compare the class of maidens with the class of gods, even the most beautiful maidens will appear ugly.[18] The questioner concludes that Hippias has specified something no more beautiful than ugly, rather than 'the Beautiful itself' ($\alpha\dot{v}\tau\dot{o}$ $\tau\dot{o}$ $\kappa\alpha\lambda\acute{o}\nu$). Only at this point in the argument does it become apparent that Socrates understands the beautiful or $\tau\dot{o}$ $\kappa\alpha\lambda\acute{o}\nu$ to be that which is beautiful in all circumstances and in all comparisons.

He also presumes that it must somehow be responsible for the beauty of all beautiful things, and he insists upon this feature as he presses Hippias for a new answer. Hippias has agreed that the human race is not beautiful in comparison with the divine, but he does not seem particularly disturbed by this fact.[19] He proceeds to give a

---

[16] Woodruff 1982, 107.

[17] I suspect there is ultimately much more to the device of the questioner than is suggested here, such that a successful interpretation of the dialogue as a whole would have to explore the possibility that the Socrates who takes part in the conversation and the questioner (the absent Socrates) make crucially different assumptions about the definitional project.

[18] Cf. *R.* 5. 479a6–7: 'is there going to be any of the various beautiful things that will not appear ugly?'

[19] Cf. Woodruff 1982, 48: 'The girl . . . is foul compared to goddesses. But why should Hippias be bothered by that? If Socrates calls her foul by herself, he will be the one who looks the fool. And if she is foul *in one comparison*, why, there are a great many other comparisons in which she is fine. She is fine "on the whole"—that is the implication of 288e.'

similar answer to the questioner's reformulated question. The questioner now asks, giving us further clues to his own metaphysical stance, what is 'the beautiful itself (αὐτὸ τὸ καλόν), by which all other things are made beautiful and appear to be beautiful when that form (εἶδος) becomes present to (προσγένηται) them' (289d2–4). Hippias responds that one will never be refuted should one say that it is gold (289d6–e6). The way he has understood the question is, again, not so much a misunderstanding as a different understanding. Gold is the beautiful thing by which all other things are adorned and whose presence makes them beautiful. The questioner's argument against this answer proceeds in much the same way as his argument against the first. He gets Hippias to admit that ivory, stone, and even fig tree wood also make things beautiful in the appropriate circumstances, while if inappropriate they make things ugly. He thereby gains the admission that gold sometimes makes things beautiful and sometimes not (290a5–291c8). Once again, however, Hippias does not seem particularly disturbed that things should be this way.

Why is Hippias not troubled by the problems with which the questioner plagues Socrates? It is not because he is ignorant or confused. To pin such labels upon him is to have adopted the Platonist perspective. Instead, the way in which he interprets and recasts the questions put to him, the type of answers he gives, and his complacency when confronted with attempts at refutation all indicate a refusal to engage in the questioner's project. This is even true, although in a somewhat more subtle sense, of his third answer, that it is fine (καλόν) for everyone everywhere to have wealth, health, honour, and long life, and to bury his parents and to be buried by his own children in a fine manner (291d9–e2). Hippias prefaces this response by saying that Socrates is searching for something that 'will never appear foul to anyone anywhere' (291d1–3), thus showing that he understands Socrates' first requirement for a proper definition. But this implies no commitment on his part to the questioner's project, as is clear from his continuing to frame his answer as something which the questioner will never be able to refute (291d6–7, 291e8–292a1). Hippias only intends to offer an answer that the questioner, on his own assumptions, will be forced to accept.[20] Hippias himself, like the

---

[20] He has adopted this stance in his previous answers as well. For example, he does not simply say that τὸ καλόν is gold but that, should one give this answer to the questioner, '*he* will be at a loss (ἀπορήσει) and will not attempt to refute (ἐλέγχειν) you' (289e2–3; cf. 287a8–b3, e3, 288a7–b3, and X. *Mem.* 4. 4. 7). In the *Meno*, when Meno objects that Socrates' proposed definition of shape as what always accompanies colour begs the question of what colour is, Socrates says that, if he were one of the clever

sight-lover, sees no need to posit a single universal that will account for all the multiple instances of beautiful things. Underpinning his refusal to enter into the questioner's project is a simple acceptance that the objects of ordinary experience may be both F and not-F. This acceptance is divorced from any feeling that one should some-how strive to overcome the world's complexity and contradictions by searching for something that is absolutely F and never not-F.

Most notably, Hippias makes precisely the kind of move I suggested is available to the sight-lover when Socrates makes the problematic shift at *Republic* 5. 476e10–477a3 from 'something-that-is' (ὄν τι) to 'what-completely-is' (τὸ παντελῶς ὄν). We saw that when the sight-lover agrees that one must know something that is, he need mean no more than that one knows something that is in one respect but that may not be in another. There is no reason for him to accept that any-thing possesses the absolute mode of being that Socrates wants to designate as 'what-completely-is'. Hippias similarly agrees that the beautiful is 'something that is' (ὄν τι, 287d1–2), but when he goes on to specify what is (the) beautiful, he specifies something that is beau-tiful in certain contexts but not in others. Here is a clear indication that Hippias would not be prepared to accept the tendentious move in Socrates' first argument directed towards the sight-lover. He is a figure who perfectly fits Socrates' description of the sight-lover in the *Republic* as 'one who accepts that there are beautiful things but nei-ther accepts that there is Beauty itself (αὐτὸ κάλλος) nor is capable of following should someone attempt to lead him towards apprehension of it' (*R.* 5. 476c2–3). This inability to be led towards apprehension of Beauty itself, however, does not result from any particular confu-sion but from a simple refusal to accept that there is any such thing. Hippias and the sight-lover are in effect unprepared to accept the key move in the argument from the possibility of knowledge. They are confronted by a person who argues that something that is F in all

types given to eristic and competitive displays, then he would respond: 'this is my answer, and if it is not correct, then it is your job to take up the statement and re-fute it (ἐλέγχειν)' (75c4–d2). Hippias answers in precisely the manner of these clever eristics. There are differences, however, in the import of the eristic stance in each of Hippias' answers. In the first, not having yet begun to grasp the meaning of Soc-rates' question, Hippias says something he thinks incontrovertibly true, something that reflects the facts of ordinary usage, in order to avoid refutation. In the second, when the assumptions grounding Socrates' question have begun to emerge during the course of the argument, his persistence in giving the same type of response, which will be attacked with the same type of argument, amounts to a deliberate rejection of those assumptions. While in the third, Hippias adopts one of those assumptions in a completely non-committal fashion for the purpose of triumphing over his opponent.

contexts and comparisons is required if we are to attain a form of knowledge that, he claims, transcends that we ordinarily experience. Faced with such claims, Hippias and the sight-lover decline to accept that there is any such thing as the F itself or what-completely-is. Nor do they regret the consequent loss of the possibility of coming to know it.[21]

GORGIAS

Since Plato's use of APK has its roots in Parmenides, it is particularly interesting to find in Gorgias' 'On What-Is-Not' (Περὶ τοῦ μὴ ὄντος)[22] a pre-Platonic treatise wherein one of Hippias' fellow sophists opposes the assumptions of the argument as it figures in Parmenides. Gorgias should be included in the class of sight-lovers since he would also want to deny that there is anything possessed of the absolute mode of being specified by Plato, and by Parmenides before him, as belonging to the proper object of knowledge. That he gains entry into the class of sight-lovers via a direct critique of Parmenides himself means that Plato will be especially concerned with responding to his specific challenge. We shall have occasion to explore aspects of this response. First, however, we need to examine Gorgias' argument against Parmenides.

In his treatise, Gorgias argues successively on behalf of three theses: nothing is; even if something is, it is unknowable; and even if something is and is knowable, it cannot be revealed to others (*MXG* 979a12–13, cf. SE, *M.* 7. 65). We shall be concerned here with the first thesis. The clearest indication of Gorgias' purpose in defending the proposition that nothing is (οὐδὲν ἔστιν) is the description of the treatise's doxographical preface (*MXG* 979a13–18, without analogue in Sextus):

καὶ ὅτι μὲν οὐκ ἔστι, συνθεὶς τὰ ἑτέροις εἰρημένα, ὅσοι περὶ τῶν ὄντων λέγοντες τἀναντία, ὡς δοκοῦσιν, ἀποφαίνονται αὑτοῖς, οἱ μὲν ὅτι ἓν καὶ οὐ πολλά, οἱ δὲ αὖ ὅτι πολλὰ καὶ οὐχ ἕν, καὶ οἱ μὲν ὅτι ἀγένητα, οἱ δ' ὡς γενόμενα ἐπιδεικνύντες, ταῦτα συλλογίζεται κατ' ἀμφοτέρων

---

[21] See Kerferd 1986 for a study of how Plato sees the inability to turn the mind toward apprehension of reality as a defining characteristic of the sophists generally. See also Goffi 1989 on Hippias' own inability.

[22] Our two sources for the treatise are *MXG* 979a10–980b21 and SE, *M.* 7. 65–87. Although DK does not even print the former, I take it to be the more important source (as do e.g. Calogero 1932, Gigon 1936, Verdenius 1942, Bröcker 1958, Migliori 1973, Newiger 1973, Wesoly 1983–4, Mansfeld 1985). Cf. Newiger 1973, 2–4, for a review of earlier opinions on the relative worth of the two reports. See also Appendix I.

(and to show that it is not, he collects what has been said by others who spoke concerning the things-that-are and made, so it seems, contradictory statements among themselves—some demonstrating that what-is is one and not many, others that it is many and not one, and some that the things-that-are are ungenerated, others that they are generated—and he draws conclusions against both sides).[23]

Jaap Mansfeld has argued decisively that 'the things-that-are' or τὰ ὄντα in Gorgias' classification 'are not in the first place the phenomenal things, but the speculative theoretical constructs of the Presocratic philosophers'.[24] In other words, Gorgias purports to demolish all previous efforts to identify some special entity or entities as ontologically and epistemologically prior to the objects of ordinary experience. In thus attacking the philosophers' 'reality', he is not denying that anything is in any way whatsoever. The beings or ὄντα of the doxographical classification are not all entities but all purportedly fundamental entities. Do away with this supposedly fundamental order of being, and (only) the being of the world of ordinary experience remains. In suggesting that Plato's argument from the possibility of knowledge depends upon certain general and deep assumptions that the sight-lover will not be prepared to accept, I introduced the possible objection that the assumption of a reality beyond appearances enjoying a mode of being more absolute and unchanging than that of the phenomenal world was universal in previous Greek thought. But now it appears that Gorgias, even more clearly than Hippias,

---

[23] Cf. *MXG* 980b19–20 and the ironic description at Gorg. *Hel.* 13 of 'those who talk of lofty matters' (μετεωρολόγοι) as substituting one *doxa* for another as they make 'things unbelievable and non-apparent' (τὰ ἄπιστα καὶ ἄδηλα) appear before the eyes of their audience's opinion. Hippias' compendium of the views of earlier thinkers (cf. Clem. Al. *Strom.* 6. 15 = 86B6 DK) has, since Snell's pioneering 1944 study, been lauded as the doxographic tradition's ur-text. However, this Gorgianic classification was arguably even more influential. Classifications sufficiently similar to be presumed to derive from Gorgias are to be found at X. *Mem.* 1. 1. 13–14, Isoc. *Orat.* 15. 268, and Pl. *Sph.* 242c–d (all of which are noted by Mansfeld 1985, 245–7; cf. Mansfeld 1986, 47 n. 9, for references to others who have noted these connections). The most important later analogue of the Gorgianic classification is that adopted by Aristotle in *Physics* 1 to structure his examination of his predecessors' views on ἄρχαι or principles (cf. esp. 1. 2. 184[b]15–25).

[24] Mansfeld 1985, 248–9, *contra* Kerferd 1955, who follows the suggestion of Calogero 1932, 197, in supposing that Gorgias is concerned with the phenomenal being of ordinary objects. Cf. Guthrie 1971, 194, who draws a conclusion similar to Mansfeld's, although not from the *MXG*'s account of the first division's doxographical preface but (less defensibly) from the alternative title 'On Nature' (Περὶ φύσεως). The essentials of this view are already to be found in Grote 1888, vii. 51–2; cf. Faggi 1926, 67–70, and Lattanzi 1932, 289–91.

would object to any attempt to isolate something that fully or completely is as what is fully knowable.

In taking exception to this assumption among his predecessors, Gorgias, as we shall see, focused upon Parmenides as something of a special target. (Thus when Plato came to revive Parmenides' basic argument he was in effect reasserting the value of that argument in the face of previous sophistic attack.) The Eleatic character of the treatise's argumentation has been almost universally recognized.[25] The *MXG* author himself points out that Gorgias employed arguments in the style of Melissus and Zeno (979a21–3). Even if, as was once maintained, this stylistic borrowing were meant as a parodic *reductio* of Eleaticism,[26] the substance of Parmenides' views might have remained untouched by such parody. Those who have seen a substantial polemic against Parmenides' Being have too often supposed it to be Gorgias' particular target throughout the treatise.[27] However, that the treatise in its entirety was not directed specifically against Parmenides should be obvious from the all-encompassing scope of the doxographical preface. Since this doxography establishes the programme for much of the treatise's first division,[28] only a few of the

---

[25] Although, not surprisingly, variously interpreted. Cf. Untersteiner 1957, 163 n. 2, Sicking 1964, 255–7, and Newiger 1973, 4–7, for selective surveys of earlier views on the treatise's overall purpose and its relation to the Eleatics.

[26] Thus e.g. Maier 1913, 223–6.

[27] Thus Nestle 1922, Calogero 1932, and Bröcker 1958 take the entire treatise to be directed primarily against Parmenides. Calogero, who recognizes that *MXG* 979a14–18 indicates 'a prima vista che si trattasse di un'antitesi non intrinseca all'-eleatismo' and yet nevertheless maintains that 'quelle dimostrazioni antitetiche, onde la realtà appare una e molteplice, eterna e transeunte, sian tutte dimostrazioni intrinseche all'eleatismo' (191–2), is criticized by Levi 1941; Bröcker, who adopts the most exclusively anti-Parmenidean interpretation, by Sicking 1964. Uniquely among discussions of Gorgias' relation to Parmenides, Cassin 1980 raises the intriguing possibility that 'On What-Is-Not' may be read, not as an attack upon Parmenides, but as 'essentiellement une répétition catastrophique' of his argument which proceeds via a radical extension of his conception of being. Cassin is primarily concerned, however, with the perspective of the *MXG*'s anonymous author; she attempts to show how the achronological order in which the treatise takes up the figures it discusses represents the author's own construction of a logical progression from Parmenides to Gorgias via Melissus and Xenophanes: 'Trouver les conditions de possibilité du discours scandaleux de Gorgias dans le model singulier dont Mélissus, puis Xénophane, répètent et transforment Parménide, voilà qui constituerait la perspective propre du traité, encore inaperçue' (30–1). Since Cassin does not herself propose that Gorgias' intention was as the *MXG* author takes it to be, much less that Plato understood Gorgias' treatise as the *MXG* author does, this is not the place to take up the details of her interpretation.

[28] The doxography's ungenerated/generated dichotomy is taken up in the arguments at 979b20–34; the one/many dichotomy, in those at 979b35–8 (at which point the text

arguments here could even conceivably have been aimed at him, namely those against the possibility that what-is is ungenerated and the possibility that it is one.[29] But even these arguments seem to target Melissus more particularly than they do Parmenides. 'If what-is is ungenerated', the *MXG* says, 'he assumes by Melissus' axioms that it is unlimited, but what is unlimited could not be anywhere . . .' (979b21 ff.). Melissus does in fact argue from the premiss that what-is is ungenerated to its being (both temporally and spatially) unlimited (30B2–B4 DK). Again, Gorgias is said to presume that if what-is is one, it must be incorporeal (ἀσώματον, 979b36). Although one might believe that Parmenides conceived of Being as incorporeal, this position is explicitly attested for Melissus (B9).[30] Therefore none of the arguments carrying out the programme established in the doxographical preface is directed specifically against Parmenides.

There is, however, an argument in the first section of the treatise where Parmenidean Being is Gorgias' target. This is the complex argument at 979a24–33 the *MXG* author calls Gorgias' 'personal demonstration' (ἴδιος ἀπόδειξις),[31] which the author says preceded the other arguments in the first division. The argument's demonstrandum is: οὐκ ἔστιν οὔτε εἶναι οὔτε μὴ εἶναι (979a24), which we may provisionally render literally as, '[it] is not, neither to be nor not to be'. The meaning of this thesis is obscure on several counts. We may move towards understanding it by looking again to the *MXG*'s report that Gorgias prefaced his demonstration of the thesis '[it] is not' or οὐκ ἔστι with a systematic collection of earlier philosophers' views

becomes corrupt). These are followed by an argument against motion at 980a1–8, suggesting that a corresponding argument against rest has been lost in the lacuna and that Gorgias' doxography may originally have included an unchanging/changing dichotomy such as we find in Aristotle.

[29] The most attractive, although ultimately unsuccessful, attempt to maintain that Gorgias' arguments throughout the first division are directed primarily against the Parmenidean conception of being (in spite of the difficulty that Gorgias also argues that what-is has not come to be, is not many, and is unmoving) remains the suggestion by Nestle 1922, 555–6, that in doing so Gorgias is employing Parmenidean arguments (e.g. SE, *M.* 7. 71 ff. ≈ Parm. B8. 7, B8. 12 ff.; *MXG* 979a38 ff. ≈ Parm. B8. 24 ff.) to reach an anti-Parmenidean conclusion.

[30] On Gorgias *contra* Melissus, cf. Calogero 1932, 214 ff.; Kerferd 1955, 20; Bröcker 1958, 433–4. Also, van Loenen 1959, 181 ff., although he goes too far in concluding that Gorgias nowhere attacks a thesis peculiar to Parmenides but argues instead throughout the first division (and even in the second and third) specifically against Melissus.

[31] Wesoly 1983–4, 23, plausibly suggests that the argument is so designated because it constitutes an original refutation of Parmenides' ontological argument, whereas the other arguments of the first division are adapted from the arguments of Parmenides' successors.

regarding τὰ ὄντα or the entities they had posited as somehow fundamental. This procedure indicates that the bracketed subject of the
thesis οὐκ ἔστι is τὰ ὄντα, so that Gorgias' first thesis claims that there
are no fundamental entities of the type posited by his predecessors.
The alternative version of the thesis given by the *MXG* author—'he
says that nothing is' (οὐκ εἶναί φησιν οὐδέν, 979a12)—has much the
same sense. It does not mean that nothing is or exists *simpliciter*
but that nothing is in the manner of the philosophers' fundamental
entities. The personal demonstration's second and third constitutive
arguments reach conclusions of this alternative form: 'nothing would
be' (οὐδὲν ἂν εἴη, 979a30), and 'not anything would be' (οὐκ ἂν εἴη
οὐδέν, 979a31–2). The conclusion of the first argument more directly
supports the suggestion that the philosophers' basic entities are the
implicit subjects of the thesis οὐκ ἔστι. For here a plural subject is supplied—τὰ πράγματα ('the things')—which I take to be the *MXG*
author's way of referring to the philosophers' ὄντα he has previously
identified as the objects of Gorgias' concern.[32]

Now, there is a certain overcompensation in the way in which
the personal demonstration's thesis is formulated, indicating that in
this argument Gorgias is concerned primarily with the fundamental
entity posited by Parmenides. If Gorgias' point here were simply that
there are no such things as the philosophers' beings, then 'it is not
there for being' (οὐκ ἔστιν εἶναι ≈ οὐκ ἔστι) would have been a sufficient demonstrandum. However, the demonstrandum in fact takes
the disjunctive form: 'it is not there *either* for being *or for not being*'
(οὐκ ἔστιν οὔτε εἶναι οὔτε μὴ εἶναι). The apparent overcompensation
of 'it is not there for not being' is best explained on the assumption
that Gorgias developed his personal demonstration as a direct and
negative counterpart to Parmenides' disjunction between being and
not-being in B2.[33] Gorgias' formulation of the thesis οὐκ ἔστι or '[it]
is not' is elliptical in precisely the same manner as ἔστιν or '[it] is'
in Parmenides B2. 3. There thus seems to be a certain tension in the
personal demonstration between the generality of its conclusions and
the specifically anti-Parmenidean stance of its argumentation. The

---

[32] *Pace* Calogero 1932, 197, who takes τὰ πράγματα as an indication that Gorgias
is concerned with the 'molteplicità empirica del reale', and Kerferd 1955, who follows Calogero's cue in taking τὰ πράγματα as indicating a concern with all phenomena.
One should not, however, place too much weight on the term πράγματα itself, for it
occurs only once in the *MXG* report and nowhere in the parallel argument in Sextus.

[33] Kerferd 1955, 7, cites Parm. B2. 3 and B6. 2–3 as 'obvious parallels' and thinks
it 'likely that Gorgias had these phrases of Parmenides in mind'. Cf. Nestle 1922,
555; Calogero 1932, 195 ff.

demonstration will, of course, be as effective against Parmenides' Being as against other would-be fundamental entities. Moreover, of all those who had chosen to posit a fundamental order of being as the reality underlying the world of ordinary experience, Parmenides was the philosopher who had been most explicit in specifying the general ontological and epistemological conditions of such a choice. Gorgias would properly have felt that attacking Parmenides' argument would allow him to generalize his conclusion beyond the non-existence of Parmenidean Being to the non-existence of all other philosophers' purportedly fundamental entities.

We may now examine in detail the argumentation of the personal demonstration to see whether it is as effective a weapon against Parmenides as Gorgias would like it to be. The demonstration's triadic structure is clearly marked by the sequence of particles μέν . . . δ᾿. . . δέ ('in the first place . . . but . . . but'). The first two arguments (979a25–8, 979a28–30) have a precise and identical arrangement. An initial assumption is followed by the statement of its consequent, the argument for that consequent, and a final statement of the conclusion. There is then a transition (979a30–1) to the third argument (979a31–3), which varies from this structure only slightly. Thus while the demonstration may seem quite complex, it does in fact have a clear and relatively simple structure. This will be apparent if we break it down into its constituent parts:

(I) Assumption: εἰ **μὲν** γὰρ τὸ μὴ εἶναι ἔστι μὴ εἶναι,
    (For, in the first place, if not-being is not being,)
    Consequent: οὐδὲν ἂν ἧττον τὸ μὴ ὂν τοῦ ὄντος εἴη.
    (what-is-not would *be* no less than what-is.)
    Argument: τό τε **γὰρ** μὴ ὂν ἔστι μὴ ὄν,[34] καὶ τὸ ὂν ὄν,
    (For what-is-not *is* what-is-not, and what-is *is* what-is,)
    Conclusion: **ὥστε** οὐδὲν μᾶλλον εἶναι ἢ οὐκ εἶναι τὰ πράγματα.
    (so that things no more are than are not.)

(II) Assumption: εἰ **δ᾿** ὅμως τὸ μὴ εἶναι ἔστι,
    (But if nevertheless not-being is,)
    Consequent: τὸ εἶναι, φησί, οὐκ ἔστι, τὸ ἀντικείμενον.
    (he says being, its opposite, is not.)
    Argument: εἰ **γὰρ** τὸ μὴ εἶναι ἔστι, τὸ εἶναι μὴ εἶναι προσήκει.
    (For if not-being is, it is fitting that being is not.)

---

[34] Aristotle may have this claim in mind when he refers to the dialectical paralogism that 'what-is-not is, for what-is-not *is* what-is-not' (ἔστι τὸ μὴ ὂν [ὄν], ἔστι γὰρ τὸ μὴ ὂν μὴ ὄν, *Rh.* 2. 24. 1402ᵃ5–6). Cf. Wesoly 1983–4, 28.

Conclusion: ὥστε οὐκ ἂν οὕτως, φησίν, οὐδὲν ἂν εἴη,
(So that in this fashion nothing, he says, would be,)

Transition: εἰ μὴ ταὐτόν ἐστιν εἶναί τε καὶ μὴ εἶναι.[35]
(unless being and not being are the same.)

(III) Assumption: εἰ δὲ ταὐτό,
       (But if they are the same,)
       Consequent: καὶ οὕτως οὐκ ἂν εἴη οὐδέν·
       (in this way also nothing would be;)
       Argument: τό τε γὰρ μὴ ὂν οὐκ ἔστι, καὶ τὸ ὄν, ἐπείπερ γε
       ταὐτὸ τῷ μὴ ὄντι.
       (for what-is-not is not and what-is also, since it is the same
       as what-is-not.)

The assumption in argument (I) appears to be taken directly from
Parmenides B2. 5: ὡς οὐκ ἔστιν τε καὶ ὡς χρεών ἐστι μὴ εἶναι. We
previously translated the line as follows: 'that it is not and it is necessary that it not be'. Gorgias, however, seems to understand the line
somewhat differently. In taking 'not-being' (τὸ μὴ εἶναι) as the subject of 'is not being' (ἔστι μὴ εἶναι) in the assumption of this argument,
he apparently presumes that the subject of the identical predicate
ἐστι μὴ εἶναι in Parmenides B2. 5b is provided by οὐκ ἔστιν in B2. 5a,
giving the sense: 'it is not and it is necessary that *what-is-not* is not
being'. This first argument then simply points out that 'not-being *is*
not being' entails that what-is-not *is*. From the conclusion that things
no more are than are not, one must be meant to infer that they are
not, which is tantamount to the conclusion in the two subsequent
arguments that nothing is. Argument (II) takes as its assumption a
simplified version of the assumption in (I) and proceeds straightforwardly to its conclusion: if not-being is (not-being) and being is
not, then nothing is. Although argument (III) begins with the rather
different assumption that being and not being are the same, it is in
fact much closer to the first two arguments than it might appear.
For the argument here also proceeds from a variation of the basic
Parmenidean premiss in (I)—here 'what-is-not is not' (τὸ μὴ ὂν οὐκ

---

[35] This premiss has been thought to echo Parm. B6. 8–9 by e.g. Calogero
1932, 203, developing the suggestion by Reinhardt 1916, 36–9, that Gorgias takes
up each of Parmenides' three ways. I am not convinced, however, that there is
any genuine connection here. In any case, Reinhardt's suggestion tallies better with
Sextus' recasting of Gorgias' argument than with the more reliable *MXG* version
(cf. Appendix I).

ἔστι)—via the minor premiss provided by the transition. Whereas (II) derived its consequent for (a truncated version of) the Parmenidean assumption via the minor premiss that being and not being are opposites, (III) derives its consequent via the minor premiss that they are the same.[36]

It is a curious feature of the personal demonstration that if one inspects the strategy of its argumentation closely enough, one finds that it does not actually succeed as the damaging response to Parmenides' ontological argument that Gorgias apparently intended it to be. Parmenides' disjunction in B2 is, in effect, 'it is for being or it is not for being' (ἔστιν εἶναι or ἔστιν μὴ εἶναι). Gorgias' demonstration seeks to establish the negation of this disjunction, that it is neither for being nor for not being, by proceeding in each of its three constitutive arguments from a version of Parmenides' second disjunct. He crucially does *not* attempt to draw any consequences from Parmenides' first disjunct in B2. 3. Instead, his strategy is to perform a *reductio* on the second disjunct that will entail the negation of 'it is for being' (ἔστιν εἶναι). Gorgias mistakenly supposes this procedure sufficient to establish the contradiction of the original Parmenidean disjunction. To see clearly the problem with the structure of Gorgias' argument, let 'Ex' represent 'it is for being' (ἔστιν εἶναι), such that E$x \lor \neg$Ex represents Parmenides' basic disjunction. By assuming $\neg$Ex, the second disjunct, Gorgias supposes he can demonstrate the negation of Parmenides' disjunction, namely, $\neg$(E$x \lor \neg$Ex). This is logically equivalent to E$x \land \neg$Ex. Thus what Gorgias has in fact demonstrated (if we are charitable to him in the details) is that *if* one assumes $\neg$Ex, one reaches the contradictory conclusion E$x \land \neg$Ex. The proper conclusion to draw from this is $\neg(\neg$E$x)$ or simply Ex, Parmenides' original thesis in B2. 3. Thus, despite his intentions to the contrary, Gorgias' personal demonstration ends up confirming Parmenides' injunction against the second path. When Gorgias sets out on this path despite this warning, he in effect shows that it leads inevitably to contradiction, thus confirming the value of Parmenides' original injunction to stay on the first path.

These subtleties aside, we can now see more clearly what Plato would probably have made of Gorgias' attack on Parmenides. He would have seen Parmenides as the first to articulate clearly the idea that there must be something possessed of an absolute mode of

---

[36] For what this account of the personal demonstration's structure in the *MXG* indicates about the relative worth of our two sources for the first division of Gorgias' treatise, see Appendix I.

being to serve as the proper object of knowledge. He would further have seen Gorgias as rejecting the existence of any such entity and consequently the possibility of any knowledge of it. In *Republic* 5, Plato adapts Parmenides' argument to his own conception of absolute being and to his own assertion of the possibility of knowledge. Yet he simultaneously gives a voice, in the figure of the sight-lover, to those who would contest the Parmenidean assumptions grounding this conception, among whom he would certainly number Hippias, possibly Antisthenes, and in all probability Gorgias. This dialectic will be taken to another level in the *Parmenides*, where the sight-lover will have developed into a figure who confronts the middle period theory with more explicitly Gorgianic scepticism. Plato will there acknowledge that Gorgias' original polemic against Parmenides has an apparent purchase against his own theory that the *Republic*'s arguments with the sight-lover were not sufficient to dispel. As we shall see, he will then push the ongoing dialectic to a further stage by giving Parmenides the opportunity to 'reply' to Gorgias.

For the moment, however, I want to concentrate a little longer on Gorgias' credentials for membership in the class of sight-lovers. We have seen that he directly challenges the first key assumption of *Republic* 5's arguments with the sight-lovers, that there is anything possessing the absolute mode of being that Plato thinks necessary for a proper object of knowledge. He will also be unprepared to accept the second key assumption, that knowledge and *doxa* can be distinguished in a purely intentional manner. In the *Encomium of Helen*, he presents the rudiments of a *doxa*-centred epistemology intended to ground his practice of rhetorical persuasion:

Anyone who has persuaded and persuades anyone about anything fashions a false account. For if everyone had regarding all matters memory of what has transpired and understanding of present events and foresight regarding what is to come, then the account one employs would not be the same as in the present circumstances, when it is neither easy to recall what has transpired nor to examine what is now nor to divine what is to come. Thus in the majority of matters the majority of people adopt *doxa* as their soul's adviser. But *doxa*, since it is insecure and unsteady, furnishes insecure and unsteady success to those relying upon it (*Hel.* 11).

Gorgias thinks the orator must of necessity restrict his arguments to the plane of *doxa* (cf. *Hel.* 9). His declaration of *doxa*'s universal sway may be in the background when Plato refers to the sight-lovers as 'lovers of *doxa*' (*R.* 5. 480a6) and when he emphasizes how their point of view is restricted to the level of *doxa*. In any case, Plato in the *Phaedrus* numbers Gorgias among those 'who saw things that are merely probable (τὰ εἰκότα) as more respectable than things true' (*Phdr*. 267a6−7). Despite this preference, in the *Helen* Gorgias does envisage the conditions necessary for knowledge. Nothing, however, indicates that knowledge as he conceives it here would be of some transcendent or absolute being. Rather, he seems to view knowledge in strictly empirical terms, as rooted in keen observation of past and present events and of the available indications of what is to come. Knowledge as Gorgias conceives it would, were it ever achieved, have as its objects the same things or states of affairs that are the objects of *doxa*.

This point is crucial, for it allows us to state more precisely why Gorgias and the sight-lovers would not be prepared to accept Plato's manner of distinguishing knowledge and *doxa* in *Republic* 5. The initial premisses of Plato's second argument with the sight-lovers were that (i) a capacity must be specified by reference to its particular class of objects, that (ii) both knowledge and *doxa* are capacities, and that (iii) knowledge and *doxa* are different. Gorgias presumably would not object to the stipulation in (i), nor would he reject (iii). He would, however, object to the attempt to include knowledge and *doxa* in the category of capacities. Although he would not want to deny that both have an intentional aspect, he would not accept their being defined by reference to the objects at which they are directed. Since he supposes that knowledge and *doxa* can have the same objects (with the qualification that humans are very rarely able to pass beyond the level of *doxa*), specifying their character as capacities will be insufficient to distinguish the two. Gorgias' manner of differentiating the two cognitive states instead takes the subject's role to be the essential factor. If a person could satisfy certain conditions, if he could exercise powers of observation and memory far beyond those typical of human beings, then one might be able to speak of him as knowing rather than merely believing. Gorgias' view of the difference between knowledge and *doxa* entails no ontological distinction among their objects. He *does* accept a contrast between reality and appearance. He says in the *Encomium of Helen* that things we see do not have the reality or nature (φύσιν) we wish them to have but instead that which they happen to have on their own (*Hel*. 15). He explains this using the example of the sight of armed soldiers inducing fear and flight. In this situation, he says, one erroneously treats future danger as present. Here Gorgias' distinction between appearance, or what is judged to be the case, and reality, or what is actually the case, in no way depends upon any concomitant ontological distinction. It is precisely because

Plato's manner of distinguishing knowledge and *doxa* in *Republic* 5 is designed to entail a distinction vis-à-vis the ontological status of their respective objects that it will be unacceptable to Gorgias or the sight-lover.

One odd feature of Plato's distinction between knowledge and *doxa* in *Republic* 5 is that previously he would have had the same kind of objections. In the *Meno* he accepts that knowledge and *doxa* can have the same objects (e.g. the road to Larissa) and thus focuses upon subjective rather than intentional criteria to distinguish them. He focuses upon their relative stability and the different means by which each is acquired. Even more peculiar is that the capacity argument's justification of the premiss that knowledge and *doxa* are different belongs, properly speaking, to the context of Plato's earlier conception. Glaucon accepts the premiss on the grounds that knowledge is unerring or infallible (ἀναμάρτητον), while *doxa* is not (*R.* 5. 477e6–7). This type of distinction is consistent with the *Meno* epistemology —one may have either a true or false belief about something, but knowledge about this thing must be true given that it is an improvement on true belief. But it seems foreign to the *Republic* 5 theory. In this context, the idea that knowledge is unerring entails that an 'erroneous' apprehension of a potential object of knowledge is not an apprehension at all and thus not any kind of knowledge. Socrates implies as much when he says that 'knowledge is by its nature directed towards what-is, to apprehend what-is as it is' (477b10–11). Given that *doxa* is now directed towards its own class of objects (what-is-and-is-not), the same should hold for it as well. There should at least be a parallel analysis of the fallibility of *doxa* and knowledge such that if a doxastic apprehension that fails in some respect can still be described as a doxastic apprehension in so far as it is directed towards an object of *doxa*, it will also be possible to have failed epistemic apprehensions. What makes *doxa* erroneous in the framework of the *Republic* 5 epistemology is not that it fails to hit upon its own proper object (which it does) but that it fails to direct itself towards the proper object of knowledge. This and other new features of the *Republic* 5 theory—including the very idea that knowledge and *doxa* are now said to have totally distinct sets of objects—have been thought so problematic that it has even been denied that the conception of *doxa* propounded here is genuinely Platonic.[37] Although this resolution is obviously too extreme, there are genuine problems in the *Republic* 5 epistemology that prompt it. We have focused upon these problems

---

[37] Thus e.g. Ebert 1974; cf. esp. 112–14 and 117 ff.

in the form of the controversial assumptions of Plato's arguments, and we have seen that because of these assumptions the arguments do not have the leverage against the sight-lovers we are initially led to expect. One of these assumptions—that there is anything possessed of the absolute mode of being Socrates designates as 'what-completely-is' or τὸ παντελῶς ὄν—is directly rooted in Plato's appropriation of Parmenides. I now want to show that the historical origins of Plato's equally problematic conception of *doxa*, of its relation to knowledge, and of the idea that each is to be defined by reference to its own specific object, are likewise to be found in this appropriation.

SIGHT-LOVERS AND MORTALS

A complex web of appropriations and associations informs the *Republic* 5 arguments. Plato adopts the essentials of a Parmenidean argument which he perceives to be substantially in accordance with his own epistemological and ontological concerns, while simultan-eously engaging with a class of contemporary or near-contemporary thinkers who not only oppose the fundamentals of his perspective but who, in at least one case, do so via a critique of Parmenides. There is yet a further level in this increasingly complex dialectic between past and present perspectives, a level at which Plato allows Parmenides to respond to the manoeuvres of his critics. He does so by describ-ing and attributing views to the sight-lovers so as to link them with the 'mortals' (βροτοί) Parmenides had criticized for their misguided beliefs.

The representation of the sight-lovers has Parmenidean over-tones from the outset. The very description of them as 'lovers of sights and sounds' may have its genesis in Parmenides' description of mortals as exercising 'aimless sight and echoing hearing' (B7. 4). We have already seen that Socrates' descriptions of the sight-lovers have immediate analogues in the *Hippias Major*'s portrayal of Hippias. These descriptions can in turn be seen to draw upon Parmenides' gen-eral diagnosis of the source of mortals' error and his specification of their resulting beliefs. Socrates' descriptions of the sight-lover as living in a dreamlike state of mind (*R.* 5. 476c2–7) and being little short of blind (6.484c6–7) have their analogues in Parmenides' descrip-tion of mortals as being carried along 'deaf, blind, and dazed' (B6. 7). Socrates says that the lovers of sights and sounds take pleasure in beau-tiful sounds, colours, shapes, and everything produced from them, even though their understanding (διάνοια) is incapable of seeing the

nature of the Beautiful itself (476b4–8, cf. c2–4). Although they possess the general cognitive faculty by which they might apprehend
absolute Beauty, they have directed their attention to another realm,
with the result that their understanding is realized only as *doxa*
rather than resolving itself into both a noetic and doxastic aspect (cf.
476d5–9). Parmenides' goddess ascribes a similar error to mortals: they
have gone astray in fixing their attention upon the world of ordinary experience when they in fact possess the cognitive capacity for a
higher form of apprehension.

Plato will thus have understood the goddess in B7 as directing
Parmenides to restrain his understanding from the objects of ordinary
mortal cognition:

> οὐ γὰρ μήποτε τοῦτο δαμῇ· εἶναι μὴ ἐόντα.
> ἀλλὰ σὺ τῆσδ' ἀφ' ὁδοῦ διζήσιος εἶργε νόημα[38]
> μηδέ σ' ἔθος πολύπειρον ὁδὸν κατὰ τήνδε βιάσθω,
> νωμᾶν ἄσκοπον ὄμμα καὶ ἠχήεσσαν ἀκουήν
> καὶ γλῶσσαν. κρῖναι δὲ λόγῳ πολύδηριν ἔλεγχον
> ἐξ ἐμέθεν ῥηθέντα

(for never let this be imposed—things that are not are. But hold your understanding back from this path of inquiry and do not let habit force you down
this familiar path, to employ aimless sight and echoing hearing and tongue.
But judge by reason the controversial argument spoken on my part).

Although it would be possible to interpret these verses in a fashion
that accords with the Platonic three-path view, by taking B7. 1–2 as
referring to the second path introduced in B2 and B7. 3–5a as referring to the third path introduced in B6, it is preferable to take the whole
of B7 as restraining Parmenides from the path of mortal understanding. Since B2. 5 by no means specified the second path as involving

---

[38] Plato twice quotes Parm. B7. 1–2, at *Sph.* 237a8–9 and again at 258d2–3. The
first quotation gives the participle διζήμενος for the noun διζήσιος attested elsewhere,
including in Plato's own second quotation. The participle is likely to be the product
of Plato's effort to integrate the lines into the sentence in which he quotes them. We
can be satisfied that he read διζήσιος. A slightly more serious problem is posed by
the reading τοῦτ' οὐδαμῇ (or perhaps τοῦτ' οὐ δαμῇ) that occurs in both quotations
in all the principal manuscript families instead of τοῦτο δαμῇ as attested *ap.* Arist.
Metaph. N. 2. 1089ᵃ4 and Simp. *in Ph.* 135, 24 and 143, 31. Here as well, however,
we should not suppose that Plato's reading differed from the more widely attested
version. He emphasizes that the lines are in metre (μετὰ μέτρων) when he introduces
the first quotation, yet the variant τοῦτ' οὐδαμῇ is unmetrical (and meaningless in context). Coxon 1986, 190–1, plausibly suggests that the words τοῦτο δαμῇ had probably already been corrupted to τοῦτ' οὐδαμῇ in the archetype of our manuscripts of
Plato. Cf. Tarán 1965, 74; Duke, Hicken, *et al.* 1995, 417, app. crit. ad *Sph.* 237a8,
and 455, app. crit. ad *Sph.* 258d2.

any supposition that things that are not are, the possibility the goddess restrains Parmenides from here can only with great difficulty be
construed as a reference to the second path. Furthermore, B7. 4–5a
seem on their own insufficient to specify another path. If, however,
one assumes that εἶναι μὴ ἐόντα ('things that are not are') at B7. 1b
is intended somehow to specify the mode of being of the objects of
a third path, then B7. 4–5a can straightforwardly be understood as
describing the conditions under which mortals direct their cognitive
attention to objects that are in this way. If B7. 1–5a are taken as referring throughout to the path along which mortals have attempted to
achieve understanding, then the error of mortals, like that of the sight-
lovers, will consist in having fixed their cognitive powers upon the
world of ordinary experience. Habit ingrained by long experience (ἔθος
πολύπειρον, B7. 3) leads one, willing or not, to rely upon the senses
instead of reason and so to turn one's understanding (νόημα ≈ διάνοια
in Plato) towards objects it cannot properly apprehend. The result is
a 'wandering understanding' (πλαγκτὸν νόον, B6. 6)—which is to say,
no knowledge or νόος at all, for the goddess describes mortals in the
same fragment as 'knowing nothing' (εἰδότες οὐδέν, B6. 4).

Because their attention is fixed on nothing stable, mortals are said
to have a 'wandering understanding' (B6. 6) and are even themselves
said to 'wander' (B6. 5, B8. 54). Plato found this image particularly
useful as a way of characterizing both the sight-lovers and the objects
of their attention. Socrates' assertion that the bulk of the masses'
opinions 'roll back and forth (κυλινδεῖται) between what-is-not and
what-genuinely-is' (479d3–5) echoes Parmenides' portrayal of the path
along which mortals wander as 'backward-turning' (παλίντροπος, B6.
9). Plato then employs the wandering image in describing what is
apprehended by *doxa* as a 'wanderer' between absolute being and
not-being (479d7–9).[39] Then, in the transitional summary of the results of the book 5 arguments beginning the next book, Socrates
contrasts the philosophers with the non-philosophers, whom he says
are 'wandering (πλανώμενοι) among a variety of things subsisting in
all manner of ways' (484b3–7). He goes on to describe 'the being that
always is' as 'not wandering (μὴ πλανωμένης) between coming-to-be
and passing-away' (485b1–3). This image of wandering is not as common in Plato as one might suppose. In a use that already reflects the
continuity of concern with Parmenides, *Phaedo* 79c–d (cf. 81a6) contrasts the soul's wandering and disturbed state when it apprehends
things via sight and hearing with the soul's apprehension via its own

[39] Cf. Crystal 1996, 357-8 and 360.

power of 'what is pure, always being, immortal, and permanent'. More pertinently, Parmenides himself, in the dialogue bearing his name, praises the young Socrates for not allowing Zeno to keep the discussion at the level of visible things so as to examine their wandering state (πλάνην) and for thus shifting the discussion to the level of intelligible reality (*Prm.* 135e1–4).[40]

The image of wandering recurs in Parmenides' poem at B8. 51b–4, the point of transition from the way of truth to the exposition of mortal opinions. By now, it should not be difficult to see how Plato is likely to have understood most elements (though not all, the naming motif in particular) in these critical lines, where the goddess specifies the nature of mortal error:

δόξας δ' ἀπὸ τοῦδε βροτείας
μάνθανε, κόσμον ἐμῶν ἐπέων ἀπατηλὸν ἀκούων.
μορφὰς γὰρ κατέθεντο δύο γνώμας[41] ὀνομάζειν,
τῶν μίαν οὐ χρεών ἐστιν, ἐν ᾧ πεπλανημένοι εἰσίν

(but from this point mortal opinions learn, listening to the deceptive ordering of my verses. For they have fixed their minds on naming two forms, neither of which[42] is necessarily, wherein they have wandered astray).

Mortals have improperly determined to name two forms (light and night), neither of which has a necessary mode of being. The difficult phrase here is χρεών ἐστιν. The neuter substantive χρεών (or χρεόν) with the copulative ἐστι either expressed or understood functions like the quasi-impersonal χρή and is typically followed by an infinitive. Since here no infinitive is expressed, the majority of modern exegetes presume that ὀνομάζειν in the previous line is to be understood again. However, in Parmenides' three other uses of the phrase, two of which are directly relevant to the present context, the accompanying infinitive is a form of the verb 'to be'. B2. 5: ἡ δ' ὡς οὐκ ἔστιν τε καὶ ὡς χρεών ἐστι μὴ εἶναι ('the other, that it is not and it is necessary that it not be'); B8. 11: οὕτως ἢ πάμπαν πελέναι χρεών ἐστιν ἢ οὐχί ('in this way it is necessary that it either is altogether or not

---

[40] Cf. also *Alc.* I 112d7–9 and 117a8–b3 (and following) where the image is used to emphasize that Alcibiades has no firm opinion and thus no knowledge concerning the nature of justice and injustice, etc.

[41] The reading γνώμας, rather than the variant γνώμαις, is accepted not only by DK but also by all of the principal recent editors, Cordero 1984, Coxon 1986, and O'Brien 1987(*a*). Cf. also the defence of γνώμας by Woodbury 1986, 2.

[42] Mansfeld 1964, 124, claims that τῶν μίαν οὐ cannot be taken as the equivalent of οὐδετέραν, as Cornford 1933, 109, proposed. However, Long 1963, 98, adduces as comparanda Aristophanes, *Thesmophoriazusae* 549, and X. *An.* 5. 6. 12 to show that μίαν οὐ may legitimately be taken to mean 'not one'.

at all'); B8. 44b–5: τὸ γὰρ οὔτε τι μεῖζον | οὔτε τι βαιότερον πελέναι χρεόν ἐστι τῇ ἢ τῇ ('for it is necessary that it be neither any greater nor any smaller at one point than at another'). B2. 5 specifies the necessary mode of (not-)being belonging to the object of the second path, while B8. 11 represents a retrospective encapsulation of the original choice in B2 between what necessarily is and what necessarily is not as the only potential objects of knowledge. In B8. 51b–4, the passage we are immediately concerned with, the goddess is diagnosing the source of mortal error. Mortals have gone astray in attempting to achieve knowledge by fixing their thought upon objects that do not have the requisite mode of being. One therefore expects the goddess's diagnosis here to point out that the objects of mortal *doxa* fail to have this absolute mode of being. The uses of χρεών ἐστιν in the comparable contexts of B2. 5 and B8. 11, and even the use at B8. 45, suggest that an infinitive of the verb 'to be' should be understood as the complement of χρεών ἐστιν here at B8. 54. One might suppose the complement is left unexpressed because ἐστιν alone is allowed to bear the sense ἐστιν εἶναι ('it is for being'). However, not only do the objects of mortal *doxa* fail to display the absolute or necessary being of the first path's object, they also fail to display the necessary (not-) being of the second path's object, in virtue of which it too satisfies the formal conditions placed upon a proper object of knowledge. Thus χρεών ἐστιν at B8. 54 needs two complements, εἶναι and μὴ εἶναι. They are left unexpressed because the focus is on the fact that the objects of *doxa* display none of the requisite necessity (either of being or of not being). Neither of the forms upon which mortals have focused their attention is necessarily. Accordingly the goddess designates the cosmology that follows as 'deceptive' (ἀπατηλόν) because it threatens to draw Parmenides' attention away from absolute being as she has just described it.

We may now be more precise about the sense of εἶναι μὴ ἐόντα in B7. 1, which we translated somewhat non-committally as 'things that are not are'. These words may likewise be presumed within the context of the present reading to pick out the non-necessary mode of being belonging to the objects of *doxa*. 'Things that are not' may be things that are F at one time but not at another, or in one context but not in another, or even that exist at one time but not at another (cf. B19. 1–2). They will not, however, be things that are not F and/or do not exist either now or at any time. That is, 'things that are not' (μὴ ἐόντα) here does not have the same sense as 'what-is-not' (τὸ μὴ ἐόν) in B2. 7, which functions as an abbreviated reference to the object of the path specified in B2. 5. For the constraint established in B2. 7

—that one could not have any apprehension of what-absolutely-is-not—holds good here as well. Mortals do have some apprehension (*doxa*) of the things they devote their attention to, and thus these things do exist in some manner. *Republic* 5. 478b6–8, at any rate, indicates that Plato would not have equated the objects of mortal *doxa* with what-is-not or τὸ μὴ ἐόν. For there he asks Glaucon, 'Does one have *doxa* of what-is-not (τὸ μὴ ὄν)? Or is it impossible even to have *doxa* of what-is-not? Think about it. Does not the person who has *doxa* direct his *doxa* at something? Or is it possible to have *doxa* but to have *doxa* of nothing?' If the 'things that are not' in B7. 1 are not to be equated with what is in no way, but rather they 'are not' in the senses indicated, then one might suppose εἶναι is to be similarly understood here, such that εἶναι μὴ ἐόντα will mean that things that are not F in one respect are F in another, and so on. But taking εἶναι in this way yields a sense that is too weak for the context. For entertaining such a view of things would involve no error obvious enough to account for the goddess's strong prohibition. If, however, εἶναι is understood in a more restricted sense such that things that are not (in the senses specified) are confusedly supposed to be in the manner appropriate to a proper object of knowledge, the goddess will have good reason to hold Parmenides back from this path. Where mortals have gone wrong, then, is not in believing that the world of ordinary experience exists but in assuming that it can constitute a proper object of knowledge.

By now it should be clear that Plato will have found ample material in Parmenides that conformed to his own view of the status of the sensible world. The adaptability of the Parmenidean material to Plato's perspective is perhaps most evident in the last lines of the proem (B1. 28–32):

> χρεὼ δέ σε πάντα πυθέσθαι,
> ἠμὲν ἀληθείης εὐκυκλέος ἀτρεμὲς ἦτορ
> ἠδὲ βροτῶν δόξας, τῆς[43] οὐκ ἔνι πίστις ἀληθής.
> ἀλλ' ἔμπης καὶ ταῦτα μαθήσεαι, ὡς τὰ δοκοῦντα
> χρῆν δοκίμως εἶναι διὰ παντὸς πάντα περῶντα

(I require you to learn all things, both the unshaken heart of well-rounded truth and the beliefs of mortals, in which there is no true persuasion. But nevertheless you shall learn these things as well, how it was necessary for the things believed to be in a believable manner passing entirely through all things).

I have refrained from emphasizing one of the most obvious features of Plato's reception, namely how straightforward it would have been

---

[43] For a defence of the reading τῆς instead of ταῖς, see Sider 1985, 363.

for him to see in Parmenides' conception of *doxa* and its objects a
direct and probably motivating counterpart for his own conception.
Making this connection has in modern times been judged the cardinal anachronism in the interpretation of Parmenides. Fear of it
has not only led scholars away from exploring the interpretation of
Parmenides underlying Plato's appropriation but has also led to an
increasingly scrupulous suppression of any feature that might be construed as 'Platonic' in the interpretation of Parmenides himself.[44] Having developed thus far a reading in accordance with Plato's reception,
we can now give voice to the heresies which this view involves for the
interpretation of B1. 30–2. Parmenides' mortals, like Plato's sight-
lovers, operate at the cognitive level of *doxa*. Plato would naturally have
seen τὰ δοκοῦντα ('the things believed') in Parmenides as an archaic
equivalent of τὸ δοξαστόν ('what is believed'), his own coinage for
referring to what is apprehended by *doxa*. In saying that it was necessary for τὰ δοκοῦντα 'to be believably' or δοκίμως εἶναι (B1. 32a), the
goddess ascribes to them a mode of being appropriate to the objects
of *doxa*.[45] When she declares that Parmenides must learn the *doxai* of
mortals, it means she will give a systematic account of those things
upon which mortals have fixed their thought.

One often encounters the idea that Plato's contrast between the
intelligible world of being and the sensible world of becoming has
its origins in a contrast between the Parmenidean and Heraclitean
perspectives.[46] This notion constitutes a reductive schematization of
his involvement with these two thinkers. Plato does not exclusively
associate Heraclitus with the world of becoming. In the *Sophist*'s

[44] Schwabl 1953, 51 n. 1, for example, declares at the outset of his study of being
and *doxa* in Parmenides that 'für Parm[enides] die (erst von Platon stammende)
Gleichsetzung: Sein = Welt der νοῦς, Doxa = Welt der Sinne abgelehnt werden muß'.
Owen is even more assiduous. For example, he criticizes Wilamowitz 1899, 204–5,
for interpreting ἐοικότα at B8. 60 in a sense similar to that at Pl. *Ti.* 29b–d and rejects
'any attempt to read *dokimôs* as "in a manner appropriate to *dokounta*"' (Owen 1960,
49 and 51; cf. Verdenius 1942, 50–1).

[45] While it may be the case that δοκίμως in its two other extant attestations
(Aeschylus, *Persae* 547; X. *Cyr.* 1. 6. 7) means something on the order of 'genuinely'
or 'really', Plato would have been unlikely to give it this sense, as he reserves such
adverbial qualifications for absolute being (as at e.g. *R.* 5. 477a3, a7, 478d6, 479d5;
cf. 478e1–3).

[46] Turnbull 1983, 279, is typical in his oversimplifying association of Parmenides
and Heraclitus respectively and exclusively with the world of being and the world of
becoming: 'It is a truism of Plato interpretation that Plato wants at once a "world"
that *is* and a "world" that *is* and *is not.* . . . to shift the metaphor, Plato must build a
philosophical house in which both Parmenides and Heraclitus can be comfortably
accommodated.'

ontological doxography, he groups Heraclitus with Empedocles as accepting that what-is is both one and many. Moreover, as I have tried to show, Plato's view of the sensible world is at least as Parmenidean as Heraclitean. I say 'at least' as Parmenidean because key features of this view have no Heraclitean analogue, as one can see even in Aristotle's presumed authoritative account of Plato's Heracliteanism. 'In his youth', Aristotle says, 'he first became familiar with Cratylus and with the Heraclitean view that all sensibles are always flowing *and that there is no knowledge (ἐπιστήμη) of them*; and he supposed these things later too' (*Metaph.* A. 6. 987ᵃ32–ᵇ1, cf. M. 4. 1078ᵇ12–15). One might well ask in what sense the view that there is no *knowledge* of sensibles or particulars is supposed to go back to Heraclitus or the so-called Heracliteans such as Cratylus. The Heracliteans would presumably claim that apprehension of the fluxy world, that being all there is, is knowledge. This is, at any rate, their thesis in the *Theaetetus*. Plato's epistemological dissatisfaction with the objects of ordinary experience must therefore be considered more Parmenidean than Heraclitean. The Heracliteans' view of knowledge, in fact, makes them plausible enough candidates for inclusion in the class of sight-lovers. It is interesting in this respect that scholars since the middle of last century have often identified Heraclitus as one particular target of Parmenides' criticism of mortal beliefs.[47] Whether or not Plato made any such identification, he will at least have seen Parmenides' criticisms of mortals as a model for his own criticism of the Heracliteans.

Modern consensus has inclined towards the view that Parmenides denies the very existence of the world as we ordinarily experience it. According to this view, what exists is described in the Way of Truth, and the subsequent cosmology is merely an elaborate description of what is in fact an illusion with no measure of reality. Plato did not take this view. His use of Parmenides indicates that he accepted that the objects of mortal *doxa* exist, only not in the way necessary to make them proper objects of knowledge. There are, of course, modern interpretations of Parmenides that accord status to the things described in the cosmological portion of the poem.[48] But there would be little

---

[47] e.g. Bernays 1885, 62 n. 1; Kranz 1916, 1174; *contra*, Reinhardt 1916, 64 ff. For further references, cf. Mansfeld 1964, 1 nn. 1 and 2.

[48] Cf. e.g. Wilamowitz-Möllendorff 1899; Reinhardt 1916; Calogero 1932, 28 ff., 42 ff.; Riezler 1934, 44 ff.; Verdenius 1942, 48 ff.; Fränkel 1946, 169–71; van Loenen 1959, 116 ff.; Chalmers 1960; Gigon 1968, 247 ff., 271 ff.; Clark 1969; Nehamas 1981, 108; Finkelberg 1986 and 1988; Curd 1992 and 1998, ch. 3. Of these, Clark 1969 perhaps comes closest to attributing to Parmenides himself a view of the status of the phenomenal world (which he argues is what Parmenides meant by τὰ δοκοῦντα at

point in attempting to catalogue where the wide variety of such interpretations seem to approximate points in the Platonic interpretation developed thus far. Part of the problem is that these modern accounts often do not make it sufficiently clear whether they mean to ascribe a subjective or objective reality to the world of ordinary experience. They often use the terms 'reality' and 'appearance' so ambiguously that one can still be left wondering whether, in according the objects of *doxa* some measure of 'reality', they are indeed allowing that they exist. The more fundamental problem is, of course, that these studies are all engaged in the first-order interpretative project of determining Parmenides' intended meaning rather than in the second-order project of examining the history of later readings of his poem. I therefore want to conclude this treatment of Plato's middle period reception of Parmenides by citing a Platonic reading from antiquity that is in essential agreement with the interpretation we have developed.

In his treatise 'Against Colotes', the Platonist Plutarch defends a number of thinkers attacked by the Epicurean Colotes in his treatise, 'On the impossibility of living according to the views of other philosophers'. Colotes apparently attributed to Parmenides what Plutarch sees as certain 'shameful sophisms' (αἰσχρὰ σοφίσματα, 1113 F), including the thesis that the universe is one in such a way that, among other things, fire, water, and 'the inhabited cities of Europe and Asia' are all abolished (1114 A–B). Colotes presumed that the goddess's account of truth precludes the existence of the world of ordinary experience and its underlying principles. Plutarch, however, says that Parmenides actually did no such thing and that one can see this from his having described the cosmic order in an account that relates how all its phenomena were produced from the intermingling of the bright and the dark (1114 B). He attacks what he sees as Colotes' maliciously

B1. 31) such as I have suggested Plato would have seen in him. Clark proposes that in Parm. B1. 30 'for the first time in philosophical thought, δόξαι is used as a technical term in contrast with Ἀλήθεια (i.e. ἐπιστήμη) to denote a kind of knowledge which is to be differentiated from that obtained through νόος, which is divine understanding' (18–19); he strongly opposes the widespread view that, according to Parmenides, the sensible world has no existence whatsoever (22, 24–5), arguing instead that 'Parmenides must mean that sensibles exist *qua* sensibles, but *they do not exist for thinking*' (27); and he notes that 'Parmenides may thus have distinguished between the objects of *Aletheia* and *Doxa*, as Plato (*Rep.* 477–80) implies a difference in kind between the objects of belief and those of knowledge' (27). Parmenides' contribution to philosophy, he declares, was to have recognized 'that δόξα and νοεῖν start from different objects of study, phenomena (αἰσθητά) and reality (νοητά) respectively' (28). For another defence of this latter thesis, see Wiśniewski 1963; and for reviews of the major stances shaping the overall debate, cf. e.g. Verdenius 1942, 45–9, and Tarán 1965, 203–10.

reductive interpretation by arguing that Parmenides was the first to distinguish the sensible and intelligible realms. The heart of Plutarch's own reading[49] is worth quoting *in extenso*:

Parmenides, even earlier than Plato and Socrates, realized that nature contains something apprehended by *doxa* (τι δοξαστόν) and also something apprehended by the intellect (νοητόν); that, moreover, what is apprehended by *doxa* is unsteady, wandering (πλανητόν) among various states and changes by virtue of growing and decaying, is different for different people's perception, and is not even always the same for the same person's perception; and that the character of the intelligible is different, for it is 'sound of limb and unshaken and ungenerated' [Parm. B8. 4][50], as he himself said, and like to itself and stable in its being. But Colotes makes petty criticisms of these things on the basis of their expression and attacks the language but not the substance when he says that Parmenides completely abolishes all things by positing one as being. Parmenides, however, abolishes neither nature. Instead, assigning to each what is appropriate, he places the intelligible in the class of what is one and being—calling it 'being' in so far as it is eternal and imperishable, and 'one' because of its likeness unto itself and its not admitting differentiation—while he locates the perceptible among what is disordered and changing. Of these it is also possible to see the criterion: 'both the sure heart of persuasive truth' [Parm. B1. 29],[51] which fastens upon the intelligible and what is the same in the same state, 'and the beliefs of mortals, in which there is no true persuasion' [B1. 30], because they involve themselves with things admitting all manner of changes, affections, and dissimilarities. Yet how could he have let perception and *doxa* remain without leaving what is apprehended by perception and *doxa*? It is not possible to say. But because it is appropriate for what-really-is (τῷ μὲν ὄντως ὄντι) to persist in being, whereas these

[49] On Plutarch's interpretation of Parmenides, see Westman 1955, 234–42, Hershbell 1972, and Isnardi Parente 1988. Westman rails against Plutarch's Platonizing (see esp. 235). Hershbell's synoptic study of all Plutarch's citations of Parmenides aims in the first place to demonstrate that Plutarch had first-hand acquaintance with Parmenides' poem, so that his treatment of the interpretation in *Col.* is primarily meant to meet the objection that the obvious Platonic influence on it tells against direct knowledge. Hershbell is nevertheless rather sympathetic to Plutarch's interpretation as a viable view of Parmenides (see esp. 202–3, 207–8). Isnardi Parente's study is unfortunately vitiated by her groundless attribution to Plutarch of the Aristotelian identification of light with being and darkness with not being, an attribution which forms the basis of her interpretation.

[50] The version of the partial line given in the text of Plutarch is: οὐλομελές τε καὶ ἀτρεμὲς ἠδ' ἀγένητον. Our other sources for the line present a puzzling variety of readings, so that what Parmenides may actually have written is much debated. Cf. Cordero 1984, 26; Coxon 1986, 61 and 195–6; and O'Brien 1987(*a*), 34.

[51] Plutarch's version of this line is ἠμὲν ἀληθείης εὐπειθέος ἀτρεκὲς ἦτορ. The reading ἀτρεκές is less widely attested than ἀτρεμές. Although εὐπειθέος is also found in Clement of Alexandria, Sextus Empiricus, and Diogenes Laertius, Simplicius' reading εὐκυκλέος is perhaps preferable as the *lectio difficilior*.

things now are, now again are not, and are always altering and exchanging their nature, he thought they required a designation different from that for what always is. Therefore his theory concerning what-is, namely, that it should be one, was not an abolition of the many perceptible things but a revelation of the distinction between them and the intelligible (1114 C–F).

Plutarch's is a fully evolved Platonist reading, for which he will have found justification in his own thorough reading of Plato. Certain purely Platonic elements have crept in that have a questionable analogue in the text of Parmenides as we possess it. Such is the association of the objects of *doxa* with disorderly motion (cf. *Ti.* 30a). Still, Plutarch's reading agrees in its general outline with Plato's own.

Where I find Plutarch's defence of Parmenides intriguing is in its attempt to recover Parmenides from what he sees as a reductive and sophistic reading. Not only does this bear witness to the polyphony of the ancient reception of Parmenides, but, more interestingly, Plutarch's defence of Parmenides against Colotes constitutes a late stage in the opposition between a Platonic and a sophistic reading of Parmenides. In turning now to Plato's later reception of Parmenides, I want to argue that such an opposition is already of fundamental importance in Plato. One of his principal concerns in certain later dialogues is to recover Parmenides from the sophistic appropriations and understandings to which he had been subjected long before Colotes.

PART II

Plato and the Sophistic
Appropriations of Parmenides

5

Parmenides' Thesis at Issue

In exploring the continuities Plato would have perceived between Parmenides' metaphysics and his own ontological and epistemological concerns during the middle period, I have tended to play down the discontinuities between the two theories. The most obvious of these is that Plato's use preserves the uniqueness of Parmenidean Being only as an attribute of each individual form. The very plurality of the forms seems a radical departure from Parmenides' monism.[1] One might, however, suppose continuity here as well. For some scholars—most prominently, Jonathan Barnes—have challenged the various considerations underpinning the general assumption that Parmenides was a monist.[2] Barnes has argued that the fragments of the 'Truth' are compatible with the existence of a plurality of Parmenidean Beings. Since the middle period forms can be seen as such a plurality, one could conclude that Plato did not think Parmenides a monist. From this perspective, one of the most interesting interpretations of Parmenides as potential pluralist is that advanced by Patricia Curd. Like Barnes, she denies that Parmenides was a 'real' or 'numerical' monist, yet she argues that he was none the less committed to what she terms 'predicational monism', the thesis that 'each thing that is can be only one thing; it can hold only one predicate, and must hold it in a particularly strong way'.[3] Unfortunately, her attempts to fit her interpretation to the text of Parmenides are, for the most part, unpersuasive. For example, although she may be correct in pointing out that Parmenides

---

[1] So Seligman 1982, 23–4, who notes two further departures—that Parmenidean Being possesses spatial properties and thus the intension of an extended being, whereas Plato primarily conceived the intension of being qualitatively; and that Plato, unlike Parmenides, tried to explain the relation of the sensible world to being (see also Seligman 1974, 6–7). Although it does seem fair enough to characterize the middle period metaphysics as departing from Parmenides in these two respects, we will want to ask whether this remains true in the later period.

[2] Barnes 1979; cf. Barnes 1982, 204–7. Among the precursors of Barnes's heterodoxy, the most important are Bäumker 1886 and Untersteiner 1955. See Barnes 1979, 2 n. 4, for an assessment of their contributions and for references to others who have either questioned Parmenides' monism or seen it as relatively unimportant.

[3] Curd 1991, 242–3 ≈ Curd 1998, 66.

B4[4] is not incompatible with there being a plurality of entities, she fails to provide a satisfactory reason for thinking that the particular point of these lines is that 'there are no predicational divisions within what is: should it be F it is all and only F with no allowances for also being G (for then it could be scattered in thought into F and G and then gathered back together into the predicational plurality FG)'.[5] If one chooses to take the forms of the verb 'to be' in B4. 2 in an exclusively predicative sense, the point would not be that what-is-F cannot be G or have other predicates but rather that what-is-F cannot be divided from what-is-F; that is, that it is unique, self-contained, and the whole of what-it-is-to-be-F. We shall, nevertheless, find an ancient view of Parmenides not unlike Curd's when we come to examine the connections between the *Sophist*'s and the *Parmenides*'s treatments of Eleaticism.

Whatever one might wish to make of the possibility that he did not view Parmenides as a monist at the time of his middle period dialogues, Plato in his later encounter with Parmenides consistently represents him as a monist (however we may want to interpret this monism). In the *Parmenides*, Socrates sums up his position as 'the all is one' (ἓν . . . εἶναι τὸ πᾶν, 128a8–b1); Zeno states his master's thesis as 'it (sc. the all) is one' (ἓν ἐστι, 128d1); and Parmenides himself prefaces his lengthy demonstration of proper dialectical method by asking, 'Shall I begin with myself and my own hypothesis, hypothesizing about the One itself (περὶ τοῦ ἑνὸς αὐτοῦ) to see what must follow if the One is (ἓν ἐστιν) and if the One is not?' (137b2–4).[6] In the *Theaetetus*, Socrates says all the sages except Parmenides may be thought to subscribe to the 'secret doctrine' that 'nothing is itself in itself one' (ἓν μὲν αὐτὸ καθ'αὑτὸ οὐδέν ἐστιν, 152d2–3). He thereby indicates that Parmenides' doctrine entails that there *is* something that is in itself one. The dialogue's subsequent references to Parmenides suggest a more restricted thesis. For later the various partisans of the secret

---

[4] Parm. B4: λεῦσσε δ' ὅμως ἀπεόντα νόῳ παρεόντα βεβαίως· | οὐ γὰρ ἀποτμήξει τὸ ἐὸν τοῦ ἐόντος ἔχεσθαι | οὔτε σκιδνάμενον πάντῃ πάντως κατὰ κόσμον | οὔτε συνιστάμενον ('yet regard things that, though far away, are firmly present to the intellect: for you will not sever what-is from cleaving to what-is, neither as scattering nor as assembling everywhere in every way according to order').

[5] Curd 1991, 253 ≈ Curd 1998, 68.

[6] I accept the emendation of *Prm.* 137b4, εἴτε ἓν ἐστιν εἴτε μὴ ἕν, to εἴτε ἓν ἐστιν εἴτε μὴ ἔστιν. Cf. Wundt 1935, 6 n. 1; Cornford 1939, 108; Meinwald 1991, 39–45. I must say, however, that there is some attraction in the proposal by Weber 1937, 8, that the non-emended text should be translated as 'la question sert de savoir s'il est un ou multiple' and that these two possibilities are to be identified with the perspectives on the One in the First and Second Deductions.

doctrine are set in opposition to the 'Melissuses' and 'Parmenideses' who maintain that 'all things are one (ἓν ... πάντα ἐστί), and it stands at rest in itself since it has no space in which it might move' (180e2–4).[7] In the final reference to the Eleatics in this dialogue, Socrates succinctly states their position as 'the all is one at rest' (ἓν ἑστὸς ... τὸ πᾶν, 183e3–4). Similarly, the *Sophist*'s Eleatic Visitor formulates the thesis of his intellectual ancestors as: 'what is called "all things" is a single being' (ὡς ἑνὸς ὄντος τῶν πάντων καλουμένων, 242d6). That is—as 244b6 makes clear—'the all is one' (ἓν τὸ πᾶν). Despite the pluralizing middle period appropriation, then, the uniqueness of Parmenidean Being becomes quite prominent in the later dialogues. We even find Plato distinguishing 'those who speak of the One' from 'those who speak of the many forms' (*Sph.* 249c11–d1).[8] This prominence is itself a sign that Plato's view of Parmenides' relevance to his own philosophical project has undergone something of a transformation.

In turning to Plato's later reception of Parmenides, our ultimate aim is to determine as best we can the view of Parmenides underlying Plato's new formulation of his doctrine as 'the all is one' (ἓν τὸ πᾶν). We shall see that behind this concise and apparently simple formulation lies quite a complex view. The *Parmenides* and the *Sophist* are the dialogues we shall be most concerned with, and it will soon become apparent that establishing the recoverable features of Plato's understanding of Parmenides in these dialogues is not as straightforward as one might hope. For in both dialogues, as we shall see, Plato is confronting various sophistic appropriations to which Parmenides had been subjected that stand in the way of the use he himself now wants to make. How Parmenides is to be understood is at issue in both dialogues. Before turning to the *Parmenides*, I want to comment briefly on how Socrates puts the interpretation of Parmenides at stake in the *Theaetetus*.

Socrates is, in this dialogue, reluctant to explore the meaning of the Eleatic thesis. This reluctance signals the difficulties in understanding what Parmenides meant when he maintained that the all is one. Having twice referred to the Eleatic thesis, Socrates bypasses

---

[7] The second thesis here, that what-is is at rest because there is no space in which it could move, reflects the specifically Melissan argument for the immobility of what-is. Cf. Simp. *in Ph.* 112, 7–10 = 30B7. 7 DK. At Pl. *Tht.* 180d7–e1, however, Socrates introduces the Eleatics by quoting a version of Parm. B8. 38 in which it is asserted that what-is is unchanging (ἀκίνητον); and in the *Sophist*, the Eleatic Visitor indiscriminately attributes the thesis that the all is at rest (τὸ πᾶν ἑστηκός) to Eleatic advocates of the One (249c10–d1, cf. 252a5–10). [8] Cf. Murphy 1937, 73.

a full consideration when he mentions it for the final time in the dialogue. As he does so, he alludes to the encounter he had with Parmenides that provides the dramatic setting for the *Parmenides*'s extended examination:

Although I would be ashamed if we were to examine in a crude way Melissus and the others who say that the all is one and at rest (ἓν ἑστὸς . . . τὸ πᾶν), I would be less ashamed than if we were thus to examine that singular being Parmenides. Parmenides seems to me, to quote Homer, to be both 'venerable and awe-inspiring'. For I encountered the man when he was quite old and I quite young, and he struck me as having a certain depth that was altogether noble. Therefore I fear that we might not understand his words and that we might fail even further in attempting to understand what he meant when he uttered them (*Tht.* 183e3–184a3).

The reference to Parmenides as 'that singular being' (ἕνα ὄντα Παρμενίδην) cleverly turns the alternative formulation of the Eleatic thesis as 'what-is is one' (ἓν τὸ ὄν) into an epithet of the one who propounded it. The interpretation of Parmenides' thesis—whether 'the all is one' or 'what-is is one'—could not be more explicitly problematized than it is by the concluding sentence of this passage. Plato would not have marked it as so deep and difficult if he presumed Parmenides' view to be equivalent to the strict monistic thesis that only one thing exists. This may be a fair representation of Melissus' view. But Socrates' greater respect for Parmenides indicates that his conception is not to be equated with Melissus'. Socrates' professed reluctance to examine Melissus' view 'in a crude way' (φορτικῶς) may be an ironic indication that he considers the view itself somewhat crude. There is, at any rate, reason to think that Aristotle understood the hesitation in this way. He appears to have thought this manner of examining Melissus quite appropriate, for in *Physics* 1. 2 he echoes the language of our passage in distinguishing Melissus' conception from Parmenides' as being rather crude (φορτικός, 185ᵃ10–11). In any case, Socrates makes it quite plain that he takes Parmenides much more seriously (as Aristotle himself does somewhat more reluctantly in the *Physics*). The distance he opens up between the two Eleatics and the declaration that he fears not understanding the deeper meaning of Parmenides' words provide a negative indication of how they are to be understood: Parmenides is not to be understood as taking the strict monistic stance that only one thing exists. How exactly he is to be understood remains unclear—the interpretation of Parmenides is not the concern of the *Theaetetus*. One naturally expects clarification in the dialogue bearing his name, but Socrates' statement, as he looks back to the conversation recorded in the *Parmenides*, that he is afraid of not understanding his full intention suggests that this clarification may not be immediately forthcoming even there. We will in fact see that the *Parmenides* puts the interpretation of Parmenides at stake in a more elaborate way.

SOCRATES, ZENO, AND PARMENIDES

Parmenides and Zeno's visit to Athens to attend the Great Panathenaea provides the dramatic occasion for the *Parmenides*. The young Socrates goes with a number of others to the house of Pythodorus, where the visitors are staying, to hear Zeno read from his famous book which he has brought to Athens for the first time. Socrates questions Zeno on the meaning and purpose of its arguments. Zeno accepts certain points that Socrates makes, while he rejects others. Socrates goes on to present a theory, closely resembling Plato's middle period theory of forms, designed to explain how it is not surprising that the objects of ordinary experience possess the contrary attributes that Zeno's arguments have shown them to possess. Parmenides then steps in to present a series of criticisms of Socrates' conception of intelligible reality. After this he proceeds to present a lengthy and involved demonstration of the kind of dialectical training Socrates needs if he is to frame a more adequate conception. I want to concentrate for now on the opening exchange between Socrates and Zeno. This exchange is carefully constructed and shows how Plato at the time of this dialogue's composition saw the interpretation of Parmenides as an arena of conflicting understandings and appropriations. In considering how the discussion of Zeno's treatise functions within the structure of the dialogue, we shall not be directly concerned with whether Plato accurately isolates the purpose of Zeno's arguments. It will nevertheless be worth while to point out how the dominance of this topic in discussions of the opening exchange has resulted in a number of unfortunate distortions.

Hermann Fränkel was one of the first to raise doubts about the feasibility of using the *Parmenides* as a guide to reconstructing Zeno's thought. He made the simple but essential point that one 'may well wonder how much authentic information Plato did possess about the real Zeno's actions and intentions and how much he, or his readers for that matter, would be interested in problems of mere historicity'.[9]

---

[9] Fränkel 1942, 125.

Despite the apparent recognition that the dialogue's representation of Zeno has other than historical aims, Fränkel persisted in maintaining that one 'can unconditionally believe what [Plato] says about the content of Zeno's work. . . . No doubt correct is the view that the book was based on Parmenides' philosophy and was meant to confirm it'.[10] It remained for Friedrich Solmsen to extend doubt to those portions of Plato's account that Fränkel rather arbitrarily presumed must be correct. He stressed even more emphatically that Plato does not introduce Zeno to give a historically accurate representation of his treatise's intention but to develop the philosophical problems with which he himself is concerned.[11] Solmsen thus set out to *discredit* Plato's account of the treatise's aims. He applied himself to this task by first 'discrediting' the account of Parmenides upon which the account of Zeno's treatise depends. Solmsen remained focused on the traditional issue of whether Plato's comments regarding Zeno and his relation to Parmenides accurately represent the substance of Zeno's thought. Rejecting the reliability of the *Parmenides*'s account, he set this text aside and attempted to develop an independent account of Zeno's aims. In doing so, however, he abandoned virtually the only substantial guide from antiquity to these aims. It is true that Simplicius, for example, makes certain conjectures about Zeno's purpose. But even if he had independent access to a version of Zeno's treatise, his dependence upon the *Parmenides* in the conjectures he makes regarding Zeno's purpose is obvious (see especially *in Ph.* 134, 2–8). The same is basically true of Proclus' remarks on Zeno in his commentary on the *Parmenides* (cf. e.g. *in Prm.* 619, 30–620, 3 Cousin), even though the extent of Proclus' knowledge of Zeno is a matter of some controversy.[12] Although Solmsen sought guidance in the comments of Eudemus and Alexander of Aphrodisias (as reported by Simplicius), he was finally forced to admit that they are questionable

[10] Fränkel 1942, 125.   [11] Solmsen 1971(*b*), 370–1.

[12] This controversy stems from Proclus' reference to Zeno's having propounded forty arguments (*in Prm.* 694, 23–5 Cousin) and from Proclus' appearing in certain passages of his commentary to provide information regarding these arguments not directly derivable from Plato or Aristotle (e.g. *in Prm.* 725, 22–39, 760, 27–761, 3, and 769, 23–770, 1 Cousin). See Dillon 1974, 1976, and 1986, as well as Morrow and Dillon 1987, xxxviii–xliii. There is perhaps more room for scepticism about Proclus' supposed lack of reliance on Plato and Aristotle than Dillon suggests. Granted that Proclus does on occasion ascribe arguments to Zeno that go beyond what we find in the exchange between Socrates and Zeno, these arguments are nevertheless often reminiscent of arguments occurring in the subsequent dialectical exercise. This may either be taken to indicate that Zeno was the ultimate source of these particular arguments in the exercise, or that Proclus is attributing arguments to Zeno on the basis of what he supposed was the Zenonian character of these arguments.

guides who probably had no first-hand acquaintance with Zeno's treatise and that it is consequently 'precarious' to be positive about Zeno's intention and motivation.[13]

Dissatisfaction with this conclusion resulted in continued efforts to treat Plato's representation of Zeno as something it patently is not in order to have it yield the necessary guidance to his historical intentions.[14] This in turn led to a neglect or glossing over of essential complexities of the exchange between Socrates and Zeno. The most unfortunate distortion has been the tendency to privilege Socrates' analysis of Zeno's purposes (127e6–128a1, 128a4–b6) over Zeno's own qualifications and corrections of this analysis (128b7–e4). Gregory Vlastos, for example, in the most influential attempt to re-establish the basic historical reliability of Plato's account in the wake of Solmsen's critique, declared that Socrates' remarks constitute the crucial segment of Plato's testimony in the *Parmenides*.[15] Vlastos listed six separate facts we would know about Zeno were Plato's testimony found trustworthy. Five of these come from Socrates' analysis. One cannot help but suspect a certain prejudice creeping in here, despite the fact that the young Socrates does not have the authority in this dialogue that the mature Socrates has in others. This bias led Vlastos to neglect the implications of Zeno's different responses to the two parts of Socrates' analysis. Zeno agrees with the point of the first part (127e6–128a1), that his arguments contend that things are not many in spite of what people commonly say. He does not, however, agree so readily with the main point in the second part of Socrates' analysis (128a4–b6), namely that he had simply upheld Parmenides' central thesis in a different form. This is one of the six key points that Vlastos isolated.[16] Although he examined in detail the extent to which each of the other five points may be considered accurate, he simply takes this point as a given. The actual situation is more complex, as one can see

---

[13] Solmsen 1971(*b*), 389 and 393.

[14] The results often barely conceal fundamental inconsistencies in attitude towards the Platonic evidence. For example, von Fritz 1974 accepts Solmsen's point that Plato's representation of the relation between Zeno and Parmenides was not meant to be historically accurate while himself maintaining that 'in a way Zeno did try to come to the help of Parmenides by showing that an analysis of the world of *doxa* led to no less strange paradoxes than an analysis of Parmenides' "real" world of undiluted being, though he did not do it exactly in the way attributed to him by Plato in order to make him serve Plato's philosophical purposes' (340–1). Prior 1978 also accepts Solmsen's criticism of earlier scholars' too ready reliance upon Plato but denies that this need imply that Plato was incorrect. He thus attempts a reconstruction of Zeno's pattern of argumentation that is supposedly independent of, but is still in the end found to confirm, Plato's analysis.   [15] Vlastos 1975, 142.

[16] Ibid. 137.

by properly considering Zeno's response. Vlastos, however, did not do so, apparently because he felt he could privilege Socrates' view over Zeno's rather different account of the history and intention of his own treatise. Predictably, Vlastos has not been alone in his prejudice in favour of Socrates. Fränkel, for example, asserted the unconditional reliability of Plato's statements regarding the contents of Zeno's treatise, including the first part of Socrates' analysis, and he accorded equal reliability to the second part. He was thus able to conclude that the 'book as a whole, so we are given to understand, is not what it seems to be, and its real essence is beyond the reach of an ordinary person'.[17] Zeno in fact tries to disabuse Socrates of such a view. But Fränkel dismissed the account of his treatise's composition and subsequent history by which Zeno does so as 'conjecture and imagination' that 'ought not to be taken literally'.

Commentators have also erroneously presumed that the meaning of Parmenides' own position, represented here by the formulation 'the all is one' (128a8–b1, cf. d1), is relatively straightforward. So, for example, Reginald Allen, compounding this error with others already touched on, can say: 'In Zeno's hands, the reductio ad absurdum is used not only to destroy a position but to establish one. Given that something exists . . . Zeno's proof that many things do not exist entails Parmenides' result that only one thing exists.'[18] The assumption here that the Parmenidean thesis means 'only one thing exists' is the product of the pervasive methodological error of assuming an interpretation of Parmenides independent of the Platonic reception. We have already seen, however, that Plato's middle period view of Parmenides is incompatible with this type of strict monist interpretation. The exercise Parmenides carries out in the latter portion of the dialogue likewise indicates his thesis is not to be understood in the trivial sense that only one thing exists. For he examines all the manifold relations of his One to other things. Apparently, this One's existence need not rule out the existence of other things. The One in fact emerges as largely responsible for the fact that other things are. Thus one should not so readily assume that Zeno's arguments against the view that many things exist, even if they do entail that only one thing exists (which is itself open to doubt), thereby entail Parmenides' thesis as Plato understands it.

It is precisely those features of the exchange between Socrates and Zeno which are most important for gauging the subtle workings

---

[17] Fränkel 1942, 125–6. Cherniss 1932, 130, displays the same prejudice.
[18] Allen 1997, 80.

of Plato's reception of Parmenides that have been unjustifiably neglected.[19] Here Plato guides the reader to the desired understanding of
Parmenides' position and the relation of Zeno's arguments to it primarily by means of Zeno's own comments on the history and intention of his treatise. When Zeno says, for example, that his treatise was
stolen and brought out against his will, we should not ask whether this
is an accurate account of its publication history, since there is no way
of determining the historical accuracy of this account. We can ask,
however, what role this odd detail plays in the dialogue. We should
ask questions of the text that it can answer. If one adheres to this principle and pays proper attention to the details of Socrates and Zeno's
conversation—particularly to the ways in which Zeno distances himself from his own treatise—one will begin to doubt whether the
treatise was in fact based on Parmenides' philosophy and meant to
confirm it. Does Zeno himself accept Socrates' characterization of his
arguments as simply saying the same thing as Parmenides in a different form? Is his treatise actually presented as an adequate defence
of Parmenides' philosophy? If so, how? If not, why not? What are the
implications of its adequacy or inadequacy for our understanding of
Plato's view of Parmenides in this dialogue? These are the kind of
questions we need to ask, and these are questions to which the text
actually provides answers.

Having heard Zeno's treatise from beginning to end, and having
then heard the first hypothesis of its first argument again, the young
Socrates decides that all its arguments are intended to demonstrate
that there are not many things (οὐ πολλά ἐστι, 127e10; οὐκ ἔστι πολλά,
127e12–128a1). Zeno agrees. Socrates then points out to Parmenides
(128a4–b6) that Zeno has surreptitiously upheld the same position
that he himself had when he maintained in his poem that 'the all is
one' (ἓν . . . εἶναι τὸ πᾶν). But at this point Zeno says to Socrates that
he is not quite correct and tries to explain the purpose of his treatise
more fully. He begins by denying what Socrates takes to be his work's
great pretensions. He notes that Socrates is wrong to presume it was
designed to conceal from the public the underlying seriousness that
Socrates imputes to it (128c2–5). In refusing to accept that his treatise was written with the profound intention Socrates feels he has
detected, Zeno is in effect denying that he was, as Socrates supposes,
secretly espousing Parmenides' thesis. Yet he does go on to describe
the treatise as having come to Parmenides' aid. It may seem that there
is some inconsistency between the three main points Zeno makes

---

[19] For an exception, see Miller 1986, 28–30, 32–6.

regarding Socrates' analysis. Zeno says (i) Socrates is right in observing that his treatise repeatedly maintains that there are not many things. 'You have', he says, 'properly grasped the intention of the entire treatise' (128a2–3). He indicates, however, that (ii) Socrates is mistaken in supposing the treatise was intended to say the same thing as Parmenides (128c2–5, cf. 128a6–b6). Yet he says (iii) the treatise was meant to defend Parmenides against his detractors. It is crucial to understanding Plato's complex characterization of the nature and purpose of Zeno's treatise that one reconcile these three points. Set out in this manner, it should be obvious that, while there is a certain tension here, these points are not absolutely inconsistent. We are, in fact, prompted to understand Zeno's arguments that there are not many things as defending Parmenides against his detractors without simply saying the same thing in a different form.

How this works itself out becomes clear in Zeno's description of his engagement with those detractors:

The treatise is in truth a sort of support for Parmenides' *logos* against those attempting to ridicule it on the ground that, if one is (ἕν ἐστι), the *logos* suffers many ridiculous results that contradict it. This treatise, therefore, argues against (ἀντιλέγει) those who say the many are, and it pays them back with the same results and worse, intending to demonstrate that their hypothesis—if many are (πολλά ἐστιν)—suffers even more ridiculous consequences than the hypothesis of there being one, if one follows the matter through sufficiently. So it was written by me in such a spirit of contentiousness (φιλονικίαν) when I was young, and someone stole it after it was written, so that it happened not to be possible to consider whether or not it should be brought forth into the light of day. Thus you are wrong in this respect, Socrates, that you do not realize it was written under the influence of youthful contentiousness (ὑπὸ νέου φιλονικίας) rather than out of more mature (πρεσβυτέρου) desire for glory (128c6–e3).

Zeno's use of the indefinite in describing his work as 'a sort of support' (βοήθειά τις) for Parmenides' *logos* marks it as an indirect defence. This indication is borne out in his subsequent description of it as a dialectical and *ad hominem* response to Parmenides' detractors in kind. By demonstrating that 'even more ridiculous consequences' follow from the hypothesis that there are many things, Zeno may seem to admit that ridiculous things also follow from Parmenides' hypothesis. Given the dialectical context of his arguments, however, no such admission is necessary. From the fact that Zeno responds to Parmenides' detractors by arguing that, if they suppose his hypothesis has ridiculous consequences, then their own presuppositions can in turn be shown to result in difficulties at least as great, one cannot legitimately infer that Zeno himself supposed Parmenides' hypothesis has ridiculous consequences.

The characterization of his tactics put in Zeno's mouth by Plato makes it easy to see why Aristotle, in his lost *Sophist*, identified Zeno as the inventor of dialectic (DL 9. 25, cf. 8. 57; SE, *M*. 7. 7). One may wonder, however, to which aspects of his own conception of dialectic Aristotle presumed Zeno's style of argument corresponded and, in particular, whether he viewed Zeno's arguments as more eristic than dialectical.[20] More relevant to our purposes is that Plato viewed Zeno as something of a sophist. In the *First Alcibiades*, Socrates reports that Pythodorus and Callias each paid Zeno a hundred minae to become clever (σοφός) and skilled in argument (ἐλλόγιμος, 119a3–6; cf. Plu. *Pericles* 4. 5). Plato would have classified Zeno's arguments as belonging to the sophistic deformation of proper dialectic he terms 'antilogic'. The *Phaedrus*'s famous designation of Zeno as the 'Eleatic Palamedes' for his ability to make the same things appear to his audience both like and unlike, both one and many, and both moving and at rest (261d6–8; cf. *Phd.* 90b9–c6, where Plato may also have Zeno in mind) marks him as a practitioner of antilogic along with Gorgias and Thrasymachus. Zeno himself in the *Parmenides* passage employs a verb to describe his manner of responding to Parmenides' detractors (ἀντιλέγει) that likewise qualifies him as a practitioner of 'antilogic' or the art of contradiction. One may also look to the beginning of the *Sophist* (216a–b), where Theodorus introduces the Eleatic Visitor as an associate of Parmenides and Zeno. Socrates worries that the Visitor may be 'some god of cross-examination' (θεὸς . . . τις ἐλεγκτικός) until Theodorus offers reassurance that he is more moderate than those who spend their time in eristic and competitive disputation (περὶ τὰς ἔριδας). Plato thus connects the rise of eristic disputation with the antinomies of Zeno.[21]

Now, there is some reason for supposing that Plato's view of Zeno's methods in the *Parmenides* conflicts with the picture of him in

---

[20] In addition to Zeno, Aristotle attributes the invention of dialectic to Socrates (*Metaph.* M. 4. 1078^b25–30), Plato (*Metaph. A.* 6. 987^b31–3), and even himself (*SE* 34. 183^b34–184^b8). On the problem of how these various attributions are to be resolved, cf. Wilpert 1956–7. That Zeno's method corresponds fairly precisely to Aristotle's conception of dialectic is maintained, for example, by Burnet 1930, 313–14, and Lee 1936, 7 and 113 ff. Moraux 1968, 293, is more careful in identifying a particular feature of dialectic for which Aristotle could have seen an antecedent in Zeno's argumentation, namely in his proceeding from the beliefs or ἔνδοξα of Parmenides' adversaries. On this point, cf. Berti 1988, 19–24.

[21] Cf. Taylor 1911, 92; Lee 1936, 118.

the *Phaedrus* and *Sophist* as a practitioner of eristic and antilogic.[22] For while Zeno's own description of his tactics against Parmenides' detractors and of his treatise's competitive and contentious tone seems perfectly consistent with his being dubbed the Eleatic Palamedes, Parmenides subsequently refers to Zeno's style of argument as representing the proper method of exercise in dialectic (135d7). The method of dialectic as Parmenides actually describes it, however, is not a direct reproduction but an adaptation of Zeno's mode of argumentation.[23] Zeno takes a single thesis and proceeds to deduce contradictory conclusions from it. The thesis itself is taken from his opponents, and the deductions are meant to constitute a *reductio* of that thesis. The dialectical procedure Parmenides proposes at 135e8–136c5 is more complex. He says it is necessary to take both a thesis and its denial and examine what follows from each in a number of definite relations. Although the conclusions drawn from the thesis (or its denial) may appear to be contradictory, it is not the expressed intention of the examination to produce contradictions. One might still suppose the Parmenidean method of dialectic is in some sense a development of the Zenonian. I think it more nearly correct to view the Zenonian method as a deformation of the Parmenidean, by which I mean a transfer of the tool of dialectic from its proper context of mutual investigation of a hypothesis to the context of competitive argument. This is, at least, how Zeno's own words in the dialogue prompt us to understand his method. When Plato has Zeno say that his treatise was written in a spirit of contentiousness (φιλονικία) when he was young, the reader should not think he is being provided with a rough date of composition. He should instead recall the *Republic*'s justification for postponing dialectical training until the guardians' thirtieth year:

So then isn't one lasting precaution this, that those who are still young are not to get a taste of this subject? For I imagine you are not unaware that when young men first get a taste of argument they play games with it, always using it for contradicting (ἀντιλογίαν), and having observed those who have engaged in refutation, they themselves refute others. . . . But a more mature person (πρεσβύτερος) would not want to share in such craziness. He will rather imitate one who wants to engage in proper dialectic (διαλέγεσθαι) and search for the truth rather than the one who plays games and contradicts others (ἀντιλέγοντα) for the sake of amusement (*R.* 7. 539b1–c8).

---

[22] So, for example, Solmsen 1971(*b*), 377. But see Cornford 1939, 67.

[23] Cornford 1939, 105–6, and Hägler 1983, 80–2, both stress that Zeno's method as adapted by Parmenides ceases to be controversialist. Cf. Cherniss 1932, 129, who calls attention to the significance of πλὴν τοῦτό γε at *Prm.* 135d8.

Compare Socrates' worries in the *Phaedo* that, in trying to win over Simmias, he is not behaving philosophically (φιλοσόφως) but contentiously (φιλονίκως) like those without proper training in dialectic (*Phd.* 91a). Zeno's repeated declaration that he wrote his treatise under the influence of youthful contentiousness (*Prm.* 128d6–7, e2) is a clear signal by Plato of a neophyte's abusive employment of dialectic.[24] Plato's characterization of Zeno's style of argument in the *Parmenides*, then, is basically consistent with that in other dialogues. He is a practitioner of antilogic, the art of contradiction that is the deformation of true dialectic. If Plato's attitude to Zeno in the *Parmenides* seems less harsh, it is because here he takes the most charitable view of Zeno's contentiousness. He resorted to this low, basically sophistic style of argument in order to pay back in kind the attacks upon his master Parmenides.

One implication of Zeno's use of antilogic is that those targeted by his arguments—Parmenides' detractors—practised it themselves. Zeno says he intended his treatise as a response to those who had attempted to ridicule Parmenides' principal thesis by showing that it has ridiculous consequences (128c7–d2). This suggests that there were certain individuals who attempted to demonstrate the ridiculous results that follow from the Parmenidean thesis that what-is is one. Proclus provides an example:

Parmenides is reported to have maintained that what-is is one (τὸ ὄν ἕν) and to have advanced this as his own particular view. Those who took hold of these words in too crude a sense (φορτικώτερον) ridiculed the view, making fun of it in various ways, including saying that if what-is is one, then Parmenides and Zeno do not both exist at the same time, but if Parmenides exists, then Zeno does not, and if Zeno exists, Parmenides does not. With other arguments of this sort they debased the view, knowing nothing of its truth (*in Prm.* 619, 21–30 Cousin).

This passage should be set alongside Plutarch's accusation that Colotes 'makes petty criticisms of [Parmenides' views] on the basis of their expression and attacks the language but not the substance when he says that Parmenides completely abolishes all things by positing one being' (*Col.* 1114 D). Zeno's description of Parmenides' detractors suggests Colotes was not the first to argue that the Parmenidean thesis of the unity of being—understood in the sense that one thing exists —leads to obvious absurdities. One might doubt whether Colotes' predecessors in this vein are those referred to by Proclus. One might

---

[24] Cherniss 1932, 130, draws attention to *Phlb.* 15d–16a to make a similar point.

even doubt the historical reliability of his report altogether. Aristotle, however, in his discussion of the Eleatics in *Physics* 1. 2, refers in passing to the proposition that what-is is one human being (185ª7, cf. 185ª24) as exemplifying a position that, like the Parmenidean thesis as he sees it, is maintained merely for the sake of argument. This example in this particular context makes it appear not improbable that arguments along the lines of the one outlined by Proclus may actually have been promulgated in Aristotle's time or earlier as a would-be *reductio* of Parmenides.

If one should no longer suppose that Zeno's arguments were directed against the Pythagorean opponents of Parmenides invented by Paul Tannery, one need not automatically accept the more plausible view of Eduard Zeller that they were directed against ordinary belief in plurality and motion.[25] Plato represents Zeno's arguments as directed against certain figures who adopted a reductive understanding of the Parmenidean thesis and purported to demonstrate its absurdity in a fundamentally eristic manner, to which Zeno responded in kind. Both those who hold that Zeno was opposing certain Pythagoreans and those who hold that he was opposing the beliefs of ordinary people feel that a chronologically plausible target must be found for his arguments. The anti-Pythagoreans have been explicit about this. Thus, for example, John Burnet: 'We know from Plato that Zeno's book was the work of his youth. It follows that he must have written it in Italy, and the Pythagoreans are the only people who can have criticized the views of Parmenides there and at that date.'[26] If the anti-Pythagorean hypothesis is rejected, the most viable candidate, from the strictly chronological point of view, appears to be ordinary belief (although others have been suggested).[27] I think we should reject the restriction

[25] Tannery 1887, ch. 10, first advanced the idea that Zeno's arguments were directed against the purportedly Pythagorean theory that the elements of physical objects incorporate the attributes of the unit, the point, and the atom. This idea was unfortunately adopted by, among others, Cornford 1922–3, 155–60, and 1939, 53–62; Burnet 1930, 314 ff.; Cherniss 1935, 43 n. 165 and 387; Lee 1936; Raven 1948, ch. 5; Zafiropulo 1950, 157–8 and ch. 3 *passim*. Zeller 1919, 747, maintained that Zeno's target was simply common opinion. Those taking this line in opposition to Tannery *et al.* include Calogero 1932, 138 ff.; van der Waerden 1940–1; Fränkel 1942, 140 n. 95; Vlastos 1953, 169–71, and 1967, 376–7; Booth 1957; Owen 1957–8, 153–6; Burkert 1972, 285–8; KRS 277 (correcting the adherence of Kirk and Raven 1957 to the anti-Pythagorean view). See Guthrie 1965, 83–5, for a survey of the controversy and further references. Barnes 1982, 234, pronounced the campaigns between the two camps over, with victory going to the latter. Unfortunately, there are still attempts to resurrect Tannery's view (e.g. Matson 1988).   [26] Burnet 1930, 314.

[27] While Tannery 1887, 249, rejected as chronologically untenable the idea that Zeno's target might be Anaxagoras or Leucippus, Solmsen 1971(*b*), 373, suggests

of chronological plausibility altogether. For it is predicated on the erroneous assumption that we can extract some kernel of historical truth regarding Zeno's actual aims from Plato's account. Figures who would have propounded arguments resembling the one preserved by Proclus would only have arisen, I take it, in the sophistic period. We know that there were opponents of Parmenides among the sophists. We have already devoted some attention to the case of Gorgias, and he will be of increasing importance as we proceed. It seems that Protagoras too may be included among Parmenides' opponents. In a work entitled 'On What-Is' (Περὶ τοῦ ὄντος)[28] he employed various arguments against those who upheld the thesis that what-is is one (ἓν τὸ ὄν). So, at least, Porphyry tells us (*ap.* Eus. *PE* 10. 3. 25). I am suggesting, then, that we have in the *Parmenides* a deliberate anachronism—that Plato presents Zeno as 'responding' to reductive attacks on Parmenides at the hands of later sophists.

Zeno has responded to certain reductive attacks upon his master's philosophy. Socrates replies to Zeno by introducing a theory that in Plato's middle period dialogues had incorporated aspects of this same philosophy. Parmenides himself presents Socrates with criticisms and corrections of his conception of intelligible reality. This series of responses presents the reader with a progressive problematization of Parmenides' thesis.[29] By structuring the responses to the thesis in the way he does, Plato indicates not only the inadequacy of the

---

without much comment that Zeno may have known the systems of Empedocles and Anaxagoras, and Furley 1967, 76–7, offers some defence for the view that Zeno was answering Anaxagoras. The *Suda*'s attribution to Zeno of an 'Exegesis of Empedocles' verses' (Ἐξήγησις τῶν Ἐμπεδοκλέους) is made somewhat less implausible by the fact (noted by Diels 1884, 359) that the term *exēgēsis* came to be used in such titles to refer to specific polemics, as in the case of the 'Exegeses of Heraclitus' (Ἡρακλείτου ἐξηγήσεις) and the 'Exegeses against Democritus' (Πρὸς τὸν Δημόκριτον ἐξηγήσεις) attributed to Heraclides Ponticus (DL 5. 88). Alcidamas *ap.* DL 8. 56 notes, furthermore, that 'Zeno and Empedocles were students of Parmenides' at the same time'. If these indications that some in antiquity may have taken Zeno to be arguing in particular against Empedocles seem unpromising, those who would like his target to have been philosophical forms of pluralism more generally might find some measure of support for this, too, having been a view taken in antiquity in the *Suda*'s attribution to him of a work 'Against the philosophers' (Πρὸς τοὺς φιλοσόφους). Whoever invented this presumably late title may even have been influenced by Pl. *Prm.* 128d2–3, where Zeno says his treatise argues 'against those advocating the many' (πρὸς τοὺς τὰ πολλὰ λέγοντας).

[28] The title does not occur in Diogenes Laertius' catalogue of Protagoras' works. Cf. Guthrie 1971, 47 n. 1, for references to the various, rather speculative attempts to identify this work with other works of Protagoras.

[29] Cf. Berti 1971 on the dialectical structure of the successive theses put forward in the dialogue.

understanding of Parmenides underlying the attacks upon him to which Zeno responds but also the inadequacy of the understanding upon which his own middle period appropriation was predicated.

The first level of understanding is implicit in the attacks of the anti-Parmenideans. The position they take, in would-be opposition to Parmenides, is that there are many things or that many things exist. They take Parmenides' thesis to be ridiculous because they understand 'one is' (ἕν ἐστι, 128d1) as meaning that there is only one thing or that only one thing exists. They would understand the companion thesis 'the all is one' (ἓν τὸ πᾶν, 128c8–b1) as meaning that everything, or all that there is, is one thing. Proclus indicates that the eristic assaults upon Parmenides' view that what-is is one were rooted in a low and vulgar interpretation of that doctrine. Plutarch declares that Colotes' analogous attack proceeded from a wilfully negligent divorce of expression from sense. Similarly, Plato indicates that the attempted demonstration by Parmenides' opponents of his thesis's ridiculous consequences is predicated upon a reductive interpretation. He does so by having Zeno distance himself somewhat from his youthful treatise. The crucial fact here is that Zeno, having confuted those who attacked Parmenides, does not feel that he has thereby directly upheld his master's teaching. By arguing that there are not many things, the contradiction of the anti-Parmenideans' thesis that there are many things, which is itself the contradiction of what they suppose to be the significance of Parmenides' thesis, Zeno does not believe he has in effect said the same thing as Parmenides. This must mean that he does not accept that Parmenides meant to say there is only one thing. Because Parmenides' detractors trivialized his thesis in their attacks, and because Zeno responded to them on their own terms, he does not think his counter-arguments directly support Parmenides. These arguments defend him by showing his opponents how ridiculous their own position is. But they do not defend him by simply saying the same thing as Parmenides in a different form. Hence Zeno's correction of Socrates. Zeno's arguments, moreover, because of their antilogical character, commit him to no particular view. Still, his refutation of Parmenides' detractors takes the reader to the second level of understanding, namely that the Parmenidean thesis is not to be understood in the sense that only one thing exists.

In responding to Zeno, Socrates differentiates the sense of 'what-is' (τὸ ὄν) in a crucial way. On the one hand, he reintroduces the anti-Parmenidean pluralists' thesis that there are many things, and he points out that it is nothing remarkable if the objects of ordinary experience partake of contrary characters such as like and unlike. But

Socrates' response to Zeno does not place him in the camp of the anti-Parmenideans. For he concerns himself with ὄντα or things-that-are (the forms) that are, not merely in the sense that they exist, but in all ways and at all times such that they are primary and fundamental to the being of other things. Parmenides praises him for not permitting the discussion to remain at the level of perceptibles but forcing it to shift to the intelligible realm (135d8–e3), presumably because Parmenides takes his own thesis to be concerned with intelligible rather than perceptible being. Socrates' theory, that is, takes the reader to the third level of understanding. Socrates' concern with the class of intelligible beings, of course, introduces Plato's own middle period appropriation of Parmenides and the kind of understanding upon which it was based. When Parmenides himself turns to criticize this theory, then, Plato is in effect calling into question his own earlier use of Parmenides.

Parmenides admires those qualities in the young Socrates that are demanded of potential guardians in the *Republic*. He twice praises his impulse towards dialectic (*Prm.* 130a8–b1, 135d2–3), and he commends his ability to grasp the intelligible (135d8–e3). These are precisely the qualities which the preliminary stages of the *Republic*'s proposed curriculum are intended to instil (*R.* 7. 533a8–10). Parmenides says Socrates at this point needs to train himself rigorously in dialectic if he is ever to apprehend the truth (*Prm.* 135c8–d6; cf. *R.* 7. 532a5–b2, e1–3). The series of difficulties he poses for Socrates demonstrates that he has attempted at too young an age and without proper training to specify the Beautiful, the Just, the Good, and each one of the forms (*Prm.* 135c8–d1). The young Socrates resembles the person described in the *Republic* as not yet possessing genuine knowledge about the forms because he cannot give a proper account of the being of each thing and survive all attempts at refuting his account without faltering in his argument (*R.* 7. 534b3–c4). Furthermore, Parmenides' description of the method of dialectic as the systematic examination of the consequences of a hypothesis and its contradiction (*Prm.* 135e8–136a2) appears to flesh out the *Republic*'s claim that dialectic is the science that examines hypotheses themselves and not merely their consequences (*R.* 7. 533c1–d1). Socrates reveals himself to be a suitable pupil for Parmenides. He is not, like the anti-Parmenideans, to be classed with the *Republic*'s sight-lovers as incapable of being led to an understanding of true being. He has, however, progressed only so far towards a proper understanding of the intelligible with his present theory. Parmenides' criticism of this theory serves as a direct indication that the middle period appropriation of Parmenides represented by that theory had itself only progressed so far in the understanding of Parmenides.

With Parmenides' criticisms of Socrates' theory we reach the fourth level of understanding. It is, like the second, largely negative. At this point in the dialogue we have little indication of where the understanding of Parmenides underlying the middle period theory of forms is in error. Nevertheless, the emphasis on Parmenides' monism suggests that the problem lies in the pluralizing nature of Plato's earlier appropriation. If Socrates shifts the focus of the discussion to intelligible being, he has still not come completely to grips with the idea that what-is is in some important sense one. This does not mean Socrates should correct his theory by reducing the plurality of forms to a single form. Parmenides does after all tell him that when philosophy takes full possession of him he will despise none of the things for which he now hesitates to posit forms (130e1–3). The implication is that, however forms are reconceived to accommodate the Parmenidean critique and the dialectical demonstration that follows, they will still be a plurality. Nevertheless, Socrates has somehow failed to understand the deeper implications of Parmenides' philosophy.

I shall not speculate at this point on what, precisely, the deeper sense of this philosophy might be. Instead, I want to develop the claim that one of Plato's concerns in the *Parmenides* is to contest certain sophistic reactions to Parmenides. I have suggested that the dialogue presents Zeno's arguments as defending Parmenides against reductive attacks by later sophists. One might suppose that attributing such anachronism to Plato tells against this proposed identification. Although one might respond to such an objection by pointing out that this type of anachronism is common in Plato, it will be more relevant to our purposes to point to one such anachronism in the *Parmenides* itself.

GORGIAS IN THE *PARMENIDES*

After pointing out various problems with the young Socrates' theory of forms, Parmenides says that one who has heard how his attempt to specify the nature of intelligible reality encounters such problems might be driven to adopt the following stance. He might maintain, first, that there are no entities such as Socrates' forms. He might say that even if there are such entities, we can have no knowledge of them. Finally, he might say that even if someone could know them, he would nevertheless be unable to communicate this knowledge to someone else:

The person hearing these problems will be at a loss and will contend that (i) these things [sc. the forms or αἱ ἰδέαι τῶν ὄντων] do not exist (οὔτε ἔστι), and that (ii) even if they should exist, it is altogether necessary that they are unknowable (ἄγνωστα) to human nature. In making these points he believes he is saying something and, as we recently said, it is amazing how difficult he is to persuade. While (ii′) it is the mark of a man of extraordinary natural ability to be able to understand that there is for each thing some general kind and a being itself in itself, (iii) it is the mark of someone still more remarkable to have discovered this and to be able to teach all these things to someone who has thoroughly examined all these difficulties (135a3–b2).

The stance Parmenides outlines here corresponds precisely to the three theses that structure Gorgias' treatise, 'On What-Is-Not'. He had declared that it is not (οὐκ ἔστι); that even if it is, it is unknowable (ἄγνωστον); and that even if it is knowable, it cannot be revealed to others (*MXG* 979a12–14).[30]

This Gorgianic scepticism vis-à-vis the existence of a stable intelligible reality should be compared both with the antagonism of Parmenides' detractors in the earlier portion of the dialogue and with Gorgias' own personal demonstration against Parmenidean Being in 'On What-Is-Not'. It is interesting in this context that Gorgias has actually been proposed as the particular target of Zeno's treatise in defence of Parmenides. Wilhelm Nestle argued that Gorgias' treatise, which he saw as directed specifically against Parmenides' conception of Being, is likely to have antedated Zeno's arguments (and Melissus') and that Plato is therefore referring to Gorgias when he has Zeno say in the *Parmenides* that his treatise was written to assist Parmenides against those who attempted to ridicule his theory.[31] This proposal has proved untenable on strictly chronological grounds. Few today would accept that Gorgias' treatise came before those of Zeno and Melissus, and the *MXG* itself indicates that Gorgias adapted

---

[30] Hays 1990, 335–7, takes this passage as the primary evidence that Plato encountered the arguments of Gorgias' treatise. This obvious and striking parallel has been virtually ignored by other commentators. Note that (ii) not only takes up Gorgias' second thesis and his specific use of the term 'unknowable' (ἄγνωστον, *MXG* 979a12, 980a18; SE, *M.* 7. 77) but also picks up the seventh and 'greatest' of Parmenides' objections to Socrates' theory, that 'entities such as we say the forms must be' are 'unknowable' (ἄγνωστα, *Prm.* 133b4 ff.); Parmenides' subsequent argument here may be viewed as an extension of Gorgias' argument for his second thesis, as given *ap.* SE, *M.* 7. 78, that 'if the things that are thought are not things-that-are, then what-is is not thought'. [31] Nestle 1922, 558 and 560–1.

certain of their arguments to his own purposes (979a21–3). Nestle's
view nevertheless shows a certain sensitivity to the representation of
Zeno's opponents in the *Parmenides* and, rather unwittingly, to the fact
that Gorgias has an important presence in the dialogue as an opponent of Parmenides and the very existence of intelligible reality.

In addition, there are certain features in Plato's characterization
of the one drawing the Gorgianic conclusions of *Parmenides* 135a–b
that subtly connect him with the *Republic*'s sight-lover. In his dis-
putatiousness (ἀμφισβητεῖν, *Prm.* 135a3–4), he believes he is saying
something (δοκεῖν . . . τι λέγειν, a6) and is remarkably difficult to
persuade (δυσανάπειστον, a7). Similarly, in the *Republic* Socrates
introduces his arguments directed towards the sight-lovers by asking
how he and Glaucon might persuade (παραμυθεῖσθαι, πείθειν, *R.* 5.
476e1) this fellow should he become difficult and dispute (χαλεπαίνη,
ἀμφισβητῇ, 476d8–9) their claim that he has only *doxa* and not knowledge; and Socrates says they will not begrudge him if he should prove
to know something (τι οἶδεν, εἰδότα τι, 476e5–6). The *Republic*'s
sight-lovers, that class of anti-metaphysicians among whom Plato
would class Gorgias, could not be persuaded to accept the basic epistemological and ontological commitments adapted from Parmenides
as grounds for the middle period theory of forms. Now in the *Parmenides*, Parmenides himself criticizes that theory in a way that
encourages the Gorgianic sight-lover to give renewed voice to his arguments against the existence of any absolute or fundamental mode of
being. Plato thus seems to acknowledge that Gorgias' original polemic
against Parmenides (as he understands it) has an apparent purchase
against his own theory that the arguments with the sight-lovers were
not sufficient to dispel.

Yet at this point Parmenides reasserts the essential demands of the
argument from the possibility of knowledge:

Nevertheless, if someone will not admit that there are general kinds of the
things that are (εἴδη τῶν ὄντων), after having considered all these objections
and others like them, and will not specify some form (εἶδος) for each individual thing, he will have nowhere to turn his intellect, since he does not admit
that there is a character (ἰδέα) for each of the things that are that is always
the same, and in this manner he will destroy the possibility of discourse altogether (*Prm.* 135b5–c2).

The dialectic Plato constructs between past and present and the structure of appropriations and rejections he builds around Parmenides has
grown quite complex by the time of the *Parmenides*, not least because
Plato now injects his own past appropriations into the battle. Gorgias

and other sophistic opponents of Parmenides, moreover, have begun to assume a heightened importance. We have already seen how Gorgias' direct attack on Parmenidean Being made him one of the best candidates for membership in the class of the *Republic*'s sight-lovers. We have been led by the *Parmenides*' opening exchange between Zeno and Socrates to identify the detractors of Parmenides targeted by Zeno's treatise with certain unspecified sophistic figures who attacked his philosophy on the basis of a reductive understanding. Finally, the voice of Gorgias has appeared after Parmenides' critique of Socrates' conception of intelligible reality to assert that there is after all no such thing. It should come as no surprise, then, that when Parmenides turns to the intricate examination of his own thesis, we encounter the Gorgianic perspective and a sophistic view of Parmenides once again, in the dialectical exercise's First Deduction (137c4–142a8).

The First Deduction proceeds from the basic assumption that the One, in so far as it is one, is not many (137c4–5). From this Parmenides infers that the One is not a whole (ὅλον) and is without parts (137c5–d3). On this basis he then infers that the One has neither beginning, middle, nor end and that it is therefore ἄπειρον or without limit (137d4–8). The One is consequently without shape, being neither straight nor spherical (137d8–138a1). The denial that the One can be characterized by these attributes directly contradicts the way Parmenides himself had described Being in his poem. He had spoken of Being as a whole (οὖλον, B8. 4, 38) and as held within the bonds of an encompassing limit or πεῖρας (B8. 30–1, cf. B8. 26, 49). As a consequence of its having a furthest limit or πεῖρας, he had described Being as like the mass of a well-rounded sphere, equally balanced in all directions from the middle (B8. 42–4).[32] Thus in the initial stages of the First Deduction we encounter an immediately apparent contrast between the characterization of the One and Parmenides' own characterization of his one Being. The contrast is important, for it indicates that something is amiss in the way the Parmenidean thesis is understood here at the outset of the deduction. The initial description of the One is in fact more reminiscent of Melissus than Parmenides. 'Therefore if it has no parts, it could have neither beginning (ἀρχήν) nor end (τελευτήν) nor middle; for such things would surely be parts of it. . . . Moreover, an end and a beginning are a limit of a thing. . . . Therefore the One is unlimited (ἄπειρον), if it has neither

---

[32] The contrast is particularly marked here, for Parmenides' own specification of Being's spherical shape as μεσσόθεν ἰσοπαλὲς πάντη (B8. 44) is reflected in 'Parmenides' ' definition of 'round' as τοῦτο οὗ ἂν τὰ ἔσχατα πανταχῇ ἀπὸ τοῦ μέσου ἴσον ἀπέχῃ (*Prm.* 137e2–3).

a beginning nor an end' (137d4–8). This directly echoes Melissus' assertion that what-is 'does not have a beginning nor an end, but it is unlimited' (ἀρχὴν οὐκ ἔχει οὐδὲ τελευτήν, ἀλλ᾿ ἄπειρόν ἐστιν, B2). Although one might be tempted to think that Plato is willing to conflate the conceptions of Melissus and Parmenides or simply ignore their differences, it seems best not to impute to him such confusion. A more acceptable, though still inadequate hypothesis would be that the First Deduction positions itself from the start as more specifically Melissan than Parmenidean such that the eventual rejection of this deduction's results constitutes a rejection of the Melissan interpretation or reworking of Parmenides. What I in fact want to argue is that, although some criticism of Melissus may be implicit in the deduction, its Melissan elements function within the context of Plato's representation of a larger Gorgianic appropriation.

The First Deduction reaches the same type of Gorgianic conclusions echoed by Parmenides after he presents his various criticisms of Socrates' theory. Although the deduction begins with the hypothesis that the One is, by the end it has concluded that the One in no way is (οὐδαμῶς ἄρα ἔστι τὸ ἕν, 141e9–10). As such, nothing can belong to the One, so that it has neither a name nor an account (λόγος). Since there can be nothing 'of' it, there can be no knowledge, perception, or opinion of or about it. All this entails that the One can be neither named nor spoken of and that it cannot be known or perceived in any way (142a1–6). In short, the First Deduction concludes that the One is not, that it is inapprehensible, and that knowledge of it is incommunicable. This is the same unacceptable Gorgianic conclusion already adumbrated by Parmenides.

The First Deduction also employs an argumentative strategy directly reminiscent of that in the first division of Gorgias' 'On What-Is-Not'.[33] The *MXG* specifies the strategy employed by Gorgias in the first division of his treatise as follows: 'For it is necessary, he says, if something is, that it is neither one nor many, neither ungenerated nor generated: so that nothing would be; for if it were something, it would be one or the other of these' (979a19–22). The *MXG*'s sub-

---

[33] Although a few other scholars have pointed to a connection between the First Deduction and Gorgias' treatise (e.g. Wahl 1926, 56–7, 59–60), Mansfeld 1985, 258–65, provides the most thorough examination to date of the specific relation between the two texts (although he is more interested in proving that the *MXG* is not Sextus' source than in the implications of Plato's use of Gorgias). Schofield 1977, 150, contrasts 'the length, subtlety, and sheer originality' of the First Deduction's arguments with 'the perfunctory character of comparable arguments in Gorgias'; but one must remember that we do not possess Gorgias' original but only imperfect summary reports by the *MXG* author and Sextus.

sequent report of arguments against change (980a2–4) and motion (980a4–9) suggests that 'neither changing nor unchanging' and 'neither moving nor at rest' also figured in the initial programme, although Gorgias' arguments that what-is is not unchanging and not at rest have dropped out of the *MXG*'s account. The arguments fulfilling this programme, namely the arguments of the treatise's first division following the personal demonstration, seek to establish that none of his predecessors' purported fundamental entities *are* by demonstrating that they have neither of the various pairs of contrary predicates. Letting 'E*x*' stand for '*x* is', we can represent Gorgias' pattern of argumentation as follows: E$x \rightarrow (\Phi x \vee \neg \Phi x)$, $\neg(\Phi x \vee \neg \Phi x)$; $\neg$Ex. Gorgias repeatedly applies this pattern by making various substitutions for the predicate variables Φ and not-Φ, specifically, generated and ungenerated, one and many, changing and unchanging. The *Parmenides*'s First Deduction likewise employs this pattern of argumentation. Parmenides argues that the One has no shape because it is neither round nor straight (137d8–138a1) and that it is nowhere because it is neither in something else nor in itself (138a2–b6). He argues that the One is neither changing nor at rest; it is not changing because it neither alters nor moves; and it does not move because it neither revolves nor undergoes locomotion (138b7–139b3). The One, he argues, is neither the same as nor different from itself or another (139b4–e6); it is neither like nor unlike itself or another (139e7–140b5); it is neither equal nor unequal, neither greater nor less (140b6–d8). It is ageless because it is neither older, younger, nor the same age as anything (140e1–141a4), and therefore it is not in time (141a5–e7). The inference from $\neg(\Phi x \vee \neg \Phi x)$ to $\neg$Ex is made at 141e7–10: 'is it then possible that something should partake of being in some way other than these?—It is not.—Therefore the One in no way partakes of being.—It seems not.—Therefore the One in no way is'. One should note that the First Deduction's argument pattern is to be contrasted with the typically Zenonian pattern. Letting 'M*x*' represent the hypothesis he attacks, 'things are many', his standard pattern of *reductio* is: M$x \rightarrow (\Phi x \wedge \neg \Phi x)$; $\neg$Mx. One might expect the Zenonian argument pattern in deductions that are indicated to be applications of Zeno's method. That we find the Gorgianic pattern instead is just one sign of his presence in the First Deduction.

Not only does this deduction's overall argumentative strategy parallel Gorgias', there are also clear correspondences at the level of individual arguments. Gorgias had argued that what-is is neither one nor many. The First Deduction begins by asserting that the One is not many and ends with the assertion that it is not one either.

A more direct use occurs in the argument that the One is nowhere because it can be neither in something else nor in itself:

Furthermore, being such, it would be nowhere: for it would be neither (i) in something else (ἐν ἄλλῳ) nor (ii) in itself (ἐν ἑαυτῷ).—How is that?—(i) If it were in something else, it would surely be encompassed (περιέχοιτο) by that in which it is, and it would touch it at many places with many parts; but since it is one and without parts and does not partake of circularity, it is impossible for it to touch at many places all round.—It is impossible.—(ii) However, if it were in itself, what encompasses it (περιέχον) would be nothing other than itself, if it were indeed in itself; for it is impossible for a thing to be in something that does not encompass it.—It is impossible.—Therefore that which encompasses would be one thing and that which is encompassed another; for the same thing will not, as a whole, suffer and produce both at once; and thus the One would no longer be one but two.—No it would not.—Therefore the One is not anywhere, being neither in itself nor in something else.—It is not (138a2–b6).

In the course of his argument that what-is is not ungenerated, Gorgias presents an argument that so closely resembles this particular argument in the *Parmenides* that Plato must have been deliberately drawing upon it. The *MXG* author tells us that Gorgias employed arguments in the style of Zeno and Melissus: 'that it is not—neither one nor many, neither ungenerated nor generated—he attempts to demonstrate in some cases in the manner of Melissus, in other cases in the manner of Zeno' (979a21–3; cf. 979b21–2, 25–6). This is just what we find him doing in the course of his demonstration that what-is is not ungenerated. The MXG author tells us that Gorgias inferred 'by the axioms of Melissus' that if what-is is ungenerated, then it must be ἄπειρον or unlimited (979b21–2). We have seen how the First Deduction begins with a similar Melissan inference to the One's being unlimited. Gorgias then argued: 'what is unlimited could not be anywhere. For neither could it be in itself (ἐν αὑτῷ) nor in another (ἐν ἄλλῳ); for in this case there would be two or more, that which is in and that which is in. But being nowhere it is nothing, according to Zeno's argument concerning place'[34] (979b23–7). Although the *MXG*'s account of the argument is quite compressed, we can see clearly enough that Plato's corresponding argument directly follows the structure of

---

[34] We do not know exactly how Zeno argued that what is nowhere is nothing. However, this was probably meant to be the conclusion of his argument against the notion of place: if everything that is is in something, i.e. place, then place too, if it is, must be in something, i.e. another place; but then this second place will also be in a place, and so *ad infinitum*; therefore, place is not. See Arist. *Ph.* 4. 1. 209ᵃ23–5, 4. 3. 210ᵇ22–5, and Eudemus fr. 78 Wehrli.

Gorgias' demonstration. Plato also picks up Gorgias' argument that if what-is is in itself, it will in fact be two things, what is in and what it is in. Because the *MXG*'s report is so elliptical, it is not clear there that the unacceptable result of what-is proving to be two things is supposed to follow from the hypothesis that it is in itself. This is, however, evident from Sextus' report: 'neither, however, is it contained in itself (περιέχεται ἐν αὐτῷ). For the same thing will be that in which and what is in it, and what-is will become two, place and body; for that in which is place, and what is in it is body. But this is absurd; therefore neither is what-is in itself' (*M*. 7. 70). Sextus also gives an argument, absent in the *MXG*, against the possibility that what-is is in something else: 'for if it is somewhere, that in which it is is other than it, and so what-is, being encompassed (ἐμπεριεχόμενον) by something, will no longer be unlimited; for what encompasses (τὸ ἐμπεριέχον) is greater than what is encompassed, but nothing is greater than the unlimited; so that what is unlimited is not anywhere' (*M*. 7. 69). Although Plato's argument on this point is rather different, presumably because he has adapted Gorgias' argument to fit into his own chain of argument, it is notable that the same terminology of 'surrounding' and 'being surrounded' recurs in both Plato and Sextus.

Parmenides goes on to argue that the One is neither changing nor at rest (*Prm*. 138b7–139b3). It appears that Gorgias likewise argued that what-is is neither changing nor unchanging. At the end of the *MXG*'s report of the first division of his treatise, we find arguments purporting to demonstrate that what-is does not change (979b38–980a8). Presumably Gorgias also argued in his typical antithetical fashion that what-is is not unchanging or at rest either, although the *MXG* report does not contain such an argument.[35] Nevertheless, in the arguments against change that the *MXG* does report, Gorgias distinguished and argued against various types of change in much the same way that Parmenides does in the First Deduction. Parmenides divides change (κίνησις) into alteration (ἀλλοίωσις) and motion (φορά), further dividing motion into revolution and locomotion; and he argues that the One cannot undergo any of these various types of change

---

[35] The text of the *MXG* becomes corrupt as it shifts to the second division's arguments that what-is is inapprehensible, although there is some doubt about where exactly to posit the lacuna or lacunae. Thus a report of Gorgias' demonstration that what-is is not at rest may have dropped out in the transmission of the text. Or it may simply be that the *MXG* author did not report this demonstration, perhaps because it was given less prominence by Gorgias himself. It is suggestive that Plato's argument that the One is not at rest is much briefer than his arguments against its undergoing various types of change.

(*Prm.* 138b8–139a3). Gorgias, though admittedly in a somewhat cruder fashion, also distinguishes and presents separate arguments against alteration (*MXG* 980a1–3) and against motion (a3–7). Parmenides takes up alteration and motion in the same order as Gorgias, and, although the correspondences between their actual arguments are not as precise as in the previous section, they still merit examination. Parmenides first argues that if the One were to undergo alteration from itself, it would no longer be one (*Prm.* 137c1–3). Gorgias argues that 'if what-is were to change, it would no longer be in the same state, but what-is would be not-being, and what-is-not would have come to be' (*MXG* 980a2–4). That is, if what-is were to change, it would no longer be what-is. Parmenides' and Gorgias' arguments are basically identical here, the difference being simply that Parmenides' subject is the One (τὸ ἕν) while Gorgias' is what-is (τὸ ὄν). Parmenides goes on at *Parmenides* 138c4–139a1 to argue against the One's undergoing motion in a pair of arguments clearly more complex than the one we find in Gorgias at *MXG* 980a4–9. Gorgias does not even distinguish between types of motion, as does Plato in arguing separately against revolution and locomotion. Nevertheless, that the fundamental notion underlying both Plato's arguments is that for the One to move it would have to have parts suggests that Plato is still drawing upon Gorgias to a certain extent, for he argues against motion on the ground that it would involve an unacceptable division of what-is.

Gorgias' presence in the First Deduction's overall argumentative strategy, in its particular arguments, and in its conclusions is so striking that Plato must have intended any reader of the dialogue to recognize it.[36] We have seen how Gorgias attacked Parmenides in his personal demonstration, and we have seen that the remainder of his

---

[36] If we possessed even a summary of Protagoras' 'On What-Is', like those we have of Gorgias' treatise, we would perhaps be able to recognize a Protagorean presence as well. This much is suggested, at any rate, by a tantalizing passage from book 1 of Porphyry's Φιλόλογος ἀκρόασις preserved *ap.* Eus. *PE* 10. 3. 24–5 (on this passage, see Heitsch 1969): 'Prosenes [a Peripatetic] said: "you have all witnessed other thefts; but that this hero himself, Plato, whose eponymous cohort we sing the praises of even today, employs many works of his predecessors (for I am ashamed to use the word 'theft' in reference to this man), you have not yet discovered." "What are you saying?" asked Callietes [a Stoic]. "I do not merely say it," he replied, "but I also furnish proof for the claim. Though the books of those born before Plato are scarce —otherwise one might perhaps observe more of the philosopher's borrowings. I by chance in my reading stumbled across Protagoras' treatise, 'On What-Is', in which I find him employing the same kind of replies against those introducing the thesis that what-is is one (ἕν τὸ ὄν)." ' Where exactly Prosenes supposes Plato has borrowed from Protagoras' attacks upon the Eleatics is not made clear, but the First Deduction of the *Parmenides* would seem one of the more likely possibilities.

treatise's first division appears to have mounted a more general attack upon his predecessors' efforts to identify certain special entities as fundamental to the being of other things. The *Parmenides*'s First Deduction suggests that Plato saw reflections of Gorgias' anti-Parmenidean stance in more parts of his treatise than the personal demonstration. It is very interesting to see Plato giving Parmenides the chance to respond to Gorgias' attack. He does so first at 135a–b by having him mark as unacceptable the Gorgianic position that there is no intelligible reality (and that even if there is, it is unknowable and inexpressible). Whereas Gorgias' personal demonstration had sought to perform a *reductio* on the Parmenidean argument from the possibility of knowledge, Plato's Parmenides now reasserts that argument against Gorgias' conclusions. These same conclusions are then reached in the First Deduction, where they are again rejected. Parmenides concludes the deduction by asking whether it is possible for things to be such with respect to the One that it is not, is inapprehensible, and is inexpressible. Aristoteles answers that it is not possible, and Parmenides begins the next deduction by expressing the hope that some different result may emerge if they return to the beginning to consider afresh the hypothesis that the One is (142a6–b2). Thus Plato in the First Deduction presents a certain sophistic appropriation of Parmenides and gives Parmenides himself the opportunity to repudiate it. We shall see that this is also the case in certain other deductions in the *Parmenides*'s exploration of Parmenides' hypothesis. First, however, we need to identify the other sophistic appropriations of Parmenides.

6

Sophistic Parmenideanism in the *Sophist*

In the *Sophist*, the Eleatic Visitor quotes Parmenides B7. 1–2 as having provided the basis for the parallel problems of appearance and
falsehood. Appearing but not really being and saying things that are
not the case both involve an assumption that what-is-not somehow
is. Parmenides, the Visitor says, expressly forbade any such assumption: 'when we were young, my boy, the great Parmenides used to
maintain this firmly from beginning to end, so saying on each occasion both in plain speech and in verse—"for never will this be made
acceptable," he says, "that things that are not are; but as you inquire[1]
restrain your thought from this path"' (*Sph.* 237a4–9). Later, at 241d,
as he sets out to explain the nature of appearance and falsehood, the
Visitor says he hopes Theaetetus will not consider him a 'parricide'
for forcibly asserting, against Parmenides' injunction, that what-is-
not *is* in some respect and that what-is *is not* in some respect. These
two passages have been central in determining the common view of
Plato's attitude towards Parmenides. For they seem to indicate that
in explaining how not-being is involved in appearance and falsehood,
Plato sees himself as directly contradicting Parmenides' 'doctrine' that
the other of being is absolute non-being.[2] Plato would thus appear
to hold something like the modern view of Parmenides as a strict

---

[1] διζήμενος. Plato himself gives the more amply attested διζήσιος when he quotes
these lines again at 258d2–3 (cf. above, Ch. 4, n. 38).

[2] The assumption that Plato is engaging in a direct refutation of Parmenides in the
Sophist is so ingrained and widespread in modern scholarship as to make citation of
specific authors superfluous. See Frère 1991, however, for a stimulating recent study
devoted specifically to how Parmenides figures in the *Sophist*. Frère poses what I take
to be the essential question: 'Comment Platon lit-il Parménide avant de le discuter?'
(127). He questions whether interpreters of Plato have taken sufficient account of what
the *Sophist* has to say concerning Parmenides and accordingly sets himself the task
'de relire le texte de Parménide à la lumière des analyses et des discussions qu'en fais-
ait . . . Platon dans le *Sophiste*' (131). Another recent study, Pelletier 1990, gives the
impression of appreciating the need to understand what Plato took Parmenides'
argument to be before addressing how the *Sophist* responds to it, but Pelletier unfortunately commits the familiar error of adopting at the outset an independent
interpretation of Parmenides (dubbing this the 'standard interpretation', for which
he appeals especially to Furth 1968) prior to examining the actual features of the
Platonic reception.

monist who thought the mixed being of the phenomenal world must in the end reduce to non-being. If this is the case, however, then Plato's view of Parmenides in the *Sophist* is incompatible with the view I have argued lies behind the *Republic* 5 appropriation and with the way I have suggested the Parmenidean thesis is successively problematized in the opening exchanges of the *Parmenides*.

One reason that Plato's middle period view of the status of *doxa* and its objects has been presumed a departure from Parmenides is that the evidence of the *Sophist* for Plato's view of Parmenides' stance on the status of appearance seems so clear. We have seen, however, that there is no discernible discontinuity in *Republic* 5 as Plato moves from the Parmenidean contrast between what-completely-is and what-is-not-at-all to isolate as the object of *doxa* the intermediate that both is and is not. We have also seen clear signs of continuity in the way Plato's description of the sight-lovers draws upon Parmenides' description of mortals. One might suppose that as he renews his engagement with Parmenides in the later dialogues, Plato comes to change his view on the status of the world of ordinary experience in Parmenides. I do not believe that this is the case. Instead, I think that the *Sophist*'s representation of Parmenides is rather more complex than it has been taken to be. We have seen that the *Parmenides*'s successive problematization of the thesis that what-is is one marks the strict monistic interpretation of this thesis as a low-level, reductive understanding. We have also seen Parmenides himself given the opportunity to reject one particular sophistic appropriation of his thesis. I want to show now that in the *Sophist* Plato is similarly concerned with confronting certain reductive understandings of Parmenides. One of Plato's aims in defeating the Sophist is to recover the Parmenidean legacy from certain sophistic appropriations to which it had been subjected. We shall see that the sophistic appropriations that figure in the *Sophist* also figure in the dialectical exercise of the *Parmenides*.

The dialogue's opening exchange between Theodorus and Socrates serves the important function of putting the Parmenidean legacy at stake at the very outset by calling into question what kind of thinkers are to be considered his legitimate heirs. Theodorus introduces the Eleatic Visitor as 'an associate of Parmenides and Zeno'[3] (*Sph.* 216a3).

---

[3] Since I shall argue that the initial exchange between Theodorus and Socrates makes the point that the followers (or purported followers) of Parmenides cannot be identified as a single homogeneous group, I think it best not to understand the phrase ἑταῖρον δὲ τῶν ἀμφὶ Παρμενίδην καὶ Ζήνωνα as including a reference to their circle of associates. The translation 'an associate of Parmenides and Zeno' is thus preferable to White's 'a member of the group who gather around Parmenides and Zeno'

That the Eleatic Visitor subsequently speaks of what Parmenides used to say 'to us when we were young' (237a5) makes it clear that the Eleatic Visitor is supposed to have been a disciple of Parmenides himself. Once Theodorus has introduced the Visitor as an associate of Parmenides and Zeno, Socrates is immediately concerned about his character and inquires whether he might be some 'god of cross-examination' (θεὸς ὤν τις ἐλεγκτικός, 216b6). Theodorus attempts to dispel Socrates' worries by assuring him that the Visitor is more moderate than 'those who devote their energy to eristic disputes' (216b8). Socrates' concern seems to be that the Visitor belongs to a certain class of disputatious thinkers who positioned themselves as representatives of Eleaticism. Theodorus seems to recognize at once those to whom Socrates is alluding. By responding that the Visitor is not one of those versed in the arts of eristic, Theodorus in effect indicates that the eristics have been most successful in appropriating the Parmenidean legacy. The Eleatic Visitor, Theodorus makes clear, does not belong to this camp. He is not an eristic but a philosopher in the true sense (216a4, cf. 216b9–c1). That he is distinguished in this way from those other contemporary representatives of Eleaticism raises the question of who Parmenides' legitimate heirs really are.

The dynamic of allusion in this opening passage may be still more involved. For one might regard Theodorus as misunderstanding what Socrates means by calling the Visitor a (potential) 'god of cross-examination'. He takes Socrates to mean that the Visitor might be an eristic rather than a true philosopher. What Socrates actually says might suggest a rather different type of Parmenidean. He is alluding

(White 1993, 1; cf. Diès 1925, 'il appartient au cercle des disciples de Parménide et Zénon', and Cornford 1935(a), 165, 'he belongs to the school of Parmenides and Zeno'). The present translation extends the systematic analysis by Radt 1980 of uses of the expression οἱ περί X to the parallel expression τῶν ἀμφὶ Π. καὶ Z. Radt shows, in the first place, that οἱ περί + acc. pronominis is an exclusive use, indicating those in the circle around X but not including X himself (e.g. Pl. R. 8. 566e2–3, γῆν διένειμε [sc. ὁ τύραννος] δήμῳ τε καὶ τοῖς περὶ ἑαυτόν). However, οἱ περί + acc. nominis proprii has an *inclusive* sense, either (1) indicating X *and* his circle/associates (e.g. Pl. Phlb. 44c1–2, ἃς νῦν οἱ περὶ Φίληβον ἡδονὰς ἐπονομάζουσιν; Cra. 440c1–3, ταῦτ' οὖν πότερόν ποτε οὕτως ἔχει ἢ ἐκείνως ὡς οἱ περὶ Ἡράκλειτόν τε λέγουσιν καὶ ἄλλοι πολλοί) or (11) functioning as a vague paraphrase for X alone (to Radt's examples of (11) may be added [Menander] Περὶ ἐπιδεικτικῶν 1. 2. 2 Spengel, referring to the φυσικοὶ ὕμνοι composed by οἱ περὶ Παρμενίδην καὶ Ἐμπεδοκλέα). Other places where οἱ ἀμφὶ X functions analogously to οἱ περὶ X in Plato are Ap. 18b3, Prt. 316d8–9, Men. 99b6, Hp. Ma. 281c5–6, Euthd. 286c2, 305d6–7, Cra. 400a1, c5, and Tht. 170c6–7. Radt 1980, 50, notes that the boundary between (1) and (11) cannot always be drawn sharply, but, for the reason indicated, τῶν ἀμφὶ Π. καὶ Z. is best understood as belonging to (11).

to *Odyssey* 9. 270–1 when he says the Visitor might be some god surreptitiously come to watch over their discussion. Plato also had Socrates allude to Homer in the *Theaetetus*, at the point where he recalls having met Parmenides as a young man and having formed an impression of him as 'venerable and awe-inspiring' (183e5–6; cf. Hom. *Il.* 3. 172, *Od.* 8. 22, 14. 234). The meeting he is referring to is, of course, that recounted in the *Parmenides* itself. Socrates' description here in the *Sophist* of the type of figure he fears the Visitor might prove to be—'one who will watch over and will cross-examine (ἐλέγξων) those of us who are weak in arguments, a sort of god of cross-examination'—might in fact be thought a fair characterization of Parmenides as portrayed in the earlier dialogue.[4] Parmenides there is anything but an eristic. If Socrates' description of the figure he fears the Visitor might be puts the reader in mind of Parmenides him-self, then Theodorus' erroneous presumption that Socrates fears the Visitor might be an eristic effectively highlights the potential difficul-ties in distinguishing the eristic from the non-eristic Parmenidean. Since the opening exchange naturally leads Socrates to the dialogue's principal theme, the distinction between the genuine Philosopher and the Sophist, we are led to expect, finally, that the examination of this larger problem will involve some sorting out of the rival claims to the Parmenidean inheritance.[5]

Socrates remarks that it is often quite difficult for people to dis-tinguish between philosophers, statesmen, and sophists, and he asks the Eleatic Visitor what people in his part of the world think. The Visitor indicates that the Eleans do distinguish the three types, but he is at first reluctant to say exactly how because of the great diffi-culty involved in clearly defining each one's nature. The company eventually agree that he should discuss the matter with Theaetetus as his respondent, and the Visitor himself proposes that they first

---

[4] Note also the reference to the *Parmenides* at *Sph.* 217c–d, where the Visitor says he prefers to employ the method of questioning that Socrates says Parmenides him-self employed on the occasion of their discussion in his youth.

[5] Bluck 1975, 31, who, noting that the *Sophist* will be concerned with responding to the linguistic legerdemain of certain thinkers who, as the Megarians seem to have done, appealed to the authority of the Eleatic tradition, is puzzled at Plato's intro-duction of the Eleatic Visitor: 'it is not obvious why Plato should choose an Eleatic as a *dramatis persona* through whom to criticize Eleatic eristic.' The present hypo-thesis should go some way towards answering his question. Cf. Cherubin 1993, who, attempting to answer the question what is Eleatic about the Eleatic Visitor, and not-ing the underlying Eleaticism of much sophistry, supposes that the introduction of the Visitor leads us 'to ask what if any the differences are between Eleatic and sophist' (215).

concentrate on defining the Sophist. After a preliminary example of
the definitional method of division he proposes to employ, followed
by a series of initial divisions characterizing the Sophist, the Visitor
and Theaetetus come to the seventh and most important attempt to
define the Sophist (232b1–236c7). Here they attempt to capture this
elusive figure by deploying the set of distinctions between reality
and appearance, knowledge and *doxa*, that Socrates had somewhat
unsuccessfully tried to force upon the sight-lovers in *Republic* 5.
They first establish that the Sophist practises the art of contradiction
(ἀντιλογική), which enables him to engage in debate on any subject
whatsoever (232b1–e5). The Sophist obviously does not have true
knowledge of every subject, but he is nevertheless capable of appearing to his audience as if he does in virtue of his 'apparent knowledge'
or δοξαστικὴ ἐπιστήμη (232e6–233d2). This apparent knowledge
consists of an ability to produce verbal images or illusions (εἴδωλα
λεγόμενα, 234c5–6; τὰ ἐν τοῖς λόγοις φαντάσματα, 234e1). In an
attempt to bring about the final capture of the Sophist, the Visitor now
divides the art of image-making or imitation (ἡ εἰδωλοποιικὴ τέχνη,
235b8–9; ἡ μιμητική, 235d1–2, 236b1) into the art of representation
(ἡ εἰκαστικὴ τέχνη), which involves production of likenesses resembling and preserving the proportions of their models (235d6–e2),
and the art of illusion or appearance (ἡ φανταστικὴ τέχνη), which
involves production of merely apparent but not genuine likenesses
(236b4–c4).

This distinction between types of verbal image-making parallels
the distinction between the genuine and spurious rhetoric in the
Phaedrus.[6] There Socrates criticized the teachers of rhetoric for holding that the aspiring orator need not know the truth about what is just
and good but only how to make things appear just and good to his
audience (*Phdr.* 272d2 ff., cf. 259e4 ff.). The orator will thus concern
himself primarily with what is plausible or persuasive (τὸ πιθανόν)
and with what is likely or reasonable (τὸ εἰκός). Since the rhetoricians
define what is likely as what appears to most people to be the case (τὸ
τῷ πλήθει δοκοῦν, 273a6–b1), they can claim that the orator need not
know the truth concerning his subject. Socrates, however, points out
that inherent in the concept of likelihood is the idea of resemblance

---

[6] Cornford 1935(*a*), 198, presumes the description of the Sophist as image-maker
should be elucidated by comparison with the attack upon art as imitation in *Republic*
10. The εἰκαστική/φανταστική distinction as drawn in the *Sophist*, however, has no
genuine analogue in the *Republic*'s discussion, and Cornford's attempts to restrict the
sense of 'likeness' in the *Sophist* in order to force the distinction upon the *Republic*
is completely *ad hoc*. Cf. the criticism of Cornford on this point by Bluck 1975, 59–60.

to truth and that as a consequence the orator who has knowledge of the truth will best be able to produce conviction in his audience (273d3–6, cf. 262a–c). Thus the *Phaedrus*'s distinction between genuine and spurious rhetoric amounts to a distinction between modes of producing conviction that is directly analogous to the *Sophist*'s division of the genus image-making into representation and illusion. Plato's basic charge against both rhetoricians and sophists is that they traffic in mere appearance without having any knowledge of the truth. This was already the accusation levelled against rhetoricians in the *Gorgias*, and it is the charge brought against the sight-lovers in the *Republic*. The attempt to define the Sophist as a producer of verbal illusions, as a practitioner of the 'phantastic' art of image-making, is thus the culmination of a long-standing concern. Plato has from at least as far back as the *Gorgias* felt it imperative to draw a defensible distinction between knowledge and belief, reality and appearance.

The rhetorician, the sight-lover, and the Sophist will attempt to respond to Plato's charge that they operate at the level of mere appearance by bringing the counter-charge that Plato's manner of distinguishing between reality and appearance is ultimately confused. Having divided the art of image-making into the production of representations and the production of appearances, the Visitor expresses some doubt about which division the Sophist should be placed in (*Sph.* 235d2–3, 236c9–10). He does not hesitate because he seriously doubts whether the Sophist should be categorized as a producer of appearances but because he knows the Sophist will attempt to elude being so defined by denying the very validity of the category of appearance. He has cleverly taken refuge, the Visitor says, in a class that is notoriously difficult to track down (236d1–3; cf. 239c6–d4). Towards the end of the dialogue, when the division of image-making is resumed at the point at which it is broken off here, the Visitor comments on this impasse: 'we said that we were at a loss over which division we should place the Sophist in. . . . And as we puzzled over this, we were thrown into even greater darkness by the emergence of an argument disputing the legitimacy of all these terms and declaring that there is no such thing as a likeness or an image or an appearance, on the ground that there is never falsehood in any way anywhere' (264c7–d2). The central portion of the dialogue is concerned with providing a coherent account of appearance and falsehood in order to overcome the Sophist's resistance to being defined as a producer of appearances.

The Visitor articulates the paired problems of appearance and falsehood as follows:

This appearing and seeming, but not being, and saying things, but not true things—all these matters have always been, and still are now, full of perplexity. For how one can say that there really are such things as making statements or having beliefs that are false, and having said this not be caught up in contradiction is, Theaetetus, altogether difficult (236e1–237a1).

The difficulty with the concepts of appearance and falsehood is that any analysis of them demands positing that what-is-not is—τὸ μὴ ὂν εἶναι (237a3–4). Parmenides, the Visitor says, expressly forbade any such possibility (237a4–9). Since Plato, at a certain point in his career, came to see the philosophy of Parmenides as the most important antecedent for his own attempt to draw the distinction between reality and appearance, it is particularly interesting to see the Sophist also appealing to Parmenides in denying the viability of the distinction. We need to try to understand the nature and background of this appeal, for doing so should make it clear that this appeal reflects the sophistic appropriations of Parmenides Plato is concerned to counter rather than his own considered view.[7] Later we will see that, not only is the appeal here inconsistent with Plato's middle period use and with his understanding of Parmenides in the *Parmenides*, it does not even prove consistent with the later representation of Parmenides in the *Sophist* itself.

THE IMPOSSIBILITY OF FALSEHOOD

One can see more or less clearly how the sophistic thesis that falsehood is impossible was supposed to derive from Parmenides. The key text is *Euthydemus* 283e7–286b6, where the sophists Euthydemus and Dionysodorus present a series of arguments intended to demonstrate the impossibility of falsehood and contradiction. These arguments

---

[7] In discussing this stretch of the *Sophist*, Bodunrin 1971, 30–1, comments: 'We are therefore to understand . . . that the sort of assumptions and arguments upon which the advocates of the theory Plato wishes to criticize base their case for the impossibility of falsehood, are the same or similar to those on which Parmenides' doctrine rests.' He points out that the basis for attributing the impossibility of falsehood thesis to Parmenides is weak and so infers that Plato is simply wrong when he signals that his sophistic opponents made assumptions similar to those of Parmenides. Bodunrin's study is helpful here in so far as it points to the complex interplay of relations among Plato, the sophists, and Parmenides (see also Bodunrin 1975). On this particular point, however, instead of supposing Plato mistaken in aligning the sophistic view with Parmenides, one should see Plato as signalling the sophistic appeal while leaving it (temporarily) open whether he sees this appeal as rooted in an adequate understanding of Parmenides.

depend upon the common Greek idiom whereby the expression 'to say what is (the case)'—τὰ ὄντα λέγειν—has the sense 'to speak the truth'. The exchange between Socrates and Hermogenes at *Cratylus* 385b2–9 provides a good example: 'come, then, tell me this: do you say there is such a thing as making true statements and false?—I do.— So then there would be true statement, and statement that is false.— Certainly.—So then the statement that speaks of what is (the case) as it is, is true, while that which speaks of it as it is not, is false (οὗτος [sc. λόγος] ὃς ἂν τὰ ὄντα λέγῃ ὡς ἔστιν, ἀληθής· ὃς δ'ἂν ὡς οὐκ ἔστιν, ψευδής)?—Yes.' A passage later in the dialogue indicates how this manner of expression can lead to the thesis that falsehood is impossible. There it has emerged that Socrates' other interlocutor, Cratylus, is willing to adopt this stance. As in the *Euthydemus*, Socrates remarks that there are now and have been in the past many who say that false statements are impossible (*Cra.* 429d1–3). Cratylus responds by asking: 'how could someone speaking of that which he is speaking of not "say what is" (τὸ ὂν λέγοι)? Or isn't this what making false statements is, "not saying what is" (τὸ μὴ τὰ ὄντα λέγειν)?' (429d4–6).[8]

Euthydemus' first argument (*Euthd.* 283e7–284a8) is designed to show that everyone always tells the truth. He gets his interlocutor Ctesippus to agree that if someone speaks falsely, he must be speaking about or mentioning the thing his speech is about, and that if he is speaking about this thing, he is not speaking about any other of the things that are. In speaking of this thing, he is speaking of something that is, so that in speaking of it he is saying what is (the case)—τὸ ὂν λέγει—that is, he is telling the truth. Ctesippus facetiously responds that whoever argues like this is not saying what is (the case)—οὐ τὰ ὄντα λέγει (284b1–2). So Euthydemus presents him with another argument (284b3–c6). He begins this time by getting Ctesippus to agree that things that are not are not (τὰ μὴ ὄντα οὐκ ἔστιν), that one cannot act or have an effect upon things that are not, and that speaking is an activity and a means of bringing about effects. Therefore no one can speak of things that are not, that is, no one can say things that are false, for this would involve acting upon things that are not. At this point Dionysodorus takes over. After the rather trivial sophism at 284c9–285a1, he argues for a corollary to the impossibility of falsehood, namely that contradiction (τὸ ἀντιλέγειν) is impossible (285d7–286b6). He gets Ctesippus to agree that everything has an account

---

[8] Cf. Procl. *in Cra.* 37, 1–4: 'Antisthenes maintained that contradiction is impossible. For, he says, every statement tells the truth. For someone speaking says something; and someone who says something says what is (the case). But one who says what is (the case) tells the truth.'

or *logos* and that a thing's *logos* must describe it as it is rather than as it is not. Support for this second premiss comes from the conclusion of Euthydemus' arguments—no one can speak of something as it is not since no one can speak of what is not. He then considers in turn the various possibilities that might arise to show that contradiction never in fact occurs. If two people give an account or *logos* of the same thing, there can be no contradiction, given that each must be speaking of it as it is. If neither person gives a *logos* of the thing, then there can be no contradiction since neither has the thing in mind at all. Finally, if only one of two people gives a *logos* of a thing, there is again no contradiction.

Even if, as seems most likely, Euthydemus and Dionysodorus were historical figures and not, as some have maintained, composite caricatures of sophistry patched together by Plato,[9] it nevertheless remains the case that many of their arguments, and in particular these against the possibility of falsehood and contradiction, draw upon earlier sophistic sources (whether the pastiche is Plato's invention or that of the brothers themselves may be ultimately indeterminable). Plato gives a clear signal of this when he has Socrates say at the conclusion of Dionysodorus' argument that he has heard it many times before because Protagoras and his associates (οἱ ἀμφὶ Πρωταγόραν) and those even older still used to employ it (286b8–c3). For Protagoras, the impossibility of falsehood and contradiction seems to have been a consequence of his measure doctrine.[10] The idiomatic expression οἱ ἀμφὶ Πρωταγόραν[11] most likely does not refer to Protagoras alone but, as indicated, has the broader sense 'Protagoras and his associates', for we know that both Gorgias and Prodicus propounded the thesis that falsehood and contradiction are impossible.

The *MXG*'s compressed account of the second principal division of Gorgias' 'On What-Is-Not' picks up after a lacuna and begins:

[9] This view was first put forward by Grote 1875, i, 536–7. Cf. Keulen 1971, 8 n. 9, for others adopting this position. Prächter 1932 argued for their historicity, expanding the arguments of Wilamowitz-Möllendorff 1919, ii, 155–6, by collecting the evidence outside the *Euthydemus* itself that could not have simply been based on Plato's portrait. Today there is general agreement that Euthydemus and probably Dionysodorus were historical figures (cf. Keulen 1971, 8 and n. 11; Canto 1989, 27–8).

[10] Cf. Pl. *Tht.* 166d ff., esp. 167d1–3; SE, *M.* 7. 60; DL 9. 51, 53. Also, Ammon. *in Cat.* 60a,16–17: 'for this man [sc. Protagoras] said that no thing has a definite nature. Therefore he also said that it is not possible for anyone to say what is false.' Rankin 1981, 25–6, noting that Protagoras is supposed to have entitled one of his treatises *Antilogiai* or 'Contradictions' and that he is reported to have held that there are at least two *logoi* on every subject, doubts whether Protagoras could have subscribed to the impossibility of contradiction thesis 'in its undiluted strength'.

[11] Cf. above, n. 3.

'. . . for all things that are thought must be, and what-is-not, if indeed it is not, cannot be thought. But if this is the case, no one could say anything false, he says, not even if one were to say that chariots are racing in the sea. For all these things would be' (980a9–12, see Appendix II). The evidence that Prodicus, too, argued against the possibility of falsehood comes from a papyrus, discovered in 1941 at Tura in Egypt, containing a previously unknown Greek commentary on *Ecclesiastes* by Didymus the Blind:[12]

A certain paradoxical opinion is reported of Prodicus, that 'contradiction is impossible'. How does he maintain this? It is contrary to everyone's belief and opinion. For everyone, when they converse, says contradictory things in both practical and theoretical affairs. He maintains dogmatically that 'contradiction is impossible'. For if two people contradict one another, they are both speaking; but it is impossible that they are both speaking with reference to the same thing. For he says that only the person who says what is true and who describes things as they are speaks of them. But the person opposing him does not speak, not [describing?] the thing [as it is?] . . . The opinion is called paradoxical, since it is contrary to everyone's opinion.

The scholars who brought this text to light employ it to counteract the tendency to see a specific attack upon Antisthenes behind Plato's discussion of the impossibility of contradiction.[13] For while Antisthenes did maintain a version of the thesis,[14] *Euthydemus* 286c indicates that the thesis was already current in certain philosophical circles at least a generation before Antisthenes.[15] The papyrus, and the portion of Gorgias' treatise just quoted, confirm this.[16]

[12] For the text translated here, see Binder and Liesenborghs 1976, 453 (also Binder 1979).

[13] Cf. Keulen 1971, 83 n. 98, for a retrospective of the debate on this point.

[14] Cf. Arist. *Metaph.* Δ. 29. 1024^{b}32–4 and Alex. Aphr. *in Metaph.* 434, 25–435, 20 = Giannantoni 1990, V A 152; Arist. *Top.* 1. 11. 104^{b}20–1 and Alex. Aphr. *in Top.* 79, 7–22 = Giannantoni 1990, V A 153; Procl. *in Cra.* 12, 18–23; DL 9. 53.

[15] Binder and Liesenborghs 1976, 456–7; cf. Keulen 1971, 82–4.

[16] Binder and Liesenborghs 1976 draws the conclusion that not even Isocrates need be referring to Antisthenes in particular, as he has generally been taken to do, when he says that 'some have grown old denying that it is possible to say what is false, or to contradict, or to utter two opposed accounts regarding the same things' (*Orat.* 10. 1). Isocrates' ascription of these theses is general and anonymous (note the plural οἱ μέν), capable of including Prodicus, Gorgias, *et al.*, as well as Antisthenes—or perhaps even in preference to him since, as Binder and Liesenborghs point out (457–8), Dionysius of Halicarnassus reports (*Isoc.* 1) that Isocrates was a student of both Prodicus and Gorgias. In any case, I shall concern myself primarily with these earlier texts and, especially, with the arguments of the *Euthydemus* rather than with Antisthenes. It simply is not true, as Hawtrey 1981, 24 (cf. 105–7), claims, that 'it is almost certainly Antisthenes who is responsible' for the sophism that contradiction is impossible.

Gorgias and Prodicus may well have been influenced by Protagoras, if he was indeed the first among the sophists to maintain that contradiction is impossible. But they will have fashioned independent arguments for the thesis, that is, arguments that do not start from Protagoras' measure doctrine. Plato himself suggests the point of departure for these alternative arguments when he has Socrates say in the *Euthydemus* that in addition to Protagoras 'those even older still' (οἱ ἔτι παλαιότεροι) denied the possibility of contradiction and falsehood. This has widely, and I think correctly, been understood as a reference to the Eleatics.[17] The key principle in Gorgias' denial of the possibility of falsehood is that 'all things that are thought must be' (ἅπαντα δεῖν γὰρ φρονούμενα εἶναι). This has clear enough analogues in Parmenides B3, τὸ γὰρ αὐτὸ νοεῖν ἐστίν τε καὶ εἶναι, and B6. 1, χρὴ τὸ λέγειν τὸ νοεῖν τ᾽ ἐὸν ἔμμεναι, which in the present context one may translate respectively as: 'for the same thing is to be thought and to be', and 'what one can speak and think of must be what-is'. Likewise, the corollary to Gorgias' principle—'what-is-not (τὸ μὴ ὄν), if it is not, cannot be thought'—has its analogue in Parmenides B2. 7, 'for you could not know what-is-not' (οὔτε γὰρ ἂν γνοίης τό γε μὴ ἐόν).[18] Prodicus' argument also seems to have its Eleatic undercurrent, particularly in the conception of truth as describing things 'as they are' (ὡς ἔχει) and of this being the only genuine form of speech.

To be in a proper position to assess Parmenides' influence on later Greek thought, we must first try to understand the interpretations of his poem underlying its subsequent appropriations. With Gorgias and Prodicus, however, application of this general principle is difficult.

---

[17] Cf. e.g. Taylor 1911, 96 n. 1; Sprague 1962, 17, and 1965, 28 n. 46; Hawtrey 1981, 110; Canto 1989, 204 n. 131. Some have supposed the reference may be to Heraclitus, since in the *Theaetetus* Plato says the Heraclitean flux doctrine lies behind Protagoras' relativism (e.g. Guthrie 1971, 182 n. 2, who in any case thinks the *Euthydemus*'s reference to earlier thinkers need not be taken seriously), but the language of Euthydemus' and Dionysodorus' arguments is decidedly more Parmenidean than Heraclitean. Keulen 1971, 87 n. 120, having argued that the Protagorean denial of the principle of contradiction was 'das zentrale systematische Motiv der sophistischen Eristik' (86), attempts to play down its probably Eleatic heritage by distinguishing between 'sophistische Eristik', for which Protagoras provides the point of departure, and 'eleatische Eristik', which bypasses the sophists to influence Eubulides and the Megarians. This kind of segregation cannot succeed, however, for although Protagoras' argument against contradiction does not seem to have been particularly Eleatic in character, this is not the case with those of Gorgias, Prodicus, and Euthydemus and Dionysodorus.

[18] On these parallels, cf. Newiger 1973, 133. Bröcker 1958, 437, tries to connect what Gorgias goes on to say in this division about seeing and hearing with Parmenides B7.

Our evidence for their actual arguments is incomplete. Even if it were better, it might still be unclear whether anything like an 'interpretation' of Parmenides lies behind their appropriations. The situation is not unlike that with Xeniades of Corinth, who should also be mentioned in this context. Xeniades is an (apparently) fifth-century thinker who seems to have reacted to Parmenides in a radical and rather idiosyncratic manner. Sextus Empiricus classifies him as a thinker who denied the existence of a criterion (*P.* 2. 18, *M.* 7. 48), attributing to him the theses that all impressions are untrustworthy (*P.* 2. 76, *M.* 7. 388) and that nothing is true (*M.* 7. 399, 8. 5). His extreme epistemological stance is coupled with equally extreme views on the nature of change; Xeniades, Sextus says, maintained that 'all things are false, and every impression and belief is false, and everything that comes to be comes to be from what-is-not, and everything that perishes passes away into what-is-not' (*M.* 7. 53 = 81 DK). Xeniades would seem to have accepted the Parmenidean analysis of change at B8. 7–21 but not the prohibition against it. It is probably futile to speculate, however tantalizing Sextus' synopsis might be, on how Parmenides might also have influenced his conclusion that all things are false. Perhaps Xeniades accepted the Parmenidean analysis of belief as erroneous in so far as it is directed towards objects that both are and are not (B6. 4–9) while simultaneously accepting the statement that belief is all-pervasive even though there is no true conviction to be found in it (B1. 30–2). Or perhaps he meant, somehow, to take the more radical step of rejecting the first path of inquiry in B2 in favour of the second. Whatever his reasoning may have been, the views Sextus attributes to him are further proof of the diversity of the sophistic engagement with the logic of Eleaticism.[19] Still, any attempt to explain and account for Xeniades' Eleaticism can be no more than speculation due to the insufficiency and potential unreliability of our evidence. This is unfortunately also the case with Gorgias' and Prodicus' arguments against the possibility of falsehood and contradiction. We cannot tell whether Gorgias' and Prodicus' 'use'

---

[19] Xeniades' encounter with Parmenides may have been influenced by those of other sophists. Attempts have been made to connect him with Protagoras (e.g. Zeller 1919, 1323–4) and, more plausibly, with Gorgias (e.g. Levi 1930, 40; Gigon 1936, 205–6; and, rather less cautiously, Untersteiner 1957, 162–3). On Xeniades, see also von Fritz 1967 and Zoumpos 1960. Zoumpos argues that Sextus' Xeniades should be identified with the Corinthian Xeniades reported to have purchased Diogenes of Sinope as tutor to his children (DL 6. 30–2, 36, 74), an identification which would place him in the first third of the 4th cent. rather than in the 5th cent. The earlier (and more likely) date has been inferred from Sextus' grouping him with other 5th-cent. figures and mentioning that Democritus referred to him.

of Parmenides consists in anything more than the most superficial transference of Parmenidean wording to the problems of falsehood and contradiction.

Fortunately, the *Euthydemus*'s more extensive arguments provide sufficient indication of how this particular sophistic appropriation *does* presume a certain interpretation of Parmenides. The arguments of Euthydemus and Dionysodorus have been variously analysed as committing the fallacy of *secundum quid*, as equivocating between existential and copulative uses of the verb 'to be', and, perhaps most accurately, as failing to recognize that reference is a necessary but not sufficient condition for truth because they fail to make a proper distinction between subject and predicate.[20] We shall be less concerned here with the analysis of the flaws in their arguments than with how these arguments use Parmenides.[21] A fifth-century sophist conducting investigations into the topic of truth and falsehood would have found something of interest in Parmenides. Euthydemus' and Dionysodorus' arguments on the theme suggest that such a sophist would have been likely to look at the following portions of his poem in the following way.[22]

---

[20] Miller 1977, 264, attributes this kind of confusion to Parmenides himself and is thus one particularly interesting case of a modern interpretation of Parmenides that parallels an ancient sophistic interpretation. Miller sees B8. 35a and B8. 36a as implying that one 'cannot hold a belief or make a statement that is true or false without securing a reference to the world' and B8.35b as adding the restriction that 'in order to make a statement about something, one must truly represent it. . . . Parmenides' dictum, so understood, permits only true affirmative statements. . . . his dictum is the result of the insight that when we make a statement we try to do two things: to secure a reference to the world and to reveal things as they are. Parmenides has failed to recognize that these two tasks are quite different.'

[21] Sprague 1962, xiii (cf. 13–14, 25, 29, 33), reasonably enough describes the two brothers as 'neo-Eleatics'. However, she sees their Eleaticism as reflecting a clash between Parmenidean monism and Plato's own metaphysics. This simple opposition is rooted in the same essentialist fallacy into which we have seen others lapse. (NB 14 n. 10, where she characterizes Plato as radically diverging from Parmenides at *R.* 5. 477a ff.) Sprague assumes at the outset a rather reductive interpretation of Parmenides and then presumes that Euthydemus' and Dionysodorus' arguments more or less directly represent his philosophy. She is criticized on this point by Stewart 1977, 33, for assuming too easily that Euthydemus and Dionysodorus are to be seen as '*bona fide* Eleatics'.

[22] Bodunrin 1971, 73, poses what I take to be the key question: 'are there aspects of Parmenides' doctrine even if he himself was not aware of them that could have led others to conclude that he . . . denied the *possibility* of falsehood?' In attempting to provide an answer to this question, however, he spends too much time attempting to extract relevant points from Owen 1960, Furth 1968, and Kahn 1969 (cf. esp. Bodunrin 1971, ch. 3), when of course none of these commentators is attempting to understand Parmenides as he seems to have been understood by those who used him

After welcoming Parmenides upon his arrival at her abode, the goddess promises to instruct him regarding both the foundation of well-rounded truth (ἀληθείης) and the opinions of ordinary humans, in which she says there is no πίστις ἀληθής or true conviction (B1. 28–30). From the start, then, it appears that the subject of her discourse is truth. When she instructs Parmenides to judge by reason alone her controversial refutation (πολύδηριν ἔλεγχον, B7. 5), she creates an expectation that the view of truth she will articulate will be, quite literally, paradoxical. A sophist propounding the paradox that falsehood is impossible would naturally have found in this description a model for his own refutation of common opinion.

Euthydemus' and Dionysodorus' arguments, as we have noted, depend on the Greeks' use of the expression τὰ ὄντα λέγειν to mean 'to speak the truth'. That is, the so-called 'veridical' sense of the verb 'to be', whereby 'what is' (τὸ ὄν, τὰ ὄντα) means 'what is so' or 'what is the case', features prominently in their arguments. If one reads Parmenides B2 with this veridical sense of the verb 'to be' in mind, one will understand him as distinguishing true thoughts and statements from false ones via a formal specification of their content.[23] There are two possible ways of thinking and speaking of a subject. One can either think or speak of one's subject as it is and consequently think or say what is the case. Or one can think or speak of one's subject as it is not and consequently think or say what is not the case. It is tempting, in this context, to understand ὅπως and ὡς in B2. 3 and B2. 5 as relative adverbs of manner, such that ὅπως ἔστιν will mean 'as it is', and ὡς οὐκ ἔστιν, 'as it is not'. This is in any case the upshot of understanding the verb 'to be' veridically here. If one takes the first path, one conceives or speaks of one's subject as it is—one thinks or says 'it is the case' (ἔστιν). If one takes the second path, one conceives or speaks of one's subject as it is not—one thinks or says 'it is not the case' (οὐκ ἔστιν).

The choice the goddess offers Parmenides has its analogue in the choice Dionysodorus offers Ctesippus in the argument against contradiction. After obtaining Ctesippus' agreement that there is a *logos* or statement corresponding to each thing, Dionysodorus asks whether this *logos* describes each thing as it is or as it is not—οὐκοῦν ὡς ἔστιν

---

to develop the impossibility of falsehood thesis. Likewise, Rankin 1981, though noting the probably Eleatic influence on the thesis that contradiction is impossible (25, 26), spends more time giving us Furth's view of Parmenides (30–1) than what might have been the sophists' view.

[23] For a reading of Parmenides giving prominence to the veridical sense of the verb 'to be', see Kahn 1969, esp. 710–13.

ἕκαστον ἢ ὡς οὐκ ἔστιν; (285e10). Dionysodorus says that the second possibility has already been ruled out by Euthydemus' earlier arguments. The language he uses in recalling their conclusion is strongly reminiscent of the goddess's words in barring Parmenides from the second path. Dionysodorus reminds Ctesippus at 286a1–3 that it has already been shown that no one speaks of anything 'as it is not' (ὡς οὐκ ἔστι) because 'no one says what is not the case' (τὸ γὰρ μὴ ὂν οὐδεὶς ἐφάνη λέγων). Likewise, Parmenides' goddess, having formally specified the content of true and false thoughts and statements, declares falsehood impossible. One cannot proceed along the path opposed to the path of truth, she says, because one can neither think nor speak of what is not the case—οὔτε γὰρ ἂν γνοίης τό γε μὴ ἐὸν . . . οὔτε φράσαις (B2. 7–8). The same prohibition seems to recur at B8. 8–9, if one ignores the immediate context: 'for one can neither speak nor conceive of it as it is not' (οὐ γὰρ φατὸν οὐδὲ νοητόν | ἔστιν ὅπως οὐκ ἔστι). The original choice and the rejection of the possibility of falsehood seem to be reaffirmed a few lines later: 'it is the case or it is not the case (ἔστιν ἢ οὐκ ἔστιν): but it has been decided, as is necessary, to dismiss the second as unthinkable and unnameable, for it is not the true path, and that the first is the true path and is genuine' (B8. 16–18). The consequence of the original choice is that the subject of all thought and speech must be what is the case. Parmenides seems to make this point directly at B6. 1: 'what one can speak and think of must be what-is' (χρὴ τὸ λέγειν τὸ νοεῖν τ' ἐὸν ἔμμεναι).[24]

One can establish more or less clearly, then, the kind of understanding of certain lines of Parmenides' poem reflected in Euthydemus' and Dionysodorus' Eleaticizing arguments. This helps us understand how the Eleatic Visitor can cite Parmenides B7. 1–2 as providing the foundation for the sophistic thesis that falsehood is impossible. The possibility of falsehood involves the assumption that what is not the case is the case or that what-is-not is available to be mentioned. Parmenides will have been taken as having denied this possibility. I presume that the sophistic use of Parmenides outlined above will seem rather inadequate. It is based on a selective reading of specific lines within the framework of a predetermined set of concerns and consequently ignores both the immediate and broader contexts of the appropriated lines. The exclusive focus on his apparent views regarding the formal content of true and false statements ignores the

---

[24] Cf. Hawtrey 1981, 99 and 111, for a view of B6. 1 as lying behind *Euthd.* 284a1–2 and 286c7–8.

crucial ontological aspects of his poem. One wonders whether all those who came to propound Eleaticizing arguments against the possibility of falsehood had read Parmenides' poem for themselves or whether they might not have been working from some selective distillation of his thought. We know that the sophists made collections of the views of earlier thinkers. Gorgias, as we have seen, prefaced his treatise 'On What-Is-Not' with a collection of previous opinions regarding the number and nature of fundamental entities (τὰ ὄντα), in which Parmenides would have figured prominently. Hippias made a collection of passages on various themes from Homer, Hesiod, the Orphic writings, and the Presocratics.[25] Perhaps most tantalizingly, Xenophon informs us that Euthydemus, too, had made a collection of the writings of the most esteemed poets and thinkers (γράμματα πολλὰ συνειλεγμένον ποιητῶν τε καὶ σοφιστῶν τῶν εὐδοκιμωτάτων, *Mem.* 4. 2. 1). It may be that Xenophon means that he had assembled a personal library of these authors' writings (in which case it is a more than likely conjecture that he had read Parmenides), but Xenophon's report can also be interpreted as indicating that Euthydemus made a collection of extracts from their works.[26]

In any case, Euthydemus' and Dionysodorus' Eleaticizing arguments represent a reductive and distorting use of Parmenides, and I presume they would have been regarded as such by Plato. Socrates says of the brothers' traffic in superficial equivocations that 'even if one were to learn many or even all things of this type, one would have no greater knowledge of how things actually are' (*Euthd.* 278b4–5). This assessment could easily have been transferred by Plato to the brothers' use of Parmenides: they display a fair degree of ingenuity

---

[25] Snell 1944 noticed that although Arist. *Metaph. A.* 3. 983^{b}27 ff., where Aristotle says there are certain people (τινες) who think the ancient theologians held views akin to Thales, had been standardly taken as a reference to Pl. *Cra.* 402b, *Tht.* 152e, 160d, and 180c, these passages in fact make no mention of Thales. Snell went on to argue that Aristotle is likely to be drawing upon a doxographical compendium by Hippias, in which he at one point connected Thales' assertion about water with the theogonies of Homer, Hesiod, and Orpheus; that Plato, too, seems to be drawing upon Hippias in his reference to Homer, Hesiod, and the Orphic verses at *Cra.* 402b–c; and that, consequently, Hippias' work played a seminal role in the development of Greek philosophical historiography. See Classen 1965 for an extension of Snell's argument to Pl. *Smp.* 178a9 ff. For a re-examination of Snell's arguments, see Mansfeld 1983. For a wide-ranging attempt to summarize and extend the work on the early traditions of doxographical writing, see Mansfeld 1986, which contains full references to work on the subject before and after Snell's study, to which should be added Patzer 1986.

[26] Such may be the sense of συνειλεγμένον, although one might have expected the verb ἐκλέγειν instead, as at *Mem.* 1. 6. 14 and Arist. *Top.* 1. 14. 105^{b}12.

in cloaking their paradoxes in an Eleaticizing pseudo-semantics, but they have neglected the thought underlying the language they have preyed upon. One might suppose Plato would want to charge this particular sophistic appropriation with the same kind of superficiality and perversity of which Plutarch accuses Colotes.

THE REDUCTION OF WHAT-IS-NOT TO WHAT-IS-NOT-AT-ALL

Protagoras' relativism provides the ontological ground for his position that contradiction is impossible. Socrates implies as much in the *Cratylus* when he explains to Hermogenes how his conventionalist theory regarding the correctness of names would seem to presume the type of relativist ontology underlying Protagoras' measure doctrine (385a–386d). Socrates also mentions in this context Euthydemus' rather bizarre thesis that 'every thing has every attribute in the same manner at the same time and at every time' (πᾶσι πάντα ὁμοίως εἶναι ἅμα καὶ ἀεί, 386d3–4), which may similarly be understood as the ontological underpinning of his thesis that falsehood is impossible. In the *Sophist*, as well, we can see the Sophist's attack on the concept of appearance as providing the ontological ground for his rejection of the possibility of falsehood. Since the latter stance is predicated upon a recognizably sophistic appropriation of Parmenides, it is natural to suppose the former is also. Moreover, the Sophist's appeal to Parmenides in attempting to elude capture by rejecting the concept of appearance goes against the grain of Plato's own use of Parmenides in the formation of his middle period metaphysics. Therefore, just as one can recognize the Parmenideanism underlying the sophists' arguments against falsehood and contradiction, one should be able to discern the sophistic Parmenideanism involved in the attack on the concepts of appearance and seeming.

In discussing Plato's engagement with those thinkers who fall into the class of 'sight-lovers', we have seen that one of their principal disagreements with him would have concerned the distinction between reality and appearance. Hippias' attention is so focused upon beautiful things that he cannot be led to conceive of Beauty itself. Antisthenes admits that there are horses but not 'Horseness'. Gorgias attempts a thoroughgoing critique of all efforts to establish something ontologically and epistemologically prior to the objects of ordinary experience. The sight-lovers, however, are not so bold as the Sophist. For in refusing to accept the existence of any being transcending appearances they do not, as does the Sophist, appeal for support to the authority of Parmenides. The Sophist's audacity consists in appealing to the very thinker who most influenced Plato's manner of distinguishing reality and appearance in denying the validity of this distinction. The sight-lover refuses to accept that there is any transcendent being corresponding to what Plato designates 'what-completely-is' ($\tau\grave{o}$ $\pi\alpha\nu\tau\epsilon\lambda\hat{\omega}\varsigma$ $\check{o}\nu$). He feels no dissatisfaction with the contradictions and complexities of a world whose population always is and is not. The Sophist's manoeuvre is a radical extension of this rejection. He hopes to achieve his aim of defeating the distinction between appearance and reality, and thereby the attempt to classify him as operating merely at the level of the former, by elevating appearance to the status of reality. That is, he seeks to elevate what-is-and-is-not to the status of what-is. He charges his would-be captor's conception of appearance as what appears to be but is not really with incoherence. Appealing to the authority of Parmenides, he will say that what-is-not is unthinkable and accordingly must be eliminated from the analysis. What survives is a quasi-Protagorean analysis of appearance: since there can be nothing that appears to be but is not, what appears to be must be. If one must eliminate 'is not' from an analysis of the 'phenomenal' world's ontological status as what both is and is not, one is left with 'what-is' or $\tau\grave{o}$ $\check{o}\nu$ *simpliciter*. One consequence of this elevation is that there is no room for any attempt to privilege something over and above appearance as 'what-completely-is' since appearance is now conceived of as what-is.

Such is the general character of the sophistic attack upon the philosopher's conception of appearance that lies at the core of the Sophist's appropriation of Parmenides and that constitutes the ontological ground for the reduction performed in the arguments against the possibility of falsehood. Notice that the application of Parmenidean logic in rejecting the conception of appearance as what both is and is not could proceed in two ways: either the *elevation* of what-is-and-is-not to the status of what-is or the *reduction* of what-is-and-is-not to what-is-not. The reduction figures somewhat more prominently in the argument of the *Sophist* than the elevation, but it is simply the means by which the Sophist seeks to secure the elevation of appearance to the status of reality. That is, the Sophist rejects the analysis of appearance as what-is-and-is-not because what involves any measure of not-being is not and is therefore inconceivable. The ontological status of what the philosopher wants to designate as appearance cannot, therefore, involve any measure of not-being but must simply be what-is.

Plato's use of Parmenides in *Republic* 5 indicates that he sees him as sanctioning neither the elevation nor the reduction but rather as according status to what-is-and-is-not as the proper object of *doxa*. In defending the conception of appearance against the Sophist's objections, Plato in the *Sophist* is returning to explore in greater depth the distinctions drawn in the arguments at the end of *Republic* 5. This return involves, among other things, Plato's confrontation of his own earlier use of Parmenides in establishing the ontological and epistemological categories of the *Republic* 5 account with a challenge to the viability of those categories that is itself rooted in an alternative and competing use. Plato's efforts to define the Sophist and to distinguish him from the Philosopher will thus involve an attempt to recover Parmenides from certain sophistic appropriations to which he had been subjected. Cornering the Sophist will involve an oblique defence of certain aspects of his own earlier understanding of Parmenides.

Plato begins his resolution of the difficulties raised in the sophistic challenge by reiterating and defending one feature of his own earlier appropriation of Parmenides. The discussion of what-is-not-at-all (τὸ μηδαμῶς ὄν) to which the Visitor turns at *Sophist* 237b7–239c3 picks up and develops the much briefer treatment of the same topic at *Republic* 5. 476e4–477a5. There Socrates had asked Glaucon whether one who knows knows something or nothing (τὶ ἢ οὐδέν), to which Glaucon responded that one who knows knows something. When then asked whether this is something that is or that is not (ὂν ἢ οὐκ ὄν), Glaucon had, in a clear echo of Parmenides B2. 7, answered: 'something that is, for how could one know something that is not?' (ὄν· πῶς γὰρ ἂν μὴ ὄν γέ τι γνωσθείη; *R.* 5. 477a1). Socrates concluded that what-is-completely is completely knowable, while what-is-not-at-all (μὴ ὂν μηδαμῇ) is altogether unknowable. He qualified this brief argument by commenting that they have sufficiently established this point even though they might consider it from other angles (477a2).

It may not be going too far to suggest that the *Sophist* looks back to this aside and fulfils its implied promise of a more extensive treatment. The *Sophist*'s discussion of what-is-not-at-all picks up the much more compressed and cursory treatment here in the *Republic*. The Visitor shows Theaetetus that it is impossible for the expression 'what-is-not-at-all' to function as a name because nothing can be designated by it. He begins this demonstration by elaborating the two points touched upon by Socrates and Glaucon in agreeing that what is known must be and must be something (must be ὄν and τι). The designation 'what-is-not' cannot, the Visitor says, be used to refer to what-is and consequently not to something (*Sph.* 237c7–d5). He then goes beyond the *Republic*'s limited treatment to point out that not speaking of something (μὴ τὶ λέγοντα) is equivalent to saying nothing at all (μηδὲν λέγειν), which is in turn equivalent to not speaking at all (237d6–e6; cf. *Cra.* 429d ff.). The Visitor then argues that since 'none of the things that are', that is, no property, can be attributed to what-is-not, and since number is a property, what-is-not should not be conceived of as either singular or plural (*Sph.* 238a1–b5). But if it is improper to speak or conceive of it as either 'what-is-not' (τὸ μὴ ὄν) or as 'what-are-not' (τὰ μὴ ὄντα), then it would seem absolutely impossible to mention or conceive of what-is-not-at-all (238b6–c11). The language of the conclusion is distinctly Parmenidean: 'it is impossible either to utter, to speak of, or to conceive of what absolutely is not (τὸ μὴ ὂν αὐτὸ καθ' αὐτό), but it is inconceivable, unsayable, unutterable, and unspeakable' (238c8–11; cf. 237b7–8, 238b6–8). This recalls precisely the lines of Parmenides echoed by Glaucon in his similar declaration at *Republic* 5. 477a1–2: 'neither could you know what-is-not, for this cannot be accomplished, nor could you pick it out' (Parm. B2. 7–8a, cf. B8. 8b–9a, 16–17).

It is a striking feature of the *Sophist*'s discussion of what-is-not-at-all that it contains no trace of sophistic Parmenideanism. The discussion here is perfectly consistent with, and even appears a direct expansion upon, the treatment of what-is-not-at-all in *Republic* 5 and, by implication, Parmenides' own treatment of what necessarily is not.[27] The Sophist appeals to Parmenides' injunction against the possibility of saying or thinking what-is-not to support his own claim that talk of something's appearing but not really being is incoherent. In investigating this claim, Plato returns to his appropriation of Parmenides in *Republic* 5, where he had followed Parmenides with regard to the utter ineffability of what-is-not-at-all. One might

---

[27] Thus Cherniss 1932, 123, can speak of the Visitor at 237a–238c as demonstrating 'in traditional Parmenidean style that *non-Being* can not be the object of thought or speech'. Cf. Ferejohn 1989, 267 and n. 26; Rudebusch 1991, 530 n. 3. Cordero 1986–7, 284–5, notes the connections between *Sph.* 237b–239c, *R.* 5. 476a (and 478b), and *Tht.* 188d; he takes it that Plato is aligning himself with Parmenides in the *Sophist*'s discussion of absolute non-being. O'Brien 1991, 328–30, goes further and uses the correspondence between the arguments at *Sph.* 237a–239c and Parm. B2. 7–8 to speak of 'l'alliance de l'Étranger et de la déesse' and thus to question whether the Visitor is in fact a parricide. He also draws attention to the fact that the series of arguments at *Sph.* 237b7–239c8 must be distinguished from the following section of the dialogue where Parmenides' condemnation of not-being is made the basis for the argument against the coherence of the concept 'image' and for the thesis that falsehood is impossible, which he says 'n'est manifestement pas parménidienne' (329 n. 13).

suppose the *Sophist*'s rather prolonged treatment of what-is-not-at-all somewhat irrelevant to the issue at hand, for the problem of appearance does not prima facie concern this but rather what-both-is-and-is-not. It is this analysis of the ontological status of appearance that the Sophist claims is confused. However, by picking up the brief discussion of what-is-not-at-all in *Republic* 5, Plato points to how his distinction between reality and appearance there was rooted in an understanding of Parmenides fundamentally different from that underlying the Sophist's appeal. The Sophist supposes, as Plato had not, that Parmenides' prohibition against the possibility of speaking or thinking of what-is-not creates serious problems for the status of things that both are and are not. We need to dwell for a while on the problems attendant upon the Sophist's collapse of the proper distinction between what-is-not (τὸ μὴ ὄν) and what-is-not-at-all (τὸ μηδαμῶς ὄν).

It will be useful to return momentarily to the *Euthydemus*. For that dialogue's third major sophism depends upon this type of collapse and obfuscation of important distinctions. Dionysodorus belittles Socrates' hope that the young Cleinias will one day become wise. Having secured Socrates' agreement that Cleinias is not now wise, Dionysodorus re-articulates Socrates' hope in the following terms. 'You want him to become what he is not', he says, 'and to be no longer what he is now' (283d2–3). From this he concludes that Socrates in fact wants Cleinias to die: 'since you wish him no longer to be what he is now (ὃς νῦν ἐστὶν μηκέτι εἶναι), you want him, so it seems, to perish' (d5–6). As with many of the sophistic arguments in this dialogue, this one is open to two levels of interpretation and response. It may be treated as a 'mere' sophism, its error diagnosed, and the problem it poses dismissed forthwith. Such is Aristotle's treatment when he classifies a version of this argument as exemplifying the fallacy of *secundum quid* (*SE* 5. 166b37 ff.); and such, more or less, is the treatment of those modern commentators who have detected further equivocations in the use of the relative pronoun ὅς and between the existential and copulative senses of the verb 'to be'.[28] But the

---

[28] Peck 1952, 47, largely follows Aristotle. Winckelmann 1833, 46 ad *Euthd.* 283d2 ὃς μέν, notes that ὅς here is used as if it were equivalent to οἷος (cf. Pl. *Phdr.* 243e2; Sophocles, *Ajax* 1259; Euripides, *Alcestis* 640) and that Dionysodorus exploits the consequent ambiguity such that 'sophisma ductum e duplici vi istius ὅς'; cf. Gifford 1905 and Hawtrey 1981, ad loc. Sprague 1962, 13 and n. 9, and Hawtrey 1981, 95–6, suppose all three fallacies operative. Sprague 1968 calls attention to the fact that Aristotle's solution to this variety of sophism is anticipated in *Dissoi Logoi* 5. 15.

argument may also be viewed as pointing to difficulties that had a more serious claim upon Plato's attention. From this point of view, Dionysodorus' leaving aside the fact that Socrates wants Cleinias to be wise is at least as significant as these various fallacies. In his educated state, Cleinias will be one who *is* wise and *is not* ignorant. That is, he will be one who is and is not. Dionysodorus, however, drops all reference to his future state of being and focuses exclusively on his future state of not-being in order to draw the conclusion that Socrates wants Cleinias not to be. Here is the analogue of the Sophist's reduction of what-is-and-is-not to what-is-not *simpliciter*. One can likewise see the analogue of the Sophist's equation of what-is-not with what-is-not-at-all in Dionysodorus' dropping of the relevant qualification 'ignorant' in the statement 'Socrates wants Cleinias not to be ignorant' in order to reach the conclusion that Socrates wants Cleinias not to be. We have already seen Euthydemus' and Dionysodorus' Eleaticism at work in the arguments that follow immediately upon this one, and it seems reasonable enough to see this argument as also reflecting a certain sophistic appropriation of the logic of Eleaticism.[29] Just as the *Sophist* is concerned with resolving the problems regarding falsehood that figure in these other arguments, so Dionysodorus' reduction in the present argument of what-is-and-is-not to what-is-not and his equation of what-is-not with what-is-not-at-all both reflect in an apparently trivializing manner the sophistic appropriation of Eleatic logic at the ontological level that Plato is also concerned to counter in the *Sophist*.

We have seen that Plato, in his own use of Parmenides at the end of *Republic* 5, was quite careful to preserve the distinctions that Dionysodorus' argument collapses. Plato has not lost sight of the relevant distinctions by the time of the *Sophist*. The situation in this dialogue is complicated, however, by the need to obscure the distinctions in presenting the problems that depend upon the sophistic reduction; there are nevertheless certain subtle indications in the midst of this obfuscation that the distinctions must be preserved. This

---

[29] Sprague 1962, 13, supposes that the argument relies on Parmenidean principles. But she supposes the relevant aspect of Parmenides' philosophy is his denial of the possibility of coming to be: 'From the Parmenidean point of view, if Cleinias is at the moment ignorant, as his friends admit, then he must remain ignorant, since this is what he *is*. If his friends say they wish him to become something else, they are really talking nonsense since nothing else exists for him to become. Therefore they can only mean that they wish for his non-existence.' This paraphrase distorts the actual mechanics of the argument to make it conform to Sprague's preconception of the 'essence of Parmenides' philosophy'. The argument in fact seems to presume the possibility of Cleinias' coming to be wise and ceasing to be ignorant.

tension informs the Visitor's attempt to specify the nature of images at 239c4–240c6. When pressed by him for a general specification of the nature of an image, Theaetetus responds that it is 'that which, in relation to the true thing, is an other (ἕτερον) such thing made like it' (240a8).[30] With this account Theaetetus comes quite close to the key element in what will be the dialogue's eventual solution to the problems of not-being. Without going into the complex details of this solution, we can simply note the relevant point that it depends on an analysis of not-being as other than or different from being rather than as the opposite of being. Thus at 257b3–4 the Visitor will say, 'Whenever we speak of what-is-not (τὸ μὴ ὄν), it seems, we are not saying that something is the opposite of what is (ἐναντίον . . . τοῦ ὄντος) but only different (ἕτερον)' (cf. 258b2–3). Why, then, does the Visitor re-involve Theaetetus in difficulties at precisely the point where he seems to be verging upon the solution? More precisely, why does the Visitor shift from Theaetetus' description of an image as an *other* (ἕτερον) like the genuine item to a description of it as the *opposite* (ἐναντίον) of the genuine? For this is precisely what he does upon receiving Theaetetus' reply (240a9–b5). One reason is that the Greek term ἕτερον is ambiguous, and Theaetetus seems not to use the sense that will ultimately be called for. He does not say that a copy is 'other than' or 'different from' the genuine item but that it is 'another item such as' the genuine one. Instead of pointing out the relevant ambiguity, though, the Visitor seizes upon Theaetetus' words to force him to admit that the copy is not 'another *genuine* item' (ἕτερον . . . ἀληθινόν, 240a9-b2) and thus that it is, *qua* not-genuine, 'the opposite of the genuine' (ἐναντίον ἀληθοῦς, b5). Since the genuine, moreover, is designated as 'really being' (ὄντως ὄν, 240b3), the Visitor concludes that the image, *qua* opposite of the genuine, must be characterized as 'not really being' (οὐκ ὄντως ὄν, b7–8). In spite of having these difficulties pressed upon him, Theaetetus persists in trying to maintain that the image 'is in some way' (ἔστι . . . πῶς, 240b9). The Visitor, however, forces him to admit that this way of speaking involves attributing to the image an intermingling of being and not-being (240b10–c2). 'The Sophist', he concludes, 'has forced us against

---

[30] Theaetetus' specification echoes Socrates' description in *Republic* 10 of how the bedmaker does not produce the Bed itself (ὃ ἔστι κλίνη) but a particular bed: 'if he does not produce what [the bed] is, he would not then produce what-is, but something such as what-is but that is not' (εἰ μὴ ὃ ἔστιν ποιεῖ, οὐκ ἂν τὸ ὂν ποιοῖ, ἀλλά τι τοιοῦτον οἷον τὸ ὄν, ὂν δὲ οὔ, 597a4–5). This particular passage comes in the context of a discussion of how 'a remarkable sophist' (596d1) can produce appearances of all things (cf. *Sph.* 233d9 ff.) but not things that really are. These connections are just a further sign of how the *Sophist* returns to problems already raised in the *Republic*.

our will to admit that what-is-not somehow is (τὸ μὴ ὂν . . . εἶναί πως)'
(240c4–5).

It is indeed the Sophist who has forced this impasse. For what
we witness in this brief transaction is the sophistic challenge to the
viability of the category of appearance proceeding via the reduction
of what-is-and-is-not to what-is-not. Precisely why this interweaving of what-is and what-is-not is unacceptable is not made explicit.
The Visitor simply moves on to the parallel problem of false belief.
(That the topics are taken up in this order is some confirmation of
the hypothesis that the attack upon appearance provides the ontological ground for the thesis that falsehood is impossible.) It is clear
enough, however, that the previous discussion of what-is-not-at-all
is meant to furnish the implicit conclusion. The Sophist has shown
that Theaetetus' analysis of the image's status involves an assertion
that what-is-not somehow is. Since it has just been shown that one
cannot attribute being under any aspect to what-is-not-at-all, this new
result is taken to be obviously incoherent. For not-being as it figures
in the analysis of image and appearance is taken as equivalent to
not-being-at-all. That is, the Sophist is permitted his characteristic
move of collapsing the distinction between what-is-not and what-is-
not-at-all. Thus what-is-and-is-not proves a conceptual chimera. If
it is not, then it can in no way be (τὸ μὴ ὄν = τὸ μηδαμῶς ὄν). Likewise,
if it is, it can in no way not be (τὸ ὄν = τὸ ὄντως ὄν). The underlying Parmenideanism of the Sophist's reduction is evident enough.
Essentially, it relies on an epexegetical understanding of B2. 3b and
B2. 5b. B2. 3 will thus be understood as indicating that whatever is
(ἔστιν) is incapable of not being (οὐκ ἔστι μὴ εἶναι). B2. 5 will be understood as indicating that whatever is not (οὐκ ἔστιν) must necessarily
not be (χρεών ἐστι μὴ εἶναι). Moreover, Parmenides will be understood as presenting a disjunction that exhausts the possible modes
of being and leaves no room for a middle term or mixed mode. The
third mode of being, that belonging to the objects of mortal opinion, will thus be understood not as a genuinely independent mode
but as reducible to the second. Which is to say that in Parmenides
appearance is rejected because it involves not-being. Thus when
Parmenides in B7. 1–2 forbids attempting to conceive of things that
are not as being, he will be understood as pointing to the inherent confusion in the conception of the objects of *doxa* as both being and not
being. If they are not, if they involve any measure of not being, then
as B2. 5 indicates they must necessarily not be and it is fundamentally mistaken to try to conceive of them as somehow being.

That Plato himself, however, wants to understand the Parmenidean
analysis of the modes of being in this way is doubtful. He suggests

his reservations vis-à-vis the sophistic reduction by indicating—even as he sets it out—how this reduction may be forestalled. We have seen how Theaetetus' attempt to specify the nature of an image already contains the seed of the dialogue's eventual response to the Sophist's attempt to collapse the distinction between what-is-not and what-is-not-at-all. Theaetetus' intuition could have been developed, had not the Visitor, arguing on the Sophist's behalf (note 240c3–5), prevented this by leading him to accept that the image is not *other than* what really is but rather its *opposite*. There is a similar prefiguration in Theaetetus' response to the Visitor's subsequent argument problematizing the nature of false belief. Employing the previous argument's substitution of 'opposite' for 'other', he gets Theaetetus to agree that false belief will involve believing 'things contrary to those which are' (τἀναντία τοῖς οὖσι, 240d6) and consequently believing 'things that are not' (τὰ μὴ ὄντα, d9). The Visitor asks Theaetetus to choose between two alternative conceptions of what this might involve: (i) believing that things which are not are not—μὴ εἶναι τὰ μὴ ὄντα, and (ii) believing that things which in no way are somehow are—πως εἶναι τὰ μηδαμῶς ὄντα (240e1–2). The disjunction is quite plainly not exhaustive. The alternatives the Visitor offers Theaetetus represent only some of the possible combinations of terms. Neither alternative, furthermore, seems coherent. The first alternative does not seem to provide an analysis of false belief at all. Believing that things which are not are not would surely be believing something true. The second alternative is simply self-contradictory. Perhaps positing this specious disjunction represents part of the Sophist's strategy for denying the possibility of false belief. Were one to opt for one of the options presented, one would find oneself forced to admit that false belief is impossible since neither in fact presents a viable analysis of the phenomenon. Theaetetus, however, is careful not to fall into the trap. He rejects the specious disjunction and chooses neither alternative. Instead, he says that for false belief to occur, it must be the case that one supposes that things which are not in some sense are—εἶναί πως τὰ μὴ ὄντα (240e3). Here again Theaetetus' naturally reflective response prefigures the problem's eventual solution.

Why does the Visitor again fail to develop the seed of the solution contained in this answer? Why does he immediately re-involve Theaetetus in difficulties?[31] One might suppose such questions

[31] Rudebusch 1991 likewise sees the Visitor as involving Theaetetus in perplexity at 237c–239b while merely pretending to be perplexed himself and suggests that this tactic is to be explained as an effective pedagogical device. Jordan 1984, 121 (criticizing Malcolm 1967, 135), finds it unpalatable that the solution to the problems here

illegitimate, on the grounds that they assume that the solution subsequently developed in the dialogue is somehow already available
to the reader. Theaetetus' responses at 240a7–8 and 240e3–4 are, of
course, striking in retrospect. But it is not necessary to have the eventual solution in mind to feel that there is something wrong with the
Visitor's shift from 'other' to 'opposite' in the first passage and with
the alternatives for the analysis of false belief he presents in the second. Theaetetus' brave attempts to avoid the traps laid for him are
alone enough to indicate that something is wrong. What is ultimately
amiss, I have been suggesting, is that the moves the Visitor makes in
these two passages are not made *in propria persona* but are representative of the kind of moves the Sophist will make in problematizing the phenomena of appearance and falsehood. In setting out the
problems and confounding Theaetetus, he is speaking on behalf of
the Sophist and making the kind of moves the Sophist will make to
elude capture (cf. 239c9–d4, 239e1–240a6, 240c3–5, 241a3–b3). The
importance of this dynamic for our purposes is that if the Visitor's
exposition does not represent his own view of the situation but that
of the Sophist, then this will also be the case with the view of Parmenides upon which this exposition depends.

This suggestion finds confirmation when one compares the *Sophist*'s
problematization of false belief with the analysis of *doxa* in the course
of the *dunamis* argument in *Republic* 5. Socrates and Glaucon have
agreed that knowledge is directed towards what-is, that knowledge
and *doxa* are separate capacities, and that consequently *doxa* must have
a separate object. They then attempt to specify the ontological status
of that object. They begin by agreeing that *doxa*'s object must be
something other than, or different from, what-is—ἄλλο τι . . . ἢ τὸ ὄν
(478b3–5). But, crucially, they do not accept, as the Visitor (speaking
on the Sophist's behalf) leads Theaetetus to do, that what is different from what-is is nothing. They *do* accept that it is impossible for
nothing or what-is-not-at-all to be the object of *doxa* and consequently
that the object of *doxa* is something (478b6–8). That is, the *Republic*
5 analysis admits precisely the possibility that the Sophist will not

should be adumbrated even as the problems are being set out (drawing particular attention to the suggestive phrasing of 240e1–6), on the grounds that 'we might reasonably expect Plato *not* to mislead the unwary reader about what he intends to prove'.
The fact is, however, that Plato has the Visitor re-involve Theaetetus in difficulties
in a way that any moderately wary reader should pick up on. If this is not what we
might 'reasonably' expect, we should then, as I have done, ask why Plato does this
rather than allow our expectations to distort the tenor of the text. For Malcolm's own,
somewhat unsatisfactory, response to Jordan's criticism on this point, see Malcolm
1985, 521.

allow: *that what is other than what-is is not nothing or what-is-not full stop but, rather, something*. This is one of the clearest instances of how Plato, in his own appropriation of Parmenides, preserved the distinctions between the three modes of being that are subsequently collapsed in the sophistic appropriation represented by the *Sophist*'s problematization of appearance and falsehood.

Plato's analysis of *doxa* in *Republic* 5 rejects the assumption that the disjunction between what-is and what-is-not is exhaustive. *Doxa* is directed towards neither what-is (τὸ ὄν) nor what-is-not (τὸ μὴ ὄν), or more properly towards neither 'what-absolutely-is' (τὸ εἰλικρινῶς ὄν) nor 'what-completely-is-not' (τὸ πάντως μὴ ὄν), but instead towards what-is-and-is-not or what participates in both being and non-being (*R*. 5. 478c6–e2). The *Sophist*, too, accepts that what-is-not can be neither an object of thought generally nor the object of (false) *doxa*.[32] More importantly, the conclusions of the *Sophist*'s initial analyses of the image's ontological status (*Sph.* 240b12–13) and of the content of false belief (240e10–241a1) correspond more or less directly to the *Republic*'s conclusion that the objects of *doxa* both are and are not. Although the terms of the analysis are much the same, in the *Sophist* this mutual participation in, or 'interweaving' of, being and not-being is presented as intensely problematic. *Both* the *Republic*'s acceptance of the possibility that the objects of *doxa* participate in both being and not-being *and* the *Sophist*'s rejection of any such interweaving are presented as extrapolations from basic Parmenidean principles. We have seen how the *Republic*'s description of the sight-lovers and the objects of *doxa* draw upon Parmenides' description of mortals and the objects upon which they have erroneously focused their cognitive attention. We have seen that there is no good reason to suppose that the *Republic*'s conception of *doxa* and its objects is suddenly departing from the appropriation of Parmenides evident in the opposition between what-completely-is and what-is-not-at-all. The *Sophist*'s appeal to Parmenides, in what is effectively a challenge to the viability of the earlier theory of *doxa*, is even more explicit. Although the *Sophist* re-examines the principal categories of that theory, in the end it re-establishes the basic validity of the distinction between reality and appearance against the Sophist's objections. Thus I think it best to resolve the conflict

---

[32] The conclusion regarding thought in general is established by *Sph.* 238c10. Although at 240d9 Theaetetus accepts the Visitor's specification of false belief as τὰ μὴ ὄντα δοξάζειν, his rejection of the Visitor's alternative analyses of this specification shows he does not understand τὰ μὴ ὄντα here as equivalent to τὰ μηδαμῶς ὄντα.

between the appropriations of Parmenides in *Republic* 5 and in the *Sophist* by acknowledging that the *Sophist*'s problematizations of the parallel phenomena of appearance and falsehood are intended to represent recognizably sophistic appropriations of the Eleatic legacy that Plato himself wants to counteract. Not only is Plato's use of Parmenides in the *Republic* at odds with the use the Visitor makes of him in mapping the territory of the Sophist's refuge, so is the representation of Parmenides later in the *Sophist* itself, in the doxographical survey at 242c–243a and in the subsequent examination of the Eleatic thesis at 244b–245e. In short, one cannot take the appeal to Parmenides at *Sophist* 237a as representing Plato's considered view of Parmenides at this time.

What, then, are we to make of the famous 'parricide'? I take it that the Eleatic Visitor's expression of concern at 241d that he may seem a parricide by contradicting the *logos* of father Parmenides in his efforts to capture the Sophist is not the unambiguous signal of Plato's departure from Parmenides most commentators have presumed it to be. I wish to advance a reading of *Sophist* 241d–242b that is both consistent with what we have said about Plato's engagement with Parmenides thus far in the dialogue and that is, I think, more attentive to the language and dynamic of the passage than other readings currently on offer. The first, crucial point to notice is that the Visitor simply does not say that hunting down the Sophist necessitates his becoming a parricide. What he actually says is rather different. He asks Theaetetus *not* to suppose that he is becoming some sort of parricide: μή με οἷον πατραλοίαν ὑπολάβῃς γίγνεσθαί τινα (241d3). The indulgence he asks of Theaetetus leads one to ask whether he is in fact going against his Eleatic upbringing. If one thinks the Sophist's appeals to Parmenidean principles represent a fair and accurate use, then one will indeed think the Visitor's subsequent analysis of the relation between being and not-being is a radical, parricidal departure. On the other hand, if one supposes the Sophist's use of Parmenides to be a reductive misappropriation, as we are given reason to believe, then the Visitor's appeal to Theaetetus might seem tinged with a certain irony. On further consideration, however, this apparent irony dissolves. The Visitor says he hopes Theaetetus will not consider him a parricide. If his arguments against the Sophist serve, at one level, to recover Parmenides from certain of the sophistic appropriations to which he had been subjected, he will in fact *not* be a parricide. His request that Theaetetus not suppose him a parricide is direct and sincere. Since he recognizes that Theaetetus might suppose that he will be contradicting Parmenides when he proceeds to argue that there is a sense in which what-is is not and what-is-not is, the Visitor takes the precaution of warning him against this.

Just as the Visitor's request at 241d3 indicates that he does not see himself as betraying the Eleatic legacy, none of his remarks immediately following about the *logos* of Parmenides indicate a direct attack on Parmenides himself. 'We must', he says, 'in defending ourselves (ἡμῖν[33] ἀμυνομένοις) put to the test (βασανίζειν) the *logos* of father Parmenides, and contend vehemently[34] (βιάζεσθαι) both that what-is-not is in some respect and conversely that what-is somehow is not' (241d5–7). What is meant here by the *logos* of Parmenides? Is the reference to his entire poem, or perhaps to his 'theory' of being and not-being? It is much more likely that the reference is to just those verses quoted above at 237a, namely Parmenides B7. 1–2. For when quoted there, they were described as a *logos* that must be put to the test (βασανισθείς, 237b2). Given that these verses have been taken from their context by the Sophist and put to uses that Parmenides neither could have envisaged nor would have sanctioned, it is a legitimate question whether putting them to the test will in actuality involve an attack upon Parmenides himself. Nowhere does the Visitor say that he will be attacking or refuting Parmenides himself. Rather, the proposed object of his refutation is always this particular *logos*. The Visitor says at 242a1–2 that they must be so bold as to apply themselves to the paternal *logos*. A few lines later, at 242b1–2, he says they should attempt to refute the *logos* if they can. The specific object of the ensuing refutation is the Sophist's denial that it is possible for what-is-not to be in any sense and for what-is somehow not to be.[35] It is the propositions that what-is-not is and what-is is not which the Visitor says must be examined and eventually accepted if it is to be possible to avoid contradiction in speaking of falsehood and images (241e1–5).[36] The Sophist has appealed to Parmenides B7. 1–2 in

---

[33] Somewhat inexplicably, von Fritz 1974, 335, supposes that ἡμῖν includes not only the Visitor and Theaetetus but Parmenides himself. Consequently, he supposes the defence is being conducted against the arguments of the Sophist rather than against Parmenides. Although I do not see how ἡμῖν can include Parmenides (although my case would be easier to make if it could), von Fritz's intuition that the defence is being conducted against the Sophist rather than against Parmenides per se nevertheless seems correct.   [34] So LSJ for βιάζεσθαι. Cf. *Sph.* 246b8.

[35] Cf. Dixsaut 1987, 217.

[36] The key phrase is τούτων γὰρ μήτ' ἐλεγχθέντων μήτε ὁμολογηθέντων (241e1–2). White 1993, 31, translates this phrase as 'unless, that is, we either *refute Parmenides' claims* or else agree to accept them'. This mistakes the sense of both τούτων and ἐλεγχθέντων. The antecedent of the plural τούτων cannot be the singular *logos* of Parmenides referred to at 241d5. The most likely antecedents are the two demonstranda specified at 241d6–7: τό τε μὴ ὂν ὡς ἔστι κατά τι καὶ τὸ ὂν αὖ πάλιν ὡς οὐκ

rejecting these propositions, and to that extent the refutation of the
Sophist will be a refutation of Parmenides' *logos*. It is a further question whether Plato supposes that the refutation of this *logos*—that is,
the rejection of the way in which the sophists had appropriated it—
will in fact constitute any serious refutation of Parmenides himself.
That it will not is suggested by the Visitor's request that Theaetetus
not think that he is becoming a parricide in the ensuing inquiry.

The treatment of not-being in the *Parmenides*'s Fifth and Sixth
Deductions provides further confirmation of Plato's perspective on the
Sophist's attempted reduction of what-is-not to what-is-not-at-all.
Before we can see how this is the case, however, we need to say some-
thing about the character of the *Parmenides*'s dialectical exercise.

ἔστι πη. Thus, apparently, Cornford 1935(*a*), 215, who translates τούτων as 'these
propositions'. What is at issue is whether the Visitor and Theaetetus can consistently
assert, against the Sophist's opposition, that what-is-not is and what-is is not. If τούτων
refers to these two propositions, then ἐλεγχθέντων cannot have the sense 'refute'. For
if the possibility that what-is-not is in some respect and what-is somehow is not were
to be refuted and rejected, then it would remain impossible to provide a consistent
analysis of false speech and belief. But this is precisely what the Visitor says one who
conducts the proposed elenchus will be able to do. That is, the correlatives μήτ'
. . . μήτε in the phrase in question do not set two alternatives in opposition but
simply connect two terms of roughly equal status. The sense of ἐλεγχθέντων here,
therefore, must be comparable to that of βασανίζειν at 241d6, and the phrase should
be translated: 'if these propositions are not examined and accepted'. The elenchus
proposed here clearly does not correspond to what has come to be known as the
Socratic elenchus, primarily because the outcome is predicted at the outset. Even as
the Visitor proposes to conduct a close examination (βασανίζειν) of Parmenides' *logos*,
he says that he and Theaetetus must arrive at the conclusion, by force if necessary
(βιάζεσθαι), that what-is-not is in some respect and what-is somehow is not.
Likewise, even as he says that these propositions must be examined (ἐλεγχθέντων),
he says an acceptable sense must be found for them (ὁμολογηθέντων). It is a further
question whether this weaker sense of ἐλεγχ- carries over into its four subsequent
uses at 242a8, b1, b2, and b4. Nothing seems to tell for or against in the first case;
and the pairing of ἔλεγχον with ἀπόδειξιν in the last perhaps tells against the stronger
sense. But the Visitor's hesitation at 242b1–2, σὴν γὰρ δὴ χάριν ἐλέγχειν τὸν λόγον
ἐπιθησόμεθα, ἐάνπερ ἐλέγχωμεν, might seem to require the stronger sense, for it
would be strange for him to doubt whether they can examine the thesis at all, though
natural enough for him to doubt their ability to refute Parmenides' *logos* (unless perhaps ἐλέγχωμεν connotes *successful* examination). It is worth pointing out that
Lesher 1984 has argued, on the basis of a thorough survey of the uses of ἔλεγχος and
ἐλέγχω from Homer and Hesiod up to the middle of the 4th cent., that Parmenides
himself in B7. 5 uses ἔλεγχος in something like this weaker sense, namely to refer to
'the orderly *examination* of each of the available ways of thinking. It is a *test* or *test-
ing* of each of them for their capacity to lead us to truth and knowledge about *to eon*'
(16–17, emphasis mine).

7

Sophistic Parmenideanism in the *Sophist* and in the *Parmenides*'s Dialectical Exercise

PARMENIDES' EXAMINATION OF HIS OWN HYPOTHESIS

Plato presents the dialectical exercise that constitutes the second part of the *Parmenides* as an examination by Parmenides himself of his own thesis (*Prm.* 137b1–4). Thus one naturally expects the exercise to have significant implications for Plato's understanding of Parmenides at this time. Unfortunately, one might also expect that determining exactly what these implications are will be quite difficult, for the second part of the *Parmenides* has been without doubt the most puzzling and controversial text in the Platonic corpus. Already in antiquity it was the locus of strong disagreement, and there have been deep divisions throughout the period of modern Platonic scholarship over the exercise's ultimate meaning. The unity of the dialogue remains the dominant problem. How does the dialectical exercise Parmenides undertakes in the second part of the dialogue relate to his critique of the theory of forms in the first part? Do the antinomies of the second part point to a solution of the difficulties raised for the theory in the first part? If so, how, and to what extent does the solution represent a revision by Plato of his earlier views? These are the central questions a thorough interpretation of the dialectical exercise must address. (There is also the issue of the exercise's relation to Plato's so-called 'unwritten philosophy', the subject of so many German and, increasingly, Italian studies.) However, since we are primarily concerned with the evidence the exercise provides for Plato's understanding of Parmenides, I shall not pretend to put forward an interpretation of the overall 'moral' of the exercise.[1] I hope, none the less, that coming

---

[1] Gill 1996 provides a recent, serviceable introduction to the dialogue, with accompanying translation, that will provide the reader with a useful point of departure for exploring these further issues. For help in approaching the dialectical exercise, one will also find useful Taylor 1896–7, Wahl 1926, Cornford 1939, Ryle 1939, Brumbaugh 1961, Owen 1970(*a*), Schofield 1977, Moravscik 1982, Hägler 1983, Meinwald 1991, and Allen 1997.

to grips with Plato's developing view and use of Parmenides in this portion of the dialogue might be thought to have some bearing on certain of the more central issues in the exercise's interpretation.

Although I shall not attempt to give an account of the exercise's overall philosophical purpose, it is nevertheless necessary to specify here at the outset certain assumptions I shall make regarding its character. I assume, first, that the exercise is serious, in the sense that it is meant to have positive doctrinal implications. It is neither some kind of elaborate joke, nor a parody of Eleatic or Megarian logic, nor is it merely a collection of fallacies to be sorted out by the budding philosopher.[2] Rather, the exercise is supposed to represent the kind of training the young Socrates needs if the truth[3] is not to escape him (135c8–d6, cf. 136c4–5, e1–3). Plato's two subsequent references to the exercise confirm its seriousness. In the *Theaetetus* Socrates describes how awestruck he had been on the occasion of their encounter by Parmenides' profundity (*Tht.* 183e3–184a2). Proclus informs us that interpreters of the dialogue in antiquity who saw it as doing something more serious and substantive than simply providing logical training[4]

---

[2] See, for example, Hardie 1936, 102–10, Ryle 1939, 97–100, and Schofield 1977, 140–2, for a defence of Plato's seriousness in composing the second half of the dialogue. The view defended by Calogero 1932, 269–311, that the exercise is a critical parody of Parmenides and Zeno no longer has serious partisans. Likewise with the view that the objections to Socrates' theory of forms put in the mouth of Parmenides represent Megarian objections to Plato's theory and that the exercise is thus a counter-attack on 'the Megarian One'. This interpretation goes back to Stallbaum 1839 and was adopted by e.g. Zeller 1922, 259 and 547–8, Burnet 1914, 253–72, Taylor 1929, ch. 14 *passim*, and 1934, 10 ff. (though he had earlier criticized this view; see Taylor 1896–7, 317–18). Despite the criticisms of, among others, Hardie 1936, 107, and Cornford 1939, 100–2 and 106, there continued to be sporadic attempts at resurrecting this view; see e.g. Karlin 1947. The less extreme position of Robinson 1942 and Ross 1951, 99–101 (both following and modifying Grote 1875, ii. 263 ff.), takes the second part of the dialogue to be simply an exercise in dialectical argument for members of the Academy without serious doctrinal implications. This view also has few recent adherents.

[3] Do we have here a glancing allusion by Parmenides to the subject of his own discourse, namely truth or ἀλήθεια (cf. B1. 29, B2. 4, B8. 51)? There seem to be other allusions, at any rate, to Parmenides' actual poem in the transitional stage of the dialogue. Zeno, for example, says that 'the many do not know' that without going through the type of comprehensive inquiry Parmenides proposes 'it is impossible to happen upon the truth and to attain genuine knowledge' (ἀδύνατον ἐντυχόντα τῷ ἀληθεῖ νοῦν σχεῖν) (*Prm.* 136e1–3), loosely echoing Parmenides' own criticisms of mortal ignorance. There also seems to be a glancing allusion to Parmenides' proem in Parmenides' comparison of himself, as he prepares to embark on an examination of his own hypothesis, to the old race horse described by the lyric poet Ibycus of Rhegium as it is about to compete in a chariot-race (136e9–137a6).

[4] Procl. *in Prm.* 630, 37–635, 27 Cousin indicates that there were in antiquity numerous interpreters who in various ways ascribed to the exercise this limited purpose of dialectical training. Although Proclus does not name the interpreters he has in mind,

cited this passage from the *Theaetetus* (*in Prm.* 635, 31 ff. Cousin). Likewise, in the *Sophist* Socrates alludes to his having been present when Parmenides went through a series of 'altogether excellent arguments' (*Sph.* 217c5–7).

I shall also assume that the exercise has something to do with Parmenides' one being. Studies subsequent to Gilbert Ryle's 1939 interpretation of the exercise as an early essay in the theory of types, that is, as an examination of certain formal concepts integral to all subject matters, have tended either to ignore or reject outright this potential historical aspect of the exercise in favour of pursuing more purely conceptual analysis. There are, indeed, good reasons to identify the subject of the exercise as the intelligible form of Unity. As we have seen, in the discussion bridging Parmenides' critique of Socrates' conception of forms and his embarking on the exercise, Parmenides says Socrates has attempted to define each one of the forms (ἐν ἕκαστον τῶν εἰδῶν) before being properly trained (135c8–d1). He nevertheless commends Socrates for not restricting his inquiries to things visible but looking instead to things that one grasps by reason and may consider to be forms or εἴδη (135d8–e4). Thus it seems reasonable enough to understand the subject of the exercise that follows as either the specifically Platonic form of Unity or more generally as the concept of Unity. One might thus suppose that the exercise actually has rather little to do with Parmenides.

Such a view would seem implicit in the numerous studies of the exercise that simply pass over the issue of its bearing upon Plato's understanding of Parmenides. Others make the point explicit. Ryle himself declared: 'The one motive which I feel fairly sure did not much influence Plato [sc. in his choice of Unity for examination] is the one usually mentioned, namely that he wished to discuss Parmenidean Monism.'[5] Likewise, William Runciman objects that there is 'no reason to suppose that Plato will put into the mouth of Parmenides anything that the historical Parmenides might have been expected to say; and the Parmenides of the dialogue is in fact made to express views with which the historical Parmenides certainly would not have agreed'.[6] The error committed in dismissing for this reason the possible relation of the exercise to Parmenides is obvious. The 'historical Parmenides' certainly would not have criticized the young Socrates'

this seems to have been a Middle Platonic view (cf. Albinus, *Isagoge* 3; Alcinous, *Didaskalikos* 6); and Dodds 1928, 135, plausibly suggests it may even go back to the New Academy.

[5] Ryle 1939, 117.   [6] Runciman 1959, 162.

theory of forms in the way we find him doing in this dialogue—
if only because he knew of no such theory. But this should not
cause us to forget the influence Parmenides had on the formation of
Plato's middle period conception of forms. If Plato now allows
Parmenides to criticize the theory he had inspired, he is in effect signalling that his own earlier appropriation somehow failed to capture
what he has now come to see as an important aspect of Parmenides'
philosophy. Our question, therefore, should not be whether the dialogue provides us with anything like an accurate representation of
Parmenides himself but rather what it can tell us about Plato's developing understanding and use of Parmenides. Since the correction
of Socrates' conception of intelligible reality, and thereby of Plato's
earlier appropriation, comes in the dialectical exercise in which Parmenides purports to examine his own thesis (137b2–4), we should
look to the exercise for evidence of Plato's new understanding of
Parmenides.

Runciman's declaration that Plato's Parmenides expresses views with
which the historical Parmenides would not have agreed somewhat
unobtrusively commits the familiar essentialist fallacy. Others more
conspicuously make the mistake. Thus Reginald Allen contends that
'Parmenides' One Being can scarcely be the subject of Parmenides'
present hypothesis. In the first place, the One Being cannot be par-
ticipated in because there is nothing else besides it. . . . Second, the
One Being precludes the possibility of "others", whereas the exercise
to follow assumes that they may exist.'[7] Allen here falls into the by
now familiar trap of presupposing an interpretation of Parmenides
independent of the actual Platonic reception and then judging Plato's
representation of Parmenides' views against it. Likewise, M. M.
McCabe asserts that the subject of the deductions should not be
identified with Parmenides' own subject since 'it is hard to see why
Parmenides would be misled into thinking that this is *his* one (*Parm.*
137b3), which excludes plural properties altogether'.[8] McCabe here
gets things the wrong way round. Given that Parmenides *does* say that
he will take up his own hypothesis for examination, we should explore
what kind of understanding of his philosophy the subsequent exercise reflects. We should not presume a view of his philosophy—that
there is nothing else apart from the One, or that the One can have only
one property—and then reject what Plato has Parmenides say in the
exercise about his own subject. (In assuming that the exercise has
something to tell us about Parmenides' one being, I do not at all mean

---

[7] Allen 1997, 208.   [8] McCabe 1994, 104.

to deny that valuable results also come from interpreting the exercise as concerned with the form of Unity or, as McCabe herself does, with what it is to be an individual. On the contrary, I hope the reading developed here by focusing on the exercise's bearing upon Plato's understanding of Parmenides will have implications for a reading with more general concerns.)

Against those who wanted to interpret the exercise as a parody of Eleaticism, W. F. R. Hardie made the telling point that it would be very odd for such an attack to be put in the mouth of Parmenides himself.[9] It would be more natural for Plato to voice through the character of Parmenides a defence and elaboration of Parmenides' philosophy as he himself understands it. This point leads to my next assumption about the nature of the exercise. Those commentators who have allowed that the exercise does have something to do with Parmenides' conception of the One have too often been confused about which portions of the exercise may be taken as representing Plato's view of that conception. This confusion has led commentators to speak of the exercise's 'refutation' of Parmenides, when it is in fact more accurate to suppose that Plato has Parmenides reject certain possible misconceptions or misappropriations of his thought. The ultimate source of this error is again a lapse into the essentialist fallacy. This lapse often leads to an assumption that Parmenides' philosophy is most accurately represented in the First Deduction. Cornford, for example, admits that what he takes to be the different senses of the hypothesis examined in the First and Second Deductions, that the One is, can both be traced back to Parmenides.[10] Yet he tends to presume that the more accurate representation of Parmenides' thought is to be found in the First Deduction, for it exhibits the One as absolutely one, unique, and without parts.[11] Cornford thus sees the First Deduction as indicating how Parmenides' own conception of the One needs to be corrected, and he interprets key points in the Second Deduction as direct criticisms of Parmenides' conception. He describes *Parmenides* 142d9–145a4, for instance, as 'a brilliant refutation of the Eleatic thesis, that a One is, and yet a plurality of beings (πολλὰ ὄντα) is irrational'.[12] Cornford sees the First Deduction as a basically

---

[9] Hardie 1936, 106; cf. Ross 1951, 95. Cherniss 1932 exemplifies the anti-Parmenidean interpretation of the exercise; he supposes that *Prm.* 137b puts it beyond doubt that 'Parmenides and his poem are the butt at which the second part of the dialogue is aimed' and so describes the exercise as 'an attack on Eleaticism by the father of the school' (130–1) and as 'a parody of the Eleatic method applied to the doctrine of Parmenides' (138).   [10] Cornford 1939, 109–10.

[11] See ibid. 134 and n. 2, 135.   [12] Ibid. 143; cf. 138, 144, 145.

accurate representation of Parmenides' own thought because he has committed the essentialist fallacy in a more thorough and explicit manner than most commentators by actually prefacing his study of the *Parmenides* with a thorough and independent interpretation of Parmenides.[13] However, it would seem to tell against this interpretation, from Plato's perspective at least, that it leads Cornford to see the most accurate representation of Parmenides' thought in the deduction where the conception of the One is, as we have seen, decidedly Gorgianic and the results of which are most explicitly rejected.

One needs to be more careful than Cornford about which of the exercise's deductions represent Plato's own understanding of Parmenides. For here, just as in the *Sophist*, Plato is concerned with recovering Parmenides from certain sophistic appropriations as well as with advancing much more explicitly than in the *Sophist* a view of Parmenides relevant to his own philosophical purposes. Thus I do not believe that the apparently conflicting results of the exercise's deductions are intended to be all mutually acceptable (nor do I think they are all to be rejected). Even if it were the case that with the appropriate qualifications the results of the deductions could be interpreted as not strictly contradictory, it remains a fact that in the course of the exercise some results are quite plainly rejected. This is clearest in the case of the First Deduction. The Neoplatonists may have thought that it presents an account of the One as a transcendent first principle, ineffable and beyond all being, and accordingly to be identified as the highest God and equated with the *Republic*'s form of the Good.[14]

---

[13] Those who suppose that Plato engages in a 'refutation' of Parmenides include Wahl 1926, 64, and Sayre 1978, 145 (representing a particularly clumsy commission of the essentialist fallacy). Others have spoken more generally of Plato's 'misrepresentation' of Parmenides; e.g. Tarán 1965, 269–71, asserts on the basis of his own analysis of Parmenides' poem that Plato's encapsulation of Parmenides' doctrine in the formula 'the all is one' or ἓν τὸ πᾶν (*Prm.* 128a8–b1) and his specification of Parmenides' subject as 'the One itself' (137b1–4) 'is not the doctrine of Parmenides' and that 'Parmenides' philosophy is incompatible with Plato's description of it'. See also Untersteiner 1955, 9–17, who attempts to explain the historical genesis of this 'misrepresentation', and Riezler 1934, 89–93 (and contrast Capizzi 1970, 45–6, 49, who accepts the accuracy of Plato's attribution of the ἓν τὸ πᾶν thesis to Parmenides). The essentialist fallacy is even committed by scholars purporting to examine the *Parmenides* for evidence of Plato's view of Parmenides. Szabó 1992, for example, while purporting to undertake such an examination, begins from his own schematic and somewhat bizarre interpretation of Parmenides, according to which his three ways are quasi-mythical expressions of the logical principles of identity, contradiction, and the excluded middle.

[14] So Proclus in the lengthy exegesis of the First Deduction that concludes his commentary on the dialogue. Cf. Procl. *Theol. Plat.* 1. 10. 41, 23–42, 2: 'so concerning the first of the hypotheses almost all have agreed with one another and deem

Plato himself, however, indicates that the results of this deduction are unacceptable. The First Deduction starts with the hypothesis that there is a One but reaches the conclusion that the One in no way is (141e9–10). At this point Parmenides indicates that this result may not be acceptable by repeating this disturbing conclusion and adding a qualification that seems to undermine the reliability of the entire previous deduction: 'as it seems, the One neither is one nor is, *if we are to trust this kind of argument*' (141e12–142a1). As we have seen, the deduction arrives at this conclusion by arguments that are often distinctly Gorgianic, and from this conclusion it infers the same type of Gorgianic consequences regarding the intelligibility and express-ibility of the One already echoed by Parmenides at the close of his critique of Socrates' conception of forms. When Parmenides con-cludes the First Deduction by asking whether it is possible for things to be like this in the case of the One, Aristoteles answers that it is not (142a6–8). Parmenides accordingly begins the next deduction by asking Aristoteles whether they should return to the original hypo-thesis in the hope that some other result may surface as they consider it afresh (142b1–2). There could be no clearer sign that the results of the First Deduction, and thus the deduction's Gorgianic conception of Parmenides' One, are repudiated.

There have nevertheless been commentators who have tried to explain away this rejection.[15] Proclus, commenting on 142a6–8,

Plato through this hypothesis to be celebrating the super-substantial principle of wholes as ineffable, unknowable, and beyond all being (τὸ ἄρρητον καὶ ἄγνωστον καὶ παντὸς ἐπέκεινα τοῦ ὄντος).' Cf. also *Theol. Plat.* 3. 8. 29, 7–30, 2, where Proclus further connects the One with what Pl. *Ep.* 2. 312e1–3 describes as the cause of all that is beautiful and with what *Phlb.* 23c7–d8 and 26e1–27c2 describe as the cause of all divinity. See Westerink and Saffrey 1968, i. lxxv–lxxxix, for a succinct exposi-tion of the history of Neoplatonic exegesis of the *Parmenides*'s exercise down to Proclus, as well as Dodds 1928, Rist 1962, and Jackson 1967 on the origins of this interpretation. Cornford 1939, 131–4 (cf. v–ix), properly criticized those of his mod-ern predecessors who attempted to revive the Neoplatonic variety of interpretation, including Wahl 1926, Wundt 1935, and Speiser 1937; on the historical circumstances and intellectual affiliations that informed Wahl's interpretation, see Saffrey 1993. Hägler 1983, 99–104, likewise opposes the Neoplatonic approach to the exercise, singling out the 'modern Neoplatonists' Speiser 1959 and Wyller 1963 for particu-lar criticism. The ancient Neoplatonic interpretations are extremely interesting as exemplifying the *use* later made of the exercise, but this use should not be confused with Plato's own intentions.

[15] For example, Lynch 1959 spends fourteen pages explaining away *Prm.* 142a6–8. Forrester 1972 is a less strained attempt to vindicate the possibility of a positive interpretation of the First Deduction in the face of Parmenides' and Aristoteles' objec-tions. He proposes that Plato means to dismiss only the portion of the deduction from 141e7 ff., where the problematic inference is drawn that only by existing in time can

recognized that this is a very unexpected conclusion that raises such doubts about the foregoing arguments that some interpreters he knew felt that Plato was in fact indicating that the One so conceived is an impossibility (*in Prm.* 62, 31–64, 7 Klibansky; cf. 1065, 3–8 Cousin).[16] Proclus devotes considerable space to reviewing his Neoplatonic predecessors' explanations of the troublesome conclusion and to setting out his own perspective on the problem (*in Prm.* 64, 11–76, 7 Klibansky). Here, however, I want to concentrate briefly on one modern attempt to discount Parmenides and Aristoteles' rejection of the First Deduction's consequences. Constance Meinwald has advanced an interpretation of the exercise according to which 'all the arguments and their conclusions are to be accepted'.[17] To explain how the contradictions among the deductions are merely apparent, she makes use of a distinction between predications that are made of a subject 'in relation to itself' or *pros heauto* and 'in relation to the others' or *pros ta alla*. In the third chapter of her study Meinwald spells out how the first type of predication indicates what holds of a subject in relation to itself or 'in virtue of a relation internal to the subject's own nature', while the second type of predication indicates what features the subject displays in virtue of its relation to other natures. Thus, taking the most important antinomy, the apparent contradictions between the conclusions drawn in the First and Second Deductions are to be explained away on the grounds that the First is considering what *pros heauto* predicates the One has while the Second is considering its *pros*

---

an object participate in being (5–6). Forrester's mistake is to suppose that 141e7–8 —'Is there, then, any way in which something could participate in being other than one of these?'—refers only to the portion of the deduction concerned with denying that various temporal attributes are predicable of the One (an assumption encouraged by Burnet's paragraph division at 141d6). But in fact the entire deduction is concerned with denying the various possible ways the One might be—that is, the question at 141e7–8 extends back over the whole deduction.

[16] Westerink and Saffrey 1974, ii. x–xii, suggest that Proclus here has in mind the Platonist Origen, on the ground that *Theol. Plat.* 2. 4. 31, 4 ff. attributes such a view to him.

[17] Meinwald 1991, 63–4. See also 20–6, where she divides interpretations of the exercise into ones that presume these contradictions are real, so that certain elements of certain deductions are to be rejected, and ones that take the contradictions among deductions to be merely apparent, so that all the conclusions of the deductions may be accepted. As representatives of the first type of interpretation, which she dubs 'rejectionism', she cites Ryle 1939, Owen 1970(*a*), Moravscik 1982, and Curd 1989. Cornford 1939 and Sayre 1983 are cited as representatives of the second type that nevertheless allow elements of rejectionism to creep in (i.e. although they do not judge the results to be actually contradictory, they reject certain results for other reasons). She presents her own interpretation as one of the second type purified of such elements of rejectionism.

ta alla predicates. One problem with this solution is that we find examples of *both pros heauto* and *pros ta alla* predicates in the Second
Deduction.[18] This is a serious problem for Meinwald's interpretation
(and one to which we shall return), but here I want to concentrate
on the inadequacy of her attempt to preserve the acceptability of the
First Deduction in spite of Parmenides and Aristoteles' comments on
its results.

She notes that in a typical Socratic dialogue, when a contradiction
emerges in the course of Socrates' discussion with his interlocutor, they
remark in one way or another on the unacceptability of such a result:
'Often the discussion extends into professions of confusion or dissatisfaction with the situation. . . . Through such passages these dialogues
provide us with (the beginnings of) an interpretative response to the
result of the dialectic.'[19] The situation regarding the *Parmenides*'s
dialectical exercise, she says, is completely different. But this simply
is not true. Parmenides and Aristoteles clearly express their dissatisfaction with the results of the First Deduction, a fact which she
acknowledges only in a footnote,[20] presumably because it directly
undermines her tenet that all the results are acceptable. One might
also ask whether the results of the First Deduction can in fact be
salvaged by the addition of the *pros heauto* qualifier. If 'the Just is
virtuous' is to count as a case of *pros heauto* predication, that is, as a
predication that holds in virtue of a relation internal to the subject's
own nature, then one might expect that 'the One is' and 'the One is
one' should also count, and yet the First Deduction ends up rejecting precisely these characterizations (141e9–12).[21] Meinwald does
not discuss these important lines but, again, only acknowledges their
threat to her interpretation in a brief footnote.[22] The First Deduction
seems to show that the One is nothing at all, which hardly seems an
acceptable conclusion regarding its nature *pros heauto* or in relation
to itself. For such reasons, then, Meinwald's rejection of 'rejectionism' cannot be judged successful.[23]

---

[18] For this point, cf. Sayre 1994, 116, who rightly concludes that 'the distribution
of *pros heauto* and *pros ta alla* predications among the several sections may not be
quite as regular as she proposes'.   [19] Meinwald 1991, 21.

[20] Ibid. 175 n. 21.   [21] Cf. Sayre 1994, 116.

[22] Meinwald 1991, 180 n. 14.

[23] Peterson 1996, who takes a generally favourable view of Meinwald's enterprise,
attempts to deal with the troublesome results of the First Deduction on her behalf
and to explain away their rejection by Parmenides and Aristoteles (178 ff.). Her efforts
in both regards are unconvincing. The rejection of the results she restricts to
Aristoteles alone, when there is every indication that Parmenides, too, finds them unacceptable. Her analysis of 'the One is not one' as meaning 'it is not *because of* Being

When Parmenides rejects the results of the First Deduction, he is rejecting the recognizably Gorgianic attempt to perform a *reductio* on his conception of the one being. When Plato has Parmenides reject the results of this deduction, he is in effect allowing him to reject a particular sophistic appropriation of his philosophy. We will see that sophistic appropriations also figure in the Fourth and Sixth Deductions, the results of which are also unacceptable. Since the results of a number of deductions prove unsatisfactory, one might wonder which of the deductions, if any, potentially represent Plato's own understanding of Parmenides. A preliminary answer to this question requires a brief analysis of the plan governing the deductions.[24] This plan is to be inferred from the revised Zenonian dialectic Parmenides presents as the proper method for examination of intelligible forms or εἴδη such as likeness, unlikeness, change, rest, coming-to-be, perishing, being, and not-being. Taking as his example the hypothesis forming the basis of Zeno's arguments, that many are, Parmenides says one must consider what follows for the many (i) in relation to themselves and (ii) in relation to the one, as well as what follows for the one (iii) in relation to itself and (iv) in relation to the many; then starting again from the negation of the original hypothesis, namely that many are not, one must consider what follows for the many (v) in relation to themselves and (vi) in relation to the one, as well as what follows for the one (vii) in relation to itself and (viii) in relation to the many (136a4–b1). The dialectical method envisaged yields eight principal deductions. When Parmenides applies this method of investigation to his own hypothesis regarding the One, this is in fact, certain relatively minor irregularities aside,[25] what we find. The dialectical exercise that takes up the remainder of the dialogue is thus comprised of eight principal deductions. Moreover, as the model structure Parmenides sets out at 136a4–b1 indicates, the deductions are naturally grouped so as to form four pairs or antinomies. Each of the paired deductions within each antinomy arrives at conclusions that conflict with those of its partner. That is, the results of the Second Deduction conflict with those of the First, the results of the Fourth conflict

or *by* Being or as *requiring* being that the One is one' (189) is exceedingly laboured and bears witness to the contortions commentators are willing to perform to uphold a deeply flawed thesis.

[24] For detailed analyses of the plan of the dialectical exercise, see e.g. Owen 1970(*a*), 349–62; Brisson and Benzécri 1989; Meinwald 1991, ch. 2; Gill 1996, 54–9 and 117–23.

[25] There is an appendix or corollary to the Second Deduction at 155e3–157b4 that some (including the Neoplatonists) have wanted to see as an independent deduction, so that the total number of deductions would be brought up to nine.

with those of the Third, and those of the Sixth and Eighth conflict, respectively, with those of the Fifth and Seventh. In each antinomy, one deduction reaches positive conclusions, the other largely negative conclusions. The 'negative' deductions are the First, Fourth, Sixth, and Eighth. The 'positive' deductions are the Second, Third, Fifth, and Seventh. The results of the First Deduction are, as we have seen, explicitly rejected, and it appears that the results of the remaining negative deductions are also to be rejected—the results of the Sixth because they directly parallel those of the First, the results of the Fourth and Eighth because they deduce the same unacceptable consequences for the others, namely that they have no attributes whatsoever. It will therefore be in the positive deductions that we can expect to find evidence for Plato's understanding of Parmenides. Among these, the Second Deduction will emerge as most important, though we shall see that the other positive deductions also reflect aspects of Plato's view.[26] However, before saying something about the implications of these deductions, I want to concentrate on the interpretations of Parmenides' hypothesis that Plato wants to reject.

[26] Work by Malcolm Schofield on the second part of the *Parmenides* constitutes an important exception to the post-Rylean tendency to dismiss the possibility that the exercise has anything to do with Parmenides (see Capizzi 1970, 58–80, for a survey of interpretations of the exercise via which he seeks to confirm that it has little to do with the historical Parmenides). Thus, for example, Schofield 1973(*b*), 8, criticizes Cornford and Brumbaugh for underestimating 'the affinity [of certain arguments in the First Deduction] with the sorts of argument employed by the historical Parmenides and his successor Zeno' (cf. Schofield 1974, 41–2). I shall have to depart, however, from Schofield's view of the first two deductions' bearing upon Parmenides (see Schofield 1972, 107–8; 1973(*a*), 44; 1974, 40; 1977, 148–9). He sees the First and Second Deductions as both employing Eleatic weapons in an *ad hominem* manner to deduce from the Parmenidean hypothesis conclusions unacceptable to an Eleatic. Yet on the whole he appears to see the First Deduction as the more accurate reflection of Eleatic principles. For it proceeds from the assumptions 'that unity excludes all plurality and divisibility' and 'that the only attributes we can or need ascribe to a thing are those which are entailed by its identifying characteristic'. Schofield presumes that it is more or less correct to see Parmenides as committed to these assumptions. While I accept that such assumptions figure crucially in the First Deduction, I believe that the Gorgianic character of the deduction and Parmenides' rejection of its results combine to suggest that Plato does not in fact think it legitimate to attribute these assumptions to Parmenides. I will argue that the Second Deduction presents a view of Parmenides that corrects the mistakes of the First, whereas Schofield sees the Second Deduction as deriving from the Parmenidean premiss conclusions that are this time even more unacceptable to an Eleatic. Schofield 1974, 42–3, sees the *Sophist* as providing the materials required to solve the problems regarding the nature of predication introduced by the First Deduction. I want to argue that Plato is already in the Second Deduction responding to the problems of the First.

NOT-BEING IN THE *SOPHIST* AND IN THE *PARMENIDES*'S FIFTH AND SIXTH DEDUCTIONS

The *Sophist*'s treatment of non-being has clear connections with the Fifth and Sixth Deductions in the dialectical exercise of the *Parmenides*.[27] Both the Fifth and Sixth Deductions proceed from the hypothesis that the One is not. However, since they understand the sense of 'is not' in quite different ways, they arrive at very different conclusions. These two ways of understanding the sense of 'is not' correspond fairly closely to the ways of understanding not-being contrasted in the *Sophist*. That is, in the Sixth Deduction 'is not' is understood in much the same way as the Sophist understands it in when he attacks the concepts of falsehood and appearance, while in the Fifth Deduction 'is not' is understood in something more like the sense that the Visitor eventually gives to it in meeting this challenge. The connections between the treatment of not-being in these two deductions and in the *Sophist* are mutually illuminating in several respects. The initial importance of these connections for our purposes is that the treatment of not-being in the negative Sixth Deduction, the results of which mirror those of the First, provides further confirmation that the reduction of what-is-and-is-not to absolute not-being is grounded in a sophistic rather than the properly Platonic understanding of Parmenides. We have already seen that the negative First Deduction reflects a particular sophistic appropriation of Parmenides. Now I want to show how the negative Sixth Deduction reflects another aspect of the sophistic engagement with Eleaticism. I shall then go on to show that this is the case with the negative Fourth Deduction as well. Parmenides and Aristoteles reject the results of the First Deduction. Those of the other negative deductions are just as unacceptable, primarily because things cannot be how these deductions conclude they must be, but also because they represent the philosophy of Parmenides in ways that Plato himself wants to repudiate.

---

[27] Dodds 1928, 134, noted that 'some of the most important discoveries of the later Platonic logic, especially the distinction between absolute and relative non-Being, appear first in the Parmenidean hypotheses'. Bondeson 1973, 17–18, draws attention to some of the similarities between *Sph.* 237b7–239b10 and the Sixth Deduction that I point out here, and he connects them with the results of the First Deduction (cf. Schofield 1977, 146). The parallels between the conclusions of the Sixth Deduction, the First Deduction, and *Sophist* 238c are also noted by e.g. Cornford 1939, 234, and Allen 1997, 336. McCabe 1994, 128 and n. 54, notes that the Fifth Deduction anticipates the *Sophist*'s eventual treatment of not-being. Schofield 1974, 42, Panagiotou 1981, McPherran 1986, and Curd 1988 also point to important connections between the *Parmenides* and the *Sophist*.

At the beginning of the Sixth Deduction, Parmenides specifies the sense of 'is not' in the following terms:

Whenever we say 'is not', does it signify anything other than the absence of being (οὐσίας ἀπουσίαν) for whatever we might say is not?—Nothing else.— So whenever we say that something is not, is it the case that we are saying that in some way it is not, while in some way it is? Or does this expression 'is not' simply signify that what-is-not is in no way at all and does not some- how have a share of being?—Most absolutely.—Therefore what-is-not could neither *be* nor in any other way at all have a share of being (163c2–d1).

The Sophist's conception of not-being as the absolute opposite of being has its manifest analogue in Parmenides' characterization of not- being in this passage. The correspondence becomes even more obvi- ous when we see that the conclusions drawn in the Sixth Deduction's display of the consequences of such an understanding of 'is not' have their analogue in the *Sophist*'s discussion of τὸ μηδαμῶς ὄν or what-is-not-at-all. Parmenides argues that if the One in no way is (οὐδαμῇ ἔστιν, *Prm.* 163d5), then it can neither come to be nor cease to be since both possibilities presume that it *is* at some point (d1–8). It cannot undergo alteration of any sort since alteration involves coming to be and ceasing to be (163d8–e2), and so it cannot be in motion (e2–3); nor can it be at rest since it cannot be thought to be in any place (e3–6). Parmenides then denies that the One can have any other attribute—not greatness, smallness, equality, similarity, dif- ference, etc.—by making the blanket assertion that 'not any of the things that are belong to it' (οὐδ' ἔστι γε αὐτῷ τι τῶν ὄντων, 163e7). What is more, the Eleatic Visitor and Theaetetus make the same point in the *Sophist* when they agree that it is impossible for 'any of the things that are' (τι τῶν ὄντων) ever to be attributed to what-is-not (*Sph.* 238a7–8). The Eleatic Visitor and Parmenides draw parallel conclu- sions from the fact that what in no way is can have no properties at all. The Visitor, as we have already seen, concludes that 'it is impos- sible either to utter or to speak of or to conceive of what absolutely is not, but it is inconceivable, unsayable, unutterable, and unspeakable' (*Sph.* 238c8–11). Parmenides concludes the Sixth Deduction with a long list of things that cannot apply to the One if it is not: ' "of that", "to that", "something", "this", "of this", "of another", "to another"; once, hereafter, now; *knowledge, opinion, perception; statement, or name*' (*Prm.* 164a7–b2). That is, if the One's not being is to be under- stood as a total absence of being, then it will have no properties at all, it will be impossible for it to stand in any relation to anything else, and it will consequently be inapprehensible and unutterable.

This series of conclusions echoes the Gorgianic conclusions of the First Deduction, namely that the One in no way is (οὐδαμῶς . . . ἔστι τὸ ἕν, *Prm.* 141e9–10) and that it can consequently not be the object of any variety of apprehension or speech (142a3–4). That is, the One neither is, nor is knowable, nor is communicable. In the Sixth Deduction Parmenides begins with the hypothesis that the One is not and goes on to conclude that one can neither have any apprehension of it nor speak about it. Although Parmenides and Aristoteles do not explicitly reject the result of the Sixth Deduction, it is just as unacceptable as that of the First. That there should be this close connection between the two deductions is just what we should expect, given that the Sixth Deduction is the structural counterpart of the First. The deductions can be grouped into pairs of antinomies (First and Second, Third and Fourth, etc.), but it is also important to recognize that each of the first four deductions examining the consequences of the hypothesis that the One is has its counterpart among the final four deductions examining the consequences of the hypothesis that the One is not (First and Sixth, Second and Fifth, Third and Seventh, Fourth and Eighth).[28]

In much the same way as, in the *Sophist*, the Eleatic Visitor's solution to the problems of not-being counters the Sophist's reduction of what-is-not to what-is-not-at-all, so the Fifth Deduction in the *Parmenides* presents a more acceptable alternative to the Sixth's understanding of not-being as the complete absence of being. Parmenides begins the Fifth Deduction by attempting to explain the semantics of statements of the form '*x* is not' (160c2–d2). He compares the statement, 'the One is not', with the statements, 'largeness is not' and 'smallness is not'. He says that one means that the thing which is not is something different in each of these statements. That is, when one says that 'largeness is not', one means that it is largeness that is not. Likewise, when one says that 'smallness is not', one means that it is smallness that is not. So, Parmenides infers, when one says that the One is not, it is clear that one means that something different from other things is not. Whether one predicates being or not-being of the

---

[28] See Sayre 1978 for a forceful demonstration of the importance of this second type of grouping. Although he overstates the case for rejecting the traditional pairing of the deductions into antinomies, he is correct in pointing out that 'no two consequences drawn from hypotheses I through IV pertain to the same object(s) in the same respect, nor any two consequences of V through VIII, but . . . for each summary consequence of I through IV there is a parallel consequence of V through VIII drawn regarding the same object in the same respect' (136–7). On some of the parallels between the Second and Fifth Deductions, see Schofield 1977, 151–2.

One, one picks out some specific thing different from other things when one mentions the One.

Plato's particular manner of expressing the point he wants to make here seems rather awkward, especially when considered from the vantage point of the *Sophist*'s eventual analysis of the semantics of not-being. In retrospect, Plato seems in this particular passage of the *Parmenides* to be finding his way towards the more precise and successful analysis of the later dialogue. That analysis is based upon a clarification of two essential points, that statements are composed of subject and predicate elements, and that statements of the form '*x* is not (F)' do not mean that *x* is in no way at all but that *x* is different from other things. We can see Plato moving towards clarification of these two points here in the *Parmenides*, and yet we can also see that he has not quite got clear about how, exactly, he needs to formulate the requisite concepts. Instead of distinguishing the subject and predicate components of the statements under consideration, he simply insists upon our having successfully mentioned or picked out something different from everything else when we say that 'largeness is not' or 'the One is not'. Again, rather than analysing its difference from everything else as a function of the predicate 'is not', he speaks of this difference as a function of our having picked out something knowable in each case. The claim that in each of the statements, 'largeness is not' and 'smallness is not', one means that what is not is something different (ἕτερόν τι λέγοι τὸ μὴ ὄν, *Prm.* 160c4) comes tantalizingly close to the central point in the *Sophist*'s analysis of the semantics of not-being, namely that when we use the expression 'not being' we are not thereby indicating that what is not is the opposite of being but only that it is different from something else (ὁπόταν τὸ "μὴ ὄν" λέγωμεν . . . οὐκ ἐναντίον τι λέγομεν τοῦ ὄντος ἀλλ᾽ ἕτερον μόνον, *Sph.* 257b3–4). That is, statements of the form '*x* is not (F)' do not mean that *x* in no way is but that *x* is different (from F). The point in the *Parmenides*, however, is not that the predicate 'is not (F)' is equivalent in sense to 'is different (from F)' but that the subjects of the two statements given as examples are different. Likewise, when he turns to a particular consideration of the hypothesis 'the One is not', Parmenides makes the point that the One is different from other things, but again this difference is taken as a consequence of successful mention of the One in the hypothesis rather than as a function of 'is not' in the hypothesis itself (*Prm.* 160d3–7). Parmenides will perhaps seem to come closest to the *Sophist*'s analysis when he says that since the things other than the One are different from it, 'the One possesses dissimilarity in relation to the others' (ἀνομοιότης ἄρα ἐστὶν αὐτῷ πρὸς τὰ ἄλλα, *Prm.* 161a6). For he seems to be employing the language of the *Sophist*'s crucial distinction between predications indicating what a thing is by itself and predications indicating what a thing is in relation to other things.[29] Again, however, difference is not attributed to the One in relation to other things in the *Parmenides* on the basis of an analysis of the semantics of 'is not' but on the basis of the presumed successful mention of the One in any statement about it.

The Fifth Deduction clearly represents an important stage in Plato's developing analysis of the problems of not-being. The relation between his approach to the problem here and the more precise analysis in the *Sophist* deserves further consideration. Nevertheless, the essential point for our purposes is that Plato in the *Parmenides*'s Fifth Deduction is suggesting a way in which the sophistic reduction of what-is-not to what-is-not-at-all may be forestalled. He is presenting a way of understanding the hypothesis that the One is not such that it does not mean that the One is in no way whatsoever. Indeed, we see Parmenides going on in the course of the deduction to argue that although the One is not in a number of respects, there are various other respects in which it is. As the One is unlike other things (161a6–b4), so it is like itself (b4–c2). The One is not equal to the others (161c3–d1), yet it is equal with respect to itself (d1–e2). Thus it emerges that the One, even if it is not, must nevertheless partake in being to some extent (161e3). Parmenides' explanation at 161e4–162b8 of how this can be the case is dense and somewhat awkward. This awkwardness, again, seems to be a result of the *Parmenides*'s as yet inadequate analysis of not-being. Parmenides' basic point is that if we are to take the hypothesis 'the One is not' as a true statement, then we must presume that the subject of this statement is something that is, for otherwise we would not know what the statement is about. So the sense of the statement 'the One is not' can be clarified by recasting it as 'the One *is* something that is not' (ἔστιν . . . τὸ ἓν οὐκ ὄν, 162a1–2) or, more precisely, 'the One has a share of being in relation to not being' (τῷ ἑνί, ἐπειδὴ οὐκ ἔστι, τοῦ εἶναι ἀνάγκη μετεῖναι εἰς τὸ μὴ εἶναι, 162b4–6). However successful one might judge the analysis here of how what is not can nevertheless be, it is at any rate clear that the Fifth Deduction is attempting to provide an account of not-being such that 'the One is not' does not mean that 'the One is in no way at all'.

[29] Cf. the key sentence, *Sph.* 255c14–15: ἀλλ᾽ οἶμαί σε συγχωρεῖν τῶν ὄντων τὰ μὲν αὐτὰ καθ᾽ αὑτά, τὰ δὲ πρὸς ἄλλα ἀεὶ λέγεσθαι; For an explanation of how the distinction introduced here is fundamental to Plato's solution of the problems of not-being in the *Sophist*, see Frede 1967 and 1992.

This latter sense, as we have seen, is that given the hypothesis in the Sixth Deduction, at the outset of which Parmenides signals quite explicitly the reduction that will be made regarding the sense of 'is not': 'so whenever we say that something is not, is it the case that we are saying that *in some way it is not, while in some way it is*? Or does this expression "is not" simply signify that what-is-not *is in no way at all* and does not somehow have a share of being?' (163c4–7). Allen comments: 'As in the thought of the historical Parmenides, the Way that is and is not has reduced to the Way that is not.'[30] Allen is at least aware of the reduction taking place here, but again, all signs are that this is not a reduction Plato would want to attribute to Parmenides himself. The sophistic reduction of what-is-and-is-not to what-is-not-at-all is, as Allen recognizes, a reduction of the mode of being specified by Parmenides' third path to that specified by his second path. This is in effect the reduction performed in the *Sophist*, where appearances are reduced to absolute non-being.

It might therefore appear quite odd that in the *Parmenides* it is the One itself that is characterized in the Fifth Deduction as both being and not being and then in the Sixth reduced to absolute non-being. This seems odd because in Parmenides the One enjoys the mode of being specified by the first path, the mode of absolute being devoid of any trace of not-being. What could be the possible motivation for performing the reduction on what-is itself and not merely upon what-is-and-is-not? What is the motivation for supposing that the One itself is not in any way? Perhaps it is this. There are numerous points in his poem where Parmenides had been perfectly willing to say that what-is or τὸ ἐόν is not various things, both by saying directly that it is not F and by saying that it is not-F. It is 'ungenerated' and 'imperishable' (B8. 2). It is 'unshaken' (B8. 4), 'unchanging' (B8. 26, 38), 'unbeginning and unceasing' (B8. 27). It is 'not endless' (B8. 32), for 'it is not lacking' (B8. 33). Now, the Fifth Deduction seeks to provide an analysis of the semantics of not-being such that it is perfectly consistent and acceptable for what-is or the One not to be all these various things while still being the things it is. The mistake of the approach taken to the Parmenidean One in the Sixth Deduction is to draw the conclusion from the fact that the One is not these various things that the One is not at all. If, however, one were of a particularly sophistic turn of mind, one might be inclined to argue that since Parmenides himself says that what-is is not F for various values of F, then what-is is not for *all* values of F. This is in effect

---

[30] Allen 1997, 336.

what Gorgias attempted to do in his personal demonstration, albeit via a different route, which goes some way towards explaining why in the Sixth Deduction we get the Gorgianic conclusion that the One is not, is unknowable, and is incommunicable.

The *Sophist* gives an account of how the reduction of what-is-not to what-is-not-at-all may be forestalled. To say of *x* that it is not need not imply a total absence of being—it is perfectly possible for *x* not to be certain things while being others. This correction of the sophistic understanding of not-being has its analogue in the Fifth Deduction's 'correction' of the Sixth. The Sixth Deduction takes 'the One is not' to mean that the One is completely devoid of all being. The Fifth Deduction, however, attempts to explain how it is possible for the One-that-is nevertheless not to be, and it emerges in this context that the One is not certain things while it is other things. That is, Plato seems perfectly willing to accept Parmenides' own statements that what-is is not various things while it is other things. The significance of this apparently pedestrian conclusion might start to become apparent if we try to understand the implications of the fact that the Fifth Deduction has its counterpart in the Second, just as the Sixth has its counterpart in the First. We noted the apparent oddity of the Sixth Deduction's attempt to reduce the One to absolute non-being. Whereas the reduction in the *Sophist* is of what-is-and-is-not to what-is-not-at-all, the reduction in the Sixth Deduction would seem to be of what-completely-is to what-is-not-at-all. But now it should be clear that this was a mistaken characterization of the reduction performed in the Sixth Deduction. There too the reduction was of what-is-and-is-not, namely the One as it had been characterized in the Fifth Deduction, to what-is-not-at-all. What now seems odd and what demands explanation is Plato's assigning of the One to the realm of what-is-and-is-not. This is how he characterizes it in the Fifth Deduction and in the structurally corresponding Second Deduction. More than anywhere else, this might seem to be the point where Plato threatens to depart radically from Parmenides.

As yet, however, we have insufficient indications of Plato's later view of Parmenides to permit a final judgement on this issue. Consideration of the *Sophist*'s examination of the Eleatic thesis (244b6–245e5) will help us to start sorting out the problems here by providing some indication of Plato's own view of Parmenides at this time. So far we have primarily paid attention to those portions of the *Sophist* and *Parmenides* that reflect uses of Parmenides' philosophy that Plato himself is unwilling to countenance. In the *Sophist*'s examination of the Eleatics, however, we shall find certain indications of how Plato wants to use Parmenides. We shall also see that this portion of the *Sophist* continues at the same time to present sophistic uses of the logic of Eleaticism that contrast with the use Plato himself wants to make and that, in so doing, it has important connections with the *Parmenides*'s dialectical exercise. The Eleatic Visitor's examination of the Eleatic thesis is in fact perhaps best understood as a miniature re-enactment of certain key portions of Parmenides' examination of his own hypothesis in the earlier dialogue. If Plato composed the *Sophist* after the *Parmenides*, then it is reasonable enough to suppose that when he comes to examine the Eleatic thesis in the later dialogue he should allude to or presume some knowledge of the earlier dialogue's more thorough examination. The compression and apparent obscurity of this difficult passage in the *Sophist* can in part be explained as a function of Plato's assumption that one will recognize its echoes of the earlier examination.[31]

THE *SOPHIST*'S FIRST CRITIQUE OF ELEATICISM AND THE *PARMENIDES*'S FOURTH DEDUCTION

The *Sophist*'s doxography of previous views on the number and nature of τὰ ὄντα or 'the things-that-are'—which we shall see is not to be understood as referring simply to things that exist but to things that are in such a way so as to be somehow fundamental to the being of other things—ascribes to its second principal group of thinkers, the Eleatics, the thesis that 'what is called "all things" is one' (242d6). This is abbreviated to Plato's standard formula 'everything is one' (ἓν τὸ πᾶν, 244b6) at the outset of the subsequent examination of the Eleatic position, and it is clear from this examination that this formula is presumed equivalent to the other standard formulation of the Eleatic thesis, 'what-is is one' (ἓν τὸ ὄν). Just as the Visitor's critique of the early pluralists constituting the doxography's first group (243d6–244b5) confronts them with the necessity of accepting that the things-that-are (τὰ ὄντα) are in some sense one, so the critique of the Eleatics confronts them with the necessity of accepting that what-is

---

[31] Perhaps because of its obscurity, this portion of the *Sophist* has received relatively little attention. The only studies I know devoted specifically to it are Guariglia 1971 and Gómez-Lobo 1974, which bear witness to the confusion that can result from failing to recognize the connection with the *Parmenides*. See Guazzoni Foà 1961, 471–2, for an example of a discussion of the critique vitiated by an essentialist approach.

(τὸ ὄν) is not just one but also many, thereby effecting the transition to the third stage of the doxography. The specific examination of the Eleatic position proceeds in two phases (244b6–d13 and 244d14–245d11), which I shall refer to as the dialogue's first and second critiques of Eleaticism.

In the first critique, the Visitor engages in an imagined mini-dialogue with the Eleatics. He begins by getting them to agree that 'what-is is one only' (244b9–10)[32] and that they call something 'being' (b12). He then asks whether what they refer to as 'being' (ὄν) is the same thing they refer to as 'one' (ἕν), that is, whether they use two names to refer to the same thing (244c1–2). This question, he says to Theaetetus, will cause advocates of the Eleatic thesis difficulties, for it forces them to admit that there are two names for the same thing in spite of their official position that what-is is only one thing (244c4–9). He then goes on, in an even more peculiar argument, to criticize them on the grounds that even saying there is a name by which one refers to the One means that there are in fact two things—the One and its name (244c11–d13).

These hardly seem the first criticisms one would want to make of the Eleatic position. One might accordingly suppose that Plato is being less than serious. Rather than dismiss the passage as not having a serious purpose because its purpose seems opaque, we should try to understand the context within which the argument functions as an intelligible response to the position. We have seen how the representation of Parmenides' position in the earlier portion of the dialogue reflects particular sophistic appropriations that posed certain problems for Plato. It is possible to understand the discussion of the Eleatic position here as functioning against the background of another sophistic engagement with Parmenides, out of which arose some of the problems regarding the nature of predication that Plato addresses in the remainder of the dialogue. The problem posed by the first critique, how one thing can have many names or predicates, is raised again at 251a5 ff., where the Visitor attributes this problem to the 'opsimaths' or 'late-learners'. They hold that it is 'impossible for what is many to be one and for what is one to be many, and they take great pleasure in forbidding one to say that a man is good, only allowing one to say that what is good is good and that what is a man

---

[32] Τόδε τοίνυν ἀποκρινέσθων. "Ἕν πού φατε μόνον εἶναι;" One might translate the question: 'do you say that there is only one thing?' But I take it that the question picks up the Visitor's stated intention to find out what the Eleatics mean by 'what-is'—τί ποτε λέγουσι τὸ ὄν; (244b6), so that εἶναι in the subsequent question is not impersonal but has the subject τὸ ὄν understood.

is a man' (251b7–c2).[33] Their position is said to be self-refuting, in so far as they must employ numerous terms and connect them in statements even to formulate it (252c2–9), a point which parallels that made against the Eleatic position in the first critique.

These late-learners have, not surprisingly, most often been identified with Antisthenes,[34] largely on the basis of Aristotle's report of his claim that 'nothing can be spoken of except by its proper *logos*, one for one' (*Metaph. Δ.* 29. 1024^{b}32–3, cf. *H.* 3. 1043^{b}23–8). Perhaps equally probable candidates for inclusion in the class of late-learners are those thinkers Aristotle elsewhere describes as having felt pressured by Parmenides' assertion that what-is is one into placing radical restrictions upon use of the verb 'to be':

> Even the more recent of the early thinkers were worried that the same thing should not turn out for them both one and many. Therefore some did away with the 'is' altogether, as for instance Lycophron,[35] while others rearranged the normal mode of expression, saying not 'the man *is* white' but 'the man has become white', and not '*is* walking' but 'walks', so as not to make what is one be many by introducing the 'is', on the ground that 'one' or 'being' is employed in only one sense (*Ph.* 1. 2. 185^{b}25–33).

Simplicius in his commentary on the passage (*in Ph.* 90, 24 ff.) explains that these thinkers in effect accepted use of 'to be' only in predications indicating what something is (τὸ τί ἐστι)—for example, 'Socrates is Socrates'—but rejected its use in predications of accident —for example, 'Socrates is white', which he says Lycophron would have changed to 'Socrates white'. The identity of the 'others' Aristotle alludes to is uncertain. Philoponus says he means Menedemus of Eretria.[36] In modern times, the Cynics, Antisthenes, the Megarians

---

[33] That there is a connection between the criticism of the Eleatics at 244b–d and the position subsequently attributed to the opsimaths is noted by Frère 1991, 139.

[34] Cf. Giannantoni 1990, i. 369–70, for references. Antisthenes has also often, and somewhat more controversially, been thought to lie behind the *Theaetetus*'s 'dream theory', at least one element of which bears comparison with predicational monism as it appears elsewhere in Plato. Socrates begins his account of the theory by saying that the primary elements of which we and everything else are composed have no account, 'for each one in itself may only be named, and it is not possible to say anything else of it, not even that it is or that it is not' (αὐτὸ γὰρ καθ' αὐτὸ ἕκαστον ὀνομάσαι μόνον εἴη, προσειπεῖν δὲ οὐδὲν ἄλλο δυνατόν, οὔθ' ὡς ἔστιν, οὔθ' ὡς οὐκ ἔστιν, *Tht.* 201e3–5).

[35] Cf. *Dam. Pr.* iii. 169, 9 ff. On Lycophron, see Hofmann 1974.

[36] *Phlp. in Ph.* 49, 18–19. Simplicius refrains from the identification, introducing the Eretrians instead as a third and separate group: 'the Eretrians were so afraid of this difficulty as to say that nothing can be predicated of anything else but each thing can only be spoken of as itself in itself, e.g. "what is a man is a man" and "what is white is white"' (*in Ph.* 91, 28–31; cf. 93, 32–3, quoting Porphyry).

Eucleides[37] and Stilpo,[38] as well as Menedemus[39] have all been proposed. We need not attempt to sort out the various claims that have
been made. For our purposes, two points are essential. First, although
Aristotle may have Stilpo and Menedemus in mind, their periods of
activity post-date Plato's. Although they continued to respond to the
supposed threat of predicational pluralism after Plato's death, Plato's
references to the problem at *Sophist* 251b–c, *Euthydemus* 303d, and
Parmenides 129a–b indicate that it was an established difficulty in his
own time. Second, as Aristotle's testimony indicates, the various
manipulations of natural language and the various restrictions placed
on the use of the verb 'to be' were in part motivated by the desire to
obey Parmenides' perceived prohibition against one thing having
many 'names' or predicates.

[37] Primarily on the basis of DL 2. 106 = fr. 24 Döring: 'he [sc. Eucleides] asserted that
the good is one though it is called by many names; for sometimes it is called wisdom,
sometimes god, and at other times intelligence, etc.' It is unclear whether this text
justifies the analysis of Eucleides' metaphysics by Findlay 1974, 14, who supposes he
held 'that there was no internal difference in [his one being] which corresponded to
the differing names applied to it. Whatever one might say of it, one was always in
effect affirming Being to be Being, Unity to be Unity, the Good to be the Good'.

[38] Primarily on the basis of Plu. *Col.* 1119 C–D = fr. 197 Döring (cf. 1120 A–B):
'Colotes . . . attacks Stilpo in tragic language and says he destroys life with his assertion that one thing cannot be predicated of another (ἕτερον ἑτέρου μὴ κατηγορεῖσθαι).
"For how shall we live, not being able to call a man good or a man a general, but
only a man a man, and, separately, good good and general general, and not being
able to speak of ten thousand cavalrymen and a secure city, but only to say that
cavalrymen are cavalrymen and ten thousand ten thousand, and likewise with the
others?"' Apelt 1891, 203 n. 2, comments: 'Es ist wohl nicht rein zufällig, daß in der
Mitteilung des Plato Soph. 251B das nämliche Beispiel gebraucht wird, wie in der
des Plutarch über Stilpo.' Cf. Simp. *in Ph.* 120, 13 ff. = fr. 198 Döring; Aristocl. *De
phil.* 7 *ap.* Eus. *PE* 14. 17. 1 = fr. 27 Döring, where the position that 'what-is is
one and the other is not' (τὸ ὂν ἓν εἶναι καὶ τὸ ἕτερον μὴ εἶναι) is ascribed to Stilpo
and the Megarians. Note also Phlp. *in Ph.* 42, 9 ff.: '[Zeno's] proof is as follows:
"Socrates, whom you say is a unit contributing to make up the plurality, is not only
Socrates, but also pale, philosophic, pot-bellied, and snub-nosed, and thus the same
man is both one and many. But the same man cannot be one and many; therefore
Socrates cannot be one."' Philoponus appears to be quoting from some lost dialogue
in which Zeno figured as an interlocutor. The respect accorded Zeno by the
Megarians makes it likely that the author is one of their number.

[39] Primarily on the basis of DL 2. 134: 'moreover he was accustomed to ask this
question: "Is what is different from another thing different?"—"Yes."—"And is
benefiting different from what is good?"—"Yes."—"So benefiting is not good."'
Menedemus is, however, reported to have held a version of the unity of virtue thesis that suggests that he *did* allow for the possibility of one thing having many names.
Cf. Plu. *Virt. mor.* 440 E: 'Menedemus the Eretrian does away with the plurality and
the differences of the virtues, since virtue is one although it uses many names. For
the same thing is spoken of as "temperance" and "courage" and "justice", just as the
same thing is spoken of as "mortal" and "human".'

Such, in brief, is the background against which we should view the Visitor's first critique of the Eleatic thesis. He is treating the Eleatic thesis that 'everything is one' (ἕν τὸ πᾶν) as it had been taken by those who understood Parmenides as forbidding predicational pluralism. He thereby raises the problem to be dealt with in the confrontation with the late-learners of how one thing can have many names. Understood predicatively, the ἕν τὸ πᾶν thesis means that every thing is one in the sense that it is one thing only or has only one predicate that can properly be asserted of it. Likewise, the proposition that 'what-is is one thing only' (244b9–10) means that each thing that is is only one thing, that is, it has only one proper predicate. With the question, 'Do you call something "being"?' (244b12), the Visitor begins to lead the predicational monist to admit that each thing has 'being' predicable of it. His next question—'Do you call what is one "being", applying two names to the same thing, or what?' (244c1–2)—forces the predicational monist to admit that what is one thing (ὅπερ ἕν) must also have 'being' predicable of it. Although the instance of 'what is one thing' in the context of this particular argument is the Eleatic One itself, the analysis here is extendable to anything else that is one, for instance Socrates or the good (to take the Megarians' examples). The Visitor forces the predicational monist to say not merely that the One is One (or that Socrates is Socrates, or that the good is good) but also that the One is 'being' or is something that is (as are Socrates and the good). The predicational monist wants to avoid any use of 'to be' other than in predications specifying what it is to be the thing in question. He makes the mistake of supposing that only the unique predicate naming a thing can be involved in specifying what it is to be that thing.

When Aristotle says that Lycophron and others were led to restrict the usage of the verb 'to be' because they assumed that 'being' is used in only one sense (ὡς μοναχῶς λεγομένου . . . τοῦ ὄντος), this is precisely what he is objecting to. It is thus quite interesting to find Aristotle attributing the same error to Parmenides. In *Physics* 1. 3 he says that part of the solution to Parmenides' argument is to recognize that he assumes 'being' is used in a single sense when it is in fact the case that it is used in several senses (ἁπλῶς λαμβάνει τὸ ὂν λέγεσθαι, λεγομένου πολλαχῶς, 186ᵃ24–5). Aristotle appears to take the view that Parmenides recognized only the use of the verb 'to be' in predications of substance. He begins the substantive portion of his treatment of Parmenides and Melissus in *Physics* 1. 2–3 by saying that since 'being' is said in many ways, one must first determine what those who say that everything is one mean by 'being';[40] one must determine whether they mean that all things are substance, or quantity, or quality (185ª20–3). By this he means that one must determine whether they understood the verb 'to be' as functioning in predications of substance, quantity, or quality. They cannot allow it to function in all these various types of predication, for this would entail a plurality of being (185ª27–9). He criticizes Melissus for supposing that 'being' indicates quantity when he asserts that what-is is unlimited, since quantity is not separable but presumes an underlying substantial subject (cf. 184ª29–ᵇ5). He appears to imply that Parmenides supposed that 'being' indicates substance. Now, Aristotle says that it is no more worth investigating whether what-is is one in the sense maintained by Parmenides than it is arguing against any other thesis propounded merely for the sake of controversy; and he even expressly calls the arguments of Parmenides and Melissus 'eristic' (185ª5–9). Aristotle in these chapters of the *Physics* is too much influenced by the sophistic appropriations of Parmenides.[41] That is, one should not look to what he says about Parmenides in this context for confirmation that Plato held the view of Parmenides as a predicational monist underlying the first critique of Eleaticism in the *Sophist*. By looking to how the Eleatic thesis is treated in the Fourth Deduction of the *Parmenides*, we can confirm that Plato both recognized the possibility of using Parmenides to support the predicational monist's position and yet did not himself want to endorse such a view.

The Fourth Deduction (159b2–160b4) considers what attributes things other than the One must have if the One is. This deduction relies upon a model of predication as naming which is very much like the Antisthenean or predicational monist conception of predication we have seen functioning in the first critique of Eleaticism. Parmenides

---

[40] It is worth remarking that his wording of this question echoes that of the Eleatic Visitor's question that begins Plato's own examination of the Eleatic position in the *Sophist*: Arist. *Ph.* 1. 2. 185ª20–2, ἀρχὴ δὲ οἰκειοτάτη πασῶν, ἐπειδὴ πολλαχῶς λέγεται τὸ ὄν, πῶς λέγουσιν οἱ λέγοντες εἶναι ἓν τὰ πάντα ≈ Pl. *Sph.* 244b6–7, παρὰ τῶν ἐν τὸ πᾶν λεγόντων ἆρ' οὐ πευστέον εἰς δύναμιν τί ποτε λέγουσι τὸ ὄν; Aristotle's treatment of the Eleatics throughout these chapters draws upon and develops Plato's two critiques of Eleaticism in the *Sophist*. A detailed demonstration of how this is so would be an appropriate subject for a separate study. Here we may just point out that the *Sophist*'s first critique of Eleaticism has its analogue in *Ph.* 1. 2. 185ª20–ᵇ5, while *Ph.* 1. 2. 185ᵇ5–25 picks up upon the *Sophist*'s second critique, and that Aristotle, like Plato, repeatedly forces the Eleatics into admitting that what-is is more than one (e.g. 185ª27–9, 185ᵇ3–4, 9–10).

[41] Cf. Cassin and Narcy 1987 for how Aristotle follows a sophistic model for interpreting Parmenides in *Metaph.* Γ. 5.

argues that the One must be separate (χωρίς) from the others and the others separate from the One by rejecting various conceptions of how the others might participate in the One that recall the conceptions of participation criticized in the first part of the dialogue. The One and the others must be separate because there is no other thing apart from them (παρὰ ταῦτα ἕτερον) in which (ἐν ᾧ) they both might be (159b6–c4). Furthermore, since what is truly one does not have parts, the One is neither in the others as a whole nor are parts of it in the others (159c5–7). This recalls the second in the series of criticisms Parmenides had made of the young Socrates' theory of forms (130e4–131c11). There he had secured Socrates' admission that each thing that participates in a form must participate in either the form as a whole or in part of it and then showed him how, because of certain difficulties, neither seems possible. Parmenides concludes that in no way can the others participate (μετέχοι) in the One (159d1), which is equivalent to saying that unity is in no way predicated of the others. He expresses this conclusion by saying: 'the others *are* one in no way' (οὐδαμῇ ἄρα ἓν τἆλλά ἐστιν, 159d3). To maintain that the others do not participate in the One or unity is in effect to rule out uses of the verb 'to be' in predications other than those of identity. One cannot say that the others *are* one, but only that the One is one. There is some indication that the conception of predication at work in this deduction is even still more restricted. For Parmenides says that, since the One and the others are separate from one another, once the One and the others have been mentioned, there is no more that can be said of them (159c1). This conception of predication as naming echoes the Antisthenean position that each thing can only be spoken of by its proper *logos* and Lycophron's recourse to eliminating all uses of the verb 'to be'. On the Fourth Deduction's conception of the admissible types of predication, all one can legitimately say of the One and the others is: 'the One [is] One' and 'the others [are] others'.

Parmenides goes on to show the extreme and unacceptable consequences of restricting possible predications in this way. If the others are not one, neither can they be many, which entails that there can be no definite number among them (159d4–e1). They are neither like nor unlike (159e1–160a3). They are neither the same nor different, neither moving nor at rest, neither coming to be nor perishing, and neither greater, less, nor equal (160a4–6). These are virtually the same consequences the First Deduction had drawn for the One itself—and as the Eighth Deduction (165e2–166c2) will draw for the others on the basis of the hypothesis that the One is not. Treating the One as entirely separate from the others and restricting admissible types of predication in the radical manner of the Fourth Deduction is tantamount to saying that the One is not, the eventual conclusion of the First Deduction. The results of the Fourth Deduction are just as unacceptable as those of the First, as is therefore its particular manner of deploying purportedly Parmenidean principles. That the same type of predicational monism we find in the Fourth Deduction underlies the *Sophist*'s first critique of Eleaticism confirms that a sophistic Parmenideanism, rather than Plato's own considered view of Parmenides, is operative in this critique. It is worth noting here that one finds predicational monism rearing its head in the course of the First Deduction. In order to argue that the One is neither like nor unlike itself or another, Parmenides lays down the principle that if the One has any property apart from being one, it would be more than one, which is impossible (ἀλλὰ μὴν εἴ τι πέπονθε χωρὶς τοῦ ἓν εἶναι τὸ ἕν, πλείω ἂν εἶναι πεπόνθοι ἢ ἕν, τοῦτο δὲ ἀδύνατον, 140a1–3).[42]

THE *SOPHIST*'S SECOND CRITIQUE OF ELEATICISM

An additional reason for supposing that the *Sophist*'s first critique of Eleaticism does not reflect Plato's own understanding of Parmenides is that the Visitor's second critique (244d14–245d11) represents the Eleatic position rather differently. This stage of the critique is more complex than the first, and appreciating its connections with the *Parmenides* is perhaps even more essential to untangling its various strands.[43] In this critique, there are several conflicting perspectives on the Eleatic position that connect in clear ways with the understandings of Parmenides represented in certain of the *Parmenides*'s deductions. These connections between the two dialogues provide the necessary criteria for determining where in this portion of the *Sophist* Plato's own view features.

One function of the Visitor's critique is to effect a transition to the position of the doxography's third group of thinkers, that what-is is

[42] Cf. Hamlyn 1955, 290–1, who points out the parallels among Antisthenes' logical doctrine that nothing may be spoken of except by its proper expression, the similar logical views of the Megarian Stilpo (cf. Plu. *Col.* 1120), and the perspective of the *Parmenides*'s First Deduction, which he sees as coming close to mirroring Parmenides' own views; and Bondeson 1976, 2–3, who notes the resemblance between the *Sophist*'s first critique of Eleaticism and *Prm.* 142a3–6 and 164a7–b2.

[43] Ross 1951, 105, briefly acknowledges that there is some connection between the *Parmenides*'s Second Deduction and *Sph.* 244b6–245e5, as had Ryle 1939, 99, and as does McCabe 1994, 108 n. 20. For less superficial discussions of the relation between the *Sophist*'s second critique and the *Parmenides*'s exercise, see Cherniss 1932, 127–8, and Schofield 1974, 42.

both many and one (ὡς τὸ ὂν πολλά τε καὶ ἕν ἐστιν, 242e1), by leading the Eleatics themselves to admit that what-is is not only one but many as well. The Visitor does not, however, go on to discuss the position of the doxography's third group but instead shifts rather abruptly to describing the conflict between the gods and giants. One reason for this apparent gap is that Plato will himself adopt a version of the third group's position that what-is is both many and one, although the sense in which he endorses it must await his analysis of the relations among the μέγιστα γένη or 'greatest kinds'. Nevertheless, an examination of the position of the doxography's third group might have been used to introduce problems to be resolved by this subsequent analysis. This purpose is, however, already served by the critique of the Eleatics, in so far as it raises the problem of how one thing can have many names or properties. One might expect that a discussion of the doxography's third group would offer a preliminary model of how this is possible. In fact, the second critique of Eleaticism already provides, albeit in tentative fashion, such a model. That is, describing Parmenides' Being as such as to have parts is for Plato a way of saying that it is capable of having more than one property attributed to it.

The Visitor begins by asking Theaetetus whether the Eleatics will say that 'wholeness' (τὸ ὅλον) is different from or the same as their one being. Theaetetus responds that they will and in fact do say that it is the same. The Visitor confirms that the Eleatic one being is a whole by quoting Parmenides' description of Being in B8. 43–5: '. . . like the mass of a sphere well-rounded on every side, balanced equally in every direction from the centre, for it is necessary that it be neither any greater nor any smaller at one point than at another.' On the basis of these lines, the Visitor infers that Parmenides' Being must be spatially extended, with a middle and extremities, and that it accordingly must have parts (244e6–7). That he directly quotes Parmenides at the outset of this portion of the discussion might seem to indicate that the Visitor's treatment of Parmenides here will somehow be more fair than in the first critique.

The second critique's description of Parmenidean being as a whole that has parts recalls the account of the hypothesis 'the One is' in the *Parmenides*'s Second Deduction.[44] There Parmenides begins by

---

[44] Plotinus' pupils Amelius and Porphyry seem to have connected the perspective on being in the *Sophist*'s second critique of Eleaticism with the *Parmenides*'s Second Deduction. In *Theol. Plat.* 1. 10, Proclus advocates his master Syrianus' interpretation of the Second Deduction, namely that it presents a synoptic account of the entire hierarchy of divine beings, against the view of Plotinus and his pupils that the One

describing the relation of 'one' and 'being' implied by the hypothesis. If the One is, he says, then the One must partake of being (142b5–6). This entails that the One's being cannot be identical with its one-ness, for otherwise it would not be the being *of* the One, and the One would not partake of this being, but the hypothesis 'the One is' would be reducible to simply ἓν ἕν or 'the One one' (142b7–c2). Here we see the threat of predicational monism asserting itself. Parmenides meets the threat by attempting to provide an account of how we can say that the One both is *one* and *is*. In the hypothesis 'the One is', he says, the 'is' signifies something different from the 'One' (142c4–5). The statement 'the One is' means that the One partakes of being (142c5–7). He expresses the idea that the One has both 'one' and 'being' predicable of it by saying that the hypothesis signifies that the One is such as to have parts. The Visitor's conclusion in the *Sophist* that Parmenides' Being must have parts echoes Parmenides' expres-sion of this important point here in the *Parmenides*.[45] Parmenides goes on to say, in a point also picked up in the *Sophist*, that the one being must be a whole (ὅλον). The way he states this point makes it clear that speaking of the one being as a whole of different parts is a way of speaking of its capacity to have more than one attribute predi-cated of it: 'if the "is" of the One-that-is is mentioned, and the "one" of the One-that-is, and being and oneness are not the same, but both are *of* the same thing, namely that which we hypothesized, the One-that-is, then is it not necessary that the one being itself is a whole and that "one" and "being" become its parts?' (142d1–5). Although Greek does not, as English does, place quotation marks around a word to indicate when we are speaking of the word itself rather than what it refers to, it does have a device for accomplishing this, namely placing the neuter article τό before a word. In these lines the neuter article is so used with the words marked with quotations in the

---

of the Second Deduction is to be identified simply with Intellect or νοῦς, the second hypostasis of the Plotinian system. Proclus opens ch. 11 by returning to the position he is criticizing: 'for let it be said, if you wish, that the conclusions of this [second] hypothesis concern what really is, and let this be granted by us at the outset. But since this is multitude and not one itself alone, as is the One prior to beings—for being has the attribute of being one (τὸ γὰρ ὂν πεπονθός ἐστι τὸ ἕν), just as both the Eleatic Visitor has instructed us on these topics in the *Sophist* and as tends to be endlessly repeated among our opponents, when they posit that the first principle is one, that Intellect is one-many, that Soul is one and many, and bodies are many and one . . .' (*Theol. Plat.* 1. 11. 47, 4–12).

[45] Compare *Prm.* 142c8–d1, σκόπει οὖν εἰ οὐκ ἀνάγκη ταύτην τὴν ὑπόθεσιν τοιοῦτον ὂν τὸ ἓν σημαίνειν, οἷον μέρη ἔχειν; with *Sph.* 244e6–7, τοιοῦτόν γε ὂν τὸ ὂν μέσον τε καὶ ἔσχατα ἔχει, ταῦτα δὲ ἔχον πᾶσα ἀνάγκη μέρη ἔχειν.

translation.[46] Thus 'one' and 'being' are terms predicated of the One-that-is (in a particularly intimate way), a relation Plato expresses by saying that they are parts of the whole, one being.[47] The Visitor's assertion in the *Sophist* that Parmenides' one being is a whole and is such as to have parts picks up on the language of the Second Deduction and suggests a way of explaining how this one being may have more than one name or more than one attribute predicated of it. Thus the second critique indicates how one might counter the understanding of Parmenides as a predicational monist.

However, as soon as the Visitor introduces a model that could explain how Parmenides' one being can have more than one property attributed to it, he immediately presents a challenge to this understanding. Surely, he says, the One itself cannot have these various properties, for what is truly one must be completely without parts (*Sph.* 245a5–9). It is important to recognize that just as the description of the one being as a whole with parts echoes the account of the One in the *Parmenides*'s Second Deduction, so this assertion that what is truly one must be completely partless picks up the account of the One in the First Deduction. There, recall, Parmenides began by declaring that if the One is, it cannot be many, and by arguing that it consequently cannot have parts and cannot be a whole (*Prm.* 137c4–d3). The *Sophist*'s second critique of Eleaticism, then, brings into direct contrast the conflicting understandings of Parmenides' hypothesis in the *Parmenides*'s First and Second Deductions. Once he has

---

[46] *Prm.* 142d1–5: εἰ τὸ ἔστι τοῦ ἑνὸς ὄντος λέγεται καὶ τὸ ἓν τοῦ ὄντος ἑνός, ἔστι δὲ οὐ τὸ αὐτὸ ἥ τε οὐσία καὶ τὸ ἕν, τοῦ αὐτοῦ δὲ ἐκείνου οὗ ὑπεθέμεθα, τοῦ ἑνὸς ὄντος, ἆρα οὐκ ἀνάγκη τὸ μὲν ὅλον ἓν ὂν εἶναι αὐτό, τούτου δὲ γίγνεσθαι μόρια τό τε ἓν καὶ τὸ εἶναι;

[47] The point would be clearer if the beginning of the passage could legitimately be translated: 'if "is" *is said of* the One-that-is, and "one" *is said of* the One-that-is'. For then it would be even more obvious that Plato is speaking of the attributes predicable of the one being. But Schofield 1973(*a*), 30, following Cornford 1939, 137 n. 1, has persuasively argued against the possibility of λέγεται plus the bare genitive being so rendered. Although I agree with Schofield on this, I do not accept his conclusion that this passage makes a point about the relation of 'one' and 'being' to the one being qualitatively different from Parmenides' earlier point about the relation of 'being' to the One at 142b7–c2. Schofield says that 'the sort of belonging in question is obviously quite different from that involved when *being* is spoken of as belonging to *the one*. For in that case *being* is treated as a property of *the one*, as Parmenides' talk of partaking (μετέχειν) shows, whereas in the present case *the one* and *being* are the component entities of the complex entity *the one that is*' (34). I think this fails to appreciate how Plato is shifting the metaphor he uses to express the predication relation, replacing talk of 'participation' with talk of 'parts' and 'whole'. This mistake is in part due to the basic failure to appreciate that τό τε ἓν καὶ τὸ εἶναι at 142d5 means ' "one" and "being" ' rather than 'one and being'.

introduced these two opposed understandings, the Visitor presents Theaetetus with a choice between them: 'is it the case, then, that what-is, having the attribute (πάθος) of unity, will thus be one and a whole —or should we not say that what-is is a whole at all?' (*Sph.* 245b4–5). The Visitor then points to some of the difficulties that arise on each conception. Although his argument becomes somewhat hard to follow at this point, it is clear enough that it proceeds in three stages: a problem for the first conception (245b7–10), a transitional problem (245c1–10), and a problem for the second conception (245c11–d11).

The problem with the first conception of what-is, as having the attribute of unity and in this way being a whole, is that it results in things being more than one: 'for if what-is has the attribute of being one in a way, it will appear that it is not the same as the One (οὐ ταὐτὸν ὂν τῷ ἑνὶ φανεῖται), and indeed all things will be more than one' (*Sph.* 245b7–9). This point echoes that made at the outset of the *Parmenides*'s Second Deduction, that the being in which the One participates is not the same as the One (ἡ οὐσία τοῦ ἑνὸς εἴη ἂν οὐ ταὐτὸν οὖσα τῷ ἑνί, *Prm.* 142b7–8). That things will be more than one if we accept that what-is can have attributes such as unity is not such a dire consequence. It is, in fact, somewhat strange that the Visitor here presents this as the problematic result of the conception of what-is as a whole of parts, for this model was initially introduced to explain how it is possible for what-is to have numerous attributes predicable of it. The connection with the Second Deduction, again, suggests that Plato understood Parmenides as capable of accommodating the conclusion that what-is is both one and many. The brevity of the objection here in comparison with those that follow may itself indicate that this is the option to be explored.

This view is in any case preferable to the view of Parmenides as a predicational monist, the unacceptable consequences of which are demonstrated in the transitional passage at *Sophist* 245c1–10. This passage considers what follows if what-is and wholeness are conceived of as separate (χωρίς—the key term in the articulation of predicational monism in the *Parmenides*'s Fourth Deduction) and distinct from one another (245c8–9). If, the Visitor says, what-is is not a whole by virtue of having this attribute, but wholeness itself is, then what-is turns out to be deprived of itself (245c1–3). This is perhaps the most opaque sentence in the whole critique. The problem is to understand whether the Visitor is still considering what-is as a whole or not. I take it that the conclusion that what-is will be deprived of itself if it does not have the attribute of wholeness only follows if it is being assumed that what-is *is* a whole. That is, this transitional section follows out the consequences of presuming that what-is is a whole though not by having the attribute of wholeness. This conception of what-is as having attributes has led to the conclusion that what-is is not just one but many. Some thinkers, as we have seen, saw this as unacceptable within the framework of Eleatic logic and so advocated predicational monism as a way of avoiding it. Their perspective reasserts itself here in the thesis that being and wholeness have separate and distinct natures. But on this conception it simply proves impossible to offer a coherent account of how what-is can be a whole while not having wholeness predicated of it. If what-is is a whole, and yet wholeness is separate and distinct from being, then what-is is deprived of itself (ἐνδεὲς τὸ ὂν ἑαυτοῦ, 245c2–3), which is tantamount to saying that what-is will not be being (ἑαυτοῦ στερόμενον οὐκ ὂν ἔσται τὸ ὄν, c5–6). This way of expressing the result makes it clear that it contradicts Parmenides himself, for he had declared that what-is 'is *not* lacking—being so it would lack everything' (ἔστι γὰρ οὐκ ἐπιδευές· [μὴ] ἐὸν δ' ἂν παντὸς ἐδεῖτο, B8. 33).

I have already suggested that the objection to the view of what-is as a whole of parts that what is truly one must be partless recalls the view of the One in the *Parmenides*'s First Deduction. The Visitor's examination of what follows from denying that what-is is a whole (*Sph.* 245c11–d11) confirms this suggestion, for this final portion of the critique reads like a miniature version of the First Deduction. If what-is is not a whole at all, then it follows that what-is is not (245c11–d1). Such is the ultimate conclusion of the First Deduction. In addition to not being, the Visitor says, what-is could never come to be, for what comes to be always comes to be a whole (245d1–6). This condenses the First Deduction's arguments against the One undergoing any type of change. Nor, the Visitor continues, should one speak of what-is as being any definite quantity, for whatever quantity it might be it would be as a whole (245d8–10). This argument has its analogue in the First Deduction's demonstration that the One cannot be the same as itself, like itself, equal to itself, and so on. Were it not for the connection of this portion of the *Sophist*'s critique with the *Parmenides*'s First Deduction, one might be tempted to think that Plato sees Parmenides as maintaining that Being is a whole and yet does not have parts, and one might feel confident in citing Parmenides B8. 22–5 as support.[48] Adopting such a position has the

---

[48] I regrettably took this view myself in Palmer 1996, 295–8, precisely because I did not consider the connections with the *Parmenides*'s deductions. Cf. Schofield 1973(*b*), 6 and n. 25, where Parm. B8. 4, 6, and 22–5, as well as Pl. *Sph.* 244d14–245b6, are cited in support of the position that Parmenidean Being is meant to be a partless whole.

unfortunate consequences that Plato will then be presumed to attribute a view to Parmenides that is essentially confused and that has little influence on his own thought. Recognizing that the *Sophist*'s critique of Eleaticism is something of a miniature re-enactment of key deductions in Parmenides' examination of his own thesis in the earlier dialogue allows us to avoid making this mistake.

The *Sophist*'s second critique of Eleaticism draws upon the conceptualization of Parmenides' one being in the *Parmenides*'s Second, Fourth, and First Deductions. It considers the possibilities (II) that what-is is a whole of parts such that it is capable of having various attributes predicated of it, (IV) that what-is is a predicational monad, and (I) that what-is is not a whole and does not have parts. The Visitor devotes most space to demonstrating the unacceptable results of the latter two conceptions, which parallel the unacceptable results of the Fourth and First Deductions. But the only objection he brings against the conception of Parmenides' one being as a whole of parts is that this leads to what-is being not just one but also many. The structure of the critique itself, I have suggested, indicates that this may not be a fatal objection, for there are signs that Plato supposed Parmenides capable of accommodating such a conception of what-is as both one and many. There are other reasons for believing this is so.

The *Sophist*'s critique of Eleaticism demonstrates the difficulties that inevitably follow if what-is is thought of as one in the sense that it admits only one proper predicate. One might suppose that Plato comes to see his own middle period conception of forms as subject to the same kind of difficulties, for it seems that these difficulties are in part a function of the particular use he had made of Parmenides in conceiving of these forms. Although this is not an uncommon view, I think it is mistaken. In the *Sophist* the friends of the forms, the representatives in the dialogue of Plato's own middle period views,[49] are twice associated with the Eleatics (249c10–d4, 252a5–10). This association is Plato's way of acknowledging the Parmenideanism of his own middle period metaphysics. The second occasion upon which he makes the association is the more important for us at the moment. It comes in the context of the Visitor's attempt to explain how we call the same thing by many names. He first considers what results if we treat each of the things that are as completely incapable of participating in or associating with anything else. This conception, he says,

---

[49] That the friends of forms are representatives of Plato's own middle period views has emerged as the majority opinion. For reviews of the debate leading to this general acceptance, see Cornford 1935(*a*), 242 ff.; Grube 1935, 295–7; Ross 1951, 105–7; Cherniss 1959, 185–7.

overturns the theories of all those whose positions on the nature of
being have been considered to this point in the dialogue, 'both of those
who maintain that the universe is in motion, and of those who make
it at rest as one [sc. the Eleatics], and those who say that the things-
that-are are in forms (κατ' εἴδη) that always remain the same in the
same state [sc. the friends of the forms]; for they all attribute being
to things, some saying that they really are moving, the others saying
that they really are at rest' (252a6–10). The Eleatics and the friends
of forms are grouped together here as the ones who say that what-is
is at rest and unchanging (as they were at 249c11–d1). The Visitor's
assertion that predicational monism overturns the theories of both the
Eleatics and the friends of forms indicates that neither theory should
be understood as a version of predicational monism. The Eleatics and
the friends of forms should be able to respond within the framework
of their respective theories to the threat posed by this crude conception of the nature of predication and so should be able to explain
how their fundamental entities can be called by more than one name.
It is at any rate the case that Parmenides' Being can legitimately be
described via the set of predicates assigned to it in the deduction of
B8, as can Plato's middle period forms in so far as they too display
the attributes of Parmenidean Being.

   This is not to say that Plato does not come to think there are problems with his middle period conception of forms and, by extension,
with the understanding of Parmenidean Being underlying it. Young
Socrates in the *Parmenides* might reasonably enough be thought a
friend of forms. He advocates a theory that is in all essential respects
a version of Plato's own middle period theory. This theory allows
him to explain how sensible objects can have numerous and often
contrary attributes. So Zeno's proofs that sensible objects are both like
and unlike, and anyone else's proof that sensibles are both one and
many, seem to him nothing remarkable. What would be remarkable,
he says, is if someone could demonstrate that 'what one is' (ὃ ἔστιν
ἕν, namely the form of Unity) is many and that the other kinds and
forms admit contrary properties (129b6–c3). One might suppose that
Socrates here bears witness to the predicational monism that Plato's
middle period theory of forms had inherited from Parmenides. I think
a more accurate analysis of Socrates' problem would focus on his
theory's inability to accommodate the possibility that forms can have
contrary attributes predicated of them, and it would focus on this as
the problematic assumption regarding the nature of intelligible reality that Plato has adopted on the basis of his earlier understanding of
Parmenides.

Socrates goes on to say that he would be surprised if someone could show him how the separate forms of likeness and unlikeness, plurality and unity, and rest and motion are capable of being mixed and separated from one another (129d6–e3). This list of forms is virtually identical to the group of the greatest kinds (μέγιστα γένη) in the *Sophist*, which the Visitor demonstrates must be allowed to blend and combine with one another to some extent.[50] In the *Parmenides*, it is Parmenides himself who meets Socrates' challenge by demonstrating in the dialectical exercise's Second Deduction how the One itself can have contrary attributes predicated of it. The Eleatic thesis in the *Sophist* that what-is is one has its analogue in the young Socrates' theory in the *Parmenides* that the forms are not subjectible to the numerous and often contrary predicates that characterize the objects of ordinary experience. That in the *Parmenides* it is Parmenides himself who corrects Socrates' theory, and that he does so by elaborating the possibility introduced in the *Sophist*'s second critique of Eleaticism that what-is is both one and many in virtue of being a whole of parts and thereby capable of admitting multiple predicates, confirms our suggestion that Plato saw Parmenides as somehow capable of accommodating the position the Visitor's critique leads him to adopt. In these two dialogues Plato is moving in the direction of introducing the type of complexities into his own conception of intelligible reality that he forces the Eleatics to admit must be integrated into their conception of the one being. Just as he had seen in Parmenides a model for his own middle period conception of intelligible reality, he comes to see Parmenides reconsidered as providing a model for his new conception of intelligible reality's necessary complexity. To see in detail how this is so, we must try to understand the view of Parmenides underlying the *Parmenides*'s important Second Deduction.

---

[50] The treatment of the greatest kinds often echoes certain arguments in the *Parmenides*'s exercise. Compare, for example, the argument at *Sph.* 255b8–c4 that being and sameness (ταὐτόν) are not identical with the argument at *Prm.* 139d2–e1 that the natures of the One and of the same (ταὐτόν) are not identical. On this argument in the *Parmenides*, see Schofield 1974, who notes in passing its obvious connection with the μέγιστα γένη (43).

PART III

Plato's Parmenides in the
Later Dialogues

8

Parmenides and Xenophanes in the *Sophist* and *Timaeus*

Our discussion of the various sophistic Parmenideanisms in both the *Parmenides* and the *Sophist* and of the role they play in introducing difficulties that Plato is concerned with resolving in the positive portions of these dialogues has given a prominent place to problems concerning the nature of predication. I have been suggesting that Plato's efforts to resolve the range of problems raised by the various sophistic appropriations of Parmenides will be grounded, at least in part, in his own rival understanding of Parmenides. This suggestion implies that Plato saw in Parmenides a model for how to develop the more complex conception of predication that enables him to explain how one thing can have many names. But we may not want to go quite so far, for Parmenides clearly does not engage in the type of philosophical reflection on the nature of predication that one finds in Plato. Nevertheless, even if Plato did not see in Parmenides an actual model for his own specific account of the nature of predication, he still may have seen him as allowing a genuine role for various types of predication and therefore as not legitimating the sophistic attempts to restrict radically the range of admissible predications.

To see how this may have been the case, we need first to appreciate that Plato understands Parmenides as speculating on the nature of the physical cosmos. Luc Brisson has emphasized this aspect of Plato's re-appropriation of Parmenides in the introduction to his recent translation of the *Parmenides*: 'Le sujet sur lequel porte la seconde partie du *Parménide* est celui sur lequel portaient les déductions de Parménide et de Zénon, à savoir l'univers considéré comme unité ou comme pluralité, et non les Formes ou l'Un.'[1] Although Brisson perhaps goes too far in insisting on this exclusive identification of the exercise's subject and is definitely too optimistic about the possibility of using the exercise as evidence for the views of the historical Parmenides, he is correct to insist upon the importance of Socrates' formulation of Parmenides' principal thesis: 'you say in your poem

---

[1] Brisson 1994, 44; cf. 3, 20–2, and *passim*.

that the universe is one (ἓν φῇς εἶναι τὸ πᾶν)' (*Prm.* 128a8–b1). This formulation of the thesis recurs in the doxographical passage of the *Sophist*, where the position of the Eleatics is captured in the phrase, ὡς ἑνὸς ὄντος τῶν πάντων καλουμένων (242d6). Although these key words tend to be translated on the lines of 'what is called "all things" is only one thing',[2] Plato probably means something more specific. For 'what is called "all things"' would seem to be the cosmos itself. That we have the plural 'all things' (τῶν πάντων) here instead of the designation for the universe more common in Greek philosophical texts, namely 'the all' (τὸ πᾶν), poses no real difficulty. As we have seen, the Eleatic thesis is formulated subsequently as the more standard 'the all is one' (ἓν τὸ πᾶν, *Sph.* 244b6; cf. 252a6–7, *Tht.* 183e3–4). Plato also uses 'the all' and 'all things' interchangeably in stating the views of the doxography's other two groups (cf. *Sph.* 243d8 and 243e3, 242e5 and 252b1). Aristotle likewise expresses the Eleatic thesis indiscriminately as 'the all is one' (e.g. *Ph.* 1. 2. 185ᵇ7) and 'all things are one' (e.g. *Ph.* 1. 2. 185ᵃ22), although when in *Metaphysics A.* 5 he echoes Plato's description of the Eleatics in the *Sophist* doxography, describing them as 'those who spoke concerning the all (περὶ τοῦ παντός) as being of a single nature' (986ᵇ10–11), he interestingly enough uses the singular. Plato, then, understood Parmenides to have held that the cosmos is in some sense one. To understand more precisely in what sense, it will be helpful to focus upon an important feature of the Platonic reception that we have not as yet discussed, namely the *Sophist* doxography's association of Parmenides with Xenophanes. We will see that there are important analogues between the positive characteristics of Xenophanes' God and the attributes of Parmenides' Being which provide the ground for the association and which Plato himself employs in a productive manner in the *Timaeus*.

The ancient doxographic tradition persistently associates Parmenides with Xenophanes. The first extant occurrence of the association comes in the doxographical passage of the *Sophist*, where the Eleatic Visitor speaks of his intellectual ancestors in the following terms: 'the Eleatic tribe that issues from us,[3] beginning with Xenophanes and even

---

[2] Thus e.g. Cornford 1935(*a*), 217: 'what we call "all things" are only one thing'; Untersteiner 1956, 49: 'la sua teoria nel senso che sia uno quelli che sono qualificati come molti'; Guazzoni Foà 1961, 469: 'non vede che un'unità in ciò che chiamiamo il tutto'; KRS 165: 'what we call all things are actually one'; Mansfeld 1986, 24: 'all things, as they are called, are one'; Cordero 1991, 99, 'ce qu'on appelle tout, est un être unique', and 103, they 'ne voient qu'unité dans ce qu'on nomme le Tout'; Lesher 1992, 211: 'what are called "all things" are really one'.

[3] Reading παρ' ἡμῶν as attested in the principal manuscripts B, T, W, and Y rather than παρ' ἡμῖν attested in Eus. Paris 1808 and the manuscripts dependent upon it (see Philip 1968, 290, for details of the manuscripts).

earlier, go through their tales on the ground that what is called "all things" is one' (242d4–7). Aristotle, too, reports the association in *Metaphysics A*. 5. In discussing those who declared the universe to be one, he says that Xenophanes was the first to tend towards this type of monism and that Parmenides is said to have been his pupil (986ᵇ21–2). The association recurs throughout the later doxography, attested in various forms in Theophrastus, Cicero, Philo Judaeus, Clement of Alexandria, Aristocles, Heraclides of Lembos, the pseudo-Plutarchan *Miscellanies*, the pseudo-Galenic *History of Philosophy*, Diogenes Laertius, Theodoretus, Simplicius, and the *Suda*.[4]

Although the dismissal of Plato's remark as merely ironic and the consequent dismissal of the association in the later doxography are now standard, this was not always the case. Zeller maintained that there was no justification for rejecting a view so well attested and so inherently probable. He accordingly held that Xenophanes was the greatest influence upon Parmenides' world-view.[5] It was Burnet who began undermining this traditional view of Xenophanes as founder of the Eleatic school, arguing that 'the certain facts of his life make it very unlikely that he settled at Elea and founded a school there', that Plato's reference in the *Sophist* passage to thinkers even earlier than Xenophanes shows his remarks to be 'playful and ironical', and that Aristotle in *Metaphysics A*. 5 reproduces Plato's statement with a literal-mindedness that misled the entire subsequent tradition.[6] Reinhardt in 1916 gave the incipient debate a radical new turn by advancing the hypothesis, based in large part upon accepting the reliability of the *MXG*'s account of Xenophanes' thought, that Xenophanes' period of intellectual activity must have post-dated Parmenides'. Reinhardt thereby sought to establish Parmenides firmly

---

[4] Thphr. *ap*. Simp. *in Ph*. 22, 26–9 = 21A31. 2 DK, and *ap*. Alex. Aphr. *in Metaph*. 31, 7–8 = 28A7 DK; Cicero, *Academica* 2. 74 = 21A25 DK; Philo Judaeus, *De providentia* 2. 39 = 21A26 DK; Clem. Al. *Strom*. 1. 64. 2 = 21A8 DK; Aristocl. *De phil*. *ap*. Eus. *PE* 14. 7. 1 = 21A49 DK; [Plu.], *Stromateis* 5 *ap*. Eus. *PE* 1. 8. 5 = 28A22 DK; [Galen], *De historia philosophica* 3 = *DG* 601, 5–6; DL 9. 21, 22 = 21A2, 28A1 DK; Theodoretus 4. 5 = 21A47 DK; Simp. *in Ph*. 28, 5–6; *Suda*, s.v. 'Parmenides' = 28A2 DK. Cf. Mejer 1978, 68 n. 3, on the likelihood that Heraclides, in his epitome of Sotion's *Diadochē*, grouped Xenophanes with the Eleatics although Sotion himself had regarded him as independent. Cordero 1991, 107–9, dismisses those sources that identify Parmenides as Xenophanes' pupil on the grounds that Parmenides (supposedly) never left Elea, while Xenophanes was (supposedly) never there; such literal-mindedness, as we shall see, misses the point of the association.

[5] Zeller 1919 (1st edn. 1856), 680 n. 1. Cf. Überweg–Prächter 1920 (1st edn. 1867), 95; Grote 1888, iv. 73–5, who accepts the association in an extreme form; Rohde 1925 (1st edn. 1893), 155–6; Wellman 1905, 2244.

[6] Burnet 1930 (1st edn. 1892), 126–7. *Contra* Burnet, see dell'Oro 1934, 287–9; Miceli 1936, 213.

as the founder of the Eleatic school. This conclusion was allowed to stand despite the near universal rejection of Reinhardt's view of Xenophanes as Parmenides' successor. Rather than returning to the view of Xenophanes as Parmenides' intellectual forebear, the possibility of any serious connection between the two strangely came to be rejected altogether. One can best see this in Werner Jaeger's influential lectures of 1936.[7] Although he rejected Reinhardt's thesis concerning the reliability of the *MXG*, he took him to have demonstrated decisively Parmenides' 'complete originality' and to have broken once and for all the connection with Xenophanes. Jaeger argued that, since the historical Xenophanes was not the Parmenideanized thinker of the *MXG*, there is no ground for the association with Parmenides. He thus concluded that the 'whole theological Eleatic Xenophanes is a chimaera' and that Xenophanes was an enlightened religious thinker influenced by Ionian natural philosophy.[8] Jaeger followed Burnet's lead in dismissing Plato's inclusion of Xenophanes among the Eleatics as 'playful and half-ironical' and in tracing the subsequent tradition's 'error' back to Aristotle.[9] More forceful attacks on the association subsequently appeared,[10] and by the 1960s the issue seemed settled. The dismissal of the *Sophist* passage as less than serious had become standard, and studies of Parmenides tended to ignore the traditional connection with Xenophanes altogether or concentrated instead on similarities that do not involve the unity thesis (for instance, similarities in their epistemological stances).[11] The state

---

[7] Later published, with revisions, as Jaeger 1947.   [8] Ibid. 51–4.

[9] Ibid. 215 n. 65.

[10] Cf. Albertelli 1939, 12–13; Heidel 1943, 267–8, 276–7; Cherniss 1951, 18 (cf. Cherniss 1935, 353–4); Corbato 1952, 5–29 (Studio I: 'Senofane Eleate?'), which implausibly denies that *Sph.* 242d attributes the unity thesis to Xenophanes; and Untersteiner 1956, CCLXXIV.

[11] Thus Tarán 1965, 3 (cf. 201, 288–9): 'Parmenides' philosophy is not doctrinally connected with the poetry of Xenophanes and . . . the ancient tradition, which maintains that it is, is probably derived from a misinterpretation of Plato's facetious remark.' Cf. Guthrie 1962, 368–9; Kerferd 1965, 135; Hölscher 1969, 61; Stokes 1971, 50–2 and ch. 3 *passim*. See also Zeller–Mondolfo 1967, 162–4, for a brief survey of the modern tendency to dissociate Xenophanes and the Eleatics, and Albertelli 1939, 49, for a partial review of opinions on the association at *Sph.* 242d. For treatment of limited correspondences, cf. e.g. Mansfeld 1964, 8–11, 120–1, 166–7; Mourelatos 1970, 120, 212 n. 51, 217. One exception during this period to the standard dismissal of Plato's association is Guazzoni Foà 1961, who asserts that 'l'importanza di Senofane nella storia del pensiero greco è anche riposta nell'aver precorso Parmenide non solo per aver asserito l'unità esteriore dell'essere (Dio) nel famoso framm. 23 . . . ma anche l'unità interiore di esso, cioè il carattere di οὖλος che diventerà attributo predicabile dell' ὄν parmenideo' (470). Instead of dismissing Plato's report as ironic, she (somewhat bizarrely) criticizes it as a reductive deformation of this genuine connection

of the question has remained largely unchanged to the present day.[12] Nevertheless, in certain quarters the association has started to receive some measure of renewed sympathy. Whereas J. E. Raven in the original 1957 edition of *The Presocratic Philosophers* maintained that Aristotle was probably misled by Plato's statement in the *Sophist*, 'which is not to be taken seriously', Malcolm Schofield in the revised 1983 edition tempers this to 'perhaps not entirely serious' and allows that there are more than merely verbal echoes of Xenophanes' theology and epistemology in Parmenides.[13]

The modern scepticism towards Plato's association of Parmenides with Xenophanes has often focused too exclusively on the relation of his remark to the historical truth concerning Xenophanes. But objecting against Plato that Xenophanes never had a close enough connection with Elea to have actually come into contact with Parmenides,[14] or even that his conception of the one God in fact has little serious affiliation with Parmenidean Being, simply misses the significance of what Plato says. Although most scholars readily acknowledge

between the two thinkers, on the ground that Plato is supposedly concerned not with the Eleatics per se but with the Megarian interpretation of Eleaticism (469, 471, following Untersteiner 1958, xxxix).

[12] Thus Barnes 1982, 84: 'There is . . . an ancient error about Xenophanes' philosophical achievement: in the *Sophist* Plato, jesting, makes Xenophanes the first Eleatic monist; Aristotle repeated the point; Theophrastus felt obliged to refer to it; and the doxographers slavishly follow their master.' Cf. Lesher 1992, 4, 102, and 190–2. In a recent re-examination of the origins of the idea of an 'Eleatic school', Cordero 1991, despite the appearance of taking a fresh approach, simply reasserts the illegitimacy of the association: 'Ce qui est certain, c'est l'origine théologique de la conception xénophanienne de l'unité, et, par conséquent, l'incohérence qui consiste à la regrouper avec trois autres philosophes [sc. Parmenides, Zeno, and Melissus] qui ne partagent pas des intérêts semblables' (104).

[13] KR 265; KRS 240–1. However, Raven's assessment at KR 165, that the phrase καὶ ἔτι πρόσθεν at *Sph.* 242d5 confirms that Plato's statement 'was not intended as a serious historical judgement' and that the 'connexion between Xenophanes and Parmenides obviously depends on the superficial similarity between the motionless one deity of the former and the motionless sphere of Being in the other' is allowed to stand (KRS 165). See also Finkelberg 1990 for a brave, if flawed, attempt to fight against the current by exploring the implications of the association for the interpretation of Xenophanes himself.

[14] The report at DL 9. 18 that Xenophanes wrote a two-thousand-line poem on the foundation of Elea has seemed suspect to many. Yet it is worth noting that there is much earlier evidence that Xenophanes had some connection with Elea. Aristotle reports the story of Xenophanes' reply, when asked by the Eleans whether they should sacrifice to and mourn Leucothea, that they should not sacrifice to her if they believed her a mortal woman and should not mourn her if they believed her a goddess (*Rh.* 2. 23. 1400[b]5–8). For a thorough discussion of the evidence connecting Xenophanes with Elea, see Ebner 1964.

that Plato's interest in his predecessors is never strictly doxographical or historical, they nevertheless remain prepared to criticize him
in cases like this for failing to provide what they presume is the accurate account of his predecessors' concerns. We should, again, attempt
to ask questions of the text that it has a chance of answering. Here
we need to ask why Plato identified Xenophanes as the forefather of
Eleatic ontology and what view of Parmenides the association with
Xenophanes implies.

To understand the precise nature of the thesis attributed to the
Eleatic school at *Sophist* 242d one must situate it within the context
of the doxography of which it forms a part. This doxography is a
classification of earlier views on the number and nature of 'beings'
or 'the things-that-are' (τὰ ὄντα). These views fall into three main
groups: (i) there is a limited plurality of beings or ὄντα; (ii) there is a
single being or ὄν; and (iii) what-is or τὸ ὄν is both one and many, a
combination of the first two views. In this classification, 'the things-
that-are' or τὰ ὄντα are obviously not just things that exist but that
subclass of entities somehow basic or fundamental to the existence of
other things.[15] Thus Aristotle, in adopting a doxographical classification in terms of first principles or ἀρχαί as his point of departure
in *Physics* 1, can say that those who inquire into the number of 'the
things-that-are' (τὰ ὄντα) are conducting an inquiry similar to his
own (184[b]22–3; cf. *Metaph. Z*. 1. 1028[b]2–6, Simp. *in Ph*. 21, 14–15).
Aristotle would seem to have the *Sophist* doxography in mind, but he
is probably not thinking only of Plato. His application of the anti-
theses one/many and changing/unchanging in classifying the opinions of earlier natural philosophers seems a direct development of
the way Gorgias classified his predecessors' views in the treatise 'On
What-Is-Not'. It may even be that Plato's doxography of earlier views
on the things-that-are is meant to be something of a response to
Gorgias', for earlier the Visitor appears to allude to Gorgias' attack on
previous philosophical speculation when he mentions those sophists
skilled at contradicting anyone who expresses any opinion concerning coming-to-be and being (γενέσεώς τε καὶ οὐσίας πέρι) (*Sph*.
232c7–10). If Plato's doxography is to some degree positioned against
Gorgias', this further corroborates that the entities Plato is concerned
with are not simply things that exist, for we have already seen that
Gorgias is concerned with would-be fundamental entities.

---

[15] Contrast the curious view of the doxography proposed by Bondeson 1976, 1–2,
that 'defining or characterizing τὰ ὄντα [*sic*] is the same as stating what entities are
the proper subject of discourse'. Instead of situating the Eleatic thesis within the context of the doxography, Bondeson allows Owen's view of Parmenides' subject to determine his view of the doxography's subject.

Within the structure of Plato's doxography, then, the Eleatics are represented as having held, not that only one thing exists, but that what is in the most fundamental or basic manner is one. It is important to recognize that this need not exclude the existence of other, non-fundamental entities. There is no suggestion that those in the first division, who are said to have posited three or two basic entities, denied the existence of other things. Far from it. The aim of these first-stage pluralists would have been to explain the being of the cosmos's varied phenomena in terms of a limited set of fundamental beings. In the absence of any indication to the contrary or any direct description of the Eleatic thesis as somehow paradoxical or exclusive, we may assume a certain continuity of perspective as the doxography moves from its first to its second division. Cornford's assumption that just the contrary must be the case is representative of scholarly views on the position of Parmenides within the doxography: 'This classification is designed to isolate from all the rest Parmenides', for he 'stands alone in denying the phenomenal world and acknowledging only one Real Thing'.[16] Cornford goes on to say: 'Plato knew that the real contrast was not between many real beings and one, but between the physical philosophers, who derived a manifold world of Nature from one or more material principles, and Parmenides, whose One Being was not material and could not generate a natural world.'[17] If Plato knew this, why does he give absolutely no indication of it? Why does he present the schema he does rather than the 'real contrast'? It simply is not the case that the classification is in any way overtly designed to isolate Parmenides. Cornford presumes this must be the point because he has himself presumed a certain interpretation of Parmenides. The inclusion of Xenophanes among the Eleatics, however, is one vital indication that Parmenides' view does not differ in

---

[16] Cornford 1935(*a*), 216. Runciman 1962, 71, recognizes that 'the historical partisans of Hot and Cold . . . did not wish to deny existence altogether to everything but Hot and Cold', noting that instead their intention 'was to draw the contrast . . . between the apparently and truly real'. He carries the distinction over into discussion of the gigantomachy: 'the issue is as to which of the contents of the universe merits the ascription of true reality (ἀληθινὴν οὐσίαν 246B8). Thus εἶναι here . . . means not "to have some sort of being" (i.e. to exist, or εἶναι πως), but "to have *real* being" ' (77). It is thus even more surprising that he, like Cornford, abandons this distinction in discussing the examination of the Eleatics, saying it is difficult to see how 244b9–10 'can be interpreted in any but the existential sense of εἶναι; and the assertion under discussion is accordingly that only one thing exists' (73). Malcolm 1967, 133 and n. 10, however, endorses the view that 'the most natural reading of the dualists' dictum "Only X and Y are" would be to take "are" as short for "are real", i.e. "Only X and Y are real (but other things may exist)" ', and he retains the distinction in briefly discussing how it functions in the examination of the monists as well as in the gigantomachy (134–5). [17] Cornford 1935(*a*), 218.

its general character from the views of the other thinkers represented in the doxography. Parmenides is manifestly *not* isolated from
Xenophanes, and we are surely not meant to presume that Xenophanes was thought by Plato to have denied the existence of the phenomenal world. Xenophanes'—and by extension Parmenides'—view
that what is called 'all things' is one is presented as a view on the
number and nature of fundamental entities. The association with
Xenophanes confirms the continuity with the rest of the doxography.
However we eventually decide to understand the sense in which Plato
felt he could attribute this view to Xenophanes and Parmenides, we
must recognize that it does not rule out the non-fundamental existence of the differentiated members of the cosmos, no more than the
position of the pluralists in the first group denies existence to things
other than their own fundamental entities.

One may develop the view of Xenophanes represented by Plato's
brief comment by comparing it with Aristotle's more extensive discussion of the Eleatics in *Metaphysics A*. 5, which is consistent with
and in several respects a direct amplification of what Plato says in the
Sophist.[18] Aristotle there implies that although the Eleatic thesis that
the universe is of a single nature is not strictly relevant to the inquiry
into the principles of the natural world, it is relevant to the higher
inquiry of theology or first philosophy. Xenophanes, he says, having
considered the entire region of the cosmos encompassed by its outermost revolution, came to the conclusion that there is a God, which
Aristotle sees as comparable to the One of the Eleatics (986^b24–5).
As already noted, he is following Plato when he describes the Eleatics as those who spoke of the universe as being of a single nature
(986^b10–11). This implies that Xenophanes' God was seen as in some
sense a cosmic entity and a unifying principle. How Aristotle could
take such a view of Xenophanes' God can best be explained, I think,
on the supposition that he understood this God as occupying the
outermost region of the heavens and from this position embracing
and exercising some imprecisely defined governing power over the
entire cosmos via the directive activity of its νόος or intellect. Xenophanes may be classed among those who spoke of the universe as
being of a single nature in so far as the directive thought of his God
is understood to be immanent throughout the cosmos. The cosmos
is therefore one, not in the sense that it is without any physical differentiation, but in so far as it is permeated by the activity of this
single divine intellect.

[18] For a full discussion justifying the remarks that follow, see Palmer 1998.

Aristotle sees Xenophanes' views on God as relevant in at least an incipient way to the project of first philosophy. He features as a crucial transitional figure, one of the first to present the type of metaphysical characterization of divinity that led to properly onto-logical speculation. With his view of God as uncreated and imper-ishable, as one and self-similar in every respect, he opened the way to the kind of metaphysical discourse we find in a more developed form in Parmenides. It is striking that each element in Parmenides' signposted summary of the characteristics of Being at the beginning of B8 has its analogue in the sparse remains of Xenophanes' posi-tive theology. Parmenides' Being is 'ungenerated and imperishable' (B8. 3). Xenophanes criticizes mortals for believing the gods are born (B14), and Aristotle reports that he held those who say the gods are born to be just as impious as those who say they die (*Rh.* 2. 23. 1399^{b}5–9). Parmenides describes what-is as 'whole and of a single nature' (οὖλον μουνογενές τε, B8. 4). Xenophanes says the God 'sees as a whole, thinks as a whole, and hears as a whole' (οὖλος ὁρᾷ, οὖλος δὲ νοεῖ, οὖλος δέ τ' ἀκούει, B24). Parmenides describes what-is as 'unshaken' (B8. 4) and says, in arguing on behalf of this attribute: 'remaining the same and in the same, it lies in itself, and thus stead-fast there it remains' (B8. 29–30). Xenophanes speaks of the God in virtually identical terms: 'always in the same place it remains moving not at all' (B26. 1). There even seems to be an analogue for Parmenides' description of what-is as perfect or complete (τελεστόν, B8. 4)[19] in Xenophanes' descriptions of God in B23 as 'greatest among gods and men' and in B25 as acting 'apart from toil', for these characterizations imply the God's perfection and self-sufficiency. These analogues provide more than sufficient basis to make Plato's association of Parmenides with Xenophanes comprehensible. Given the way Xenophanes' God appears to have been understood in the fourth century, these analogues provide further confirmation of the fact that Plato would have understood Parmenides' Being as a cosmic entity of some kind.

In the *Timaeus*, Plato endows the intelligible living creature and the body of the cosmos that the demiurge models upon it with attri-butes of Xenophanes' God and Parmenides' Being in a way that verifies that he understood both as cosmic entities. The clearest echo of Parmenides in the *Timaeus* comes in the argument for the cosmos's sphericity. Having argued that the shape most appropriate to the

---

[19] Following Tarán 1965, 93–5, and Cordero 1984, 188 n. 31, in accepting Cov-otti's proposed reading ἠδὲ τελεστόν as an improvement on the transmitted variants.

living creature would be that encompassing all shapes, Timaeus says that 'he fashioned it rounded and spherical, extending equally from the middle in every direction to the extremities, of all shapes the most perfect and the most similar to itself' (σφαιροειδές, ἐκ μέσου πάντη πρὸς τὰς τελευτὰς ἴσον ἀπέχον, κυκλοτερὲς αὐτὸ ἐτορνεύσατο, πάντων τελεώτατον ὁμοιότατόν τε αὐτὸ ἑαυτῷ σχημάτων, 33b4–6). This seems a clear adaptation of Parmenides B8. 42–4: 'it is perfected like the mass of a sphere well-rounded on every side, balanced equally in every direction from the centre' (τετελεσμένον ἐστί | πάντοθεν εὐκύκλου σφαίρης ἐναλίγκιον ὄγκῳ, | μεσσόθεν ἰσοπαλὲς πάντη). Proclus quotes Parmenides B8. 43–4 in his commentary on the *Timaeus* passage (*in Ti.* 160 D).[20] Diels, conversely, quotes Plato's words as the best commentary on Parmenides' image of the sphere.[21] The lines Plato echoes here are the same lines he had quoted at the beginning of the *Sophist*'s second critique of Eleaticism, which we saw was informed by the perspective on Parmenides' Being in the Second Deduction of the *Parmenides*. Thus this passage of the *Timaeus* on its own supports the idea that Plato's use of Parmenides in these other two dialogues presumes that his one being is a cosmic entity.

Although commentators have standardly drawn attention to the parallel between *Timaeus* 33b4–6 and Parmenides B8. 42–4,[22] it is less frequently noticed that parallels with Parmenidean Being suffuse Plato's accounts of the intelligible living creature and of the cosmos in so far as it is made to resemble it.[23] The intelligible living creature is 'perfect' (τελέον, *Ti.* 30d2 ≈ Parm. B8. 4, τελεστόν; B8. 42, τετελεσμένον). The demiurge made this cosmos one and 'the only member of its kind' (μονογενής ≈ Parm. B8. 4, μουνογενές)[24] so that

---

[20] Proclus also makes reference to Empedocles' *Sphairos*. Olerud 1951, 43, suggests that Empedocles provides the most direct model for Plato's conception. However, the elements in Emp. B27. 3–4, B27a, and B28 that would appear to be echoed by Plato figure more prominently in Parmenides. Plato's use of Empedocles is more conspicuous elsewhere, notably in the four-element theory (*Ti.* 31b–32c) and in the mutual binding of the elements by *philia* (32c2); cf. Hershbell 1974. On the *Timaeus*'s use of Emp. B29, see below.   [21] Diels 1897, 88.

[22] In addition to Diels, cf. e.g. Karsten 1830, 120; Stenzel 1917, 117 n. 2; Cornford 1937, 54; Olerud 1951, 45–6; Mortley 1969, 344; Ballew 1974, 202; Guthrie 1978, 280. Taylor 1928, ad *Ti.* 33b4–5, calls these lines 'possibly a conscious echo' of Parm. B8. 42–4; he is less cautious when he comes to comment on the term ἰσοπαλές at *Ti.* 63a1, which he sees as 'an echo of Parmenides' description of τὸ ἐόν as a sphere which is μεσσόθεν ἰσοπαλὲς πάντη'.

[23] Though see Theiler 1924, 68; Sinnige 1968, 188–91.

[24] For a defence of μουνογενές at Parm. B8. 4a (as *ap.* Simplicius, Clement, Theodoretus, and Philoponus), accompanied by a survey of the attested variants and the various readings adopted by modern editors and commentators, see Tarán 1965,

it might resemble the intelligible living creature in respect of its uniqueness (*Ti*. 31a7–b3, cf. 34b5, 69c2).[25] The cosmos is composed of the entirety of the four elements so that it may be one and 'perfect' (τέλεον, 32c5–33a2).[26] These epithets recur in the dialogue's final, hymnic description of the cosmos: 'this cosmos has become a visible living creature embracing what is visible, a perceptible god that is an image of the intelligible, most great and most good, most beautiful and most perfect, this one heaven single in its kind' (κάλλιστός τε καὶ τελεώτατος . . . εἷς οὐρανὸς ὅδε μονογενὴς ὤν, 92c6–9, cf. 68e3). It has no organs of perception, respiration, or digestion so that it may be self-sufficient rather than in need of anything (αὔταρκες . . . μᾶλλον ἢ προσδεὲς ἄλλων, *Ti*. 33d2–3, cf. 34b7 ≈ Parm. B8. 33). Although the cosmos is in motion, unlike the intelligible living creature, the description of its rotation does nevertheless preserve aspects of Parmenides' description of Being's unchanging nature: 'turning it around in the same way in the same place and in itself (κατὰ ταὐτὰ ἐν τῷ αὐτῷ καὶ ἐν ἑαυτῷ), he made it move revolving in a circle' (*Ti*. 34a3–4) ≈ Parmenides B8. 29, 'remaining the same and in the same place with respect to itself' (ταὐτόν τ' ἐν ταὐτῷ τε μένον καθ' ἑαυτό). Finally, the cosmos is described in summary as 'equal in every direction from its centre and whole and complete' (πανταχῇ . . . ἐκ μέσου ἴσον καὶ ὅλον καὶ τέλεον, *Ti*. 34b1–2), again recalling Parmenides B8. 42–4.[27]

---

88 ff. O'Brien 1987(*b*), 320 (cf. 333), argues for accepting οὐλομερές (as *ap*. Plu. *Col*. 1114 c), taking up the suggestion of Festugière *ap*. DK, i. 496, ll. 38–40, and Burnet 1930, 174 n. 4, that μουνογενές infiltrated the text of Simplicius *et al*. under the influence of Pl. *Ti*. 31b3 and 92c9. It seems at least as likely, however, that the parallel in Plato supports rather than tells against μουνογενές, given Plato's numerous adaptations of Parmenidean language in this portion of the dialogue.

[25] On the argument for the cosmos's uniqueness, see Fraisse 1982, Keyt 1971, Mohr 1985, 9–52, Parry 1979 and 1991, and Patterson 1981.

[26] Plato's argument for the uniqueness of the cosmos here, that there was nothing left over from which another such world could come to be, accords with Parmenides' own assertion of the uniqueness of Being at B8. 12–13a: οὐδέ ποτ' ἐκ μὴ ἐόντος ἐφήσει πίστιος ἰσχύς | γίγνεσθαί τι παρ' αὐτό ('nor will the force of conviction ever allow anything to come to be alongside it from what-is-not'). Plato goes on to argue that the cosmos is ageless and free from disease, a point that has its analogue in Melissus B7.

[27] These are some of the more obvious analogues. There may be a less direct correspondence at *Ti*. 31b4 ff., where the elements fire and earth are privileged in the account of the demiurge's creation of the cosmos's body. Guthrie 1978, 276 n. 3, supposes that 'Plato's start from fire and earth may reflect once again his great respect for Parmenides'. If the influence of Parmenides is at play here, then this passage may have in turn influenced Aristotle's identification of Parmenides' Light and Night with fire and earth at *Metaph*. A. 5. 986ᵇ34. For other less immediately apparent analogues, see Broniak 1987 and Ballew 1974, which argues that there is a set of epistemological

Since certain features of Xenophanes' God have their analogue in the attributes of Parmenides' Being, certain of these Parmenidean attributes of the intelligible living creature and of the visible cosmos modelled upon it have Xenophanean resonances as well. There are, however, important Xenophanean attributes of the cosmic living creature that have no analogue in Parmenides. For example, Timaeus argues that the demiurge created the cosmic living creature (i) with neither eyes nor hearing, for there was nothing visible or audible outside it; (ii) with no organs of respiration or digestion, for there was no air or nourishment outside it; and (iii) with neither hands nor feet, for the rotating motion proper to its spherical shape and to the activity of its intelligence or *νοῦς* did not require them (33b7–34a7). This third point is often seen as an adaptation of Empedocles B29: 'for two branches do not spring from its back, it has no feet, no swift knees, no organs of reproduction, but it was a sphere and equal to itself in every direction.'[28] If Plato had Empedocles in mind, he would have also perceived how Empedocles draws upon his Italian predecessors —upon Parmenides himself for the image of the sphere, and in other respects upon Xenophanes' criticisms of anthropomorphic views of the divine. Timaeus' first and second points are more clearly Xenophanean. Diogenes Laertius reports that Xenophanes' God 'sees as a whole, hears as a whole, and does not breathe' (*ὅλον δὲ ὁρᾶν καὶ ὅλον ἀκούειν, μὴ μέντοι ἀναπνεῖν*, DL 9. 19). The first two phrases clearly reflect Xenophanes' own words in B24: 'it sees as a whole, it thinks as a whole, and it hears as a whole' (*οὖλος ὁρᾷ, οὖλος δὲ νοεῖ, οὖλος δέ τ' ἀκούει*). The third phrase in Diogenes' report may well come from the close of a lost Xenophanean hexameter.[29] Timaeus' denial that the cosmic living creature has specific organs of perception also seems to be an adaptation of Xenophanes B24.[30] The most important Xenophanean aspect of the cosmic living creature is its animate nature and endowment with the cognitive faculty of intellect or *νοῦς*. Timaeus begins his account of the cosmos by declaring that it must

correspondences, since in both Parmenides and the *Timaeus* 'the notions of straight and circular are applied both to the universe and to men's thought about it' and that the principle 'like knows like' is prominent in both (189).

[28] Cf. e.g. Cornford 1937, 56; Olerud 1951, 43–4; Guthrie 1978, 280.

[29] Cf. Babut 1974, 412–14. Timaeus' argument that there is nothing outside the cosmic living creature for it to breathe is most likely a correction of a Pythagorean conception. Cf. Arist. *Ph.* 4. 6. 213^{b}22–4. The presumption by Tannery 1887, 125 ff., that Xenophanes was himself criticizing Pythagoras on this point is called into question by Burkert 1972, 280–1, on the ground that the conception of the heaven's breathing in the surrounding *πνεῦμα* appears to belong to a later phase of Pythagorean cosmology.   [30] So Cornford 1937, 55.

be considered a living creature provided with both soul and intelligence (ζῷον ἔμψυχον ἔννουν τε, *Ti.* 30b7–8). Endowing the cosmic living creature with intelligence gives it a Xenophanean attribute without analogue in Parmenides.[31]

This important Xenophanean addition to the generally Parmenidean conception of the cosmic living creature has an interesting analogue in the *Sophist*, in the revision the Eleatic Visitor suggests the friends of forms should make to their own Eleatic conception of being. We have seen that the Eleatic Visitor twice groups the friends of forms with the Eleatics, thereby pointing to the Parmenideanism of Plato's middle period metaphysics (*Sph.* 249c10–d4, 252a6–10). When he does so at the end of his imagined discussion with the friends of forms, he implies that any correction of their views will apply to the Eleatics as well. One interim conclusion via which the Visitor gets the friends of forms to revise their ontology may appear rather bizarre. He leads them to admit that being's coming to be known by the soul entails its being affected and to this extent undergoing some change (248b2–e4). At this point the Visitor abruptly asks: 'are we really to be so easily convinced [sc. by the friends] that change and life and soul and thought do not belong to what-completely-is (τὸ παντελῶς ὄν),[32] that it neither lives nor thinks, but, reverend and holy, devoid of intelligence, is changeless and motionless?' (248e6–249a1). He asserts that what-completely-is must be considered to be ensouled (ἔμψυχον) and to possess intelligence, life, and soul—νοῦς, ζωή, and ψυχή (249a9–10). Those who have occasioned to comment on this assertion while discussing the argument in which it occurs have either not noticed or played down how strange and puzzling it really is.[33] I do not pretend to understand it fully myself. We do

---

[31] Though note Theophrastus' tantalizing and rather puzzling remark at *Sens.* 4 that according to Parmenides, ὅλως δὲ πᾶν τὸ ὂν ἔχειν τινὰ γνῶσιν ('all that is generally possesses some intelligence'). Guthrie 1978, 280, sees Empedocles B134 as having 'contributed the conception of a great Mind pervading the whole cosmos', thus ignoring the more important Xenophanean antecedent (upon which Empedocles, again, may have been seen by Plato as having drawn). Timaeus' references to the animate cosmos as itself a god (34b8, 68c4) might be thought another Xenophanean element unparalleled in Parmenides.

[32] This formidable designation occurs at only one other place in the Platonic corpus, namely at *R.* 5. 477a3, in the midst of Plato's Parmenideanizing presentation of APK.

[33] So e.g. Frank 1985, Keyt 1969, 4–5, Owen 1966, 338; though see Seligman 1982, 27–9, on how the *Timaeus* takes up the Visitor's remarks here, and generally on how the *Timaeus* employs the *Sophist*'s conception of being as no longer belonging, as in the middle period metaphysics, only to the realm of the intelligible and unchanging. For Proclus' comments on the passage, see *Theol. Plat.* 3. 6. 26, 12–27, 8.

nevertheless seem to have a rather striking parallel with Timaeus' Xenophanean description of the cosmic living creature as endowed with both soul and intelligence (ἔμψυχον ἔννουν τε). The Visitor even argues for attributing these properties to what-completely-is in a manner closely resembling Timaeus' account of the demiurge's decision to endow the cosmos with life and intelligence. The Visitor reasons that if what-completely-is is to have intelligence, it must have life, and to have these it must have soul (*Sph.* 249a4–8). Likewise, the demiurge, having decided that the cosmos must possess intelligence, reasoned that it must first have soul, which must reside in a body (*Ti.* 30b1–5; cf. *Phlb.* 30c9–d3).

The demiurge creates the cosmic body so that the visible cosmos may be endowed with soul and intellect and thereby be as good as possible (*Ti.* 30a2–c1). Thus after his account of the creation of the cosmic body, Timaeus explains how the demiurge created the cosmos's soul (34b10–37c5) and subsequent to this how, again to make the visible cosmos as like its intelligible model as possible, he created time as the changing image of the intelligible living creature's eternity (37c6–d7). Timaeus then comments upon how we carelessly apply past- and future-tensed predicates to this eternal, intelligible being: 'we say that it was, and is, and will be, but only "is" belongs to it according to the true way of speaking' (37e5–38a1). Timaeus' words here directly recall Parmenides B8. 5–6: 'nor was it ever, nor will it be, since it is now all together, one, continuous'.[34] Not surprisingly, Parmenides' assertion has been taken to mean a variety of things.[35] Some have argued that he is not especially concerned with temporal distinctions and that he does not mean to deny that what-is has a past and a future. Instead, he means only to deny the creation and destruction of what-is—or more accurately, that what-is ever enjoyed an existence in the past that is now over or that it will ever begin an existence in the future, the argument against these possibilities coming in B8. 19–20.[36] I myself find this view attractive, but it does not seem to be the view implied in Plato's appropriation.

---

[34] Pl. *Ti.* 37e5–38a1: λέγομεν γὰρ δὴ ὡς ἦν ἔστιν τε καὶ ἔσται, τῇ δὲ τὸ ἔστιν μόνον κατὰ τὸν ἀληθῆ λόγον προσήκει. Parm. B8. 5–6: οὐδέ ποτ' ἦν οὐδ' ἔσται, ἐπεὶ νῦν ἔστιν ὁμοῦ πᾶν, | ἕν, συνεχές. Cf. Taylor 1928, ad *Ti.* 37e3–38b5; Cornford 1937, 102; Tarán 1965, 175 n. 1.

[35] See Sorabji 1983, 99–108, for a survey and discussion of the various proposed interpretations. See also the references to earlier views on the subject in Schofield 1970.

[36] This view is advanced by Fränkel 1968, 191 n. 1, and Tarán 1965, 175–88. It has been most ably defended by Schofield 1970, against the criticisms of Fränkel by Owen 1966, 320–2, and of Tarán by Kahn 1968, 127–9. See also O'Brien 1980.

Among the various types of view one might take were one to accept that Parmenides is making some point about the relation of what-is to time, there are two that I take to be most important. Parmenides might be attempting to express the idea that what-is is not in time at all, that it exists atemporally or timelessly so that it admits no temporal predicates whatsoever. On this view, not only are past- and future-tensed predicates inadmissible, but grammatically present-tense predicates such as 'is' when asserted of what-is are logically tense-less, meaning that they do not actually refer to a particular time. Alternatively, Parmenides might be presuming that grammatically present-tense predicates, when asserted of what-is, do remain logically tensed and do refer to a particular time. One might well find it difficult to admit the second possibility as a coherent conception of eternity, for when stripped of its relation to past and future the idea of the present seems to lose its meaning. It appears, none the less, that Plato meant to attribute this type of eternity to the *Timaeus*'s intelligible living creature, which accordingly implies that he understood Parmenides' Being as likewise always being in the now. Consideration of Plato's use of Parmenides in *Timaeus* 37e–38a led Owen to question whether Parmenides actually managed to isolate a use of the verb 'is' entirely free from tense-affiliations. For whereas Parmenides wants to do away with past and future tenses, he insists upon saying that it is *now* (νῦν ἔστιν, B8. 5). Thus Owen says that Parmenides 'wants to maintain its existence in the present while admitting no use for the statement that it existed in the past or will do so in the future'.[37] This is, at least, how Plato's appropriation of Parmenides' language in his description of the intelligible living creature in the *Timaeus* suggests he understood Parmenides.

We can refine our understanding of how Plato viewed Parmenidean Being's relation to time by considering the *Parmenides*'s account of the temporal predicates admitted by the One. Now, one might suppose that the analogue of the *Timaeus*'s denial of the applicability of temporal predicates to the intelligible living creature is to be found in the First Deduction. Timaeus explains that 'was' and 'will be' cannot be predicated of the intelligible living creature because what is always unchangingly in the same state becomes neither older nor younger (*Ti.* 38a1–5). In the *Parmenides*'s First Deduction, Parmenides argues at some length that the One cannot be either older or younger than anything, including itself, with the consequence that the One does not partake of time and is not in time (*Prm.* 140e1–141d6).

---

[37] Owen 1966, 332; see also 329–30.

Thus neither can it be said of the One that it 'was', 'has become', or 'was becoming', nor can it be said that it 'will be', 'will become', or 'will have become' (141d7–e7). However, the First Deduction also denies that the One admits present-tense predicates. Not only can the One not be older or younger than anything, it cannot even be the same age as anything, including itself. Thus in addition to ruling out 'was', 'will be', and the rest, Parmenides also rules out 'is' and 'is becoming' as implying that the One partakes of present time, whereas in the *Timaeus* only past- and future-tensed predicates are denied to the intelligible living creature. Timaeus clearly allows us to say that it 'is', just as Parmenides himself had. Thus the First Deduction is not the proper place in the *Parmenides* to look for an analogue for the *Timaeus*'s Parmenidean account of the intelligible living creature's relation to time.

We find in the *Parmenides*'s Second Deduction a use of Parmenides more in keeping with that in the *Timaeus*. The Neoplatonists appreciated that there is an affiliation between these two texts. Plotinus and his followers supposed that Plato is speaking of Intellect or the second hypostasis both in his account of the One in the Second Deduction as well as in the *Timaeus*'s account of the demiurge and of the intelligible living creature itself, in so far as they identified it with the demiurge (cf. e.g. Plot. 3. 9. 1, 5. 1. 8, 5. 9. 9; Procl. *Theol. Plat.* 1. 10. 42, 4–9).[38] Thus Proclus can say: 'Timaeus traces all things back to the Demiurge, Parmenides traces them to the One, and there is an analogous relation between the Demiurge and the contents of the cosmos, and the One and all things whatsoever, <the Demiurge being a kind of one> but not One in the absolute sense' (*in Prm.* 642, 20–643, 2 Cousin, trans. Morrow and Dillon; cf. Dam. *Pr.* 2. 57, 4–58, 18 Ruelle). One need not endorse any of the particular Neoplatonic interpretations to appreciate their recognition that there is a connection between the Second Deduction and the portion of the *Timaeus* with which we are presently concerned. Particularly important for us is that both texts represent key Platonic uses of Parmenides. As we turn to the relevant portion of the Second Deduction, however, the

---

[38] Plotinus identified the accounts of the One in the first three deductions of the *Parmenides* with the three hypostases, the One, Intellect, and Soul, and subsequent Neoplatonic exegesis of these deductions developed and systematized this interpretation. See Procl. *in Prm.* 1051, 34–1064, 12 Cousin for an account of the history of this development. Proclus himself, following his master Syrianus, sees the Second Deduction as providing an account of the entire hierarchy of divine beings (see e.g. *Theol. Plat.* 1. 10–12, 3. 1. 23–6). On Plotinus', Proclus', and Damascius' views of the connections between the *Parmenides* and the *Timaeus*, see Trouillard 1970.

fact that it is itself not well understood means that we shall have to spend some time in making sense of the deduction in order to make sense of how it reflects Plato's understanding of Parmenides.

The analysis of the One's relation to time occupies the final movement of the Second Deduction (*Prm.* 151e3–155d6). Despite the daunting length and complexity of this stretch of the deduction, it has a clearly discernible structure that follows a programme introduced by the discussion's first sentence: 'so, then, does the One also partake of time? Is it, and does it come to be, younger and older, both than itself and than the others, and neither younger nor older, either than itself or than the others, partaking as it does of time?' (151e3–6 ≈ 155c4–7). This sentence introduces four general demonstranda: (A) the One is and becomes younger and older than itself; (B) the One is and becomes younger and older than the others; (C) the One is and becomes neither younger nor older than itself; and (D) the One is and becomes neither younger nor older than the others. Each of these general demonstranda contains within itself four distinct theses. (A), for example, yields: (A1) the One *is younger* than itself; (A2) the One *is older* than itself; (A3) the One *becomes younger* than itself; and (A4) the One *becomes older* than itself. The programmatic sentence 151e3–6 thus contains in total sixteen distinct theses. Each of these receives its own demonstration in the course of the deduction, with the beginning and conclusion of each successive argument being clearly marked. This whole stretch of the deduction thus breaks down as follows:

A3: the One becomes younger than itself, and
A4: the One becomes older than itself (152a3–b2);
A2: the One is older than itself (152b2–d5);
A1: the One is younger than itself (152d6–8).
C1–C4: the One neither is nor becomes older or younger than itself (152e3–10).
B2: the One is older than the others (153a1–b7);
B1: the One is younger than the others (153b8–d5).
D1: the One is not younger than the others, and
D2: the One is not older than the others (153d5–154a2);
D3: the One does not become younger than the others, and
D4: the One does not become older than the others (154b1–c5).
B3: the One becomes younger than the others (154c6–155b2);
B4: the One becomes older than the others (155b2–4).

Parmenides concludes this series of demonstrations by saying that since the One partakes of time and of becoming older and younger, it must also partake of the past, the future, and the present, and therefore 'the One was, is, and will be, and it came to be, comes to be, and will come to be' (155c8–d5).

This conclusion appears to belie directly the suggested connection with the *Timaeus*, where 'is' alone is permissible in statements regarding the intelligible living creature. We should not be too hasty, however, to dismiss the connection with the *Timaeus*. Instead, we need to distinguish the various aspects and relations in which Parmenides speaks of the One in order to establish the apparently contradictory results of this portion of the deduction. Plato himself is often more explicit here than in other portions of the exercise about these various aspects and relations. For example, (D3) and (D4) are the contradictories of (B3) and (B4) when stated without qualification. But Plato takes great pains to make it clear that (D3) and (D4) hold in so far as the difference in age between the One and the others remains constant, whereas (B3) and (B4) hold in so far as the ratio of the One's age to the age of the others decreases continually over time. (Let a_1 be greater than a_2 by amount d. After time t has elapsed, $a_1 + t$ remains greater than $a_2 + t$ by amount d. But the ratio $a_1 + t : a_2 + t$ is less than the ratio $a_1 : a_2$.) Plato also makes it clear that, from a certain perspective, the One may be spoken of as having a past and a future as well as a present, while from another perspective the One should be spoken of only in the present. Just as from a certain perspective the One can be said to become younger and older than the others, while from another the One should not be said to become younger or older than the others, so there is a perspective from which the One will be viewed as admitting past-, present-, and future-tensed predicates, while there is another perspective from which it should be spoken of only in the present tense. Our task at the moment is to determine what distinguishes these ways of viewing the One and how they might relate to Parmenides' conception of Being.

We might suppose that the relevant distinction would contrast the One considered in relation to itself with the One considered in relation to the others. We might accordingly attempt to explain the admissibility of past- and future-tensed predicates as a function of the One's relation to the others. If we consider the One in relation to the present state or arrangement of the others, then it is legitimate to say that the One *was* before the others came to be in this state, that it *is* at the same time as the others are in this state, and that it *will be* after the others are no longer in this state. However, the suggestion will be, when we speak of the One in relation to itself, we can only speak of it in the present tense. Now, this is a useful suggestion, for it seems correct to point to the One's changing relation to the others to explain the sense in which it admits the predicates of various tenses. The contrast between considering the One in relation to itself and in relation to others does not, however, go far enough, for there seems to be a sense in which the One considered in relation to itself will admit predicates of various tenses.

The programmatic first sentence of this portion of the deduction distinguishes between consideration of the One in relation to itself and in relation to the others (ἑαυτοῦ καὶ τῶν ἄλλων, 151e4–5; αὐτοῦ καὶ τῶν ἄλλων, 155c5), but it also distinguishes between consideration of the One as being and as coming to be (ἐστί τε καὶ γίγνεται, 151e3–4; cf. 155c5–6). If we look carefully at Parmenides' expression of the conclusion that the One admits past-, present-, and future-tensed predicates, we see that this is in virtue of its being considered in its aspect *qua* coming-to-be: 'since the One partakes of time and of *coming-to-be* (γίγνεσθαι) older and younger, is it not necessary that it also partakes of the past, the future, and the present?' (155c8–d2). I take it that the reason the One considered in relation to itself in its aspect *qua* coming-to-be admits the full range of tensed predicates is that considering the One from such a perspective involves conceptualizing it as, so to speak, divided or apart from itself: saying the One becomes older than itself involves comparing the One at one time with the One at a previous time.

In the demonstration of A2, however, Parmenides makes an effort to explain how the One considered in its aspect *qua* being is always in the now.[39] He says that the One *is* older whenever in coming to be it is 'at the present time' (κατὰ τὸν νῦν χρόνον) between 'was' and 'will be' (152b2–4). In proceeding from past to future it will not skip over the present, so that when the One encounters the present, at that time it stops *coming to be* older and simply *is* older (152b4–c2). He rejects the conception of the One advancing in time and so coming to be between the present and future on the ground that it cannot be allowed to pass by the present (152c2–7). Thus, again, whenever it is 'at the present', it stops becoming and is at that point whatever it happened to be becoming, so that whenever the One encounters the present it stops becoming older and simply is at that point older

---

[39] Notice that in the A-arguments the relational tag 'than itself' features more prominently in A3 and A4's consideration of the One in its aspect *qua* coming-to-be (152a5, twice at a8, b2) than in the consideration of the One in its aspect *qua* being, where it appears in the transition from A2 to A1 (152d5, 7). In argument A2, Parmenides plays down the relative character of the predicates 'older' and 'younger' as far as possible so as not to consider the One as other than itself.

(152c7–d4). In this portion of the deduction Plato in the voice of Parmenides is attempting to articulate a conception of the One, in relation to itself in its aspect *qua* being rather than becoming, as existing exclusively in the present. The clearest possible statement of the One's being eternally present comes at the end of A1 and A2: 'the "now" is always present to the One throughout its entire being; for it always is now whenever is it' (τό γε μὴν νῦν ἀεὶ πάρεστι τῷ ἑνὶ διὰ παντὸς τοῦ εἶναι· ἔστι γὰρ ἀεὶ νῦν ὅτανπερ ᾖ, 152d8–e2). Although one might be inclined to question the coherence of this conception, there seems no denying that Plato is asserting here that from this particular perspective the One exists in an eternal present. Owen argued that this was Parmenides' own conception on the ground that he insists upon saying in B8. 5 that 'it is *now*'; and he pointed out that in the *Timaeus* passage where Plato adapts this conception he 'is apparently ready to drop the word "now" from timeless propositions, but he imports "always" in its place'.[40] Here in the corresponding portion of the *Parmenides* we see Plato not only not dropping the word 'now' but, like Parmenides, insisting upon saying 'the One is now' and explaining what this means and from what perspective it is true.

Thus this portion of the *Parmenides*'s Second Deduction confirms what the *Timaeus* has already led us to believe, namely that Plato understood Parmenides B8. 5 as asserting the eternal presence of what-is. That is not all. The Second Deduction's analysis of the One's relation to time crucially depends upon the idea that the One can be considered from various perspectives and in different aspects. Considering the One from the perspective of its relation to the others and in its aspect *qua* coming-to-be, we can say that it 'was', 'is', and 'will be'. Considered, however, from the perspective of its relation to itself in its aspect *qua* being, it can only be said that it 'is'. That this distinction between the One in its aspect *qua* coming-to-be and in its aspect *qua* being is important to Plato finds confirmation in the fact that such a distinction also figures in *Timaeus* 37c–38b. What is said there of the intelligible living creature's relation to time corresponds to what is said of the One's relation to time *qua* being in the *Parmenides*, while what is said of the visible cosmos in this portion of the *Timaeus* corresponds to what can be said of the One in its aspect *qua* coming-to-be. The nature of the intelligible living creature is eternal (*Ti.* 37d3), it enjoys 'an eternity that abides in unity' (37d6), and its eternal existence in the present means that it is without past and future (37e5–38a1). By contrast, it is legitimate to make past- and

---

[40] Owen 1966, 333.

future-tensed statements about the visible cosmos modelled upon the intelligible living creature, for it belongs to the class of generation proceeding in time (τὸ δὲ ἦν τό τ' ἔσται περὶ τὴν ἐν χρόνῳ γένεσιν ἰοῦσαν[41] πρέπει λέγεσθαι, 38a1–2). Furthermore, Timaeus says that it is fitting for what remains always unchangingly in the same state 'neither *to become* older nor younger through time' (οὔτε πρεσβύτερον οὔτε νεώτερον προσήκει γίγνεσθαι διὰ χρόνου, 38a3–4).[42] This assertion has its most direct parallel in the *Parmenides* in theses C1–C4, but notice that it is also consistent with both theses A3 and A4, that the One in its aspect *qua* coming-to-be becomes older and younger in relation to itself, and with theses A1 and A2, that the One in its aspect *qua* being may be said to *be* older and younger.

It may seem odd that in the Second Deduction's treatment of the One's relation to time Plato has Parmenides distinguish between the One in its aspect *qua* coming-to-be and in its aspect *qua* being, for it may seem that he could have found nothing in Parmenides corresponding to this type of distinction. We shall see, however, that Plato could quite reasonably have read Parmenides in a way that makes such a distinction central. The portion of the *Parmenides* we have been discussing is our first indication that as we turn to developing an interpretation of the relevant portions of Parmenides' poem within the parameters set by what we have been able to recover of Plato's later reception, we need to consider the possibility that Parmenides may be seen as presenting accounts of Being from different perspectives. What is more, the fact that the *Timaeus*'s description of

[41] With this use of the term 'proceeding' (ἰοῦσαν) and that at *Ti.* 37d6–7, where time itself is described as the image eternally proceeding according to number (κατ' ἀριθμὸν ἰοῦσαν αἰώνιον εἰκόνα) of eternity itself, compare the denial in the *Parmenides*'s demonstration of A1 that the One is proceeding (προϊόν) through time (152c2–6), along with the premises in the demonstration of A3 that the One participates in proceeding time (πορευομένου τοῦ χρόνου, 152a3–4) and that the One itself proceeds according to time (προέρχεται κατὰ χρόνον, 152a5).

[42] Timaeus continues at 38a4–5: 'and neither is it fitting for it to come to be, nor to have come to be now, nor to be in the future hereafter' (οὐδὲ γενέσθαι ποτὲ οὐδὲ γεγονέναι νῦν οὐδ' εἰς αὖθις ἔσεσθαι). Here Plato seems to be echoing Parm. B8. 19–20: 'and how could it be in the future? And how could it come to be? For if it came to be, it is not, nor if it is ever going to be in the future' (πῶς δ' ἂν ἔπειτα πέλοιτο ἐόν; πῶς δ' ἄν κε γένοιτο; | εἰ γὰρ ἔγεντ', οὐκ ἔστ', οὐδ' εἴ ποτε μέλλει ἔσεσθαι). (See Coxon 1986, 202 ad loc. for the text of l. 19a.) It is striking that in the last clause Plato breaks off the sequence of polyptotic uses of the verb 'to become' by shifting to the verb 'to be' (ἔσεσθαι instead of γενήσεσθαι), for this parallels, and is likely motivated by, Parmenides' own reference at B8. 19–20 to the possibility of future being instead of future becoming. The parallel suggests that Plato would have understood Parmenides' argument as pointing out the incompatibility of the use of past- and future-tensed predicates with the present-tense thesis 'it is'.

the intelligible living creature corresponds in certain ways to the *Parmenides*'s account of the One in its aspect *qua* being, while the description of the visible cosmos modelled upon the intelligible living creature corresponds to the account of the One *qua* coming-to-be, suggests that if we do indeed find it possible to read Parmenides as describing Being from different perspectives, we might expect that these descriptions provide accounts of Being in its intelligible and in its perceptible aspects.

9

Plato's Parmenides

I shall suggest that Plato understood Parmenides as presenting in the deduction that comprises the bulk of B8 a description of the cosmos in its intelligible aspect *qua* being. This description is compatible with a description of the cosmos considered from another perspective as a differentiated world system. We shall also see that the possibility of considering the cosmos from different perspectives and describing it in its different aspects relates in important ways to the problem of how one thing can have many names.

It will be useful to begin straightway with an interpretation of the relation between the cosmos in its aspects *qua* intelligible Being and *qua* sensible plurality. Crucial to an explication of this relation will be an understanding of how the theme of naming functions in the poem. We may begin with the relatively straightforward articulation of the theme in B19:[1]

οὕτω τοι κατὰ δόξαν ἔφυ τάδε καί νυν ἔασι
καὶ μετέπειτ᾽ ἀπὸ τοῦδε τελευτήσουσι τραφέντα·
τοῖς δ᾽ ὄνομ᾽ ἄνθρωποι κατέθεντ᾽ ἐπίσημον ἑκάστῳ

(thus according to *doxa* these things grew, now are, and hereafter from this point will end once developed: and upon them humans have placed a name giving its mark to each).

Simplicius tells us that these verses came at the end of the cosmological portion of Parmenides' poem (*in Cael.* 558, 8). Presumably 'these things' refers to the heaven, aether, sun, moon, stars, and so on mentioned in the cosmological programme of B10 and B11. The goddess is marking the fulfilment of her promise that Parmenides will learn the nature and origin of the various celestial phenomena.[2] This promise itself picks up the one originally made at the end of the proem that he will learn not only Truth but also 'how it was necessary for

---

[1] Cf. Owens 1975, 16, who likewise begins from this fragment because 'it has not evoked controversy about its prima facie sense'.

[2] Thus 'grew' (ἔφυ, B19. 1) picks up 'whence they came into being' (ὁππόθεν ἐξεγένοντο, B10. 3), 'whence it grew' (ἔνθεν ἔφυ, B10. 6), and 'started to come into being' (ὡρμήθησαν | γίγνεσθαι, B11. 3–4).

the things believed to be in a believable manner passing entirely through all things' (B1. 31–2). B19's description of the celestial phenomena as having grown, being now, and bound to perish hereafter marks them as possessing the mode of being appropriate to objects of *doxa* or 'the things believed' (τὰ δοκοῦντα). They are not, note, denied being altogether: the goddess is perfectly willing to say that they 'now are'. The phrase 'according to *doxa*', however, seems to place some qualification on their being (and having come to be). One is naturally put in mind of the goddess's declaration at the end of the proem that there is no 'true trust' to be found in mortal beliefs (B1. 30). Understanding the character of the action attributed to humans in the last line of B19 should cast some light on the qualification placed upon the being of the celestial phenomena and why mortal beliefs regarding them are untrustworthy.

The goddess says human beings established names that assigned a distinguishing characteristic to each thing. The crucial words here are ἐπίσημον ἑκάστῳ, which I have translated as 'giving its mark to each'. These words specify exactly what is involved in the act of naming. The adjective ἐπίσημος is standardly used to indicate that the noun it modifies is an object bearing a distinguishing mark or sign (σῆμα). Thus coins may be described as χρυσὸς ἐπίσημος or 'marked gold' because of the stamp they have received.[3] Likewise, the stamp itself that a coin bears is referred to by the substantives ἐπίσημα and ἐπίσημου,[4] which may also be used of the device on a shield.[5] Parmenides' use of the adjective ἐπίσημος at B19. 3 is somewhat uncharacteristic. Instead of using the adjective to describe what has been given the distinguishing mark or sign, he actually uses it as a modifier of what *gives* the distinguishing mark or sign—in this case the names mortals employ. Parmenides' atypical usage ὄνομ'. . . ἐπίσημον, 'a name that gives its mark', stresses that names themselves are the bearers of the marks set upon things. Naming, then, is an act of bestowing upon an object linguistic σήματα, which are distinguishing marks or signs by which the object may be identified and known.

If we turn now to the passage in the poem where naming figures most prominently (B8. 38–41, 53–9), we find that this same bestowal of marks or signs is an essential feature of naming:

> οἷον, ἀκίνητον τελέθει· τῷ παντ(ὶ) ὄνομ'ἐστίν
> ὅσσα βροτοὶ κατέθεντο πεποιθότες εἶναι ἀληθῆ,

---

[3] Hdt. 9. 41. Cf. Thucydides 2. 13; X. *Cyr.* 4. 5. 40.
[4] e.g. Simonides 157 Bergk, Plu. *Theseus* 6.
[5] e.g. Hdt. 9. 74; Aristophanes, *Thesmophoriazusae* 659; Euripides, *Phoenissae* 1107.

γίγνεσθαί τε καὶ ὄλλυσθαι, εἶναί τε καὶ οὐχί,
καὶ τόπον ἀλλάσσειν διά τε χρόα φανὸν ἀμείβειν.
μορφὰς γὰρ κατέθεντο δύο γνώμας ὀνομάζειν,
τῶν μίαν οὐ χρεών ἐστιν, ἐν ᾧ πεπλανημένοι εἰσίν·
τἀντία δ' ἐκρίναντο δέμας καὶ σήματ' ἔθεντο
χωρὶς ἀπ' ἀλλήλων, τῇ μὲν φλογὸς αἰθέριον πῦρ,
ἤπιον ὄν, μέγ' ἐλαφρόν, ἑωυτῷ πάντοσε τωὐτόν,
τῷ δ' ἑτέρῳ μὴ τωὐτόν· ἀτὰρ κἀκεῖνο κατ' αὐτό
τἀντία, νύκτ' ἀδαῆ, πυκινὸν δέμας ἐμβριθές τε

(alone, unchanging it is; for the all, there is every name such as mortals have bestowed, believing them to be true, both coming to be and perishing, both being and not [being], and changing place and exchanging bright colour. For they have fixed their minds on naming two forms, neither of which is necessarily, wherein they have wandered astray. But they distinguished things opposite in form and assigned them *signs* separate from one another, for one of which the aetherial fire of flame, being gentle, most light, the same as itself in every direction but not the same as the other; but that is in itself the opposite, dark night, dense in form and heavy).

I have here accepted Theodor Ebert's transposition of B8. 34–41 immediately after B8. 52,[6] such that B8. 38–41 and 53 ff. form a continuous passage. I have also given the text of B8. 38 as it is given by Plato at *Theaetetus* 180d7–e1, with the slight alterations of placing a comma after οἷον, a semicolon after τελέθει, and changing Plato's infinitive εἶναι to the indicative ἔστιν (see Appendix III). Most ancient citations of the line give the elided form πάντ', which virtually all modern commentators presume is an elision for the neuter nominative plural πάντα. The most significant feature of Plato's reading of the line is its indication that he took the elided form to be the dative singular παντί (the elision of the final syllable is still necessary for the line to scan properly). When πάντ' is taken as an elision of πάντα, there is a potential uncertainty about the sense of τῷ just before it. The word can be used in an absolute sense to mean 'therefore' or 'on this account', as at B8. 25. Or it can be used as a relative pronoun picking out the object of mortal naming, in this case 'what-is' in the line

---

[6] Ebert 1989 presents a convincing case for the transposition. He notes that the relation of B8. 34–41 to the surrounding argument has often been thought unclear, that in particular it cannot be understood as a summary recapitulation or as an argument for the programme's μουνογενές (as e.g. Tarán 1965, 139–44, attempts to argue), and that the criticism of mortal naming at B8. 38b–41 seems out of place. The transposition both removes the interruption in the continuous argument for the last attribute set out in the programme and resolves the problems of the subjectless κατέθεντο and of the apparently functionless γάρ in B8. 53.

immediately preceding.[7] On Plato's reading, τῷ is simply the dative form of the article with the dative πάντι. This reading gives a sense quite close to the second option just mentioned, except that it makes it even clearer what Plato takes to be the object of mortal naming, namely the universe itself. Here we have further confirmation, then, that Plato understood Parmenides' Being as some kind of cosmic entity. I accordingly translate: '*for the all*, there is every name such as mortals have bestowed, believing them to be true, both coming to be and perishing, both being and not [being], and changing place and exchanging bright colour.'

In B8. 53 and following the goddess undertakes to explain how the fundamental choice mortals have made in assigning signs or σήματα to the cosmos has resulted in their describing it via the representative set of names catalogued at B8. 40–1. Mortals, she says, resolved to name two forms (B8. 53). This naming, as in B19, involves the bestowing of signs or σήματα: mortals distinguished things opposed in form and established distinguishing marks for them (σήματ' ἔθεντο, B8. 55). Let us call these two forms Light and Night. If we look carefully at what Parmenides says, the opposition between Light and Night does not appear to be a naturally given distinction. Light and Night do not seem to be independently distinct forms to which mortals simply assign the respectively appropriate marks or signs.[8] Instead, Light and Night themselves belong to the set of marks or signs that mortals bestow upon the object of their naming—the universe or what-is. The antecedent of the relative 'for one of which' (τῇ μέν, B8. 56) is one of the two forms, so that B8. 56b–9 constitutes a catalogue of the signs mortals bestowed upon these forms. That Light and Night do not have independent status but belong to the set of signs mortals have used in their description of the universe finds confirmation in B9, which appears to recapitulate the action described at B8. 53–9: 'and yet since *all things have been named light and night*, and the names corresponding to their respective powers have been given to these things and those, the universe is full of light and obscure night together' (αὐτὰρ ἐπειδὴ πάντα φάος καὶ νὺξ ὀνόμασται | καὶ τὰ κατὰ σφετέρας δυνάμεις ἐπὶ τοῖσί τε καὶ τοῖς, | πᾶν πλέον ἐστὶν ὁμοῦ φάεος

---

[7] So e.g. Woodbury 1958, 149, who provides examples of the construction ὀνομάζειν ἐπί τινι and identifies the reference of τῷ as 'the real world'; and Owens 1975, 18, who bases his interpretation on taking τῷ as a relative 'referring to the whole and immobile being that was mentioned in the two preceding lines'.

[8] Cf. Owens 1975, 17: 'naming would be implicit in what makes one thing distinct from another. It would not be the mere labelling of a distinctive status already recognized for the thing in priority to the naming.'

καὶ νυκτὸς ἀφάντου, B9. 1–3). Here again, as in Plato's version of B8. 38, the object of mortal naming is the universe itself (πάντα, B9. 1 ≈ πᾶν, B9. 3).

In much the same way as an ἐπίσημα may be the mark or symptom indicating the nature of a disease (e.g. Hp. *Morb. Sacr.* 8, *Epid.* 1. 18; Arist. *HA* 6. 18. 572ᵇ32) or the sign by which one can tell of a coming change in the weather (e.g. Thphr. *Sign.* 10 *et passim*), 'episemantic' names serve to indicate the nature of that to which they are given. Mortals have established a certain set of descriptive names for the physical world so that its various phenomena may be distinguished and known. But they have gone astray in establishing signs by which things may be known only in isolation from and in opposition to other things. Their error consists in having assigned the cosmos distinguishing marks or signs that obscure its essential lack of change and differentiation. When the goddess begins her own description of what-is with a catalogue of its properties, she calls these properties also 'signs' or σήματα (B8. 2). The marks that distinguish the nature of the cosmos in her account are: uncreated and imperishable, whole, single in kind, unchanging, and complete. The signs or marks that mortal names have bestowed upon what-is—coming to be and perishing, being and not being, changing place and appearance—stand in contrast with the set of signs or marks via which the goddess describes what-is.

In this connection it is useful to compare the idea, common in early Greek thought on the relation between the human and divine spheres, that gods and mortals use different names for the same things.[9] Two types of example stand out. First, there are cases where the distinction is made vis-à-vis the objects of ritual and sacrifice. Thus Pherecydes is reported to have said that mortals call the offering-table τράπεζα, whereas the gods call it θυωρόν (DL. 1. 119 = fr. 74 Schibli). The same type of distinction is made by the Athenian comic poet Sannyrion (fr. 1 Kock): 'we gods call the barley-cake πελανόν, which you mortals (βροτοί) piously call ἄλφιτα.' It is a sign of their reverence that mortals employ the term ἄλφιτα because in so doing they refrain from using the term proper only to the sacred context. The more directly relevant type of case involves the use of different names for celestial phenomena. Two such examples occur in the

---

[9] Cf. Pl. *Cra.* 391c8–392b2, where Socrates introduces three Homeric examples: *Il.* 20. 74, 14. 291, and 2. 811–14. Other Homeric instances are *Il.* 1. 403–4, *Od.* 10. 305, 12. 61. Cf. also Pl. *Phdr.* 252b, *Cra.* 400d6–e1, *Phlb.* 12c1–3. West 1966, 387–8, lists other examples and provides references to discussions of the phenomenon; cf. also Heubeck 1949–50 and Clay 1972.

fragments of the Hesiodic *Astronomia*: '. . . which mortals (βροτοί) call "the Pleiads" . . .' (Hes. fr. 288), and '. . . which the race of humans upon the earth calls "the Hyades" . . .' (Hes. fr. 291. 4). The corresponding divine names are not preserved in these fragments. One does find an example of this type in the Orphic Rhapsodies: 'he devised another boundless earth, which immortals call "*selēnē*", but earth-dwellers call "moon"' (*OF*, fr. 91. 1–2; cf. the many names of the moon in *OF*, fr. 201). The theme of divine versus mortal names also has its place among the early philosophers. For example, the divinely inspired Empedocles declares that there is, properly speaking, no generation (φύσις) nor death of mortal things but only mixing and unmixing, 'though the name φύσις has been given to these things by humans' (B8). Here we may actually have an echo of Parmenides' assertion that mortals have bestowed the names 'coming-to-be' and 'perishing' upon things. The contrast between human and divine names plays a somewhat different, though still central, role in Heraclitus B67: 'the god is day night, winter summer, war peace, satiety hunger; it undergoes alteration in just the way that fire whenever mixed with spices is named in accordance with the scent of each one.' Here a whole series of opposed names is assigned in human language to what is from the divine point of view a single entity.[10] The theme of naming in Parmenides may be seen as functioning against the background of this traditional contrast. The goddess has reworked it into something much more elaborate by producing a whole complex series of divine and mortal names and corresponding signs that produce starkly opposed descriptions of the cosmos.

What I am suggesting, then, is that the goddess's own account (the 'Truth') and the account she goes on to present in the cosmological portion of the poem (the 'Doxa') are related to one another as accounts of the self-same object, the cosmos itself, from the divine and human perspectives respectively.[11] The names mortals employ are not 'mere' or empty names without referent.[12] They refer to and describe the same thing that the goddess describes in the 'Truth', only from

[10] To make a similar point, Schwabl 1953, 56, cites Aeschylus, *Prometheus Vinctus* 212–13: ἐμοὶ δὲ μήτηρ οὐχ ἅπαξ μόνον Θέμις | καὶ Γαῖα, πολλῶν ὀνομάτων μορφὴ μία.

[11] Cf. Robinson 1979, 56–7, and Austin 1990. On the parallels with Heraclitus, see Robinson 1989.

[12] Cf. Woodbury 1958, 149: 'The names that mortal men institute, although false and deceptive, are not mere fancies or illusions of the mind. They are accounts of the one real world.' Despite this, Woodbury continues to waver on the question of whether mortals are actually committed to the world's existence.

a different perspective and with a different set of assumptions about its nature. Their description of what-is represents it in its changing and differentiated aspect. Their apprehension of what-is in this aspect is accordingly restricted to the level of opinion or *doxa*. The goddess, by contrast, describes what-is via a set of signs that reveal it to Parmenides' understanding in its unchanging and undifferentiated aspect. Considered in this aspect, what-is constitutes a proper object of knowledge. Aristotle in *Metaphysics A. 5* appears to view the relation between the two accounts in this sort of way. Parmenides, he says, seems to have had a conception of formal unity (986^b18-19); and after a compressed account of the reasoning by which he arrived at this view (986^b27-31), Aristotle goes on to say: 'but being compelled to follow the phenomena, and presuming that what-is is one[13] in accordance with reason (κατὰ τὸν λόγον) but many in accordance with perception, he posits two causes and principles . . .' (986^b31-4; cf. Thphr. *Phys. Op.* fr. 6 *ap.* Alex. Aphr. *in Metaph.* 31, 7 ff.). Aristotle appears to understand Parmenides as having provided two accounts of the same object, one in its intelligible aspect, according to which what-is is one, and another in accordance with perception, according to which what-is is a plurality.

The account we have given thus far of the relation between the 'Truth' and the 'Doxa' is in accordance with the parameters of the later Platonic reception. An important passage in this context which we have not yet discussed is *Sophist* 243d6–244b5, the Eleatic Visitor's critique of the doxography's first-stage pluralists that precedes his critique of Eleaticism. Both critiques are implicated in the dialectical structure of the doxography, implying as it does that each successive stage of speculation on the number and nature of fundamental entities is an advance developing directly in reaction to the previous stage(s). This point is clearly stated with reference to the third stage of speculation represented by Heraclitus and Empedocles. For the Visitor says they recognized that the surest course was to weave together the positions of both previous stages by saying that what-is is both many and one (242d7–e1). Although no such genetic analysis of the Eleatic theory is presented within the confines of the doxography itself, the conclusion of the subsequent critiques of the first-stage pluralists and the monists indicates that there has been a similar dialectical progression from one group to the next. Theaetetus comments

[13] Accepting Christ's proposal τὸ ὂν ἓν μέν (cf. Alex. Aphr. *in Metaph.* 45, 3) for the transmitted τὸ ἓν μέν.

on the increasingly greater difficulties their theories have encountered (245e3–5), presumably referring not only to a progression within the series of questions put to each group but also to a progression from one group to the next. A dialectical relation between the first-stage pluralists and the second-stage monists is definitely implied in the criticisms the Visitor puts to the first group. That is, the Visitor's critique of the doxography's first-stage pluralists provides some evidence for the kind of considerations Plato sees as having led to the monism of the Eleatics and of Parmenides in particular.

The Visitor begins by asking what the pluralists mean when they say that all things *are* Hot and Cold or some other pair of principles (243d8–e2). He then quickly presents two possibilities the pluralists might entertain about the relation of being to their two principles. First, he asks whether being should be considered a third thing alongside these two principles (243e2–4). This possibility receives no further consideration. The Visitor instead presents another option, that being might be identified with one of the pluralist principles. On this option, however, it would seem impossible to say that both *are*—or even to maintain that there is a duality, since in saying that the principle not identified with being *is*, one is effectively reducing it to the principle identified with being (243e4–6). That is, with this second argument, the Visitor presents a consideration designed to force monism on the pluralists. It is perhaps significant that whereas in the doxography itself there were numerous varieties of pluralism catalogued in the first division, the Visitor singles out for examination a view according to which there are two principles, Hot and Cold. Perhaps he is simply avoiding irrelevant complexities. But there may be some point in his focusing on two rather than some other number of entities and on Hot and Cold rather than some other pair. Aristotle, suggestively, identifies Hot and Cold with the principles of Parmenides' own dualist cosmology (*Metaph. A.* 5. 986^{b}33–4).[14] Likewise, the second option presented the early pluralists for explaining the relation of their principles to being—'for surely you do not call one of the two "being" and yet say that they both are' (*Sph.* 243e4–5)—may be compared with Aristotle's statement that Parmenides, having posited the two principles Hot and Cold, 'ranges the Hot with

---

[14] Aristotle may also have Parmenides in mind at *GC* 2. 9. 336^{a}3 ff. Although Aristotle in the *Metaphysics* further specifies the principles of Parmenides' cosmology as fire and earth (cf. *GC* 2. 3. 330^{b}13), the influence of the more general identification is still to be seen at e.g. Thphr. *Sens.* 3; DL 9. 22; Stobaeus, *Eclogae* 1. 25. 1. 8a = Aëtius 2. 43 (349 *DG*); Simp. *in Ph.* 31, 3–7 = schol. in Parm. B8. 56–9.

being and the other with not-being' (*Metaph. A.* 5. 987ª1–2). There is little or no evidence that Parmenides himself made any such iden-tification,[15] and Aristotle has often been criticized for introducing this apparent distortion. It may well be, however, that he was influenced to some degree by Plato on this point.

The Visitor goes on to present the pluralists with a third option for explaining the relation of their two principles to being. This option, even more manifestly than the second, is designed to effect the dialectical transition from pluralism to monism. Plato devotes more space to this option, apparently because he sees it as representing the type of reflection upon earlier systems that led Parmenides to the thesis that what-is is not many but one. The Visitor presents the pluralists with the option of saying that both their principles *are* without positing being as separate from them or identical with only one of them. He shows that in this case, too, their two principles must reduce to one. 'Do you want to call the both of them "being"?', he asks. 'Perhaps', says Theaetetus, responding on their behalf. 'But, my friends,' the Visitor says, 'in this way also the two things most obvi-ously might be said to be one' (*Sph.* 243e8–244a2). The point here seems to be, simply put, that the duality of principles can be said to be one *qua* being. Being is not a third principle alongside Hot and Cold, but in so far as these both *are*, they are in this respect one. This particular argument against the pluralists is meant to suggest to them that their plurality of entities may be subjected to a deeper level of ontological analysis. This is a very Parmenidean criticism of the pluralist ontologies.

The *Sophist*'s criticism of early pluralism, accordingly, should be considered at least as important for understanding Plato's view of Parmenides as the subsequent critique of the Eleatic thesis itself, for it suggests a view of the origins of that thesis and thereby a view of the relation between the principles of Parmenides' cosmology and his One Being. Whereas mortals have fixed their thought upon the cosmos in its differentiated aspect, the goddess enjoins Parmenides to fix his own thought upon the cosmos in its properly intelligible aspect *qua* being. Only by adopting this latter perspective may he grasp its perfection. Thus she describes her cosmological account as 'deceptive' (B8. 52) not because it is false, nor because it describes a non-existent state of affairs, but because if one remains at this level

---

[15] Such evidence as may be found depends upon understanding B8. 54a, τῶν μίαν οὐ χρεών ἐστιν, to mean 'one of which it is not necessary [to name]', and then infer-ring (as does Zeller 1919, 701–3) that it is necessary to name the other form and that, if so, it must be identified with being.

of description, as mortals do, one fails to penetrate to the underlying unity and perfection of the cosmos.[16]

All this suggests that we may want to read the diagnosis of mortal error at B8. 53–4 rather differently from how we did in discussing the *Republic* 5 appropriation. Just above, I translated the lines, μορφὰς γὰρ κατέθεντο δύο γνώμας ὀνομάζειν, | τῶν μίαν οὐ χρεών ἐστιν, ἐν ᾧ πεπλανημένοι εἰσίν, as: 'for they have fixed their minds on naming two forms, neither of which is necessarily, wherein they have wandered astray.' This translation reflects our previous interpretation of the difficult phrase, τῶν μίαν οὐ χρεών ἐστιν. However, Hans Schwabl has advocated a way of understanding this phrase that would be in basic accordance with the analysis of the pluralists' error that has emerged from our examination of the *Sophist*'s critique of the doxography's first group. He translates B8. 53–4 thus (emphasis mine): 'denn sie legten ihre Meinung dahin fest, zwei Formen zu benennen, *von denen die Eine nicht notwendig ist*, in diesem Punkte sind sie in die Irre gegangen.'[17] Schwabl thus understands the goddess's criticism of mortal beliefs in B8. 50–9 as directed, not against positing the two principles Light and Night per se, but against the failure to grasp that in so far as both these principles 'are' they have a deeper, unconditional unity in being.[18] According to his view, the unity

---

[16] This general type of view of the relation between the goddess's two accounts has not been without its modern advocates, though they have constituted the minority opinion. For example, Hussey 1990, 31, 32–3, and 36, speaks of the first part of the goddess's account as revealing 'the essential structure of reality' and of mortal opinions as 'a "most probable" opinion about those non-essential features of the world that are really given in sense-experience'; mortals, he says, have characteristically made the mistake of treating the material side of things as an object of knowledge. Here Hussey is departing rather radically from his earlier view on the relation of the two accounts (cf. Hussey 1972, 78–99, esp. 97–9), where he substantially follows Owen 1960. The reading I have offered also agrees incidentally in certain key respects with those of Schwabl 1953, Chalmers 1960, and Owens 1974. Chalmers compares B8. 24b with B9. 3–4 so as to suggest that 'the World of Belief occupies the same space' as the spherical universe of the Truth; 'in his poem [Parmenides] shows us what is fundamentally the same Universe as viewed by a goddess in the Way of Truth and by mortals in the Way of Opinion' (15). However, Chalmers dismisses the potential relevance of the distinction between intellect and sensation, saying that it 'may not have occupied the foremost place in Parmenides' thought', and consequently veers onto another track to argue that 'the basic distinction between the two worlds is the distinction between Eternity and Time' (15–16). Owens takes Arist. *Metaph. A.* 5. 986^b28–33 as the impetus for arguing that the physical world 'is strictly one and immobile as it is understood in human reasoning, but is multiple and mobile as perceived by the senses' (379–80).

[17] See Schwabl 1953, 54 ff., for a defence of this understanding, along with Mansfeld 1964, 122–31, for a development of it. Cf. Diels 1897, 93; Cherniss 1951, 21 and n. 101; Tarán 1965, 220 ff.   [18] See Schwabl 1953, 55.

underlying the two principles *is* being. He sees this as confirmed by B9. 4, where Parmenides says that 'nothing (μηδέν ≈ τὸ μὴ ὄν) is with neither' of the two.[19]

The task now is to see how the goddess's account in accordance with Truth as presented in B8 may have been read by Plato as a demonstration of the nature of things in their aspect *qua* being, that is, in accordance with the principle that 'it is' announced at B8. 2. By this point in the poem it has been established that, for there to be knowledge in the strict sense, there must be an object enjoying the absolute mode of being specified in B2. 3: 'it is and is not for not-being.' Throughout B8 the goddess refers to this object as 'what-is' or 'Being' (τὸ ἐόν, B8. 3, 19, 33, 35, 37, 47). She undertakes to describe its nature as it presents itself to the apprehension of the intellect or νόος. In reading these lines, we shall want to ask not only how this conception is borne out but also whether anything in the account given here rules out the existence of the kind of multiplicity within the cosmos that is apparent to the senses. We shall want, that is, to ask whether this description of the cosmos in its aspect *qua* being is incompatible with its differentiation in an alternative aspect. We shall also want to take account of the evidence provided by the *Parmenides*'s important Second Deduction for how Plato understood certain of the properties of Being in this demonstration.

The deduction of Being's properties begins at B8. 6–11 with two arguments against its genesis:

> τίνα γὰρ γένναν διζήσεαι αὐτοῦ;
> πῇ πόθεν αὐξηθέν; οὐδ' ἐκ μὴ ἐόντος ἐάσσω
> φάσθαι σ' οὐδὲ νοεῖν· οὐ γὰρ φατὸν οὐδὲ νοητόν
> ἔστιν ὅπως οὐκ ἔστι. τί δ' ἄν μιν καὶ χρέος ὦρσεν
> ὕστερον ἢ πρόσθεν, τοῦ μηδενὸς ἀρξάμενον, φῦν;
> οὕτως ἢ πάμπαν πελέναι χρεών ἐστιν ἢ οὐχί

(for what birth will you seek of it? How and from where grown? 'From what-is-not' I shall allow you neither to say nor to think: for it is not to be said nor thought that it is not. And indeed what need could have urged it, beginning from nothing, to grow later instead of before? In this way it is necessary that it either is altogether or not at all).

With the argument that there could have been no generation of what-is from what-is-not, Parmenides is at one level simply articulating and applying the axiom that Aristotle correctly speaks of as the 'common opinion' of all the early natural philosophers, that there can

---

[19] Ibid. 64–5.

be no genesis from nothing or what-is-not (*Ph.* 1. 4. 187ª27–9; cf.
Metaph. A. 3. 983ᵇ11–13). Parmenides is in a position to give this
axiom added force in that his principle is Being itself, which he has
already argued cannot be conceived of as not being. Water, air, or some
other such principle might easily be conceived of as not being or as
having come to be from something else, but this is not the case with
Being itself. The conclusion that what-is must necessarily be altogether
means both that it has not gradually emerged or come to be and that
it is the totality of what is. B8. 12–13a establishes that what-is is all
there is: οὐδέ ποτ' ἐκ μὴ ἐόντος ἐφήσει πίστιος ἰσχύς | γίγνεσθαί τι παρ'
αὐτό ('nor will the force of conviction ever allow anything to come to
be alongside it from what-is-not'). We may pause to note that the disjunctive form of the conclusion at B8. 11—'it is necessary that it either
is altogether *or not at all*'—is suggestive of the gap that we previously
pointed out in the general argument from the possibility of knowledge and that features in Parmenides' version of the argument in B2.
That is, 'or not at all' here does not merely represent some vaguely
conceived counterfactual possibility. Rather, it is an acknowledge-
ment of the genuine possibility that there is no such thing as what the
goddess is describing as the proper object of knowledge. *If* there is,
however, it is necessary that it be altogether and in every way.

This initial series of arguments establishes for what-is the first
pair of marks or σήματα set out by the goddess in her programme
for the deduction: 'that Being is ungenerated and imperishable'
(ὡς ἀγένητον ἐὸν καὶ ἀνώλεθρόν ἐστιν, B8. 3; cf. the conclusions at
B8. 13b–14, 21). Consequently, the first two marks or σήματα she
will indicate mortals have established in their descriptions of the
world—'coming-to-be and perishing' (B8. 40)—are banned from a
description of the world as Being. Does this mean that there is no
genesis or destruction in the cosmos whatsoever? On the face of it,
no. The goddess will employ the language of genesis in the cosmogon-
ical portion of the poem. In the programmatic fragments from the
cosmology, for example, she promises to describe 'from whence there
came to be' the aether and all the 'signs' (σήματα) in it (B10. 1–3),
how the heaven itself 'grew' (B10. 6), and how the earth and the various celestial bodies 'were impelled to come to be' (B11). There is
no contradiction here. What is argued in B8. 6–14 is that Being itself
did not come to be (and by implication will not perish). The coming-
to-be of the aether, the ouranos, the earth, and the remaining phenomena apparent in the cosmos in no way implies that Being itself
comes to be. 'Ungenerated and imperishable' and 'coming-to-be and
perishing' are two pairs of marks or σήματα attributed to the same

object. The two pairs of properties may contradict one another, but they may still be attributed to the same object provided that they are done so in different respects.

One way of consistently maintaining that the cosmological manifestations of Being come to be while Being itself has not done so would be to identify Being as what persists through the various changes involved. One might object that the principles of Parmenides' cosmology that underlie its various phenomena are clearly Light and Night rather than Being. Still, there are certain indications in the poem that Being underlies Light and Night themselves and as such persists through the various changes in the cosmos. Certain of the properties of Being recur in the description of Light and Night. As Being is 'all alike' (πᾶν . . . ὁμοῖον, B8. 22), so Light is 'the same as itself in every direction' (ἑωυτῷ πάντοσε τωὐτόν, B8. 57). As what-is is absolutely continuous because 'all is full of being' (πᾶν ἔμπλεόν ἐστιν ἐόντος, B8. 24), so there is no void in the cosmos because 'the universe is full of light and obscure night together' (πᾶν πλέον ἐστὶν ὁμοῦ φάεος καὶ νυκτὸς ἀφάντου, B9. 3). Just as what-is-not is banished from the description of the cosmos *qua* Being, so there is no 'nothing' among Light and Night (B9. 4). There is also evidence that the attributes of Being recur in the later stages of the cosmogony. For example, there are striking parallels between the goddess's description of how necessity holds Being within limits and her promise to teach Parmenides how necessity bound the heaven to provide the limit of the astral region:

$$\text{κρατερὴ γὰρ ἀνάγκη}$$
$$\text{πείρατος ἐν δεσμοῖσιν ἔχει, τό μιν ἀμφὶς ἐέργει}\quad\text{(B8. 30b–1)}$$

(for a powerful necessity holds it in the bonds of a limit that restrains it all about);

$$\text{εἰδήσεις δὲ καὶ οὐρανὸν ἀμφὶς ἔχοντα}$$
$$\text{ἔνθεν ἔφυ τε καὶ ὥς μιν ἄγουσ᾿ ἐπέδησεν ἀνάγκη}$$
$$\text{πείρατ᾿ ἔχειν ἄστρων}\quad\text{(B10. 5–7)}$$

(and you will know too whence grew the surrounding heaven and how a necessity directing it bound it to hold the limits of the stars).

Given that the two parts of the poem are alternative descriptions of the same object, it is perhaps not surprising that there should be this type of recurrence.

This recurrence should be seen as at least a partial basis for what the *Sophist*'s criticisms of the doxography's first-stage pluralists suggest was Plato's view of the relation between the duality of principles and the one Being in Parmenides. The argument there—that, in so far as Hot and Cold both *are*, they are in this respect one—was designed to suggest to the pluralists that their principles might be subjected to a deeper level of analysis, thereby effecting the transition to the monist ontology. The recurrence of the attributes of Being in the descriptions of Light and Night (and of the cosmos's structure) points to this type of intimate connection between Being or what-is and Light and Night. The phenomena available to perception, that is, the aspects of the cosmos upon which mortals have focused their cognitive attention, and in terms of which they have constructed their accounts of it, are manifestations of Being in its non-permanent and therefore non-essential aspect. This idea is clearest at B8. 36b–9 (the last part of which has been discussed above):

οὐδὲν γὰρ <ἢ> ἔστιν ἢ ἔσται
ἄλλο πάρεξ τοῦ ἐόντος, ἐπεὶ τό γε Μοῖρ' ἐπέδησεν.
οἷον, ἀκίνητον τελέθει· τῷ παντ(ὶ) ὄνομ' ἐστίν
ὅσσα βροτοὶ κατέθεντο πεποιθότες εἶναι ἀληθῆ

(for nothing else either is or will be apart from Being, since Fate has bound it. Alone, unchanging it is; for the all there is every name such as mortals have bestowed, believing them to be true . . .).

The goddess has just reasserted that genuine knowledge must have Being as it object (B8. 34–6a). Here she declares that there is nothing except Being. It is the totality of what-is. It is what mortals have described by bestowing upon it the various marks or σήματα they have erroneously taken to be its essential properties. The first argument of the 'Truth', then, demonstrates that 'ungenerated and imperishable', rather than 'coming-to-be and perishing', belong to the class of marks or σήματα that indicate the nature of the cosmos in its aspect *qua* Being. This demonstration does not entail that there are no processes of genesis and destruction within the cosmos but merely that, should one choose to focus upon these manifestations of Being, the perfection of what-is will not present itself to one's understanding.

10

Plato's Parmenides and the *Parmenides*'s Second Deduction

The remaining portion of the Truth describes the further perfections of Being considered in itself rather than in its manifestations. The properties it is shown to have in itself are all present in the Second Deduction's account of the One-that-is. Rather than take up these properties as they occur in Parmenides' poem and demonstrate how they are attributed to the One-that-is in the *Parmenides*, however, I want instead to follow through certain arguments in the Second Deduction itself in order to show how it reflects Plato's use of Parmenides. In discussing the relation of the *Sophist*'s second critique of Eleaticism to this deduction, we have seen how Parmenides expresses the idea that the One has both 'one' and 'being' predicable of it by saying that the hypothesis that the One is signifies that the One is such as to have parts. Describing the One as a whole having different parts is a way of speaking of its capacity to have more than one property predicated of it. This basically spatial model of predication may well seem unfortunate, and its infelicity might be thought responsible for some of the tortured ambiguities of the Second Deduction. But since Plato develops this spatial model of predication via his appropriation of Parmenides, we need to try to come to grips with the problems it poses.

Consider, for example, the stretch of analysis at *Parmenides* 142d9–143a2.[1] Parmenides has just prior to this passage introduced the idea that the hypothesis 'the One is' implies that the One is such as to have parts. Specifically, what this hypothesis refers to, 'one being', is a whole whose parts are 'one' and 'being'. Saying that the One is such as to have parts is a way of expressing the idea that the One is capable of having various predicates. 'The One is.' 'The One partakes of being.' ' "Being" is a part of the "one being".' All these statements express the idea that 'being' is predicated of the One. Likewise, 'the

---

[1] See Schofield 1973(*a*) for an interpretation of this passage as making a principally *ad hominem* point against Eleaticism (via generally invalid argumentation). For a more charitable view of the argument, see Curd 1990, 19–25.

One is one', 'the One partakes of oneness', and ' "one" is part of "one being" ' all express the idea that 'one' is predicated of the One.[2] Some of these ways of putting the point may seem unfortunate. Some seem to express the relation in question less clearly than others. In particular, describing 'one' and 'being' as parts of the one being or the One-that-is has potentially uncomfortable spatial connotations. The discussion between Parmenides and Aristoteles at 142d9–143a2 is starting to bring out these connotations:

What of this then? As for each of these parts of the One-that-is, namely 'one' and 'being': is 'one' ever absent from the part 'being', or 'being' from the part 'one'?—They could not be.—Therefore each of the parts also has in turn both 'one' and 'being', and the part comes to be composed of at least two parts again. And it is always so, by the same reasoning: whatever part comes to be always has these two parts. For what is one always has 'being', and what is always has 'one'. So that what is always becoming two is necessarily never one.—By all means.—Therefore would not the One-that-is be in this way unlimited in multitude?—Apparently.

This will all seem inexplicably puzzling unless one appreciates how Plato is pressing and teasing out the physical implications of the spatial model of predication. If 'one being' is a whole, then it can be divided. If it is divided into what have been identified as its predicate parts, namely 'one' and 'being', then each of these parts both is and is one. The part 'one' is, and the part 'being' is one. Each of the parts of 'one being', that is, is one being. The same division can be performed on each of these parts 'one being' with the same result. Each of the parts of the parts 'one being' is one being, and so on. This is obviously a special kind of division. 'One' and 'being' may be identified as the predicate parts of 'one being'. Even so, it seems wrong to suppose that these parts can be divided out of the 'one being' and kept separate from one another. It in fact seems that part of the point of our passage is that this kind of division cannot strictly speaking be carried out. This is because 'one' and 'being' stand in a special kind of relation to the whole, 'one being'.

Perhaps we can clarify this point by taking a less abstract example and by considering a wider range of types of predicate parts. Consider the water in a lake. Let the water in the lake be wet, blue, water, rippling, liquid, cold, green, still, lukewarm, and so on. Some of these properties are contraries, for example blue and green. But let the water in the lake be blue here and green there, rippling here and still there, and so on. We can say that 'wet', 'blue', 'water', etc., are all

---

[2] For an account of how the One itself is one, cf. Nehamas 1982, 358–64.

predicated of the water. Plato would appear to want to speak of wet, blue, water, etc., as all being parts of the water. If the water is a whole that has various predicate parts, then it can in some sense be divided. That the water is a spatially extended body also entails the possibility of its being divided. The relation between these two kinds of divisibility may not be exactly clear, but let us in any case concentrate for the moment on the second kind. Suppose we divide the water in the lake into two bodies of water and continue this process of division further and further. (Let us not worry here about what happens when we carry out the division past the molecular level.) The initial divisions may produce partial bodies of water that display all the properties that the whole body of water in the lake did when we started. At some point, however, we will end up with a partial body of water that is, say, cold but not lukewarm, or blue but not green, or still but not rippling. Some parts of the water may not be lukewarm, or may not be green, or may not be rippling. What we will not end up with, however, are parts of the water that are not liquid, not wet, or not water. Every part into which we divide the water in the lake will be wet, liquid, and water. These predicate parts *reduplicate* or *persist* all the way down through the series of divisions.

Because of this reduplication or persistence, it makes less sense to speak of dividing the water into parts that are water and parts that are wet than it does to speak of dividing the water into parts that are blue and parts that are green. The fact that some predicate parts reduplicate all the way down while others do not suggests that we are dealing with two different types of predicate parts. The reduplicating predicate parts appear to be more intimately connected with what it is to be a body of water than the non-reduplicating ones. One might be inclined to say that the reduplicating predicate parts are essential properties of water, while the non-reduplicating predicate parts are non-essential or accidental properties. I hesitate to characterize the difference in exactly these terms, however, for it is unclear that 'wet', 'liquid', and 'water' are in fact all predicates indicating essential properties of water. They do not seem to be predicates of a sufficiently similar type to warrant grouping them together in precisely this manner. Would these predicate parts all belong in a definition of 'water'? Would any of them? ('Liquid' seems the only potentially viable candidate.) What about the predicate 'being'? The body of water we started with certainly *is*, so that it will admit having 'being' predicated of it. Furthermore, it is clear that each of the parts into which we could conceivably divide the body of water will also *be*. So 'being' belongs to the set of reduplicating predicate parts that includes 'wet', 'liquid',

and 'water'. However, we are unlikely to include 'being' in a definition of 'water', and we may even be uncertain whether we would
want to call being an essential property of water.

Nevertheless, the conceptual division we have carried out does suggest that in the case we have been considering 'being', 'wet', 'liquid',
and 'water' belong together under some description. For we have seen
how, in relation to water at least, they do not behave like the predicates 'blue', 'cold', 'still', etc. Plato himself does not speak of essential properties. Instead, he speaks of what is said of or predicated of
a thing *kath' hauto*, with respect to the thing itself or in virtue of that
thing being what it is. However widely 'being', 'wet', 'liquid', and
'water' may differ as types of predicate, it makes sense to think of them
all as predicated of a body of water in virtue of itself or *kath' hauto*.
Thus the kind of conceptual division we have undertaken with the
example of a body of water appears to constitute a tool for distinguishing between *kath' hauto* and non-*kath' hauto* predicates. This
tool is quite crude, however, for we can easily think of cases somewhat different from the water in a lake where it will be of no use
at all in making this type of distinction. Let us say a certain person
is 'female', 'intelligent', 'dark-haired', 'human', 'hazel-eyed', 'two-
footed', 'beautiful', 'near-sighted', and so forth. It seems impossible
in this case to imagine carrying out a conceptual division aimed at
determining which of these predicates are said of the person just in
virtue of her being a person or the person she is. Generally, the conceptual division of things into their predicate parts will not be an
effective way of differentiating between the *kath' hauto* and non-*kath'
hauto* predicates of things belonging to natural kinds, for example,
human beings, horses, caterpillars, or even of things like tables and
chairs.

It would be worth trying to explain why the conceptual division of
wholes into their predicate parts is feasible in the case of some wholes
but not others. All I want to do here, however, is point out that the
One-that-is behaves more like a body of water than a person. In returning to the case Parmenides is actually examining, it will be helpful to
remind ourselves that the one being is in some sense a cosmic entity.
Consider the body of water now, not as a whole to be subjected to
division into its predicate parts, but as one of the parts into which the
world itself as a whole might be divided. Among the body of water's
predicate parts are 'being', 'one', 'water', 'liquid', 'wet', 'green', 'rippling', 'cold', etc. Of these the only ones that will have reduplicated
themselves all the way down through every division of the cosmos itself
taken as a whole are 'one' and 'being'. In the same way that we spoke

of the water in the lake as 'wet', 'blue', 'water', etc., so we can speak of the cosmos itself as 'one', 'being', 'earth', 'air', 'fire', 'water', 'planets', 'stars', 'humans', 'green', 'still', and on and on indefinitely. The cosmos can have all these properties predicated of it since they all describe parts or manifestations of it. But if we perform the same type of conceptual division upon the cosmic whole that we did upon the body of water, the only predicate parts in this particular list that reduplicate themselves and persist in each and every part into which we divide it are 'one' and 'being'. This analysis suggests, then, that 'one' and 'being' belong among the cosmos's *kath' hauto* predicates, those things said of the totality of what there is simply in virtue of its being what it is. If all this seems a strange way to speak of things, it may be because we harbour an Aristotelian preference for metaphysical principles whose paradigm instances are natural kinds. I have been trying to suggest, if only in the most basic manner, how one might conceive of things were one to give precedence instead to unity and being as principles. For this is in effect what Plato's use of Parmenides leads him to do. In *Parmenides* 142d9–143a2 Plato is considering the Parmenidean cosmic entity characterized as one and being. This one being is resistant to the attempt to divide it conceptually into its predicate parts 'one' and 'being', for each part into which it can be divided both is and is one: 'each of the parts also has in turn both "one" and "being", and the part comes to be composed of at least two parts again. And it is always so, by the same reasoning: whatever part comes to be always has these two parts. For what is one always has "being", and what is always has "one" ' (142e3–7).

Although Plato's conceptual division of the one being might seem to go against Parmenides' own declaration that what-is is not divisible,[3] this is not actually so. Rather, the demonstration of the one being's resistance to the type of division envisaged here via a demonstration of how its predicate parts 'one' and 'being' persist through every possible division should be seen as Plato's way of making much the same point Parmenides himself makes in B8. 22–5 when he declares what-is to be indivisible:

> οὐδὲ διαιρετόν ἐστιν, ἐπεὶ πᾶν ἐστιν ὁμοῖον·
> οὐδέ τι τῇ μᾶλλον, τό κεν εἴργοι μιν συνέχεσθαι,
> οὐδέ τι χειρότερον, πᾶν δ' ἔμπλεόν ἐστιν ἐόντος.
> τῷ ξυνεχὲς πᾶν ἐστιν· ἐὸν γὰρ ἐόντι πελάζει

---

[3] So e.g. Cornford 1939, 139, who sees the passage as envisaging a conceptual division of the notion of 'One Entity' and supposes that its 'reasoning is valid against Parmenides, who declared that a "One Being" must be indivisible, and yet asserted that "what can be thought can be" '.

(nor is it divisible, since it is all alike; nor is it any more in some place nor any less, which would prevent it from being continuous, but it is all full of being. Therefore it is all continuous: for being draws near to being).

Parmenides will have been understood as saying here that the cosmos in its aspect *qua* being is indivisible because if one attempts to divide it even conceptually one finds that it is, *qua* being, entirely alike and indistinguishable. After no possible division does one find that some part of it has being more than another. On the contrary, since it is entirely full of being, every potential part *is* as much as any and all others. Thus the cosmos, considered in its aspect *qua* being, is a continuous and undifferentiated whole. This is not to say that it is undifferentiated in other aspects. Parts of it are bright and fiery, others dark and cold. Certain structures and things within it come to be, while others perish. Things move and change colour. These are some of the properties of the cosmos in its differentiated aspect that Parmenides himself mentions. But they are not properties of the whole that persist in whatever parts into which the whole could conceivably be divided. Nor are the parts of the cosmos whose creation Parmenides describes in his cosmology—the heaven, the aether, the stars, sun, moon, planets, the earth itself, and all the living creatures upon it. The predicate parts of the totality of what-is that persist in each of these are 'one' and 'being'.

In the next portion of the Second Deduction (143a4–b8),[4] Plato adds to these the property of difference. Parmenides begins here by restating that the One partakes of being and has thus appeared to be many—that is, has predicate parts, with all this implies. He then asks Aristoteles to consider the One itself alone in itself without the being it partakes of. If the One is not being but partakes of being, he says, then the One's being is one thing and the One itself another. He then analyses how it is that the One and being are different from one another. It is not in virtue of its unity that the One is different from being, nor is it in virtue of its being that being is other than the One. They are instead different from one another in virtue of difference and otherness (τῷ ἑτέρῳ τε καὶ ἄλλῳ ἕτερα ἀλλήλων). Thus difference is not the same as the One or being. It is instead a third thing in addition to them, in virtue of which each is different from the other. This analysis of how the One is not being (μὴ οὐσία τὸ ἕν, 143b2) in terms of the One being different from or other than being prefigures to some extent the more fully developed analysis of not-being in the Fifth Deduction, in much the same way as predicational monism

---

[4] On which, see Curd 1990, 26–9.

appears initially in the First and then is developed more fully in the Fourth Deduction.

Furthermore, the way 'difference' is introduced here alongside 'one' and 'being' foreshadows the way the Eleatic Visitor, in discussing the greatest kinds in the *Sophist*, introduces 'same' and 'different' as additional kinds or characters alongside 'being', 'rest', and 'change'. Each of these latter three, he says, is different from the other two and the same as itself (254d14–15). After establishing that 'same' and 'different' are distinct kinds not to be identified with any of the other three (254e2–255e2), he says that difference 'pervades all the kinds: for each one is different from the others, not in virtue of its own nature, but in virtue of partaking of the character of difference' (255e3–6).[5] Parmenides is making a similar point in the Second Deduction when he says that it is not in virtue of its unity that the One is different from being, nor in virtue of its being that being is different from the One, but that they are different from one another in virtue of 'difference' (*Prm.* 143b3–6).[6] The Visitor in the *Sophist* goes on to make a number of statements involving the five greatest kinds to show the various ways they do and do not combine with one another. One conclusion emerging from this examination of how the kinds combine is that 'being' and 'difference' pervade all the kinds, including one another (*Sph.* 259a5–6; cf. 253c1–3, 254b10–c1). Each of the kinds, indeed each and every thing that is, will combine with or partake of 'being'. Each thing that is will have 'being' predicated of it. Likewise, each kind, and every thing that is, will combine with or partake of 'difference', that is, have 'difference' predicated of it, for there are innumerable things from which each thing is different.

In his view of the all-pervasive character of being, Plato finds himself in particular allegiance with Parmenides. Plato's concern with the all-pervasive character of difference, on the other hand, is not an area where he would perceive a continuity of concern with Parmenides. For, as the Visitor makes clear in the *Sophist*, things always partake of 'difference' in relation to other things, whereas Parmenides is concerned with the character of being in relation to itself. At 255c14–d1 the Visitor draws the distinction between things that are said in relation to, or in virtue of, themselves and things that are always said in relation to other things, and he points out that 'difference' belongs to the latter class (τὸ δέ γ'ἕτερον ἀεὶ πρὸς ἕτερον).[7] He repeats this point

---

[5] On how difference pervades all the forms, see Nehamas 1982, 352–7.

[6] This connection is also noted by Allen 1997, 261.

[7] This passage provides the cornerstone for Frede's 1967 interpretation of Plato's use of the verb 'is' in the *Sophist* (see esp. 12–36). Frede's distinction between a use

regarding the character of difference when, having shown that 'not-being' does not signify the complete opposite of being but only what is different, he quotes Parmenides B7. 1–2 for the second time in the dialogue and says that he and Theaetetus have disobeyed Parmenides by going further in their inquiries than the prohibition expressed in these lines would have them do: 'we have not only shown that things that are not are, but we have also revealed the character that "not-being" happens to have; for having demonstrated that the nature of "difference" both is and is divided out over all the things that are in relation to one another (ἐπὶ πάντα τὰ ὄντα πρὸς ἄλληλα), we have dared to say, regarding each part of it set in opposition to something that is, that this itself is genuinely "not-being"' (258d5–e3). Now, this claim to have gone beyond Parmenides does not mean that he has been 'refuted' in any serious way. The Visitor says that he and Theaetetus have disobeyed Parmenides' prohibition by focusing their attention upon things that are not as well as things that are. This has involved focusing upon the all-pervasive character of difference that things that are exhibit in relation to other things. Parmenides' goddess had warned him against doing anything of this sort, directing him instead to concentrate upon the character of what-is in relation to itself. Again, though, the Visitor has not refuted Parmenides by disobeying him in this way. The Visitor has instead simply done what he describes himself and Theaetetus as having done. 'We have disobeyed Parmenides by proceeding beyond the limits of his prohibition' (258c7–8). 'We have shown him more than he bade us consider by continuing to inquire further than his prohibition would have us' (258c10–11).

These comments might serve as a fair enough description of what Plato has done in the *Parmenides*'s Second Deduction by demonstrating the pervasive character of 'difference' at 143a4–b8. Parmenides had instructed his audience to focus upon what-is in relation to itself and upon the all-pervasive character of being. Plato has done so both in the Second Deduction and in the *Sophist*, but he has also drawn attention to how what-is may be conceived of in its differentiated aspect or as partaking of 'difference' in relation to other things. In the remainder of the Second Deduction he will continue to give an account of the characters the One displays in relation to itself, echoing Parmenides' own account of Being as he does so, but he will also give an account of the character the One displays in relation to

of 'is' in statements indicating what something is by itself and a use of 'is' in statements indicating what something is by standing in a certain relation to something else has proved both influential and controversial (Frede 1992, 401–2, responds to certain of his critics and offers some clarification of his original distinction).

other things, thereby going beyond Parmenides' account of Being in relation to itself. Plato's refusal to abide by the limits of Parmenides' injunction, therefore, does not consist in his having demonstrated that 'not-being' should not be understood as indicating the complete absence of being or the opposite of being. Where he has gone beyond Parmenides is in his willingness to explore the relations things may have via partaking of difference in relation to other things. For this involves focusing one's attention upon what-both-is-and-is-not rather than solely upon what-is. Thus when the Visitor says at *Sophist* 258e6–259a1 that we should not allow anyone (τις—not Parmenides) to tell us that what-is-not is the opposite of being (τοὐναντίον τοῦ ὄντος) since we have long since bid farewell to whatever is opposed to being, this should not be understood as an indication of where he sees himself as departing from Parmenides. He is instead indicating that the sophistic appropriation of Parmenides whereby what-is-not has been reduced to what-is-not-at-all has finally been forestalled.

Let us return, then, to the *Parmenides*'s Second Deduction and to the point on which Plato finds himself in allegiance with Parmenides, the all-pervasive character of being. After the portion of the deduction in which he introduces 'difference' alongside 'one' and 'being', Plato proceeds to an argument often referred to as the generation of number (*Prm.* 143c1–144a9). Taking the various possible pairings of 'one', 'being', and 'difference', he says that the members of each pair can collectively be referred to as 'both' and therefore as 'two'. Each member of each pair is 'one'. If any 'one' is added to any 'two', the total is 'three'. That there are 'two' and 'three' means that there are also 'twice' and 'thrice' and thus 'twice two', 'thrice three', 'twice three', 'thrice two', and so on, generating all the numbers. Here we have yet another conceptual generation of a plurality from the hypothesized 'one being'. Important for our purposes are the conclusions of this generation rather than its actual mechanics. These conclusions are: if number is, there are many things, indeed an unlimited multitude of things, that are; number, unlimited in multitude, also partakes of being; and if every number partakes of being, each part of number partakes of being as well (144a5–9). In short, although the conceptual division of the one being via the generation of number from it yields a limitless plurality, each and every member of this resultant plurality *is*. As in the previous conceptual division of the one being at 142d9–143a2, so here too being persists all the way down through the series of divisions producing an ever greater number of entities.

We have seen how part of the point of the previous attempt to divide the one being into its predicate parts 'one' and 'being' was that

the characteristics of the one being so designated persist in any part
of it one might single out. They are characteristics of the whole that
pervade all possible limited manifestations of that whole. The idea
of the all-pervasive character of 'one' and 'being' receives perhaps its
clearest statement at the close of the generation of number's conceptual division of what-is. Being, Parmenides says, has been portioned
out over all the many beings resulting from this division and is absent
from none of them, neither from the smallest nor from the largest
(144b1–3). This portioning out of being means that it is divided into
parts and that it has in fact an unlimited number of parts (144b4–c1).
Parmenides then argues that 'one' will be predicated of every part
into which being may be divided. Since there is no part of being that
is not one part, and since whatever is must always, so long as it is, be
one part, 'one' will be predicated of every part of being (144c2–8).

This analysis of how being and unity are present to each of the
limitless number of things that are puts Parmenides in a position to
deal with one of the problems he had previously raised regarding
Socrates' account of how particulars participate in forms. In the second of the series of objections he brought against Socrates' theory,
Parmenides had asked whether each thing participating in a form
participates in the whole form or in part of it (131a4–5). At the point
in the Second Deduction we have now reached, he asks Aristoteles
to consider whether, while being one, it is in numerous places simultaneously as a whole (144c8–d1). Aristoteles, in one of his longest
and most thoughtful responses in the exercise, says that when he considers this possibility he sees that it is impossible (144d1–2). He is
clearly right to do so, for the totality of being is not present in each
and every individual thing that is. This suggests that despite Socrates' previous brave attempts to maintain that there is a way in which
a form as a whole can be in each thing participating in it (131a8–b6),
Plato does not in fact mean this to be a feasible option. Parmenides
leads Socrates to the alternative that each thing participating in a
form participates in part of the form by introducing the analogy of a
sail spread over many people, whereby part of the sail would be over
one person and another part over another (131b7–c4). The analogy
implies that forms are themselves divisible into parts, that things
participating in a form participate in part of it, and that only a part
of the form, not the whole of it, is present in each thing participating
in it (131c5–7). Parmenides then puts a question to Socrates that
leads him to reject this option: 'So are you willing, Socrates, to say
that our one form is in truth divided into parts, and will it still be
one?' (131c9–10). Socrates does not think this possible. Parmenides'

question to Socrates raises the issue we need to focus on in considering the Second Deduction's account of how 'being' and 'one'
are divided so as to be in many things simultaneously.[8] The fundamental problem with the idea that they are in numerous things simultaneously by being divided into parts is that it makes it difficult to
continue conceiving of each of them as one. Such is the force of the
question that baffles Socrates. Given that Parmenides in our present
passage is returning to the issues involved in the problem he had raised
for Socrates' conception of participation, we naturally expect that
his discussion here of 'being' and 'one' as divided into parts should
reflect at least part of the solution to this problem.[9] I do not propose
to discuss how the solution in the case of 'one' and 'being' may or may
not extend to other forms. Presumably one needs to examine other
forms in the same way Parmenides examines the One. I would not
hazard a guess regarding what might result. Our focus continues to be
Plato's use of Parmenides. It seems that Parmenides was understood
as providing a model for how being can be parcelled out among the
various things that are and yet remain one.

One implication of the way this stretch of the Second Deduction progresses is that Plato recognizes that Parmenides is more
fundamentally concerned with being than with unity. Unity is a property of being in Parmenides, and it is treated as such here. Plato's
Parmenides begins with the fact that being is portioned out among
all the limitless number of things that are. He then goes on to argue
that since unity is a property of each and every part of being, it is
equally portioned out among all the things that are. One reason he proceeds from how 'being' is divided to how 'one' is isomorphically
divided, it seems, is that it is relatively simple to conceive of the totality of being as divided among the various particular things that are.
Parmenides himself provides the model for how this works. Consider
a division of Being or what-is into two discrete entities. We can follow Parmenides and call them Light and Night. Each of these *is*.
Neither, however, has the whole of Being in itself alone. Light is not
the whole of what-is, for there is more Being than that in Light. The
remainder of Being is in Night. Thus Being is portioned out among

---

[8] Weber 1937, 9, notes that in the first part of the dialogue the possibility that a
participant participates in the whole of a form is rejected within the space of four lines,
while the possibility that a participant participates in part of a form receives 26¼ lines
of discussion, and that there is a similar proportion in the corresponding passage of
the Second Deduction.

[9] Cf. Curd 1990, 29–31, which rightly points out that Plato does not adequately
elucidate his conception of participation or predication as a part/whole relation.

Light and Night and is absent from neither. We can speak of it as divided into a part that is in Light and a part that is in Night. One could take ever more complex divisions and give the same kind of account. One could speak of how Being is divided among the stars, sun, moon, earth, the planets, and the remaining population of the cosmos.

We now need to ask the type of question Parmenides had put to Socrates. Can we say that there is any sense in which Being can be divided into the parts corresponding to Light and Night and yet still remain one? We have in effect already answered this question. Being may be parcelled out among Light and Night, and indeed among all the limitless number of things that are, while still being one in relation to itself. For consider how Being is divided into parts that are distinguishable as Light and Night. It can only be so divided by attaching differentiating marks to it that themselves bring about its having distinguishable parts. Being can only be conceived of as divided into parts if we conceive of it as something other than being, as Light and Night or what have you. One can describe what-is in terms of the opposition Light and Night so that it becomes possible to say that part of what-is is in Light and part of what-is is in Night. Thus as Light and Night, Being has distinguishable parts. But simply as Being, or just in virtue of its own nature, Being remains one and, as Parmenides himself says, indivisible. Here we come back to the Eleatic Visitor's suggestion, in that portion of the *Sophist*'s second critique of Eleaticism which we have seen corresponds to the present deduction, that 'nothing prevents what is divided into parts having the attribute of unity over all its parts, and in this manner being one, as being all and whole' (τό γε μεμερισμένον πάθος μὲν τοῦ ἑνὸς ἔχειν ἐπὶ τοῖς μέρεσι πᾶσιν οὐδὲν ἀποκωλύει, καὶ ταύτῃ δὴ πᾶν τε ὂν καὶ ὅλον ἓν εἶναι, 245a1–3).

It is in large part because being is conceived of along Parmenidean lines as the actual being of the cosmos itself that it makes sense to speak of each of the things that are as having a portion of being while it remains a single and undifferentiated whole with respect to itself or in virtue of its own nature. The divisibility of 'one' into parts would seem rather more complicated to grasp had Plato not taken pains to emphasize here how unity is always a property of anything that is. It hardly seems to make sense to speak of 'one' as divided, any more than it would to speak of 'same' or 'different' as being divided. If we can make any sense at all of this way of speaking, it is only in virtue of the fact that 'one' can be predicated of a number of things. To say that 'one' is divided into parts is simply a way of saying that there are a number of things of which it can be predicated. Plato tries to give some explanation of how this happens to be the case by indicating that 'one' will belong to each and every part into which being itself can conceivably be divided.

Although not present in each of the things that are as a whole, the One-that-is nevertheless is a whole when considered in its own right. Having examined some of the consequences of being and unity's being parcelled out among all the things are, Plato now at 144e8–145b5 considers some of the consequences of the One-that-is being a whole, as if to reassert that being when considered in relation to itself remains one. This portion of the argument also reminds us that, however much the deduction is concerned with models of predication, the One is still conceived of as a spatially extended entity like Parmenides' own Being. This perhaps explains why the echoes of Parmenides here are particularly strong. He demonstrates that the One is limited; that it has a beginning, middle, and end; and that it consequently has a certain shape. The arguments plainly draw upon Parmenides B8. 30–3 and 42–4 (which on Ebert's transposition form a continuous passage):

> κρατερὴ γὰρ ἀνάγκη
> πείρατος ἐν δεσμοῖσιν ἔχει, τό μιν ἀμφὶς ἐέργει,
> οὕνεκεν οὐκ ἀτελεύτητον τὸ ἐὸν θέμις εἶναι·
> ἔστι γὰρ οὐκ ἐπιδευές· [μὴ] ἐὸν δ' ἂν παντὸς ἐδεῖτο.
> αὐτὰρ ἐπεὶ πεῖρας πύματον, τετελεσμένον ἐστί
> πάντοθεν εὐκύκλου σφαίρης ἐναλίγκιον ὄγκῳ,
> μεσσόθεν ἰσοπαλὲς πάντῃ

(for a powerful necessity holds it in the bonds of a limit that restrains it all about, wherefore it is right that what-is is not endless: for it is not lacking —being so it would lack everything. But since there is a furthest limit, it is perfected like the mass of a sphere well-rounded on every side, balanced equally in every direction from the centre).

Plato more or less directly adapts Parmenides' own chain of argument. Plato's Parmenides argues that the One is limited in so far as it is a whole because its parts are parts of a whole, its parts are therefore encompassed by the whole, and what encompasses provides a limit (*Prm.* 144e8–145a1). Parmenides also begins with the notions of encompassing and limit (B8. 30–1). The consequence that Being is 'not endless' or οὐκ ἀτελεύτητον (B8. 32) and the analogous point that, since there is a furthest limit, it is perfected or has an end (τετελεσμένον ἐστί, B8. 42) are also taken over by Plato's Parmenides, who goes on to argue that since the One is limited, it has extremities, and that since it is a whole, it has a beginning, middle, and an end or τελευτή (*Prm.*

145a4–b1). From here he proceeds to argue that since the middle of the One must be equidistant from its extremities (≈ Parmenides' μεσσόθεν ἰσοπαλές, 'balanced equally from the centre'), the One must have some shape, whether straight or round or a mixture of the two (145b1–5).[10]

The portion of the Second Deduction stretching from 145b to 151e comprises a complex series of arguments that attribute various properties to the One. This portion of the deduction falls into seven main sections, in each of which apparently incompatible properties are attributed to the One. We shall see, however, that these properties are not in fact incompatible, for they are not all attributed to the One considered from the same perspective. Before identifying the different perspectives in which the One is considered here, however, it will be helpful to set out the basic plan of this portion of the deduction:

(I) The One is in itself (ἐν ἑαυτῷ) and in another (ἐν ἄλλῳ) (145b6–e6):
    (A) in itself (145b7–c7);
    (B) in another (145c7–e3).
(II) The One is at rest and changing (145e7–146a8):
    (A) at rest (145e8–146a3);
    (B) changing (146a3–6).
(III) The One is the same as (ταὐτόν) and different from (ἕτερον) itself and the others (146a9–147b8):
    (A) same as itself (146b2–c4);
    (B) different from itself (146c4–d1);
    (C) different from the others (146d1–5);
    (D) same as the others (146d5–147b6).
(IV) The One is like (ὅμοιον) and unlike (ἀνόμοιον) itself and the others (147c1–148d4):
    (A) like the others (147c2–148a6);
    (B) unlike the others (148a6–c3);
    alternative argument for IV A and B (148c3–d1);
    (C) like itself and (D) unlike itself (148d1–4).
(V) In contact and not in contact with itself and the others (148d5–149d7):

---

[10] Since Parmenides himself concluded that Being is spherical, the appropriate shape for the cosmic entity he is describing, one might well ask why Plato refrains from going so far here at the end of an argument that in other respects follows Parmenides quite closely. I suspect a proper answer to this question would have to make reference to the *Timaeus*'s intricate account of the composition of the world soul, in which the bands of soul material compounded from being, sameness, and difference in harmonic proportions are split and formed into circles (*Ti.* 35a–36d).

(A) in contact with the others, and **(B) in contact with itself** (148d6–e4);

(C) not in contact with itself (148e4–149a3);

(D) not in contact with the others (149a3–d5).

(VI) Equal and unequal to itself and the others (149d8–151b7):

(A) equal to the others (149d9–150d8);

(B) equal to itself (150e1–4);

(C) greater and smaller than, i.e. unequal to, itself (150e5–151a2);

(D) greater and smaller than, i.e. unequal to, the others (151a2–b5).

(VII) (corollary to VI) Of equal measures and parts to, and of greater and fewer measures and parts than, itself and the others (151b7–e2).

Each of the sections in bold type has a discernible analogue in Parmenides' own deduction of the properties of Being.[11] As the One is in itself (ἐν ἑαυτῷ) and the same (ταὐτόν) as itself, so Parmenides says of Being: 'remaining the same and in the same, it lies in itself' (ταὐτόν τ' ἐν ταὐτῷ τε μένον καθ' ἑαυτό τε κεῖται, B8. 29). As the One is at rest, so Parmenides' Being is 'unchanging' (ἀκίνητον, B8. 26). Parmenides says that Being 'is all alike' (πᾶν ἐστιν ὁμοῖον, B8. 22), that because of its homogeneity and continuity 'being draws near to being' (ἐὸν . . . ἐόντι πελάζει, B8. 25), and that there is no absence of being within it, 'which would prevent it reaching to what is like' (τό κεν παύοι μιν ἱκνεῖσθαι | εἰς ὁμόν, B8. 46–7). So in the Second Deduction Plato's Parmenides shows that the One is like itself and that it is in contact with itself. Finally, the One is equal to itself, as Parmenides says that Being is 'from every side equal to itself' (οἷ . . . πάντοθεν ἶσον, B8. 49).

The properties of the One here in the *Parmenides* that reproduce the properties Parmenides himself had attributed to Being are all predicated of the One considered in a particular aspect. To understand exactly what this aspect is, it will be useful to return to the earlier part of the deduction and consider the means Plato employed there for expressing what we might speak of as various types of predication. The deduction begins by speaking of predication as participation. There the statement, 'the One is', is analysed as: 'the One partakes of being' (142b5–6). As Parmenides says a few lines later: ' "the One partakes of being"—this would be what is expressed when someone says in brief that the One is' (142c5–7). As we have seen, this analysis leads

[11] Cf. Raven 1965, 222.

Parmenides to speak of predicates as parts. The statement, 'the One is', comes to be understood as indicating that the One-that-is is such as to have parts: the predicate parts of the one being are 'one' and 'being' (142c8–d9). The subsequent conceptual division at 142d9–143a2 implies that some predicate parts of x are parts of x in virtue of x's being what it is, and it suggests the following analysis of the statement, 'the One is': the One has the property of being by virtue of being one. The subsequent thought experiment at 143a4–b8 introduces a means of speaking of predicates that do *not* belong to something in virtue of its being what it is. Especially important is 143b3–6: 'so then if being is one thing, and the One another, neither is the One different from being by being one, nor is being other than the One by being being, but they are different from one another by difference and otherness' (οὐκοῦν εἰ ἕτερον μὲν ἡ οὐσία, ἕτερον δὲ τὸ ἕν, οὔτε τῷ ἓν τὸ ἓν τῆς οὐσίας ἕτερον οὔτε τῷ οὐσία εἶναι ἡ οὐσία τοῦ ἑνὸς ἄλλο, ἀλλὰ τῷ ἑτέρῳ τε καὶ ἄλλῳ ἕτερα ἀλλήλων). This suggests the following analysis of the statement, 'the One is different from being': the One has the property of being different from being by virtue of difference. That is, the One can have the property of being different from being, but this is not to be conceived of as a property the One has simply in virtue of its own nature. If one had to specify exactly what it is in virtue of which the One has this property, one would presumably say that it is in virtue of the relation obtaining between the One and being, which is what Plato himself seems to be expressing by saying it is in virtue of 'the difference' (τῷ ἑτέρῳ).

Thus the early stages of the Second Deduction present a way of distinguishing between, on the one hand, properties the One has in virtue of being what it is or in virtue of its own nature and, on the other hand, properties it has though not just in virtue of being what it is. This distinction is important in the subsequent series of arguments at 145b6–151e2 enumerating the various properties of the One. Each of the properties with an analogue among the properties of Parmenidean Being is a property attributed to the One in virtue of its own nature. This might lead one to expect the remaining properties to be properties the One has though not in virtue of its own nature. If things were this simple, the Second Deduction would have to be less complex and bewildering than it actually is. For, on this view, there should be two arguments instead of four in each of the sections III to VI. That there are in fact four arguments in each section points to there being a second distinction operative in these sections. What this second distinction is should be clear enough from the above outline: the deduction not only considers the properties the One has in relation to itself but also properties it has in relation to other things.

We must be careful to keep clear about how this second distinction differs from the first. This second distinction between (2a) properties the One has in relation to itself versus (2b) properties it has in relation to other things is not the same as the previous distinction between (1a) properties the One has in virtue of its own nature versus (1b) properties it has though not in virtue of its own nature. We can see the difference in the prior analysis of the statement, 'the One is different from being'. In this case the One has the property of difference not (2a) in relation to itself but (2b) in relation to something else, in this case being, and it has this property (1b) not in virtue of its own nature (but in virtue of difference). Both these features of the One's display of the property of difference were reflected in the analysis of the statement suggested by 143b4–5, namely that the One has the property of being different from, or in relation to, being not in virtue of being one but in virtue of difference. We can likewise explain the prior analysis of the statement, 'the One is', as a case where the One has a property, namely being, (1a) in virtue of its own nature and (2a) in relation to itself. These two distinctions thus yield four possible aspects in which properties may be attributed to the One: (2a + 1a) in relation to itself and in virtue of its own nature; (2a + 1b) in relation to itself but not in virtue of its own nature; (2b + 1b) in relation to the others and not in virtue of its own nature; and (2b + 1a) in relation to the others and in virtue of its (and their) own nature(s). The arguments in the stretch of the Second Deduction with which we are now concerned show how the One considered in these various aspects has various properties.

I am suggesting, therefore, that the apparently contradictory properties attributed to the One in the Second Deduction are not genuinely contradictory, for these properties are attributed to the One in different aspects. I find unfathomable the view one sometimes encounters that this deduction attributes properties to the One indiscriminately.[12] The deduction repeatedly distinguishes by numerous

---

[12] So e.g. McCabe 1994, 102–3, says that the Second Deduction 'rules in every-thing—we can say whatever we like about the One, without restriction (in particular, without let or hindrance from the law of noncontradiction)'. Although McCabe offers some discussion of the conception of properties as parts in relation to the First and Second Deductions (which she considers in light of a set of concerns rather different from our own), her failure to appreciate the distinctions among various types of predicates operative in the Second Deduction leads her astray. For example, she says: 'Any property (of the one) whatsoever will be a member of the collection in the

means the respects in which the One can be said to have various properties. Parmenides concludes the arguments of section I, for instance, with the words: 'therefore *in so far as* (ᾗ μέν) the One is a whole, it is in another; *but in so far as* (ᾗ δέ) it happens to be all the parts that are, it is in itself' (145e3–4). We shall examine presently some of the ways Plato expresses the specific qualifications that account for the deduction's apparent contradictions.

The idea that properties can be attributed to something in different aspects is not new with the *Parmenides*. It will suffice to mention just one of the more important earlier places where this idea is prominent. In book 4 of the *Republic* Plato articulates the principle of non-contradiction in the following terms: 'it is clear that the same thing will not be willing to do or suffer opposite things in virtue of the same thing and in relation to the same thing simultaneously' (δῆλον ὅτι ταὐτὸν τἀναντία ποιεῖν ἢ πάσχειν κατὰ ταὐτόν γε καὶ πρὸς ταὐτὸν οὐκ ἐθελήσει ἅμα, 436b8–9). The crucial phrases in this articulation of the principle are κατὰ ταὐτόν and πρὸς ταὐτόν, which I have translated as 'in virtue of the same thing' and 'in relation to the same thing' because I would like to think they are not simply synonymous but reflect the kind of aspectival distinction I have suggested is operative in the *Parmenides*. One reason it is difficult to tell whether this is in fact the case is that the two examples Plato introduces to clarify what he means both involve only the first of these qualifications. He does not make clear what he means by the second, apparently because it is not a relevant aspect in the examples he discusses, which involve the simultaneous attribution of the properties motion and rest to the same object. It is noteworthy that these properties figure in section II of the Second Deduction, where the 'in virtue of' but not the 'in relation to' qualification is operative. In any case, although Plato does not discuss both qualifications here in the *Republic*, the fact that he does not use the phrases κατὰ ταὐτόν and πρὸς ταὐτόν interchangeably in discussing his examples and that both recur in his concluding restatement of the principle (436e9–437a2) seems to confirm that they represent a genuine distinction regarding the aspects under which a property may be attributed to something. This distinction among aspects need not necessarily be identical to the one I have proposed is operating in the Second Deduction. The important thing is that we can see Plato concerned with two aspectival distinctions prior to the

same way, since we lack any distinction between one sort of property and another. . . . So the properties that might be thought to explain identity will be no more and no less than the accidental features of it' (112). I hope it will be clear that this altogether mischaracterizes the Second Deduction.

Parmenides and that the terms in which he speaks of them are already suggestive of the *Parmenides*'s conception.

One of the main reasons the *Parmenides*'s Second Deduction continues to be bewildering when one progresses through it with these distinctions in mind is that Plato employs various means to express how properties are attributed to the One in these several aspects. Even though it seems clear enough in 142d9–143b8 that Plato is concerned with the two distinctions we have isolated, he does not express them as clearly as we have just done. Likewise, in the series of deductions that follow he does not employ a simple and uniform terminology to express the aspects of predication with which he is concerned. One can see clearly enough, despite his often odd and contorted manner of speaking of these aspects, that the two distinctions we have identified define the perspective on the One in each of the various arguments. One can see, in particular, that the 'Parmenidean' properties are all attributed to the One considered in relation to itself and in virtue of its own nature. Since we are concerned with Plato's use of Parmenides in this deduction, these are the properties with which we shall be primarily concerned. But in so far as I have suggested that Plato will have seen Parmenides as allowing for the possibility that Being may also have other properties that do not reveal its essential nature, we will want to say something about how other properties are attributed to the One in the remaining portions of the deduction.

Before discussing some of these arguments in detail, I want to clarify my view of the relevant distinctions by commenting on one recent and influential account that gives a rather different explanation of what is going on in the Second Deduction. Constance Meinwald has argued that the key distinction for resolving the apparent contradictions of the dialectical exercise is one between what she terms *pros ta alla* and *pros heauto* predication. A paradigm statement-pattern in her account of *pros ta alla* predication is: A is B *pros* C. An example of a statement conforming to this pattern would be: 'the One is unlike *pros* Unlikeness'. This type of statement is useful in giving an account of the features displayed by individuals, for the *pros ta alla* relationship is useful for referring to the nature to which an individual's display of a certain feature is conformable. The paradigm statement-pattern for *pros heauto* predication is again: A is B *pros* C. In this type of predication, however, since '*pros* C' indicates a *pros heauto* predication, C will be the nature of A itself, and thus B will mark the predicate(s) that A has in relation to its own nature. *Pros heauto* predicates hold of A in virtue of having the proper connection

with A's own nature, rather than with the nature of other things as in
pros ta alla predication. Meinwald expresses this point with reference
to the One by saying that 'the One is X in relation to itself when being
X is part of being one'.[13] Her account of *pros heauto* predication
leaves room for the One to have more than just the single predicate
'one' in virtue of its own nature. The simple case is: A is A in relation to A's own nature. For example, we can say that the One is one
in relation to the One's nature. But statements of the following form
are also possible: A is B in relation to A's own nature. This second
kind of statement is possible when being B is part of what it is to
be A.

Meinwald sees the Second Deduction as concerned with establishing what follows for the One *pros ta alla* from the hypothesis that
the One is. To maintain successfully both that the Second Deduction is concerned throughout with establishing *pros ta alla* results
and that these results do not contradict one another, Meinwald is
forced to introduce a distinction within her conception of *pros ta alla*
predication. There are problems with the distinction,[14] but the most
critical failure of her view is that, even if we accept her particular
account of the distinction between *pros ta alla* and *pros heauto* predication, it simply is not true that the deduction is concerned solely
with *pros ta alla* predications. Consider argument III A that the One
is the same as itself. Parmenides begins with a classification, designed
to be exhaustive, of how one item can stand in relation to (πρός)
another. There are four possibilities for how X can stand in relation
to Y. Either (i) X is the same as Y, or (ii) X is different from Y, or
(iii) X is a part of Y, or (iv) X is the whole of which Y is a part.
Parmenides then considers which of these applies to how the One

---

[13] Meinwald 1991, 67.

[14] The distinction she makes (see Meinwald 1991, 100–5 and ch. 5 *passim*) would
have it that there are two kinds of *pros ta alla* truths grounded in two kinds of facts.
The first kind concerns an item's own display of a feature, while the second kind concerns other things displaying the item in question as a feature. Without even commenting on whether or not this is in fact the type of distinction required to sort out
the apparent contradictions of the Second Deduction, one can see that the proposed
extension of the notion of *pros ta alla* predication is in itself highly problematic.
Meinwald's original model of *pros ta alla* predication involved X's having certain predicates in relation to other things, whereas the extension she proposes casts X in the
role of a predicate something else has. The result is that this extension of the original model no longer concerns properties X itself displays, which amounts to its no
longer being concerned with X's *pros ta alla* predicates. Meinwald herself verges on
acknowledging the problematic character of her proposed extension when she says
of a case where certain subjects display Justice, 'We might perhaps say that in such
a case the predicate holds of Justice indirectly' (111).

stands in relation to itself. Ruling out (ii), (iii), and (iv), he arrives at this conclusion: 'if therefore it is neither different nor a whole nor a part *in relation to itself* (πρὸς ἑαυτό), is it not necessary that it is the same *as itself* (ταὐτὸν . . . ἑαυτῷ)?' (146c2–4; cf. 146b7). Or consider the brief argument VI B that the One is equal to itself. Having shown that the One is equal to the others because neither of them have largeness nor smallness in them (we will say more presently about how exactly this is supposed to be the case), Parmenides says: 'moreover, the One itself would also be in this state *in relation to itself* (πρὸς ἑαυτό); having neither largeness nor smallness in itself, it would neither be exceeded by nor exceed itself, but being equally it would be equal *to itself* (ἴσον . . . ἑαυτῷ)' (150e1–4). One would presume that someone interested in something she calls *pros heauto* predication would have something to say about these passages.

Unfortunately, however, Meinwald does not actually discuss *any* of the arguments in the long stretch of the Second Deduction running from 145b to 151e. She might well be able to display sufficient interpretative ingenuity to bring the results here into line with her account of the Second Deduction as establishing exclusively the One's *pros ta alla* properties. Perhaps she could find the means to argue that, despite Plato's using the phrase πρὸς ἑαυτό or 'in relation to itself', the One's being the same as and equal to itself are actually cases of *pros ta alla* predication. It seems preferable, however, simply to accept that some of the properties attributed to the One in the Second Deduction are attributed to it in virtue of its own nature. If we do not accept this, we blind ourselves to Plato's signals of his Parmenidean inheritance. For, again, the properties the One has in virtue of its own nature and in relation to itself are precisely those adapted from Parmenides' deduction of the properties of Being.

Consider again the argument VI B that the One is equal to itself: 'moreover the One itself would also be in this state *in relation to itself* (πρὸς ἑαυτό); having neither largeness nor smallness in itself, it would neither be exceeded by nor exceed itself, but being equally it would be equal to itself' (150e1–4). Not only does Plato here attribute a distinctly Parmenidean property to the One, he does so in a way that echoes a stretch of Parmenides' own argument. The point that the One is neither larger nor smaller than itself recalls Parmenides' assertion at B8. 23–4 that Being is neither any 'more' (μᾶλλον) nor any 'less' (χειρότερον) since this would prevent it from holding together. After the declaration of Being's sphericity, this point recurs in a slightly different form, more directly in line with argument VI B, at B8. 44b–9:

τὸ γὰρ οὔτε τι μεῖζον
οὔτε τι βαιότερον πελέναι χρεόν ἐστι τῇ ἢ τῇ.
οὔτε γὰρ οὐκ ἐὸν ἔστι, τὸ κεν παύοι μιν ἱκνεῖσθαι
εἰς ὁμόν, οὔτ᾽ ἐὸν ἔστιν ὅπως εἴη κεν ἐόντος
τῇ μᾶλλον τῇ δ᾽ ἧσσον, ἐπεὶ πᾶν ἐστιν ἄσυλον·
οἷ γὰρ πάντοθεν ἶσον, ὁμῶς ἐν πείρασι κυρεῖ.

(for it is necessary that it be neither any greater nor any smaller at one point than at another. For neither is there not-being, which would prevent it reaching to what is like, nor is Being such that it could be more than Being in one aspect and less in another, since it is all inviolate: for from every side equal to itself, it turns out to be equally within limits).

At B8. 23–4 the general principle that Being is neither greater nor smaller had been used to rule out variations in the cosmos's internal density. Here Parmenides begins by restating this general principle (B8. 44b–5) and then using it to deny that Being could be greater or smaller *than itself*. In the same way Plato's Parmenides first says that the One has neither largeness nor smallness in itself and then infers that it cannot by exceeded by nor exceed itself. Both Parmenides himself and Plato's Parmenides then draw the conclusion that Being/the One is equal to itself.

I want to return, then, to how our two distinctions regarding the aspects in which a subject can have various predicates function in the series of arguments at *Parmenides* 145b6–151e2 establishing the properties of the One. We have distinguished between (1a) properties a subject has in virtue of itself or its own nature and (1b) properties a subject has though not in virtue of itself or its own nature. In what follows I will speak of 'in virtue of itself' and 'not in virtue of itself' in general as 'type 1' qualifications and of particular expressions of these qualifications as 'type 1' qualifiers. We have also distinguished between (2a) properties a subject has in relation to itself and (2b) properties a subject has in relation to other things. I will speak here of 'type 2' qualifications and qualifiers. These two distinctions make possible a conception of the One as something other than a predicational monad, namely as an entity with a nature that enables it to have a number of properties in relation to itself in virtue of this nature and an even greater collection of properties, in relation both to itself and other things, that are not in virtue of its own nature.[15]

---

[15] Although I have criticized Meinwald's account of the distinction among types of predicate operative in this deduction, I hope it will be clear that reflection on her argument has been a valuable spur to the development of my own, somewhat simpler view. Frede 1967 and Schofield 1974 have also been particularly helpful in this process.

The two instances of the phrase 'in relation to itself' (πρὸς ἑαυτῷ) in arguments III A and VI B are clearly type 2 qualifiers. If one pays close attention to the qualifications expressed in the course of the whole series of arguments, one will observe that type 2 qualifications are made explicit more often than type 1 qualifications. One sees this, for example, in the initial sentences of sections III to VI, where the sections' demonstranda are announced. III: 'moreover it must be the same *as itself* (ἑαυτῷ) and different *from itself* (ἑαυτοῦ), and likewise it must be both the same *as* and different *from the others* (τοῖς ἄλλοις)' (146a9–b1). IV: 'therefore it is both like and unlike *both itself and the others* (ἑαυτῷ τε καὶ τοῖς ἄλλοις)' (147c1–2). V: 'consider how it stands regarding the One being in contact *with itself and the others* (αὑτοῦ καὶ τῶν ἄλλων) and regarding its not being in contact' (148d5–6). VI: 'therefore is it both equal and unequal *to itself and to the others* (αὑτῷ τε καὶ τοῖς ἄλλοις)?' (149d8–9). While the type 2 qualifiers are consistently expressed in these statements, the type 1 qualifiers are consistently absent. In the sentences stating the demonstranda of sections I and II, no type 2 qualifications are expressed since both sections consider the One only in relation to itself. Although one might thus expect some expression of the type 1 qualifications, this expectation appears to be disappointed. I: 'so, therefore, being like this will it not be both in itself and in another?' (145b6–7). II: 'indeed, is it not necessary that the One, being of such a nature, both changes and remains at rest?' (145e7–8). Throughout the actual arguments of each section, moreover, type 2 qualifications such as we see in the initial sentences are much more frequently expressed than type 1 qualifications. Perhaps this is natural, given their prominence in Parmenides' programmatic statement at 136a4–c5. The type 1 qualifications are of more immediate interest to us, however, given that Plato would have seen in Parmenides a model for the distinction he wants to make between properties the One has in virtue of its own nature and properties that may also be attributed to it without belonging to it in virtue of its own nature.

The arguments of section II, which demonstrate that the One is both at rest and changing, are free from any overt qualifications. Yet it is clear that both rest and change are being attributed to the One considered in relation to itself rather than in relation to others and that this accounts for there being only two arguments in this section. It also seems clear enough that argument II A considers what holds of the One in virtue of its own nature, while argument II B considers what holds of the One not in virtue of its own nature. One can also see that Plato is drawing upon Parmenides both for the properties

themselves and for the sense in which they are each attributed to the
One. As we have already noted, the predicate 'at rest' in II A has its
counterpart among the properties of Parmenidean Being, namely
that it is 'unshaken' (ἀτρεμές, B8. 4) and 'unchanging' (ἀκίνητον, B8.
26). The argument Plato gives Parmenides here recalls Parmenides'
own argument: 'it is surely at rest, if indeed it is in itself (ἐν ἑαυτῷ
[from I A]); for being in one and not changing from this, it would be
in the same (ἐν τῷ αὐτῷ), in itself.—Yes it is.—And what is always
in the same (ἐν τῷ αὐτῷ) must surely always be at rest.—Certainly'
(*Prm.* 145e8–146a3). Compare Parmenides' B8. 29–30: 'remaining
the same and in the same, it lies in itself, and thus steadfast there it
remains' (ταὐτόν τ' ἐν ταὐτῷ τε μένον καθ' ἑαυτό τε κεῖται | χοὖτως
ἔμπεδον αὖθι μένει). It is tempting to suppose that Plato would have
understood Parmenides' phrase 'in itself' (καθ'ἑαυτό) as specifying the
aspect in which Being is unchanging, namely in virtue of its own
nature. The property of change attributed to the One in II B has
its Parmenidean analogue among the marks or σήματα that mortals
have placed upon Being in their misguided account of it—coming to
be and perishing, changing place and colour (B8. 40–1). Here too
Parmenides provides the model for how this property can be attributed to the One, for as we have seen in examining the role of naming in his thought, these marks are assigned to the cosmic entity but
are not such as to reveal its essential aspect as Being.

One might suppose that this account of how rest and change
are attributed to the One is inconsistent with the declaration at
Sophist 250c6–7 that 'being is in virtue of its own nature neither at
rest nor changing' (κατὰ τὴν αὐτοῦ φύσιν ἄρα τὸ ὂν οὔτε ἔστηκεν οὔτε
κινεῖται). For I have been claiming that in this section of the Second
Deduction rest *is* supposed to be a property that the One, which is
so intimately connected with being, has in virtue of its own nature.
However, this sentence from the *Sophist* simply provides us with an
opportunity to note a distinction between two kinds of predicate
a subject may have in virtue of its own nature. Consider the statements, (i) 'the One is the One', (ii) 'the One is one', and (iii) 'the One
is at rest'. All three statements may be considered as attributing to the
One properties it has in virtue of its own nature, with the following
qualification. The first statement goes beyond attributing a property
to the One that it has in virtue of its being what it is by also identifying the One or picking out the thing that it is. When the Eleatic
Visitor in the *Sophist* says that being is not at rest in virtue of its own
nature, he means to say that being and rest are not identical. To be
is not to be at rest. This does not, however, mean that being could

not have the property of rest in virtue of its own nature. (Whether we should suppose that this actually is the case, as it seems to be with the One, is perhaps unclear, though the Visitor's amazement that being does not have one of the contrary predicates 'motion' and 'rest' (250c12–d3) suggests that there is a sense in which being is at rest.) One might try to express the distinction between these two kinds of predication via a distinction between senses of the verb 'to be'. One might want to say that our first statement employs the 'is' of identity, while our second and third statements employ a more ordinary copulative or predicative 'is'.[16] Although attempts to discriminate between such senses of the Greek verb εἶναι have rightly come under attack, we do appear to need some means of distinguishing statements of identity from other statements indicating what holds of a subject in virtue of its own nature. As important as this particular distinction may be, and however we might want to express it, more important to the *Parmenides*'s Second Deduction is our type 1 distinction between predicates belonging to a subject in virtue of its own nature and predicates belonging to a subject though not in virtue of its own nature. If alongside our three statements above we set a fourth, (iv) 'the One is in motion', we see that the distinction between statements of identity and other predicative statements, important as it may be, cuts at the wrong point; for it would have us group statements (ii), (iii), and (iv) together as predicative as against the identity statement (i), when it is more natural to group statements (i), (ii), and (iii) together so as to distinguish them from (iv). This more natural grouping is what our type 1 distinction yields. We may perhaps want to introduce a further distinction of (i) versus (ii) and (iii), but only subsequent to the more fundamental division between statements indicating the properties belonging to a subject in virtue of its own nature and statements indicating the properties belonging to a subject though not in virtue of its own nature.

Thinking about the relation between the contradictory properties attributed to the One in section II of the Second Deduction and the corresponding contradictory marks or σήματα set upon Being in the two accounts of it given by Parmenides himself would seem to confirm the importance of the type 1 qualifications in this section even if they are not explicitly signalled in the text. Now we need to ask where and how these qualifications are in fact expressed. Perhaps the best place to begin is with argument VI A, which establishes that the

---

[16] For appeals to this type of distinction in interpreting the *Sophist*, see e.g. Ackrill 1957 and Owen 1970(*b*).

One is equal to the others. Here Parmenides' general strategy is to show that the One is neither greater nor less than the others and must therefore be equal to them. He begins his argument by asking: 'if the One were greater or less than the others, or if the others were in turn greater or less than the One, then they would not be any greater or any less than one another *just by the One being one* and *by the others being other than one*, that is, *by their very own natures* (αὐταῖς γε ταύταις ταῖς οὐσίαις), would they?' (149d9–e4). Here we have as clear an expression as one could want of the idea that the One and the others would not be greater and less than one another in virtue of their own natures (the second variety of type 1 qualification). It is apparently possible, however, for the One and the others to be equal in virtue of their respective natures, for Parmenides' next step is to say: 'but if, *in addition to being such as they are*, they *also* were to have equality, they would be equal in relation to one another' (149e4–5). This argument, then, considers the One and the others in virtue of their own natures and in relation to one another. This is one of the more curious combinations of the two types of aspectival qualifications, a fact which partly explains why the demonstration of what results from considering the One in this light takes up the major part of section VI.

Such is the overall character of argument VI A. We still need to focus, however, on the manner in which it expresses the type 1 qualification. Much of the remainder of the argument is occupied with explaining what it means for 'largeness' and 'smallness' to be predicated of the One but not in virtue of its own nature. This explanation begins with Parmenides declaring that they are forms or εἴδη. Parmenides then considers whether smallness ever comes to be *in* the One (εἰ ἄρα ἐν τῷ ἑνὶ σμικρότης ἐγγίγνεται, 150a1–2). This seems to be a somewhat peculiar idiom for expressing the possibility that smallness might be a property attributed to the One in virtue of its own nature. We have returned to the spatial model of predication in a somewhat different guise. Parmenides proceeds to dismiss the possibility that smallness could ever be in the One by arguing that it could be neither in the whole of the One nor in part of it (150a2–b4). This is his way of establishing that the One is not small in virtue of its own nature, a point that seems correct enough. The actual conclusion generalizes to all things that are: 'therefore smallness will never be *in* any of the things that are' (οὐδενί ποτε ἄρα ἐνέσται τῶν ὄντων σμικρότης, 150b5). None of this means that 'small' can never be predicated of either the One or anything else. The argument in fact begins by presuming that this is possible. It only means that 'small' is never predicated of the One or other things simply in virtue of their own natures. The property of smallness, that is, always requires the second variety of type 1 qualification. The same holds for the property of largeness. It can never be *in* the One or other things (150b7–c3).

We can generalize Parmenides' manner of expressing the point that the One will not be small in virtue of its own nature. Statements of the form 'F is not in x' (e.g. smallness is not in the One), in cases where it is possible that F can be predicated of x, can be used to indicate that x is F *not* in virtue of x's own nature. Likewise, statements of the form 'F is in x' can be used to indicate that x is F in virtue of x's own nature. This expression of type 1 qualifications in terms of one thing's being 'in' another extends beyond argument VI A. Most importantly, it seems to be the case that the initial pair of properties in section I of the deduction—'in itself' ($\dot{\epsilon}\nu\ \dot{\epsilon}\alpha\upsilon\tau\hat{\omega}$) and 'in another' ($\dot{\epsilon}\nu\ \ddot{\alpha}\lambda\lambda\omega$)—are not only properties subject to type 1 qualifications but simultaneously provide a model for expressing this type of qualification. 'x is in itself (x)' would thus be a way of indicating that x is predicated of x in virtue of its own nature. 'x is in another' would be a way of indicating that x is predicated of something else in virtue of that thing's nature.

The suggestion that 'in itself' and 'in another' play some such role seems to be confirmed by the fact that a number of the subsequent arguments derive more or less directly from I A and I B, not haphazardly, but such that properties the One has in virtue of its own nature derive from its being 'in itself' (II A—at rest; V B—in contact with itself), while properties the One has though not in virtue of its own nature derive from its being 'in another' (II B—changing; III B—different from itself; and apparently V A—in contact with the others, if 'in the others' or $\dot{\epsilon}\nu\ \tau o\hat{\imath}\varsigma\ \ddot{\alpha}\lambda\lambda o\iota\varsigma$ at 148d8 functions like 'in another' or $\dot{\epsilon}\nu\ \ddot{\alpha}\lambda\lambda\omega$). An exception to this pattern is VI C, where from the One's being in itself it is inferred to be greater and less than (i.e. unequal to) itself. One might examine the details of arguments I A and I B for clarification regarding how, exactly, the One's property of being in itself functions as a model for speaking of properties it has in virtue of its own nature and its property of being in another functions as a model for speaking of properties it has though not in virtue of its own nature. I am not sure, however, that this would be a profitable approach to the issue. For it seems that we need to preserve some distinction between how this section *argues* that the One has these particular properties and how they might function more generally as a way of distinguishing types of predication. A full interpretation of the Second Deduction would have to explore in much greater depth how the concepts of whole and part so prominent in this section and in several other key passages (some of which we have examined in a preliminary manner) function within Plato's overall conception of the nature of predication at this time. A proper exploration of this theme would take us too far beyond our present purposes.[17] What I want to do at the moment, then, is take a particular section of the Second Deduction, show that its four constitutive arguments are determined by the conjunction of type 1 and type 2 qualifications, and then return to how Plato may have seen a model for these qualifications in Parmenides.

Take as an example section III, where Plato's Parmenides argues that the One is the same as and different from itself and the others. We have already seen how argument III A, that the One is the same as itself, considers what holds of the One in relation to itself and in virtue of itself. Argument III B, that the One is different from itself, considers what holds of the One in relation to itself though not in virtue of itself, inferring this, again, from I B's conception of the One as in something different (ἐν ἑτέρῳ τινι, 145d8). Argument III C, that the One is different from the others, considers what holds of the One in relation to the others and not in virtue of itself. These three arguments are all brief and draw their conclusions quite quickly. Argument III D, however, demonstrating in what way the One is the same as the others, takes up more space than the first three combined. This is partly because considering the One, as it does, in relation to the others and in virtue of its (and their) own nature(s) involves adopting a rather complex view of the One, and partly because here we get an interesting explanation of how difference, unlike sameness, will never be a property of a thing in virtue of that thing's own nature.

The argument begins with an assertion that sameness and difference are opposites (146d5–6). Next Parmenides and Aristoteles agree that sameness will never be in what is different nor difference in what is the same (ταὐτὸν ἐν τῷ ἑτέρῳ ἢ τὸ ἕτερον ἐν ταὐτῷ, 146d7). The point is not just that the same thing cannot be both same and

---

[17] To mention just one difficulty, one would want to give some account of how the conception of predication here as a part–whole relationship compares with the *Sophist*'s description of the parts of 'difference' being divided out among the various things that are different (*Sph.* 257c–258a). On the implications of this connection, see Allen 1997, 272–3. See also Allen's more general discussion of the Second Deduction's model of predication as a relation between part and whole at 246–50 and 275–9.

different. Rather, our analysis of the relation of 'being in' suggests this means that 'sameness' will never be predicated of what is different in virtue of its being different and that 'difference' will never be predicated of what is the same in virtue of its being the same. Parmenides' next point picks up on this latter implication to move towards the claim that 'difference' will never be predicated of anything in virtue of its own nature (a principle with an obvious bearing upon the previous two arguments, III B and III C). He says that if difference will never be in what is the same, then difference can be in none of the things that are for any length of time: for if it were in something for some length of time, that thing would be the same for that length of time, and difference cannot be in what is the same (146d8–e4). Again, this is not to say that 'difference' cannot be predicated of anything whatsoever, only that it cannot be predicated of a thing in virtue of its own nature (cf. *Sph.* 255c14–d1). Sameness, however, does seem to be a property predicable of something in virtue of its own nature. The upshot of all this within this particular argument is that difference is not 'in' either the One or the things other than the One, and that the One and the others are accordingly not different from one another in virtue of themselves (*Prm.* 146e4–147a1). (The language here corresponds to that we have seen employed at the beginning of argument VI A to express the idea that the One and the others are neither greater nor less than one another in virtue of their own natures.) This might seem sufficient to establish that the One and the others are somehow the same. Before drawing this conclusion, however, Parmenides stresses that he is considering what holds of the One and the others respectively just in virtue of their own natures by introducing the point that the others do not partake of the One (147a3–4). This point allows him to deduce that they are the same by returning to III A's classification of the possible ways one thing can stand in relation to another. That the One and the others are not different has already been established. That the others do not partake of the One means that they are not parts of the One nor it parts of them. The only possibility remaining is that they are the same. We can only make sense of this claim, I suggest, by appreciating that this argument is considering what holds of the One and the others in relation to one another when they are each considered in virtue of their own natures.

Although sections IV, V, and VI are in certain respects more complex, when one works through them in detail one finds that the perspectives adopted in their four constitutive arguments are likewise determined in each case by the four possible conjunctions of type 1 and type 2 qualifications. Reading the arguments here in light of the relevant qualifications makes them appear less fallacious than they have often been accused of being. However, rather than wandering further from our primary subject by demonstrating this in detail, I want to start bringing our discussion of Plato's use of Parmenides to a close by considering the extent to which Plato may have seen these two types of qualification operating in Parmenides' own philosophy. Let us start by returning to Parmenides' description of the two forms that provide the basis for mortals' description of the cosmos (B8. 55–9):

> τἀντία δ᾽ ἐκρίναντο δέμας καὶ σήματ᾽ ἔθεντο
> χωρὶς ἀπ᾽ ἀλλήλων, τῇ μὲν φλογὸς αἰθέριον πῦρ,
> ἤπιον ὄν, μέγ᾽ ἐλαφρόν, ἑωυτῷ πάντοσε τωὐτόν,
> τῷ δ᾽ ἑτέρῳ μὴ τωὐτόν· ἀτὰρ κἀκεῖνο κατ᾽ αὐτό
> τἀντία, νύκτ᾽ ἀδαῆ, πυκινὸν δέμας ἐμβριθές τε

(but they distinguished things opposite in form and assigned them signs separate from one another, for one of which the aetherial fire of flame, being gentle, most light, the same as itself in every direction but not the same as the other; but that is in itself the opposite, dark night, dense in form and heavy).

What interests us here is how mortals are said to have assigned the marks or σήματα (or even predicates) 'same' and 'not same' to the single form Light. It is the same as, or in relation to, itself (ἑωυτῷ . . . τωὐτόν), and not the same as, or in relation to, the other form, Night (τῷ δ᾽ ἑτέρῳ μὴ τωὐτόν). Here, then, are instances in Parmenides of type 2 qualifiers expressed via the same terms we find in the Second Deduction. We also have here instances of properties attributed to the two forms in virtue of their own natures. In its own nature the first form is 'the aetherial fire of flame, being gentle, most light'. It may even be that 'the same as itself in every direction' is meant to be included as well among the properties this first form has in virtue of its own nature. Likewise, the second form in its own nature is 'dark night, dense in form and heavy'. Here we find a phrase that may easily be understood as an overt expression of this type 1 qualification —κατ᾽ αὐτό or 'in (virtue of) itself'. Thus in the space of these few lines we have what may quite straightforwardly be understood as instances of both varieties of type 2 qualification, 'in relation to itself' and 'in relation to another', and of the first variety of type 1 qualification, 'in virtue of its own nature'.

We have also seen in the course of our examination of the Second Deduction that the properties Parmenides demonstrates must be attributed to Being in his own deduction at B8. 1–51 all appear to have been understood by Plato as attributable to Being in virtue of its own nature. For all the analogous properties of the One in Plato's deduction are attributed to it in virtue of its own nature (and in relation to itself). Are there any potential instances in Parmenides of properties attributed to Being that would merit the second variety of type 1 qualification? I hope by now it is obvious that there are. For our previous discussion of mortal naming has shown that *all* the marks or σήματα bestowed upon Being by mortals belong to this class. 'For the all, there is every name such as mortals have bestowed, believing them to be true, both coming to be and perishing, both being and not being, and changing place and exchanging bright colour' (B8. 38b–41). B9 suggests that to these properties should be added Light and Night themselves. These are all properties that may be attributed to Being although not in virtue of its own nature. Considering how the distinctions among types of predication operative in the Second Deduction of the *Parmenides* may have been inspired in part by Plato's reflection upon Parmenides allows us to give more specific content to the notion that Plato will have understood Parmenides' 'Truth' as an account of the nature of the cosmos in its essential aspect *qua* Being and the 'Doxa' as an account of the self-same object that fails to reveal its essential nature. We are thereby able to justify the claim that emerged in our consideration of Plato's representation of Parmenides in other portions of the *Parmenides*, and in various parts of the *Sophist*, that the Second Deduction is the most important text for an understanding of Plato's later view of Parmenides.

It is difficult to know how much further one might pursue Plato's reception of Parmenides. Although we now have a fair idea of how Plato understood Parmenides at various stages of his philosophical career, we have merely begun to consider the implications that this progressive engagement might have for a better understanding of Plato's own thought. I hope that some readers will see the preceding account of Plato's later uses of Parmenides as a step towards clarification of certain problems in the development of Plato's metaphysics. Rather than pursue these difficult issues here, however, we shall now bring our inquiry to a close, drawing together some of the conclusions we have reached and commenting briefly on the status of the interpretation of Parmenides we have developed.

It is sometimes suggested that the critique of the conception of the One in the *Parmenides*'s First Deduction is equally damaging to Parmenidean Being and Plato's own middle period forms. We are now in a position to see that this is not correct. The First Deduction shows how an attempt to conceive of the One as one only, that is, as admitting only the property of 'oneness' or unity in virtue of its own nature, inevitably breaks down. By the end of this deduction, even the cardinal property of unity is denied the One. This *reductio* in effect shows the untenable character of the predicational monist's conception of the One. Its key premiss, articulated at the outset, is that the One is neither a whole nor has parts. Just as the Second Deduction's description of the One as a whole of parts serves to explain how the One can have more than one attribute predicated of it, so this premiss in the First Deduction amounts to treating the One as a predicational monad. We have seen this conception of the One articulated more clearly in the Fourth Deduction. We have also seen how the conclusions of the Fourth Deduction mirror those of the First, how there are traces of predicational monism in the language of the First Deduction itself, and how both these deductions are re-enacted in miniature in the *Sophist*'s critique of Eleaticism. Most importantly, we have seen how the First Deduction exemplifies the Gorgianic perspective on Parmenides. This makes it highly improbable that Plato would have supposed this deduction's account of the One to be a proper representation of either Parmenides' or his own middle period conception of the nature of intelligible reality.

Just as Plato's Parmenides responds to the Gorgianic conclusions that he says one might be tempted to draw from his criticisms of Socrates' conception of intelligible reality with a reassertion of the argument from the possibility of knowledge that formed the cornerstone of Plato's middle-period use of Parmenides, so he marks as unacceptable the similarly Gorgianic conclusions of the First Deduction. Plato gives Parmenides the chance to respond to this sophistic deformation by allowing him to provide an alternative account of his one being in the Second Deduction. We began our inquiry by calling attention to the fact that Plato's middle period forms display all the key properties of Parmenidean Being. The One continues to have these properties in the Second Deduction. Collectively, these properties might be thought to constitute a proper specification of what it is for the One to be what it is. If we ask, then, what Plato learned from his continued reflection on Parmenides' philosophy as he composed the later dialogues, we should first acknowledge that in key respects his view of Parmenides' achievement remains unchanged. Much of Plato's work in the later dialogues involves re-articulating the essentials of his earlier use in light of a more direct confrontation with competing sophistic appropriations. The *Parmenides*'s Second Deduction, however, does in fact mark an advance in Plato's understanding of Parmenides, in so far as it demonstrates by extrapolation from

Parmenides just what the young Socrates says he would be amazed to learn—that the One is both many and capable of supporting apparently contrary attributes. This deduction shows that in addition to the properties the One has in virtue of its own nature and in relation to itself, there are a number of other properties it has in different aspects. We have seen how Plato would have found a model for his complex account of the various and seemingly conflicting properties of the One in Parmenides' own apparently conflicting accounts of the nature of the cosmos in its aspect *qua* being and in its aspect as a differentiated world system. It is no accident, therefore, that Parmenides, who provided the inspiration for so many aspects of the middle-period conception of forms, should also be the one who introduces these further refinements in the dialogue that bears his name.

I have tried to give an account of Plato's reception of Parmenides which captures some of its depth and character. It must be conceded, however, that Plato's interaction with Parmenides is a phenomenon the full complexity of which is ultimately bound to elude us. I have none the less tried to capture some of this complexity by developing readings of the relevant portions of Parmenides' poem within the parameters set by Plato's intricate representation and use of his predecessor. At no point have I claimed that these readings present a more accurate view of Parmenides himself than others presently on offer. Such a claim would be warranted only if one believed that Plato understood Parmenides as he intended to be understood. I have in fact proceeded on the premiss that what Parmenides may actually have intended is to a large degree irrelevant to a proper account of his influence on Plato. When I have gone beyond the direct indications of Plato's understanding to present fuller readings of Parmenides' poem, I have done so both as a means of furthering our understanding of the Platonic reception and to show how the words of the poem can plausibly support a Platonic reading. Although this reading may not be a completely accurate reflection of Parmenides' own philosophy, we may perhaps agree that Plato's use is in the end fairer than those uses underlying the various sophistic appropriations of Parmenides which he was forced to confront.

Even here, appreciating the polyphony of Parmenides' reception during this period remains important. All students of ancient philosophy will readily acknowledge the diversity of the uses and interpretations of Plato by later philosophers. These uses constitute the substance of Plato's influence, and their diversity bears witness to the power of his philosophy. It is somewhat ironic, then, that scholars have been less inclined to explore the variety of uses made of the

philosopher whom Plato saw as his most important Presocratic predecessor. It is a sign of the power of Parmenides' philosophy that it
too influenced later thinkers in ways that he himself could never have
imagined. Any attempt to describe his influence based on an account
of what one presumes he must have meant only betrays his legacy. I
hope that the reception-orientated account I have given of a particular chapter in that legacy restores a measure of his true importance in
the history of philosophy. I also hope it will point the way to further
work on his influence. A properly reception-orientated approach to
his influence on Presocratic philosophy, for example, might well lead
to significant revisions in our understanding of the history of early
Greek thought. Finally, I would like to think that the approach I
have taken to this one particular interaction could be extended to other
cases of intellectual influence. I will be content, however, if I have
achieved the more modest aim of indicating the full complexity of
Plato's uses of Parmenides.

Appendix I

MXG vs. Sextus on the first division of Gorgias' 'On What-Is-Not'

Gigon's view that the two presentations of Gorgias' treatise in the *MXG* and Sextus Empiricus differ so fundamentally that one cannot tell which more accurately reflects what Gorgias wrote[1] is demonstrably false. Inspection of their respective accounts of the treatise's first division shows how Sextus has rearranged the material at his disposal. Sextus says (*M.* 7. 66) that the argument for the thesis 'nothing is' (οὐδὲν ἔστιν) proceeded via a *reductio* performed on each alternative in the following progression: 'if something is, either (A) what-is is, or (B) what-is-not is, or (C) both what-is and what-is-not are' (εἰ γὰρ ἔστι <τι>, ἤτοι τὸ ὂν ἔστιν ἢ τὸ μὴ ὄν, ἢ καὶ τὸ ὂν ἔστι καὶ τὸ μὴ ὄν). This structure reflects Sextus' own systematization of Gorgias' arguments. The *MXG* provides a more accurate representation of Gorgias' own order. The *MXG* author himself tells us that the arguments fulfilling the doxography's programme came after Gorgias' personal demonstration (979a23–4, b20). Apart from Sextus' reshuffling, however, the arguments in the two reports match up remarkably well. Sextus gives two arguments on behalf of B at *M.* 7. 67 that correspond directly to arguments I and II in the *MXG*'s account of the personal demonstration.[2] Sextus then presents a series of arguments for A that proceed from the assumptions that if what-is is, then it must be either eternal or generated or both (*M.* 7. 68–72), and that it must be either one or many (73–4). These arguments, though more detailed than what we find in the *MXG*, obviously correspond to the arguments there based on the doxography (*MXG* 979b20–38; Sextus gives no argument corresponding to that concerning motion at 980a1–8). Sextus finally gives an argument for C at *M.* 7. 75–6, which corresponds to argument III in the *MXG*'s personal demonstration.[3]

It is noticeable that Sextus does not follow the order suggested by his own statement of the overall structure. Instead, he gives the arguments for B before those for A and C. What has happened is fairly clear. The most reasonable explanation for why he gives the B arguments before the A arguments is that this is how the arguments actually came in the summary of the treatise from which he worked. The C arguments also came earlier in the summary, but Sextus could not allow what he took to be the arguments *contra* the conjunction 'both what-is and what-is-not are' to precede those

---

[1] Gigon 1936, 192–3.   [2] Cf. Calogero 1932, 194, 199; Kerferd 1955, 9.
[3] Cf. Calogero 1932, 201–2.

contra its component 'what-is is'. He thus split up the arguments of the personal demonstration.[4] Migliori has gone so far as to suggest that the *MXG* is actually the summary of the treatise from which Sextus worked,[5] although this seems doubtful. Kerferd admits that arguments I and II in the MXG's personal demonstration are equivalent to Sextus' arguments for B at *M.* 7. 67, but he thinks the obvious similarities between the *MXG*'s argument III and Sextus' arguments for C at *M.* 7. 75–6 are to be explained on the assumption that 'Gorgias may have used the same argument in different connections and in effect repeated himself'. Kerferd thus concludes that 'there is no reason to think that the arguments were differently arranged in the two versions'.[6] The present explanation is preferable in that it is more economical.

[4] So, basically, Calogero 1932, 204–7; Bröcker 1958, 428–9; and Wesoly 1983–4, 25.   [5] Migliori 1973.

[6] Kerferd 1955, 19, 23.

Appendix II

Gorgias on the impossibility of falsehood

... ἅπαντα δεῖν γὰρ τὰ φρονούμενα εἶναι, καὶ τὸ μὴ ὄν, εἴπερ μή ἐστι, μηδὲ φρονεῖσθαι. εἰ δ' οὕτως, οὐδὲν ἂν εἴποι ψεῦδος οὐδείς, φησιν, οὐδ' εἰ ἐν τῷ πελάγει φαίη ἁμιλλᾶσθαι ἅρματα. πάντα γὰρ ἂν ταῦτα εἴη. This is the text of *MXG* 980a9–12 as established by Buchheim's 1989 edition, which generally agrees with that of Newiger's 1973 edition,[1] except that Buchheim prefers ταῦτα codd. to Apelt's ταύτῃ in line 12 and suppresses the supplement <, εἰ τὸ ὄν φρονεῖται,> in line 9. Cook Wilson thought some such supplement necessary for the sense of the argument and proposed either (i) inserting εἰ τὸ ὄν φρονεῖται (or its equivalent) before ἅπαντα or (ii) after εἶναι in line 10.[2] Newiger adopts (ii) even though he admits that this protasis is perhaps merely to be understood.[3]

I find both Cook Wilson's original conjecture and Newiger's acceptance of it unattractive. Given that γάρ indicates that ἅπαντα δεῖν and what follows is to explain whatever came before in the lacuna, (i) does not make sense. *Contra* (ii), there is no indication that any supplementation at this point would be legitimate. Newiger's admission that the supplemented protasis is perhaps merely to be understood here shows how weak this conjecture is. Furthermore, since Newiger then goes on, in a fine bit of circular reasoning, to base his conjecture for what has been lost in the lacuna before ἅπαντα upon the need to provide a basis for the supplemented premiss εἰ τὸ ὄν φρονεῖται,[4] it is clear that some other account of what is likely to have come in the gap is needed. I would propose an *exempli gratia* reconstruction along the following lines: (a) εἰ δὲ καὶ ἔστιν φησιν ἄγνωστον εἶναι. (b) εἰ γὰρ τὰ φρονούμενα οὐκ ἔστιν ὄντα, τὸ ὄν οὐ φρονεῖται. (c) εἰ δὲ οὕτως, τὸ ὄν ἄγνωστον ἐστίν. (d) ἔτι δὲ εἰ τὰ φρονούμενα ἔστιν ὄντα, τὸ ὄν οὐ φρονεῖται. (a) is adapted from 979a11. (b) is taken from Sextus' account of the second division, where he quotes the line twice (*M.* 7. 77, 78).[5] (c) is the direct consequence of (b). Finally, (d) is the thesis contrary to (b) supported by the

---

[1] Both, for example, adopt Apelt's conjecture εἴποι for εἶναι codd. in l. 12; cf. Newiger 1973, 127 ff.   [2] Cook Wilson 1893, 34.

[3] Newiger 1973, 125.   [4] Ibid. 125 ff., cf. 141.

[5] Sextus obviously recasts Gorgias' argument to suit his own purposes. After quoting (b), he first presents his own argument for the validity of the conditional inference (*M.* 7. 77) then proceeds to his own demonstration (note *M.* 7. 78, ὡς παραστήσομεν) of the truth of the antecedent τὰ φρονούμενα οὐκ ἔστιν ὄντα by showing the absurdities resulting from its denial. Here he adapts Gorgianic material more accurately represented in *MXG*: SE, *M.* 7. 79 ≈ *MXG* 980a9–12; 7. 80 ≈ 980a12; 7. 81–2 ≈ 980a14–19.

arguments that follow in the surviving portion of the text: 980a9–10, ἄπαντα
δεῖν γὰρ . . . μηδὲ φρονεῖσθαι, provides the (roughly Parmenidean) ground for
the antecedent in (*d*), and what follows in the *MXG* report supplies the
demonstration of the consequence that τὸ ὂν οὐ φρονεῖται (≈ τὸ ὂν ἄγνωστον
ἐστίν). The overall structure of this division would thus conform to Gorgias'
general preference for antithetical arguments. One should note that although
Gorgias is prepared to employ an argument against the possibility of falsehood, the fact that it might have been embedded in this type of dialectical
structure makes it unclear whether he felt himself committed to the thesis.

Appendix III

Plato's quotation of Parmenides at *Theaetetus* 180d7–e1

I presume that the line quoted by Plato is a version of Parmenides B8. 38.[1] There is some uncertainty whether Plato's version of the line begins with οἷον (as *ap*. Simp. *in Ph*. 29, 18 and 143, 10) or οἶον (as *ap*. Anon. *in Tht*. col. 70, 41). There is, furthermore, some division of opinion among those accepting οἷον as to whether it merely serves to introduce Plato's quotation or is actually supposed to be part of the quotation.[2] If the latter, then οἷον seems preferable to οἶον,[3] and it in fact seems likely enough that the reading οἶον is simply a scribal error for οἷον.[4]

The reading of the end of this line is one of the more problematic issues in textual criticism of Parmenides. The two most widely endorsed versions are: (i) τῷ πάντ᾽ ὄνομ᾽ ἔσται, and (ii) τῷ πάντ᾽ ὀνόμασται. Woodbury argues for the authenticity of ὀνόμασται (as *ap*. Simp. *in Ph*. 87, 1 E).[5] This somewhat peculiar form, perfect passive with loss of temporal augment, occurs also at Parmenides B9. 1. He advocates this reading against the reading accepted by Diels, ὄνομ᾽ ἔσται (as *ap*. Simp. *in Ph*. 87, 1 a; cf. ὄνομα ἔσται loc. cit. F and οὔνομα ἔσται loc. cit. D). ὀνόμασται is also accepted by Long, Mourelatos, KRS, and Sider, who notes that the manuscript evidence for this reading is somewhat stronger than had been previously reported.[6] ὄνομ᾽ ἔσται, by Tarán, Cordero, Coxon, and O'Brien.[7]

Since it seems impossible to make sense of Plato's εἶναι in the context of the surrounding lines, I presume Plato has changed an indicative form to an infinitive to integrate the line more smoothly into his own text. The question is then whether the indicative form Plato read or remembered was the future ἔσται or the present ἐστίν. The sense of the future ἔσται has often been thought problematic, and the present ἐστίν does occur *ap*. Simp. *in Ph*. 146, 11 a. Although the Aldine edition is admittedly not the best authority, it may just be possible that ΕΣΤΑΙ is a corruption of an original ΕΣΤΙΝ (and perhaps that uncertainty about the sense of the future in antiquity led

---

[1] *Contra* Cornford 1935(*b*), followed by Woodbury 1958, 148–9 and 153 ff., and 1986, 5–6.

[2] See Dixsaut 1987, 246–53, for a valuable discussion of this and other problems posed by the quotation and a survey of the various solutions that have been proposed.

[3] Cf. Woodury 1958, 148 and 158 n. 10.

[4] Cf. Duke, Hicken, *et al*. 1995, ad loc.   [5] Woodbury 1958, 147 ff.

[6] Long 1963, 96–7; Mourelatos 1970, 181–9; KRS 252; Sider 1985, 366.

[7] Tarán 1965, 129 ff.; Cordero 1984; Coxon 1986; O'Brien 1987(*a*).

to the emendation ὀνόμασται, which in turn was emended to ὠνόμασται, as *ap.* Simp. *in Ph.* 146, 11 DEF). Although this particular account of the progressive corruption is speculative, it remains likely enough that Plato read or remembered ἐστίν. Plato quotes the line in making the point that the Eleatics subscribe to the thesis that the universe is at rest (ἑστὸς τὸ πᾶν), and this point is secured by the first half of the line. Since the second half of the line is not directly relevant to this point,[8] there is no need to attempt a translation of the line as quoted in isolation from the context of the whole fragment.[9]

[8] Cf. Woodbury 1986, 7.

[9] For a survey of the bizarre results to which attempting to do so can lead, see Dixsaut 1987, 249–50. I cannot see that Dixsaut's own suggestion—'ce qui est immobile, que cela soit nom pour le tout'—is any less strange than those she criticizes.

References

ACKRILL, J. L. 1957. 'Plato and the copula: *Sophist* 251–59'. *Journal of Hellenic Studies*, 77: 1–6.

ADAM, J. (ed.). 1963. *The Republic of Plato, Edited with Critical Notes, Commentary and Appendices*, 2nd edn. revised by D. A. Rees, 2 vols. Cambridge: Cambridge University Press.

ALBERTELLI, P. 1939. *Gli Eleati: Testimonianze e frammenti*, Filosofi antichi e medievali. Bari: Laterza.

ALLEN, R. E. 1959. 'Anamnesis in Plato's *Meno* and *Phaedo*'. *Review of Metaphysics*, 13: 165–74.

—— (ed.). 1965. *Studies in Plato's Metaphysics*. London: Routledge & Kegan Paul.

—— 1997. *Plato's Parmenides: Translated with Comment*, 2nd edn. New Haven: Yale University Press.

—— and FURLEY, D. J. (eds.). 1975. *Studies in Presocratic Philosophy*, ii: *The Eleatics and Pluralists*. London: Routledge & Kegan Paul.

ANNAS, J. 1981. *An Introduction to Plato's Republic*. Oxford: Clarendon Press.

APELT, O. 1891. *Beiträge zur Geschichte der griechischen Philosophie*. Leipzig: Teubner.

AUSTIN, S. 1990. 'Parmenides' reference'. *Classical Quarterly*, NS 40: 266–7.

BABUT, D. 1974. 'Sur la théologie de Xénophane'. *Revue philosophique de la France et de l'étranger*, 164: 401–40.

BALLAUFF, T. 1963. *Die Idee der Paideia: Eine Studie zu Platons 'Höhlengleichnis' und Parmenides' 'Lehrgedicht'*, 2nd edn., Monographien zur philosophischen Forschung, 7. Meisenheim and Glan: Hain.

BALLEW, L. 1974. 'Straight and circular in Parmenides and the "Timaeus"'. *Phronesis*, 19: 189–209.

BARNES, J. 1979. 'Parmenides and the Eleatic One'. *Archiv für Geschichte der Philosophie*, 61: 1–21.

—— 1982. *The Presocratic Philosophers*, 2nd edn., The Arguments of the Philosophers. London: Routledge & Kegan Paul.

—— 1988. 'The Presocratics in context', critical notice of Osborne, 1987. *Phronesis*, 33: 327–44.

BÄUMKER, C. 1886. 'Die Einheit des parmenideischen Seienden'. *Jahrbucher für klassische Philologie*, 133: 541–61.

BENITEZ, E. 1996. '*Republic* 476d6–e2: Plato's dialectical requirement'. *Review of Metaphysics*, 49: 515–46.

BERMANN, K. 1979. 'The interpretation of Parmenides by the Neoplatonist Simplicius'. *Monist*, 62: 30–42.

BERNAYS, J. 1885. 'Heraklitische Studien', in H. Usener (ed.), *Gesammelte Abhandlungen von Jacob Bernays*, i (Berlin: Hertz): 37–64.

BERTI, E. 1971. 'Struttura e significato del "Parmenide" di Platone'. *Giornale di metafisica*, 26: 497–527.

—— 1988. 'Zenone di Elea inventore della dialettica?' *La parola del passato*, 43: 19–41.

BICKNELL, P. J. 1964. 'Aristotle's comments on the Parmenidean One'. *Acta Classica*, 7: 109–12.

BINDER, G. 1979. 'Heidnische Autoritäten im Ecclesiastes-Kommentar des Didymos von Alexandrien'. *Revue belge de philologie et d'histoire*, 57: 51–6.

—— and LIESENBORGHS, L. 1976. 'Eine Zuweisung der Sentenz οὐκ ἔστιν ἀντιλέγειν an Prodikos von Keos', in C. J. Classen (ed.), *Sophistik*, Wege der Forschung, 187 (Darmstadt: Wissenschaftliche Buchgesellschaft): 452–62.

BLUCK, R. S. 1961. *Plato's Meno, with Introduction and Commentary*. Cambridge: Cambridge University Press.

—— 1975. *Plato's Sophist: A Commentary*, G. C. Neal (ed.). Manchester: Manchester University Press.

BODUNRIN, P. O. 1971. 'Plato and his Contemporaries on the Possibility of Falsehood'. Ph.D. thesis, University of Minnesota.

—— 1975. 'The *koinonia genon* and Plato's philosophical objectives in the *Sophist*'. *Museum Africum*, 4: 47–51.

BONDESON, W. B. 1973. 'Non-being and the One: some connections between Plato's *Sophist* and *Parmenides*'. *Apeiron*, 7/2: 13–22.

—— 1976. 'Some problems about being and predication in Plato's *Sophist* 242–249'. *Journal of the History of Philosophy*, 14: 1–10.

BOOTH, N. B. 1957. 'Were Zeno's arguments directed against the Pythagoreans?' *Phronesis*, 2: 90–103.

BRANCACCI, A. 1990. *Oikeios logos: La filosofia del linguaggio di Antistene*, Elenchos, 20. Naples: Bibliopolis.

BRANDWOOD, L. 1990. *The Chronology of Plato's Dialogues*. Cambridge: Cambridge University Press.

—— 1992. 'Stylometry and chronology', in R. Kraut (ed.), *The Cambridge Companion to Plato* (Cambridge: Cambridge University Press): 90–120.

BRISSON, L. 1994. *Platon, Parménide: Traduction inédite, introduction et notes*. Paris: Flammarion.

—— and BENZÉCRI, J.-P. 1989. 'Structure de la seconde partie du *Parménide* de Platon'. *Cahiers de l'analyse des données*, 14: 117–26.

BRÖCKER, W. 1958. 'Gorgias contra Parmenides'. *Hermes*, 86: 425–40.

BRONIAK, C. J. 1987. 'Heraclitus, Parmenides, and Plato on living the good life'. *Dialogue*, 30: 28–37.

BROWN, G. 1945. 'The alleged metaphysics in the *Republic*'. *Aristotelian Society Supplement*, 19: 165–92.

BROWN, L. 1986. 'Being in the *Sophist*: a syntactical enquiry'. *Oxford Studies in Ancient Philosophy*, 4: 49–70.

BRUMBAUGH, R. S. 1961. *Plato on the One: The Hypotheses in the Parmenides*. New Haven: Yale University Press.

BURKERT, W. 1969. 'Das Proömium des Parmenides und die Katabasis des Pythagoras'. *Phronesis*, 14: 1–30.

—— 1972. *Lore and Science in Ancient Pythagoreanism*, trans. E. L. Minar, Jr. Cambridge, Mass.: Harvard University Press.

BURNET, J. 1914. *The History of Greek Philosophy*, part I: *Thales to Plato*. London: Macmillan.

—— 1930. *Early Greek Philosophy*, 4th edn. London: Black.

CALOGERO, G. 1932. *Studi sull' Eleatismo*. Rome: Tipografia del senato.

CAMERON, A. 1938. *The Pythagorean Background of the Theory of Recollection*. Menasha, Wis: Banta.

CANTO, M. 1989. *Platon, Euthydème: Traduction nouvelle, introduction et notes*. Paris: Flammarion.

CAPIZZI, A. 1970. *Socrate e i personaggi filosofi di Platone*. Rome: Ateneo.

CASSIN, B. 1980. *Si Parménide: Le traité anonyme De Melisso Xenophane Gorgia*, Cahiers de philologie, 4. Lille: Presses universitaires de Lille.

—— and NARCY, M. 1987. 'Parménide sophiste: la citation aristotélicienne du fr. XVI', in P. Aubenque (gen. ed.), *Études sur Parménide*, ii (Paris: J. Vrin): 277–93.

CHALMERS, W. R. 1960. 'Parmenides and the beliefs of mortals'. *Phronesis*, 5: 5–22.

CHERNISS, H. 1932. 'Parmenides and the *Parmenides* of Plato'. *American Journal of Philology*, 53: 122–38.

—— 1935. *Aristotle's Criticism of Presocratic Philosophy*. Baltimore: Johns Hopkins University Press.

—— 1951. 'The characteristics and effects of Presocratic Philosophy'. *Journal of the History of Ideas*, 12: 319–45. Reprinted in Furley and Allen (eds.), 1970: 1–28.

—— 1959. 'Plato (1950–1957)', part 1. *Lustrum*, 4: 5–308.

CHERUBIN, R. 1993. 'What is Eleatic about the Eleatic Stranger?', in G. A. Press (ed.), *Plato's Dialogues: New Studies and Interpretations* (Lanham, Md.: Rowman & Littlefield): 215–36.

CLARK, R. J. 1969. 'Parmenides and sense-perception'. *Revue des études grecques*, 82: 14–32.

CLASSEN, C. J. 1965. 'Bemerkungen zu zwei griechischen "Philosophiehistorikern"'. *Philologus*, 109: 175–81.

CLAY, J. 1972. 'The Planktai and moly: divine naming and knowing in Homer'. *Hermes*, 100: 127–31.

COOK WILSON, J. 1892–3. 'Apelt's pseudo-Aristotelian treatises'. *Classical Review*, 6: 16–19, 100–7, 156–62, 209–14; 7: 33–9.

COOPER, N. 1986. 'Between knowledge and ignorance'. *Phronesis*, 31: 229–42.

CORBATO, C. 1952. *Studi Senofanei*, extract from *Annali Triestini*, 22.1a. Trieste: Editrice Università di Trieste.

CORDERO, N.-L. 1979. 'Les deux chemins de Parménide dans les fragments 6 & 7'. *Phronesis*, 24: 1–32.

—— 1984. *Les deux chemins de Parménide: Édition critique, traduction, études et bibliographie*. Paris: J. Vrin; Brussels: OUSIA.

CORDERO, N.-L. 1986–7. 'Le non-être absolu dans le "Sophiste" de Platon'. *Annuaire de l'École pratique des Hautes Études, V^e section, sciences religieuses,* 95: 282–5.

—— 1987. 'L'histoire du texte de Parménide', in P. Aubenque (gen. ed.), *Études sur Parménide,* ii (Paris: J. Vrin): 3–24.

—— 1991. 'L'invention de l'école éléatique: Platon, *Sophiste,* 242D', in P. Aubenque (gen. ed.), M. Narcy (ed.), *Études sur le Sophiste de Platon,* Elenchos, 21 (Naples: Bibliopolis): 91–124.

CORNFORD, F. M. 1922–3. 'Mysticism and science in the Pythagorean tradition'. *Classical Quarterly,* 16: 137–50; 17: 1–12. Reprinted in Mourelatos (ed.), 1993: 135–60.

—— 1933. 'Parmenides' two ways'. *Classical Quarterly,* 27: 97–111.

—— 1935(*a*). *Plato's Theory of Knowledge: The Theaetetus and the Sophist of Plato Translated with a Running Commentary.* London: Routledge & Kegan Paul.

—— 1935(*b*). 'A new fragment of Parmenides'. *Classical Review,* 39: 122–3.

—— 1937. *Plato's Cosmology: The Timaeus of Plato Translated with a Running Commentary.* London: Routledge & Kegan Paul.

—— 1939. *Plato and Parmenides: Parmenides' Way of Truth and Plato's Parmenides Translated with an Introduction and a Running Commentary.* London: Routledge & Kegan Paul.

COULOUBARITSIS, L. 1987. 'Les multiples chemins de Parménide', in P. Aubenque (gen. ed.), *Études sur Parménide,* ii (Paris: J. Vrin): 25–43.

COXON, A. H. 1986. *The Fragments of Parmenides, Phronesis* supplementary volume, 3. Assen: Van Gorcum.

CRYSTAL, I. 1996. 'Parmenidean allusions in *Republic* V'. *Ancient Philosophy,* 16: 351–63.

CURD, P. K. 1988. 'Parmenidean clues in the search for the Sophist'. *History of Philosophy Quarterly,* 5: 307–20.

—— 1989. 'Some problems of unity in the first hypothesis of the *Parmenides*'. *Southern Journal of Philosophy,* 27: 347–59.

—— 1990. '*Parmenides* 142b5–144e7: the "unity is many" arguments'. *Southern Journal of Philosophy,* 28: 19–35.

—— 1991. 'Parmenidean monism'. *Phronesis,* 36: 241–64.

—— 1992. 'Deception and belief in Parmenides' *Doxa*'. *Apeiron,* 25: 109–33.

—— 1998. *The Legacy of Parmenides: Eleatic Monism and Later Presocratic Thought.* Princeton: Princeton University Press.

DELL' ORO, A. 1934. 'Precedenti al principio dell'unità del mondo in Parmenide'. *Historia: Studi storici per l'antichità classica,* 8: 279–89.

DENYER, N. 1991. *Language, Thought and Falsehood in Ancient Greek Philosophy,* Issues in Ancient Philosophy. London: Routledge.

DIELS, H. 1884. 'Gorgias und Empedokles'. *Sitzungsberichte des königlichen preussischen Akademie der Wissenschaften:* 343–68.

—— 1897. *Parmenides Lehrgedicht griechisch und deutsch, mit einem Anhang über griechische Thüren und Schlösser.* Berlin: Reimer.

DIÈS, A. (ed.). 1925. *Platon, œuvres complètes*, viii, 3: *Le Sophiste*. Paris: Belles Lettres.

DILLON, J. 1974. 'New evidence on Zeno of Elea?' *Archiv für Geschichte der Philosophie*, 56: 127–31.

—— 1976. 'More evidence on Zeno of Elea?' *Archiv für Geschichte der Philosophie*, 58: 221–2.

—— 1986. 'Proclus and the forty logoi of Zeno'. *Illinois Classical Studies*, 11: 35–41.

DIXSAUT, M. 1987. 'Platon et le logos de Parménide', in P. Aubenque (gen. ed.), *Études sur Parménide*, ii (Paris: J. Vrin): 215–53.

DODDS, E. R. 1928. 'The *Parmenides* of Plato and the origin of the Neoplatonic "One"'. *Classical Quarterly*, 22: 129–42.

DÖRING, K. 1972. *Die Megariker: Kommentierte Sammlung der Testimonien*, Studien zur antiken Philosophie, 2. Amsterdam: Grüner.

DÜMMLER, F. 1882. 'Antisthenica', inaugural dissertation, Bonn. Reprinted in his *Kleine Schriften*, i (Leipzig: Hirzel, 1901): 10–78.

—— 1889. *Akademika: Beiträge zur Literaturgeschichte der sokratischen Schulen*. Giessen: Ricker.

EBERT, T. 1974. *Meinung und Wissen in der Philosophie Platons: Untersuchungen zum 'Charmides', 'Menon' und 'Staat'*. Berlin: de Gruyter.

—— 1989. 'Wo beginnt der Weg der Doxa? Eine Textumstellung im Fragment 8 des Parmenides'. *Phronesis*, 34: 121–38.

EBNER, P. 1964. 'Senofane a Velia'. *Giornale di metafisica*, 19: 797–812.

FAGGI, A. 1926. 'L'"essere" e il "non essere" nella sofistica greca'. *Atti della Reale Accademia delle Scienze di Torino, classe di scienze morali, storiche e filologiche*, 61.

FEREJOHN, M. T. 1989. 'Plato and Aristotle on negative predication and semantic fragmentation'. *Archiv für Geschichte der Philosophie*, 71: 257–82.

FERGUSON, J. 1963. 'Sun, line and cave again'. *Classical Quarterly*, NS 13: 188–93.

FEYERABEND, B. 1984. 'Zur Wegmetaphorik beim Goldblättchen aus Hipponion und dem Proömium des Parmenides'. *Rheinisches Museum*, 127: 1–22.

FIELD, G. C. 1930. *Plato and his Contemporaries: A Study in Fourth-Century Life and Thought*. London: Methuen.

FINDLAY, J. N. 1974. *Plato: The Written and Unwritten Doctrines*. London: Routledge & Kegan Paul.

FINE, G. 1978. 'Knowledge and belief in *Republic* V'. *Archiv für Geschichte der Philosophie*, 60: 121–39.

—— 1990. 'Knowledge and belief in *Republic* V–VII', in S. Everson (ed.), *Epistemology*, Companions to Ancient Thought, 1 (Cambridge: Cambridge University Press): 85–115.

—— 1993. *On Ideas: Aristotle's Criticism of Plato's Theory of Forms*. Oxford: Clarendon Press.

FINKELBERG, A. 1986. '"Like by like" and two reflections of reality in Parmenides'. *Hermes*, 114: 405–12.

FINKELBERG, A. 1988. 'Parmenides: between material and logical monism'. *Archiv für Geschichte der Philosophie*, 70: 1–14.

—— 1990. 'Studies in Xenophanes'. *Harvard Studies in Classical Philology*, 93: 104–67.

FORRESTER, J. W. 1972. 'Plato's *Parmenides*: the structure of the first hypothesis'. *Journal of the History of Philosophy*, 10: 1–14.

FRAISSE, J.-C. 1982. 'L'unicité du monde dans le *Timée* de Platon'. *Revue philosophique de la France et de l'étranger*, 172: 249–54.

FRANK, D. H. 1985. 'On what there is: Plato's later thoughts'. *Elenchos*, 6: 5–18.

FRÄNKEL, H. 1925. 'Xenophanesstudien'. *Hermes*, 60: 174–92.

—— 1942. 'Zeno of Elea's attacks on plurality'. *American Journal of Philology*, 63: 1–25, 193–206. Revised version in Fränkel, 1968, trans. and reprinted in Allen and Furley (eds.), 1975: 102–42.

—— 1946. Critical notice of Verdenius, 1942. *Classical Philology*, 41: 168–71.

—— 1968. *Wege und Formen frühgriechischen Denkens: Literarische und philosophiegeschichtliche Studien*, 3rd edn. Munich: Beck.

FREDE, M. 1967. *Prädikation und Existenzaussage: Platons Gebrauch von '. . . ist . . .' und '. . . ist nicht . . .' im Sophistes*, Hypomnemata, 18. Göttingen: Vandenhoeck and Ruprecht.

—— 1992. 'The *Sophist* on false statements', in R. Kraut (ed.), *The Cambridge Companion to Plato* (Cambridge: Cambridge University Press): 397–424.

FRÈRE, J. 1991. 'Platon lecteur de Parménide dans le *Sophiste*', in P. Aubenque (gen. ed.), M. Narcy (ed.), *Études sur le Sophiste de Platon*, Elenchos, 21 (Naples: Bibliopolis): 127–43.

FRIEDLÄNDER, P. 1969. *Plato*, i: *An Introduction*, trans. H. Meyerhoff, 2nd edn. Princeton: Princeton University Press.

FRITZ, K. VON 1943. 'Nóos and νοεῖν in the Homeric poems'. *Classical Philology*, 38: 79–93.

—— 1945–6. 'Noῦs, νοεῖν and their derivatives in Presocratic philosophy'. *Classical Philology*, 40: 223–42; 41: 12–34. Reprinted in Mourelatos (ed.), 1993: 23–85.

—— 1967. 'Xeniades', in G. Wissowa, W. Kroll, *et al.* (eds.), *Paulys Realencyclopädie der classischen Altertumswissenschaft*, 2nd ser. ix, 2 (Stuttgart: Druckenmüller): 1438–9.

—— 1974. 'Zeno of Elea in Plato's *Parmenides*', in J. L. Heller and J. K. Newman (eds.), *Serta Turyniana: Studies in Greek Literature and Palaeography in Honour of A. Turyn* (Urbana, Ill.: University of Illinois Press): 329–41.

FRUTIGER, P. 1930. *Les mythes de Platon: Étude philosophique et littéraire*. Paris: Alcan.

FURLEY, D. J. 1967. *Two Studies in the Greek Atomists*. Princeton: Princeton University Press.

—— 1973. 'Notes on Parmenides', in E. N. Lee, A. P. D. Mourelatos, and R. M. Rorty (eds.), *Exegesis and Argument: Studies in Greek Philosophy*

Presented to Gregory Vlastos, Phronesis supplementary volume, 1 (Assen: Van Gorcum): 1–15.

—— and ALLEN, R. E. (eds). 1970. *Studies in Presocratic Philosophy*, i: *The Beginnings of Philosophy*. London: Routledge & Kegan Paul.

FURTH, M. 1968. 'Elements of Eleatic ontology'. *Journal of the History of Philosophy*, 6: 111–32. Reprinted in Mourelatos (ed.), 1993: 241–70.

GADAMER, H.-G. 1950. 'Zur Vorgeschichte der Metaphysik', in *Anteile: Martin Heidegger zum 60. Geburtstag* (Frankfurt: Klostermann): 51–79.

GERSHENSON, D. E., and GREENBERG, D. A. 1962. 'Aristotle confronts the Eleatics: two arguments on the One'. *Phronesis*, 7: 137–51.

GIANNANTONI, G. (ed.). 1990. *Socratis et Socraticorum Reliquiae*, 4 vols., Elenchos, 18. Naples: Bibliopolis.

GIFFORD, E. H. 1905. *The Euthydemus of Plato*. Oxford: Clarendon Press.

GIGON, O. 1936. 'Gorgias "Über das Nichtsein"'. *Hermes*, 71: 186–213.

—— 1968. *Der Ursprung der griechischen Philosophie: Von Hesiod bis Parmenides*, 2nd edn. Basel and Stuttgart: Schwabe.

GILL, M. L. (with P. Ryan). 1996. *Plato: Parmenides*. Indianapolis: Hackett.

GOFFI, J.-Y. 1989. 'Ce que Platon reproche à Hippias'. *Revue de philosophie ancienne*, 7: 235–45.

GÓMEZ-LOBO, A. 1974. 'Platon *Sofista* 244b6–d12'. *Dialogos*, 10: 131–7.

GONZALEZ, F. J. 1996. 'Propositions or objects? A critique of Gail Fine on knowledge and belief in *Republic* V'. *Phronesis*, 41: 245–75.

GOSLING, J. C. B. 1968. '$\Delta \acute{o} \xi a$ and $\delta \acute{v} v a \mu \iota s$ in Plato's *Republic*'. *Phronesis*, 13: 119–30.

GROTE, G. 1875. *Plato and the Other Companions of Socrates*, 3rd edn., 3 vols. London: Murray.

—— 1888. *A History of Greece, from the Earliest Period to the Close of the Generation Contemporary with Alexander the Great*, 6th edn., 10 vols. London: Murray.

GRUBE, G. M. A. 1926. 'On the authenticity of the *Hippias Major*'. *Classical Quarterly*, 21: 134–48.

—— 1935. *Plato's Thought*. London: Methuen.

GUARIGLIA, O. N. 1971. 'Platon, *Sofista* 244b6–245e2: la refutacion de la tesis eleática'. *Dialogos*, 7: 73–82.

GUAZZONI FOÀ, V. 1961. 'Senofane e Parmenide in Platone'. *Giornale di metafisica*, 16: 467–76.

GUÉRARD, C. 1987. 'Parménide d'Élée chez les Néoplatoniciens', in P. Aubenque (gen. ed.), *Études sur Parménide*, ii (Paris: J. Vrin): 294–313.

GUTHRIE, W. K. C. 1962. *A History of Greek Philosophy*, i: *The Earlier Presocratics and the Pythagoreans*. Cambridge: Cambridge University Press.

—— 1965. *A History of Greek Philosophy*, ii: *The Presocratic Tradition from Parmenides to Democritus*. Cambridge: Cambridge University Press.

—— 1971. *The Sophists*. Cambridge: Cambridge University Press.

—— 1975. *A History of Greek Philosophy*, iv: *Plato, the Man and His Dialogues: The Earlier Period*. Cambridge: Cambridge University Press.

GUTHRIE, W. K. C. 1978. *A History of Greek Philosophy*, v: *The Later Plato and the Academy*. Cambridge: Cambridge University Press.

HACKFORTH, R. 1952. *Plato's Phaedrus, Translated with Introduction and Commentary*. Cambridge: Cambridge University Press.

—— 1955. *Plato's Phaedo, Translated with Introduction and Commentary*. Cambridge: Cambridge University Press.

HÄGLER, R.-P. 1983. *Platons 'Parmenides': Probleme der Interpretation*, Quellen und Studien zur Philosophie, 18. Berlin: de Gruyter.

HAMLYN, D. W. 1955. 'The communion of forms and the development of Plato's logic'. *Philosophical Quarterly*, 5: 289–302.

HARDIE, W. F. R. 1936. *A Study in Plato*. Oxford: Clarendon Press.

HAWTREY, R. S. W. 1981. *Commentary on Plato's 'Euthydemus'*. Philadelphia: American Philosophical Society.

HAYS, S. 1990. 'On the skeptical influence of Gorgias' *On Non-Being*'. *Journal of the History of Philosophy*, 28: 327–38.

HEIDEL, W. A. 1943. 'Hecataeus and Xenophanes'. *American Journal of Philology*, 64: 257–77.

HEITSCH, E. 1969. 'Ein Buchtitel des Protagoras'. *Hermes*, 97: 292–6.

HERSHBELL, J. 1972. 'Plutarch and Parmenides'. *Greek, Roman and Byzantine Studies*, 13: 193–208.

—— 1974. 'Empedoclean influences on the *Timaeus*'. *Phoenix*, 28: 145–66.

HEUBECK, A. 1949–50. 'Die homerische Göttersprache'. *Würzburger Jahrbücher für die Altertumswissenschaft*, 4: 197–218.

HINTIKKA, J. 1980. 'Parmenides' *cogito* argument'. *Ancient Philosophy*, 1: 5–16.

HOFMANN, H. 1974. 'Lykophron der Sophist', in G. Wissowa, W. Kroll, *et al.* (eds.), *Paulys Realencyclopädie der classischen Altertumswissenschaft*, Supplementband, 14 (Munich: Druckenmüller): 265–72.

HÖLSCHER, U. 1969. *Parmenides, vom Wesen des Seienden: Die Fragmente, griechisch und deutsch*, Theorie, 1. Frankfurt: Suhrkamp.

HUSSEY, E. 1972. *The Presocratics*, Classical Life and Letters. London: Duckworth.

—— 1990. 'The beginnings of epistemology: from Homer to Philolaus', in S. Everson (ed.), *Epistemology*, Companions to Ancient Thought, 1 (Cambridge: Cambridge University Press): 11–38.

ISNARDI PARENTE, M. 1988. 'Il Parmenide di Plutarco'. *La parola del passato*, 43: 225–36.

JACKSON, B. D. 1967. 'Plotinus and the *Parmenides*'. *Journal of the History of Philosophy*, 5: 315–28.

JAEGER, W. 1947. *The Theology of the Early Greek Philosophers*, trans. E. S. Robinson, Gifford Lectures 1936. Oxford: Clarendon Press.

JOËL, K. 1893. *Der echte und der Xenophontische Sokrates*, i. Berlin: Gaertners.

JORDAN, R. W. 1984. 'Plato's task in the *Sophist*'. *Classical Quarterly*, NS 34: 113–29.

KAHN, C. H. 1968. Critical notice of Tarán, 1965. *Gnomon*, 40: 123–33.

—— 1969. 'The thesis of Parmenides'. *Review of Metaphysics*, 23: 700–24.

—— 1979. *The Art and Thought of Heraclitus: An Edition of the Fragments with Translation and Commentary*. Cambridge: Cambridge University Press.

—— 1981. 'Some philosophical uses of "to be" in Plato'. *Phronesis*, 26: 105–34.

—— 1985. 'The beautiful and the genuine: a discussion of Paul Woodruff, *Plato, Hippias Major*'. *Oxford Studies in Ancient Philosophy*, 3: 261–87.

—— 1988. 'Being in Parmenides and Plato'. *La parola del passato*, 43: 237–61.

KARLIN, E. 1947. 'The method of ambiguity'. *New Scholasticism*, 21: 154–91.

KARSTEN, S. 1830. *Xenophanis Colophonii Carminum Reliquiae*, Philosophorum Graecorum Veterum, i, 1. Amsterdam: Muller.

—— 1835. *Parmenidis Eleatae Carminis Reliquiae*, Philosophorum Graecorum Veterum, i, 2. Amsterdam: Muller.

KERFERD, G. B. 1955. 'Gorgias on nature or that which is not'. *Phronesis*, 1: 3–25.

—— 1965. 'Recent work on Presocratic philosophy'. *American Philosophical Quarterly*, 2: 130–40.

—— 1986. 'Le sophiste vu par Platon: un philosophe imparfait', in B. Cassin (ed.), *Positions de la Sophistique* (Paris: J. Vrin): 13–25.

—— 1991. 'Aristotle's treatment of the doctrine of Parmenides'. *Oxford Studies in Ancient Philosophy*, supplementary volume: 1–7.

KEULEN, H. 1971. *Untersuchungen zu Platons 'Euthydem'*, Klassisch-Philologische Studien, 37. Wiesbaden: Harrassowitz.

KEYT, D. 1969. 'Plato's paradox that the immutable is unknowable'. *Philosophical Quarterly*, 19: 1–14.

—— 1971. 'The mad craftsman of the *Timaeus*'. *Philosophical Review*, 80: 230–5.

KIRK, G. S., and RAVEN, J. E. 1957. *The Presocratic Philosophers*. Cambridge: Cambridge University Press.

—— —— and SCHOFIELD, M. 1983. *The Presocratic Philosophers*, 2nd edn. Cambridge: Cambridge University Press.

KRÄMER, H. J. 1959. *Arete bei Platon und Aristoteles. Zum Wesen und zur Geschichte der platonischen Ontologie*, Abhandlungen der Heidelberger Akademie der Wissenschaften, Philosophisch-historische Klasse, 6. Heidelberg: Carl Winter.

—— 1969. 'ΕΠΕΚΕΙΝΑ ΤΗΣ ΟΥΣΙΑΣ: Zu Platon, Politeia 509B'. *Archiv für Geschichte der Philosophie*, 51: 1–30.

KRANZ, W. 1916. 'Über Aufbau und Bedeutung des parmenideischen Gedichts'. *Sitzungsberichte des königlichen preussischen Akademie der Wissenschaften*, 47: 1158–76.

LATTANZI, G. M. 1932. 'L'attegiamento gnoseologico di Gorgia nel "περὶ τοῦ μὴ ὄντος ἢ περὶ φύσεως"'. *Rendiconti della Reale Accademia Nazionale dei Lincei, classe di scienze morali, storiche e filologiche*, 6th ser. 8: 289–92.

LEE, H. D. P. 1936. *Zeno of Elea: A Text, with Translation and Notes*, Cambridge Classical Studies, 1. Cambridge: Cambridge University Press.

LESHER, J. 1981. 'Perceiving and knowing in the *Iliad* and *Odyssey*'. *Phronesis*, 26: 2–24.

—— 1983. 'Heraclitus' epistemological vocabulary'. *Hermes*, 111: 155–70.

—— 1984. 'Parmenides' critique of thinking: the *poludêris elenchos* of fragment 7'. *Oxford Studies in Ancient Philosophy*, 2: 1–30.

—— 1992. *Xenophanes of Colophon, Fragments: A Text and Translation with a Commentary*, *Phoenix* supplementary volume, 32. Toronto: University of Toronto Press.

LEVI, A. 1930. 'Il problema dell'errore nella filosofia greca prima di Platone'. *Athenaeum*, NS 8: 27–44.

—— ('D. Viale'). 1941. 'Studi su Gorgia'. *Logos*, 24: 154–91.

—— 1948. 'Parmenide, Platone, la scienza moderna e il problema dell' intelligibilità dell'esperienza'. *Scientia*, 83: 79–82.

—— 1970. *Il problema dell'errore nella metafisica e nella gnoseologia di Platone*, G. Reale (ed.). Padua: Liviana.

LIBRIZZI, C. 1950. *I problemi fondamentali della filosofia di Platone*, Il pensiero antico, 1. Padua: CEDAM.

LIEBRUCKS, B. 1949. *Platons Entwicklung zur Dialektik: Untersuchungen zum Problem des Eleatismus*. Frankfurt: Klostermann.

LOENEN, J. H. M. M. VAN 1959. *Parmenides, Melissus, Gorgias: A Reinterpretation of Eleatic Philosophy*. Assen: Van Gorcum.

LONG, A. A. 1963. 'The principles of Parmenides' cosmology'. *Phronesis*, 8: 90–107.

LYNCH, W. F. 1959. *An Approach to the Metaphysics of Plato through the Parmenides*. Washington: Georgetown University Press.

McCABE, M. M. 1994. *Plato's Individuals*. Princeton: Princeton University Press.

McPHERRAN, M. L. 1986. 'Plato's reply to the worst-difficulty argument of the *Parmenides—Sophist* 248A–249D'. *Archiv für Geschichte der Philosophie*, 68: 233–52.

MAIER, H. 1913. *Sokrates: Sein Werk und seine geschichtliche Stellung*. Tübingen: Mohr.

MALCOLM, J. 1967. 'Plato's analysis of τὸ ὄν and τὸ μὴ ὄν in the *Sophist*'. *Phronesis*, 12: 130–46.

—— 1985. 'On what is not in any way in the *Sophist*'. *Classical Quarterly*, NS 35: 520–3.

MALCOLM, N. 1968. 'On the place of the *Hippias Major* in the development of Plato's thought'. *Archiv für Geschichte der Philosophie*, 50: 189–95.

MANSFELD, J. 1964. *Die Offenbarung des Parmenides und die menschliche Welt*, Wijsgerige teksten en studies, 9. Assen: Van Gorcum.

—— 1983. '*Cratylus* 402a–c: Plato or Hippias?', in L. Rossetti (ed.), *Atti del Symposium Heracliteum 1981*, i: *Studi* (Rome: Ateneo): 43–55. Reprinted in Mansfeld, 1990: 84–96.

—— 1985. 'Historical and philosophical aspects of Gorgias' "On What is Not"', in L. Montoneri and F. Romano (eds.), *Gorgia e la sofistica, Siculorum gymnasium*, 38: 243–71. Reprinted in Mansfeld, 1990: 97–125.

—— 1986. 'Aristotle, Plato, and the Preplatonic doxography and chronography', in G. Cambiano (ed.), *Storiografia e dossografia nella filosofia antica* (Turin: Tirrenia Stampatori): 1–59. Reprinted in Mansfeld, 1990: 22–83.

—— 1990. *Studies in the Historiography of Greek Philosophy*. Assen: Van Gorcum.

MANSION, S. 1953. 'Aristote, critique des Éléates'. *Revue philosophique de Louvain*, 51: 165–86.

MATSON, W. I. 1988. 'The Zeno of Plato and Tannery vindicated', *La parola del passato*, 43: 312–36.

MEINWALD, C. 1991. *Plato's Parmenides*. New York and Oxford: Oxford University Press.

MEJER, J. 1978. *Diogenes Laertius and his Hellenistic Background, Hermes* Einzelschriften, 40. Wiesbaden: Steiner.

MICELI, R. 1936. 'Dall' "essere" degli Eleati al "non-essere" dei sofisti'. *Archivio della cultura italiana*, 5: 191–224.

MIGLIORI, M. 1973. *La filosofia di Gorgia: Contributi per una riscoperta del sofista di Lentini*, Scienze umane, 10. Milan: CELUC.

MILLER, F. D. 1977. 'Parmenides on mortal belief'. *Journal of the History of Philosophy*, 15: 253–65.

MILLER, M. H., JR. 1986. *Plato's Parmenides: The Conversion of the Soul*. Princeton: Princeton University Press.

MOHR, R. D. 1985. *The Platonic Cosmology*, Philosophia Antiqua, 42. Leiden: Brill.

MORAUX, P. 1968. 'La joute dialectique d'après le huitième livre des *Topiques*', in G. E. L. Owen (ed.), *Aristotle on Dialectic: The Topics*, Proceedings of the 3rd Symposium Aristotelicum (Oxford: Clarendon Press): 277–311.

MORAVSCIK, J. 1970. 'Learning as recollection', in G. Vlastos (ed.), *Plato: A Collection of Critical Essays*, i: *Metaphysics and Epistemology* (Garden City, NY: Doubleday): 53–69.

—— 1982. 'Forms and dialectic in the second half of the *Parmenides*', in M. Schofield and M. C. Nussbaum (eds.), *Language and Logos: Studies in Ancient Greek Philosophy Presented to G. E. L. Owen* (Cambridge: Cambridge University Press): 135–53.

MORRISON, J. S. 1955. 'Parmenides and Er'. *Journal of Hellenic Studies*, 75: 59–68.

MORROW, G. R., and DILLON, J. 1987. *Proclus' Commentary on Plato's Parmenides*. Princeton, NJ: Princeton University Press.

MORTLEY, R. J. 1969. 'Plato's choice of the sphere'. *Revue des études grecques*, 82: 342–5.

MOURELATOS, A. P. D. 1970. *The Route of Parmenides: A Study of Word, Image and Argument in the Fragments.* New Haven: Yale University Press.

—— (ed.). 1993. *The Pre-Socratics: A Collection of Critical Essays*, 2nd edn. Princeton: Princeton University Press.

MURPHY, N. R. 1937. 'Plato, *Parmenides* 129 and *Republic* 475–480'. *Classical Quarterly*, NS 31: 71–8.

NATORP, P. 1890. 'Aristoteles und die Eleaten'. *Philosophische Monachshefte*, 26: 1–16, 147–69.

—— 1894. 'Antisthenes (10)', in G. Wissowa (ed.), *Paulys Realencyclopädie der classischen Altertumswissenschaft*, i, 2 (Stuttgart: Metzlerscher): 2538–45.

—— 1903. *Platons Ideenlehre: Eine Einführung in den Idealismus.* Leipzig: Dürr.

NEHAMAS, A. 1975. 'Confusing universals and particulars in Plato's early dialogues'. *Review of Metaphysics*, 29: 288–306.

—— 1979. 'Self-predication and Plato's theory of Forms'. *American Philosophical Quarterly*, 16: 93–103.

—— 1981. 'On Parmenides' three ways of inquiry'. *Deucalion*, 33–4: 97–111.

—— 1982. 'Participation and predication in Plato's later thought'. *Review of Metaphysics*, 36: 343–74.

NESTLE, W. 1922. 'Die Schrift des Gorgias "Über die Natur oder über das Nichtseiende" '. *Hermes*, 57: 551–62.

NEWIGER, H. J. 1973. *Untersuchungen zu Gorgias' Schrift 'Über das Nichtseiende'.* Berlin: de Gruyter.

O'BRIEN, D. 1980. 'Temps et intemporalité chez Parménide'. *Études philosophiques*: 257–72.

—— (with Frère, J.). 1987(*a*). *Le poème de Parménide: Texte, traduction, essai critique, Études sur Parménide*, P. Aubenque (gen. ed.), i. Paris: J. Vrin.

—— 1987(*b*). 'Problèmes d'établissement du texte', in P. Aubenque (gen. ed.), *Études sur Parménide*, ii (Paris: J. Vrin): 314–50.

—— 1991. 'Le non-être dans la philosophie grecque: Parménide, Platon, Plotin', in P. Aubenque (gen. ed.), M. Narcy (ed.), *Études sur le Sophiste de Platon*, Elenchos, 21 (Naples: Bibliopolis): 317–64.

OLERUD, A. 1951. *L'Idée de macrocosmos et de microcosmos dans le Timée de Platon: Étude de mythologie comparée.* Uppsala: Almqvist & Wiksells.

OSBORNE, C. 1987. *Rethinking Early Greek Philosophy: Hippolytus of Rome and the Presocratics.* London: Duckworth.

OWEN, G. E. L. 1957–8. 'Zeno and the mathematicians'. *Proceedings of the Aristotelian Society*, 58: 199–222. Reprinted in Allen and Furley (eds.), 1975: 143–65.

—— 1960. 'Eleatic Questions'. *Classical Quarterly*, NS 10: 84–102. Reprinted in Allen and Furley (eds.), 1975: 48–81.

—— 1966. 'Plato and Parmenides on the timeless present'. *Monist*, 50: 317–40.

—— 1970(*a*). 'Notes on Ryle's Plato', in O. P. Wood and G. Pitcher (eds.), *Ryle: A Collection of Critical Essays* (Garden City, NY: Doubleday): 341–72.

—— 1970(*b*). 'Plato on not-being', in G. Vlastos (ed.), *Plato: A Collection of Critical Essays*, i: *Metaphysics and Epistemology* (Garden City, NY: Doubleday): 223–67.

OWENS, J. 1974. 'The physical world of Parmenides', in J. R. O'Donnell (ed.), *Essays in Honour of Anton Charles Pegis* (Toronto: Pontifical Institute of Mediaeval Studies): 378–95.

—— 1975. 'Naming in Parmenides', in J. Mansfeld and L. M. de Rijk (eds.), *Kephalaion: Studies in Greek Philosophy and its Continuation Offered to Professor C. J. de Vogel*, Philosophical Texts and Studies, 23 (Assen: Van Gorcum): 16–25.

PALMER, J. A. 1996. 'Aspects of Plato's Reception of Parmenides'. Ph.D. thesis, Princeton University.

—— 1998. 'Xenophanes' ouranian God in the fourth century'. *Oxford Studies in Ancient Philosophy*, 16: 1–32.

PANAGIOTOU, S. 1981. 'The *Parmenides* and the communion of kinds in the *Sophist*'. *Hermes*, 109: 167–71.

PARRY, R. D. 1979. 'The unique world of the *Timaeus*'. *Journal of the History of Philosophy*, 17: 1–10.

—— 1991. 'The intelligible world-animal in Plato's *Timaeus*'. *Journal of the History of Philosophy*, 29: 13–32.

PATTERSON, R. 1981. 'The unique worlds of the "Timaeus"'. *Phoenix*, 35: 105–19.

PATZER, A. 1986. *Der Sophist Hippias als Philosophiehistoriker*. Freiburg: Alber.

PECK, A. L. 1952. 'Plato and the ΜΕΓΙΣΤΑ ΓΕΝΗ of the *Sophist*'. *Classical Quarterly*, NS 2: 32–56.

PELLETIER, F. J. 1990. *Parmenides, Plato, and the Semantics of Not-Being*. Chicago: University of Chicago Press.

PELLIKAAN-ENGEL, M. E. 1974. *Hesiod and Parmenides: A New View on their Cosmologies and on Parmenides' Proem*. Amsterdam: Hakkert.

PETERSON, S. 1996. 'Plato's *Parmenides*: a principle of interpretation and seven arguments'. *Journal of the History of Philosophy*, 34: 167–92.

PHILIP, J. A. 1968. 'The apographa of Plato's "Sophistes"'. *Phoenix*, 22: 289–98.

PRÄCHTER, K. 1932. 'Platon und Euthydemos'. *Philologus*, 87: 121–35.

PRAUSS, G. 1966. *Platon und der logische Eleatismus*. Berlin: de Gruyter.

PRIOR, W. J. 1978. 'Zeno's first argument concerning plurality'. *Archiv für Geschichte der Philosophie*, 60: 247–56.

RADT, S. L. 1980. 'Noch einmal Aischylos, Niobe fr. 162 N.² (278 M.)'. *Zeitschrift für Papyrologie und Epigraphik*, 38: 47–58.

RANKIN, H. D. 1981. 'Ouk estin antilegein', in G. B. Kerferd (ed.), *The Sophists and their Legacy*, *Hermes* Einzelschriften, 44 (Wiesbaden: Steiner): 25–37.

RAVEN, J. E. 1948. *Pythagoreans and Eleatics: An Account of the Interaction between the Two Opposed Schools during the Fifth and Early Fourth Centuries B.C.*, Cambridge Classical Studies. Cambridge: Cambridge University Press.

—— 1965. *Plato's Thought in the Making: A Study of the Development of his Metaphysics.* Cambridge: Cambridge University Press.

REALE, G. 1978. 'Il concetto di opinione (doxa) e le ragioni della sua svalutazione teoretica negli Eleati e in Platone', in M. Sordi (ed.), *Aspetti dell'opinione pubblica nel mondo antico*, Contributi dell'Istituto di Storia antica, 5 (Milan: Vita e pensiero): 7–32.

REEVE, C. D. C. 1988. *Philosopher-Kings: The Argument of Plato's Republic.* Princeton: Princeton University Press.

REINHARDT, K. 1916. *Parmenides und die Geschichte der griechischen Philosophie.* Bonn: Cohen.

RIEZLER, K. 1934. *Parmenides: Text, Übersetzung und Interpretation*, Frankfurter Studien zur Religion und Kultur der Antike, 5. Frankfurt: Klostermann.

RIST, J. M. 1962. 'The Neoplatonic One and Plato's *Parmenides*'. *Transactions and Proceedings of the American Philological Association*, 93: 389–401.

ROBIN, L. 1919. 'Sur la doctrine de la réminiscence'. *Revue des études grecques*, 32: 451–61.

—— (ed.). 1954. *Platon, œuvres complètes*, iv, 3: *Phèdre*, 4th edn. Paris: Belles Lettres.

—— 1968. *Platon*, 2nd edn., Les grands penseurs. Paris: Presses universitaires de France.

ROBINSON, R. 1942. 'Plato's *Parmenides*'. *Classical Philology*, 37: 51–76, 159–86. Reprinted with revisions in Robinson, 1953: 223–80.

—— 1953. *Plato's Earlier Dialectic*, 2nd edn. Oxford: Clarendon Press.

ROBINSON, T. M. 1975. 'Parmenides on the ascertainment of the real'. *Canadian Journal of Philosophy*, 4: 623–33.

—— 1979. 'Parmenides on the real in its totality'. *Monist*, 62: 54–60.

—— 1989. 'Parmenides and Heraclitus on what can be known'. *Revue de philosophie ancienne*, 7: 157–67.

ROHDE, E. 1925. *Psyche: Seelencult und Unsterblichkeitsglaube der Griechen*, ii, 10th edn. Tübingen: Mohr.

RÖLLIG, F. W. 1900. 'Zum Dialoge Hippias Major'. *Wiener Studien*, 22: 18–24.

ROSS, W. D. 1951. *Plato's Theory of Ideas.* Oxford: Clarendon Press.

RUDEBUSCH, G. 1991. '*Sophist* 237–239'. *Southern Journal of Philosophy*, 29: 521–31.

RUNCIMAN, W. G. 1959. 'Plato's *Parmenides*'. *Harvard Studies in Classical Philology*, 64: 89–120. Reprinted in Allen (ed.), 1965: 149–84.

—— 1962. *Plato's Later Epistemology*, Cambridge Classical Studies. Cambridge: Cambridge University Press.

RYLE, G. 1939. 'Plato's *Parmenides*'. *Mind*, 48: 129–51, 303–25. Reprinted with afterword in Allen (ed.), 1965: 97–147.

SAFFREY, H.-D. 1993. 'Jean Wahl et le *Parménide* de Platon'. *Revue des sciences philosophiques et théologiques*, 77: 399–404.

SAYRE, K. 1978. 'Plato's *Parmenides*: why the eight hypotheses are not contradictory'. *Phronesis*, 23: 133–50.

—— 1983. *Plato's Late Ontology: A Riddle Resolved*. Princeton: Princeton University Press.

—— 1994. Critical notice of Meinwald, 1991. *Noûs*, 28: 114–16.

SCHLEIERMACHER, F. 1855. *Platons Werke*, 3rd edn., 3 vols. Berlin: Reimer.

SCHOFIELD, M. 1970. 'Did Parmenides discover eternity?' *Archiv für Geschichte der Philosophie*, 52: 113–35.

—— 1972. 'The dissection of unity in Plato's *Parmenides*'. *Classical Philology*, 67: 102–9.

—— 1973(*a*). 'A neglected regress argument in the *Parmenides*'. *Classical Quarterly*, NS 23: 29–44.

—— 1973(*b*). 'Eudoxus in the "Parmenides"'. *Museum Helveticum*, 30: 1–19.

—— 1974. 'Plato on unity and sameness'. *Classical Quarterly*, NS 24: 33–45.

—— 1977. 'The antinomies of Plato's *Parmenides*'. *Classical Quarterly*, NS 71: 139–58.

—— 1988. Critical notice of Osborne, 1987. *Isis*, 79: 537–8.

SCHWABL, H. 1953. 'Sein und Doxa bei Parmenides'. *Wiener Studien*, 66: 50–75.

SELIGMAN, P. 1974. *Being and Not-Being: An Introduction to Plato's Sophist*. The Hague: Nijhoff.

—— 1982. 'Being and forms in Plato', in P. Morewedge (ed.), *Philosophies of Existence, Ancient and Medieval* (New York: Fordham University Press): 18–32.

SHARPLES, R. 1985. *Plato, Meno: Edited with Translation and Notes*. Warminster: Aris and Phillips.

SICKING, C. M. J. 1964. 'Gorgias und die Philosophen'. *Mnemosyne*, 4th ser. 17: 225–47.

SIDER, D. 1985. 'Textual notes on Parmenides' poem'. *Hermes*, 113: 362–6.

SINNIGE, T. G. 1968. *Matter and Infinity in the Presocratic Schools and Plato*, Philosophical Texts and Studies, 17. Assen: Van Gorcum.

SNELL, B. 1924. *Die Ausdrücke für den Begriff des Wissens in der vorplatonischen Philosophie*, Philologische Untersuchungen, 29. Berlin: Weidmann.

—— 1944. 'Die Nachrichten über die Lehren des Thales'. *Philologus*, 96: 119–28.

—— 1953. *The Discovery of the Mind: The Greek Origins of European Thought*, trans. T. G. Rosenmeyer. Oxford: Blackwell.

SOLMSEN, F. 1971(*a*). 'Parmenides and the description of perfect beauty in Plato's *Symposium*'. *American Journal of Philology*, 92: 62–70.

—— 1971(*b*). 'The tradition about Zeno of Elea re-examined'. *Phronesis*, 16: 116–41. Reprinted in Mourelatos (ed.), 1993: 368–93.

SORABJI, R. 1983. *Time, Creation and the Continuum: Theories in Antiquity and the Early Middle Ages*. London: Duckworth.

SORETH, M. 1953. *Der platonische Dialog Hippias Major*, Zetemata, 6. Munich: Beck.

SPANGLER, G. A. 1979. 'Aristotle's criticism of Parmenides in *Physics* I'. *Apeiron*, 13: 92–103.

SPEISER, A. 1959. *Ein Parmenideskommentar: Studien zur platonischen Dialektik*, 2nd edn. (1st edn., 1937). Stuttgart: Köhler.

SPRAGUE, R. K. 1962. *Plato's Use of Fallacy: A Study of the Euthydemus and Some Other Dialogues*. London: Routledge & Kegan Paul.

—— 1965. *Plato, Euthydemus: Translated with an Introduction*. Indianapolis and New York: Bobbs-Merrill.

—— 1968. 'A Platonic parallel in the *Dissoi Logoi*'. *Journal of the History of Philosophy*, 6: 160–1.

—— 1971. '*Symposium* 211A and Parmenides frag. 8'. *Classical Philology*, 66: 261.

STALLBAUM, G. 1839. *Platonis Parmenides cum Quattuor Libris Prolegomenorum et Commentario Perpetuo*. Leipzig: Libraria Lehnholdiana.

STENZEL, J. 1917. *Studien der Entwicklung der Platonischen Dialektik von Sokrates zu Aristoteles: Arete und Diaeresis*. Breslau: Trewendt & Granier.

STEVENS, A. 1990. *Postérité de l'Être: Simplicius interprète de Parménide*, Cahiers de philosophie ancienne, 8. Brussels: OUSIA.

STEWART, M. A. 1977. 'Plato's sophistry'. *Aristotelian Society Supplement*, 51: 21–44.

STOKES, M. C. 1971. *One and Many in Presocratic Philosophy*. Washington: Center for Hellenic Studies.

—— 1992. 'Plato and the sightlovers of the *Republic*'. *Apeiron*, 25: 103–32.

SZABÓ, A. 1955. 'Eleatica'. *Acta Antiqua*, 3: 67–102.

—— 1992. 'La filosofia degli Eleati e il *Parmenide* di Platone', in V. Vitiello (ed.), *Il 'Parmenide' di Platone*, Laboratorio, 8 (Naples: Guida): 31–46.

TANNERY, P. 1887. *Pour l'histoire de la science hellène: De Thalès à Empédocle*. Paris: Alcan.

TARÁN, L. 1965. *Parmenides: A Text with Translation, Commentary, and Critical Essays*. Princeton: Princeton University Press.

—— 1985. 'The text of Simplicius' commentary on Aristotle's Physics', in I. Hadot (ed.), *Simplicius: Sa vie, son œuvre, sa survie*, Peripatoi, 15 (Berlin: de Gruyter): 246–66.

TARRANT, D. 1928. *The Hippias Major Attributed to Plato, with Introductory Essays and Commentary*. Cambridge: Cambridge University Press.

—— 1955. Critical notice of Soreth, 1953. *Classical Review*, 69: 52–3.

TAYLOR, A. E. 1896–7. 'On the interpretation of Plato's *Parmenides*'. *Mind*, 5: 297–326, 483–507; 6: 9–39.

—— 1911. *Varia Socratica, First Series*, St Andrews University Publications, 9. Oxford: Parker.

—— 1928. *A Commentary on Plato's Timaeus*. Oxford: Clarendon Press.

—— 1929. *Plato: The Man and His Work*, 3rd edn. London: Methuen.

—— 1934. *The Parmenides of Plato: Translated into English with Introduction and Appendices*. Oxford: Clarendon Press.

TELOH, H. 1976(*a*). 'The isolation and connection of the Forms in Plato's middle dialogues'. *Apeiron*, 10: 20–34.

—— 1976(*b*). 'Parmenides and Plato's *Parmenides* 131a–132c'. *Journal of the History of Philosophy*, 14: 125–30.

THEILER, W. 1924. *Zur Geschichte der teleologischen Naturbetrachtung bis auf Aristoteles*. Zurich: Hoenn.

TROUILLARD, J. 1970. 'L'âme du *Timée* et l'Un du *Parménide* dans la perspective néoplatonicienne'. *Revue internationale de philosophie*, 24: 236–51.

TUGWELL, S. 1964. 'The way of truth'. *Classical Quarterly*, NS 14: 36–41.

TURNBULL, R. G. 1983. 'Episteme and doxa: some reflections on Eleatic and Heraclitean themes in Plato', in J. P. Anton and A. Preus (eds.), *Essays in Ancient Greek Philosophy*, ii (Albany, NY: State University of New York Press): 279–300.

ÜBERWEG, F. 1920. *Grundriss der Geschichte der Philosophie der Altertums*, 11th edn., edited and enlarged by K. Prächter. Berlin: Mittler.

UNTERSTEINER, M. 1955. 'L'essere di Parmenide è οὖλον non ἕν'. *Rivista critica di storia della filosofia*, 10: 5–23.

—— 1956. *Senofane, testimonianze e frammenti: Introduzione, traduzione e commento*, Biblioteca di studi superiori, 33. Florence: La nuova Italia.

—— 1957. *The Sophists*, trans. K. Freeman. Oxford: Blackwell.

—— 1958. *Parmenide: Testimonianze e frammenti*, Biblioteca di studi superiori, 38. Florence: La nuova Italia.

VERDENIUS, W. J. 1942. *Parmenides: Some Comments on his Poem*, trans. A. Fontein. Groningen: Wolters.

VLASTOS, G. 1946. 'Parmenides' theory of knowledge'. *Transactions and Proceedings of the American Philological Association*, 77: 66–77.

—— 1953. 'Raven's "Pythagoreans and Eleatics"'. *Gnomon*, 25: 29–35. Reprinted in Allen and Furley (eds.), 1975: 166–76.

—— 1965. '*Anamnesis* in the *Meno*'. *Dialogue*, 4: 143–67.

—— 1967. 'Zeno', in P. Edwards (ed.), *The Encyclopedia of Philosophy* (New York: Macmillan): 369–79.

—— 1975. 'Plato's testimony concerning Zeno of Elea'. *Journal of Hellenic Studies*, 95: 136–63.

VRIES, G. J. DE 1969. *A Commentary on the Phaedrus of Plato*. Amsterdam: Hakkert.

WAERDEN, B. L. VAN DER 1940–1. 'Zeno und die Grundlagenkrise der griechischen Mathematik'. *Mathematische Annalen*, 117: 141–61.

WAHL, J. A. 1926. *Étude sur le Parménide de Platon*, 2nd edn. Paris: Rieder.

WEBER, A. 1937. *Essai sur la deuxième hypothèse du Parménide*, Exposés d'histoire et philosophie des sciences, 8, Actualités scientifiques et industrielles, 546. Paris: Hermann.

WELLMAN, E. 1905. 'Eleatische Philosophie', in G. Wissowa (ed.), *Paulys Realencyclopädie der classischen Altertumswissenschaft*, v, 2 (Stuttgart: Metzler): 2244–5.

WESOLY, M. 1983–4. 'L'"argomento proprio" di Gorgia'. *Annali dell'Istituto Italiano per gli Studi Storici*, 8: 15–45.

WEST, M. L. (ed.). 1966. *Hesiod: Theogony*. Oxford: Clarendon Press.

WESTERINK, L. G. (ed.), and SAFFREY, H.-D. (trans.). 1968, 1974, 1978, 1981. *Proclus: Théologie Platonicienne*, 4 vols. Paris: Belles Lettres.

WESTMAN, R. 1955. *Plutarch gegen Kolotes: Seine Schrift 'Adversus Colotem' als philosophiegeschichtliche Quelle*, Acta Philosophica Fennica, 7. Helsinki: Suomalaisen Kirjallisuuden Kirjapaino.

WHITE, N. P. 1993. *Plato, Sophist: Translated, with Introduction and Notes*. Indianapolis: Hackett.

WILAMOWITZ-MÖLLENDORFF, U. VON 1899. 'Lesefrüchte'. *Hermes*, 34: 203–6.

—— 1919. *Platon*, 2 vols. Berlin: Weidmann.

WILPERT, P. 1956–7. 'Aristoteles und die Dialektik'. *Kant-Studien*, 48: 247–57.

WINCKELMANN, A. W. 1833. *Platonis Euthydemus*. Leipzig: Hartmann.

WIŚNIEWSKI, B. 1963. 'La théorie de la connaissance de Parménide'. *Studi italiani di filologia classica*, NS 35: 199–204.

WOODBURY, L. 1958. 'Parmenides on names'. *Harvard Studies in Classical Philology*, 63: 145–69.

—— 1986. 'Parmenides on naming by mortal men: fr. B8.53–56'. *Ancient Philosophy*, 6: 1–11.

WOODRUFF, P. 1982. *Plato, Hippias Major: Translated, with Commentary and Essay*. Oxford: Blackwell.

WUNDT, M. 1935. *Platons Parmenides*, Tübinger Beiträge zur Altertumswissenschaft, 25. Stuttgart: Kohlhammer.

WYLLER, E. A. 1963. 'Platons *Parmenides*: Form und Sinn'. *Zeitschrift für philosophische Forschung*, 17: 202–26.

ZAFIROPULO, J. 1950. *L'école éléate: Parménide, Zénon, Mélissos*, Collection d'études anciennes. Paris: Belles Lettres.

ZELLER, E. 1919. *Die Philosophie der Griechen in ihrer geschichtlichen Entwicklung dargestellt*, i, 1: *Allgemeine Einleitung, vorsokratische Philosophie*, 6th edn., edited and enlarged by W. Nestle. Leipzig: Reisland.

—— 1922. *Die Philosophie der Griechen in ihrer geschichtlichen Entwicklung*, ii, 1: *Sokrates und die Sokratiker, Plato und die alte Akademie*, 5th edn., edited and enlarged by W. Nestle. Leipzig: Reisland.

—— 1967. *La filosofia dei Greci nel suo sviluppo storico*, i, 3: *Gli Eleati*, edited and enlarged by R. Mondolfo, A. Capizzi (ed.). Florence: La nuova Italia.

ZOUMPOS, A. N. 1960. 'Zwei Nachrichten über Xeniades von Korinth'. *Ẑiva Antika*, 10: 16.

Index Locorum

1. 11. 47, 4–12   175 n. 44
2. 4. 31, 4 ff.   155 n. 16
3. 1. 23–6   200 n. 38
3. 6. 26, 12–27, 8   197 n. 33
3. 8. 29, 7–30, 2   154 n. 14

Sannyrion
  fr. 1 Kock   211

Semonides
  1. 3–5   25 n. 16

Sextus Empiricus
Adversus mathematicos
  7. 7   101
  7. 48   129
  7. 53   129
  7. 60   126 n. 10
  7. 65–87   66 n. 22
  7. 65   66
  7. 66–72   255
  7. 67   256
  7. 69–70   115
  7. 71 ff.   69 n. 29
  7. 73–4   255
  7. 75–6   255–6
  7. 77–8   109 n. 30, 257
  7. 79–82   257 n. 5
  7. 111   11
  7. 112–14   22
  7. 388   129
  7. 399   129
  8. 5   129
Outlines of Pyrrhonism
  2. 18   129
  2. 76   129

Simonides
  157 Bergk   208 n. 4

Simplicius
in Aristotelis Categorias
  208, 28–32   57
  211, 15–21   57
in Aristotelis de Caelo
  558, 8   207
  558, 11–17   34 n. 3
in Aristotelis Physica
  21, 14–15   190
  22, 26–9   187 n. 4
  28, 5–6   187 n. 4
  29, 18   259
  31, 3–7   214 n. 14

87, 1   259
90, 24 ff.   168
112, 7–10   93 n. 7
120, 13 ff.   169 n. 38
134, 2–8   96
135, 24   78 n. 38
143, 10   259
143, 31   78 n. 38
146, 11   259–60

Solon
  13. 65–70   25 n. 16
  17   25 n. 16

Sophocles
Ajax
  1259   138 n. 28

Stilpo
  fr. 27 Döring   169 n. 38
  fr. 197 Döring   169 n. 38
  fr. 198 Döring   169 n. 38

Stobaeus
Eclogae
  1. 25. 1. 8a   214 n. 14

Suidas
s.v. 'Parmenides'   187 n. 4

Theodoretus
  4. 5   187 n. 4

Theognidea
  141–2   25 n. 16

Theophrastus
De sensibus
  3   214 n. 14
  4   197 n. 31
  26   27 n. 21
De signis tempestatum
  10   211
φυσικαὶ δόξαι
  fr. 6   213

Thucydides
  2. 13   208 n. 3

Tzetzes, Joannes
Historiarum variarum chiliades
  7. 605–9   57 n. 7

General Index